Pedagogical Translanguaging

BILINGUAL EDUCATION & BILINGUALISM

Series Editors: **Nancy H. Hornberger** *(University of Pennsylvania, USA)* and **Wayne E. Wright** *(Purdue University, USA)*

Bilingual Education and Bilingualism is an international, multidisciplinary series publishing research on the philosophy, politics, policy, provision and practice of language planning, Indigenous and minority language education, multilingualism, multiculturalism, biliteracy, bilingualism and bilingual education. The series aims to mirror current debates and discussions. New proposals for single-authored, multiple-authored, or edited books in the series are warmly welcomed, in any of the following categories or others authors may propose: overview or introductory texts; course readers or general reference texts; focus books on particular multilingual education program types; school-based case studies; national case studies; collected cases with a clear programmatic or conceptual theme; and professional education manuals.

All books in this series are externally peer-reviewed.

Full details of all the books in this series and of all our other publications can be found on http://www.multilingual-matters.com, or by writing to Multilingual Matters, St Nicholas House, 31–34 High Street, Bristol BS1 2AW, UK.

BILINGUAL EDUCATION & BILINGUALISM: 132

Pedagogical Translanguaging

Theoretical, Methodological and Empirical Perspectives

Edited by
**Päivi Juvonen and
Marie Källkvist**

MULTILINGUAL MATTERS
Bristol • Blue Ridge Summit

DOI https://doi.org/10.21832/JUVONE7376

Library of Congress Cataloging in Publication Data
A catalog record for this book is available from the Library of Congress.
Names: Juvonen, Päivi, editor. | Källkvist, Marie, editor.
Title: Pedagogical Translanguaging: Theoretical, Methodological and
   Empirical Perspectives/Edited by Päivi Juvonen and Marie Källkvist.
Description: Bristol, UK; Blue Ridge Summit, PA: Multilingual Matters,
   2021. | Series: Bilingual Education & Bilingualism: 132 | Includes
   bibliographical references and index. | Summary: "This book presents
   cutting-edge qualitative case-study research across a range of
   educational contexts, as well as theory-oriented chapters by
   distinguished multilingual education scholars, which take stock of the
   field of translanguaging in relation to the education of multilingual
   individuals in today's globalized world"—Provided by publisher.
Identifiers: LCCN 2021022372 (print) | LCCN 2021022373 (ebook) | ISBN
   9781788927369 (paperback) | ISBN 9781788927376 (hardback) | ISBN
   9781788927383 (pdf) | ISBN 9781788927390 (epub)
Subjects: LCSH: Multilingual education. | Translanguaging (Linguistics) |
   Education and globalization.
Classification: LCC LC3715 .P427 2021 (print) | LCC LC3715 (ebook) | DDC
   370.117—dc23 LC record available at https://lccn.loc.gov/2021022372
LC ebook record available at https://lccn.loc.gov/2021022373

British Library Cataloguing in Publication Data
A catalogue entry for this book is available from the British Library.

ISBN-13: 978-1-78892-737-6 (hbk)
ISBN-13: 978-1-78892-736-9 (pbk)

Multilingual Matters
UK: St Nicholas House, 31–34 High Street, Bristol BS1 2AW, UK.
USA: NBN, Blue Ridge Summit, PA, USA.

Website: www.multilingual-matters.com
Twitter: Multi_Ling_Mat
Facebook: https://www.facebook.com/multilingualmatters
Blog: www.channelviewpublications.wordpress.com

The policy of Multilingual Matters/Channel View Publications is to use papers that are natural, renewable and recyclable products, made from wood grown in sustainable forests. In the manufacturing process of our books, and to further support our policy, preference is given to printers that have FSC and PEFC Chain of Custody certification. The FSC and/or PEFC logos will appear on those books where full certification has been granted to the printer concerned.

Typeset by SAN Publishing Services.
Printed and bound in the UK by the CPI Books Group Ltd.

Contents

Contributors

Valentina Carbonara completed her PhD in Linguistics and Second Language Acquisition in 2017 from the University for Foreigners in Siena. She has a background as an Italian as second language teacher. With her colleague Andrea Scibetta, she coordinates the project 'L'AltRoparlante: translanguaging educational practices for the management of the superdiversity in class', which was awarded the European Language Label in 2018. Her research interests include teaching Italian as a second language, early language education, CLIL, bilingualism and translanguaging.

Jim Cummins is a Professor Emeritus at the Ontario Institute for Studies in Education of the University of Toronto. His research focuses on literacy development in educational contexts characterized by linguistic diversity. In numerous articles and books, he has explored the nature of language proficiency and its relationship to literacy development with particular emphasis on the intersections of societal power relations, teacher–student identity negotiation and literacy attainment in multilingual classrooms.

Henrik Gyllstad is an Associate Professor of English Linguistics at the Centre for Languages and Literature, Lund University, Sweden. His work broadly focuses on lexical aspects of second language acquisition, bi- and multilingualism and language testing and assessment. More specifically, he has investigated cross-linguistic influence in second language lexical and phraseological processing and carried out validation studies of vocabulary size tests. His work has been published in prominent journals such as *Applied Linguistics*, *ITL International Journal of Applied Linguistics*, *Language Learning* and *Studies in Second Language Acquisition* and in *The Routledge Handbook of Vocabulary Studies*.

Nancy H. Hornberger is a Professor Emerita of Education at the University of Pennsylvania, USA. She is an educational linguist and educational anthropologist researching on multilingual language education policy and practice in immigrant and Indigenous communities. With sustained commitment and work with Quechua speakers and bilingual intercultural education in the Andes beginning in 1974, she has also taught, lectured, collaborated and advised internationally. A prolific author and editor, her books include *Continua of Biliteracy* (2003), *Can Schools Save Indigenous Languages? Policy and Practice on Four Continents* (2008) and *Honoring Richard Ruiz and his Work on Language Planning and Bilingual Education* (2017).

Francis M. Hult is a Professor of Education at the University of Maryland, Baltimore County (UMBC). His research explores multilingualism in policy and practice drawing upon ethnographic and discourse analytic approaches. He has published widely on educational linguistics, language policy and linguistic landscapes. Recent books include *Language Policy and Language Acquisition Planning* (with Siiner and Kupisch), *Research Methods in Language Policy and Planning* (with Johnson) and a forthcoming second edition of the *Handbook of Educational Linguistics* (with Spolsky).

Päivi Juvonen works as a Professor of Swedish as a second language at Linnæus University, Sweden, and as a Visiting Professor of Swedish at Sámi University of Applied Sciences in Kautokeino, Norway. Her research is in the area of applied linguistics, focusing on language contact, multilingualism in education, second language development and language policy and practice.

Marie Källkvist is an Associate Professor of English Linguistics at Lund University and Visiting Professor of English at Linnæus University, Sweden. Her research is in the area of applied English linguistics, focusing on multilingualism in education, second language acquisition and language policy and practice.

Berit Lundgren is an Associate Professor Emerita of Education at Umeå University, Sweden. Her current research includes literacy and language in school development, focusing on migrants' learning of Swedish as an additional language, translanguaging, critical literacy and identity formation. Her literacy studies are conducted in schools, while her language and identity studies focus on adults.

Anne Pitkänen-Huhta is a Professor of English (language learning and teaching) at the University of Jyväskylä, Finland. She is also the Vice Dean of the Faculty of Humanities and Social Sciences. Her research focuses broadly on issues related to practices of additional language learning and teaching, including multiliteracies and multilingualism in language education. Her research interests also connect to early language learning and language teacher education. Her research employs ethnographic, discourse analytic and visual methods.

Anne Reath Warren is a Senior Lecturer in education with a focus on multilingualism and newcomers' learning at Uppsala University, Sweden.

Her research interests include the development of multilingual literacies in educational contexts, including multilingual tutoring for newcomers in schools and mother tongue instruction. She currently works with in-service teacher education and collaborates with mother tongue teachers, tutors and municipalities to improve learning conditions for multilingual and newcomer students.

Jenny Rosén is an Associate Professor of Swedish as a second language at the Department of Language Education at Stockholm University, Sweden. Her research interests are multilingualism, second language learning and literacy in policy and practice in varied educational settings. She is currently working on collaborative research projects with teachers in adult education in Sweden.

Erica Sandlund is an Associate Professor of English Linguistics at Karlstad University. Her research interests center on social interaction in institutional settings and encompass L2 classrooms, L2 oral proficiency tests and workplaces. Methodologically, most of her work lies within the field of Conversation Analysis, with a particular interest in social practices in the context of doing learning, instruction and reflection. Additionally, she has conducted several studies on professional training and workplace interaction, including performance appraisal interviews and teachers' professional development. She is a researcher in the project MultiLingual Spaces, which combines experimental, ethnographic and interactional methods.

Andrea Scibetta is a Post-Doc fellow at the University for Foreigners of Siena and a Chinese language lecturer at the University of Florence. In 2017, he completed his PhD in Linguistics and Second Language Acquisition at the University for Foreigners of Siena. With his colleague Valentina Carbonara, he coordinates the project 'L'AltRoparlante: translanguaging educational practices for the management of the superdiversity in class', which was awarded the European Language Label in 2018. His scientific activity concerns Chinese, L2 Italian teaching to Chinese students, the promotion of Chinese in Italian schools and multilingual education.

Jessica Sierk is an Assistant Professor of Education at St. Lawrence University in Canton, New York. Her research on the New Latinx Diaspora attends to issues of educational equity, looking at how a particular place and its demographics reproduce features of the larger society within which it is situated to advantage certain individuals while disadvantaging others. Her scholarly work seeks to describe how the broader sociopolitical and sociocultural contexts related to race and whiteness in the United States influence students' identities, worldviews and aspirations.

Oliver St John is a Senior Lecturer, Teacher Educator and Researcher at Örebro University, Sweden. He has taught and initiated research within the fields of second language acquisition and pedagogy. His current research focuses on 'Swedish for immigrants' (SFI) learning environments and, through action research alongside SFI teachers, explores the kind of pedagogical support that enables newly arrived adult migrants to succeed in learning Swedish as a second language and participate meaningfully in Swedish society. A crucial question within this context is the use of the students' mother tongues as a learning asset for adapting to the surrounding language.

Pia Sundqvist is an Associate Professor of English Language Education at the University of Oslo, Norway and of English Linguistics at Karlstad University, Sweden. Sundqvist's main research interests are in the field of applied English linguistics, with a focus on informal language learning, the assessment of L2 oral proficiency and English language teaching in multilingual classrooms. She is an expert on learning through extramural English activities, in particular through gaming.

Gudrun Svensson is an Associate Professor of Swedish as a second language at Linnaeus University, Sweden. She has a background as an upper secondary school teacher, after which she earned her PhD at Lund University, Sweden, on language variation among multilingual youth. Since then, her work has focused on multilingualism and pedagogical translanguaging in schools. Currently, she researches classrooms, parental inclusion in schools and teacher education. She also does consultancy work for the National Agency for Education, specifically for enhancing learning in multilingual schools. Her research is framed by discourse and interaction theory.

Åsa Wedin holds a PhD in Bilingualism and is a Professor in Educational Work at Dalarna University, Sweden. With a background as a primary school teacher, Wedin's main research interests are in multilingualism and literacy in education. In Tanzania, she has carried out research on literacy practices in primary school, and in Sweden, she conducted research on literacy and interactional patterns in classrooms and on conditions for multilingual students' learning. Her research is ethnographically inspired, particularly using linguistic ethnography and theoretical perspectives where languaging is studied as social and cultural practices and where opportunities for learning are related to questions of power.

Foreword: Teaching and Researching in Linguistically and Culturally Diverse Classrooms

How do we teach in linguistically and culturally diverse classrooms? I pose this question each year in my graduate course on language diversity and education at Penn. We go on to explore answers in terms of making multiple cultural, linguistic, literate discourse practices available in our classrooms, drawing on my Continua of Biliteracy framework to analyze examples in the literature and imagine possibilities for such practices and classrooms. This volume on pedagogical translanguaging and multilingual practices asks essentially the same question and offers theoretical, methodological and empirical answers from studies in Sweden, Italy, the US and Finland. A selection of papers originally presented at the Third Swedish Conference on Translanguaging, held at Linnaeus University in April 2019, the studies herein show and tell us about the infusion of multilingual practices into formerly monolingual classrooms or schools. Frequent calls are made throughout the volume for these studies and practices to be taken up by others and diffused more widely; it is to the authors' and editors' great credit that much of the how-to of pedagogical translanguaging and multilingual practices in classrooms is readily available to the reader in these pages.

Multilingual practices have been going on a long time, indeed centuries, but the turn of this century saw a veritable explosion of terminology for fluid multilingual and multimodal communicative practices, by now a well-rehearsed list including metrolingualism, polylanguaging, polylingual languaging, heteroglossia, codemeshing, translingual practice, hybrid language practices, multilanguaging, flexible bilingualism, dynamic bilingualism, dynamic languaging and translanguaging.[1] Multiple and overlapping meanings attributed to these terms include communicative practice, pedagogical approach, neurolinguistic or cognitive phenomenon, theory of language and sine qua non for equitable education and social justice (see Jim Cummins, this volume, for a clear-eyed and helpful review on translanguaging). My purpose here is not to tackle this abundant landscape of terminology but rather to offer a personal view on this volume's contributions from the vantage point of my research and teaching with the Continua of Biliteracy framework (discussed below).

Several volume authors document and evaluate processes and outcomes of shifts in pedagogical practice and language ideology in the Swedish context of increasingly multilingual classrooms including recently arrived migrant adolescent and adult students, whether they be classes of the state-funded Language Introduction Programme (LIP) geared to preparing recently arrived adolescent students for an exam that will permit them to enter upper secondary school, Swedish for Immigrants (SFI) classes teaching adult newcomers foundational skills in Swedish, increasingly multiethnic English as Additional Language (EAL) classrooms in schools or indeed entire schools. The Swedish studies are complemented by Jessica Sierk's exploration of teachers' ideologies about multilingualism in two schools of the New Latinx Diaspora in midwestern US, Carbonara and Scibetta's case of monolingual teachers learning to adopt translanguaging practices in Italian mainstream public primary school classrooms as part of the authors' teacher–researcher collaborative L'AltRoparlante Project and Anne Pitkänen-Huhta's overview of the Finnish policy and classroom context for multilingualism in language education with particular attention to the siloed nature of educational policy and practice for Finland's 'old' multilingualisms (Finnish–Swedish bilingualism, minoritized Sámi, Roma and Sign languages, foreign language education) and the missing attention to the 'new' multilingualisms and linguistic resources recent migrants bring including Arabic, Chinese, Estonian, Farsi, Kurdish, Russian and Somali.

Gudrun Svensson documents teacher change processes in a Swedish primary and middle school, analyzing how teachers, principals and she as researcher collaboratively effected schoolwide transformation from monolingual to multilingual pedagogy over a six-year period; Jenny Rosén and Berit Lundgren likewise document teacher change processes in their collaborative professional development with teachers in SFI adult migrant education. In chapters that directly address methodological challenges in documenting the processes or outcomes of teachers' adopting pedagogical translanguaging practices and/or heteroglossic ideologies, volume editors Marie Källkvist and Päivi Juvonen recount how accommodation to participant fluidity and the concomitant need for adequate time to complete the research played crucial roles in their four-year research projects on inclusive language practices in multilingual student groups in Swedish secondary schools; likewise, Pia Sundqvist and co-authors consider the challenges and successes in mapping teacher beliefs and practices about multilingualism through the MultiBAP questionnaire they developed.

In addition to these studies on teacher change processes as they shift from monolingual to multilingual and translanguaging pedagogies, three additional studies analyze the nuances of these practices and pedagogies in Swedish multilingual classroom contexts. Åsa Wedin's account of 'languaging mathematics' in an LIP classroom for recently arrived adolescent immigrant students in Sweden highlights the 'shuttling between registers, modes and languages in the negotiation of meaning' observable there. Likewise, Anne Reath Warren's linguistic ethnography of LIP Tutoring in the Mother Tongue interactions analyzes in minute detail the richness and complexity of multilingual, multimodal negotiation of meaning in 'semiotic assemblages [...] connecting languages that students understand [here, Dari], Swedish, images, gestures, objects and spaces'. Along similar lines, Oliver St John analyzes the discourse of Multilingual Language Assistance (MLA) in SFI classrooms among adult immigrants with little schooling and variable degrees of literacy, demonstrating how the assistants do MLA by means of 'multilingual moves' including transposing teacher talk/performance, multilingual linking between participants, contextualizing instructional content and thresholding student performance.

What does the Continua of Biliteracy lens bring to our reading and understanding of these cases of pedagogical translanguaging and multilingual practices? The Continua of Biliteracy framework, recently dubbed CoBi (Antia, 2019), was developed originally from my literature review and research in multilingual schools and communities of Philadelphia beginning in the 1980s and has been subsequently applied by me and others in contexts of immigrant and Indigenous education around the world (including several chapters herein). It offers a heuristic for understanding learners' fluid and dynamic communicative repertoires and how multilingual classroom practice can best support their development and strengthening. Organized around three-dimensional, intersecting and nested spaces of the continua of context, media, content and development of biliteracy, the framework offers an analytical heuristic for understanding and shaping bi/multilingualism and multimodality as practiced and nurtured in individuals, classrooms, programs, schools, communities, societies and indeed in any instance of biliteracy use and development, where biliteracy is defined as 'any and all instances in which communication occurs in two (or more) languages in or around writing' (Hornberger, 1990: 213).

Continua of Biliteracy

traditionally <u>less</u> powerful <-------------> traditionally <u>more</u> powerful

<u>Contexts of biliteracy</u>

micro <---> macro

oral <---> literate

bi(multi)lingual <------------------------------> monolingual

<u>Development of biliteracy</u>

reception <--> production

oral <--> written

L1 <---> L2

<u>Content of biliteracy</u>

minority <---> majority

vernacular <---> literary

contextualized <------------------------------------> decontextualized

<u>Media of biliteracy</u>

simultaneous exposure <-------------------------> successive exposure

dissimilar structures <---------------------------------> similar structures

divergent scripts <---------------------------------> convergent scripts

Figure 1. The Continua of biliteracy. From Hornberger & Skilton-Sylvester 2000: 99. Reprinted with permission from Taylor & Francis.

From the CoBi framework illustrated in Figure 1, I posit that the more learners' and users' contexts of language and literacy use allow them to draw from across the whole of each and every biliteracy continuum, the greater are the chances for the complete development and expression of their language and literacy (Hornberger, 1989, 2003, 2016). In short, the continua model suggests that a full picture of multilingual, multiethnic classroom teaching and learning includes *how* (development), *where* and *when* (context), *by what means* (media) and *what* (content) language and literacy practices are deployed and supported in the classroom.

Holly Link and I discussed CoBi in relation to translanguaging, noting that from a sociolinguistics of globalization perspective, the four dimensions of the continua can be best understood in the following parallels – context as scaled, spatiotemporal spaces, media as communicative repertoires, development as translanguaging and content as transnational literacies including funds of knowledge (Hornberger & Link, 2012). Bringing the CoBi lens to this volume, then, focuses the lens on multilingual practices as the media of biliteracy, i.e. the communicative repertoires of teachers and students in the multilingual classroom – the complexes of linguistic, communicative, semiotic resources they draw on and develop; the volume's attention to pedagogical translanguaging turns the CoBi lens on biliteracy development as it unfolds in the individual, classroom and wider contexts. Sociolinguistic and ethnographic assumptions within the continua model about the fluidity of language varieties and scripts, and the multiple paths and varying degrees of expertise in individuals' communicative repertoires, entail attention not just to different languages, dialects, styles and discourses but also to different communicative modes including oral, written and digital ones, as they are acquired and used – usually in hybrid languaging practices and crisscrossed paths of acquisition.

The chapters of this volume, and indeed the global uptake of translanguaging pedagogies, reflect an increased sense of urgency worldwide to transform classrooms and schools into spaces that support and nurture language practices of multilingual and especially language minoritized learners. This is not to say that multilingual classroom discourse research and practice have been a blank slate until now; quite the contrary, there is a lineage of research on multilingual classroom discourse that has without doubt contributed to today's explosion of attention.

So let me back up a little, as we do also in my course, considering four strands woven through our growing understandings of multilingual classroom discourse in support of biliteracy across the past several decades: fluid use of language and literacy; meaning-based use of language and literacy; pedagogical practices reflective of community-based language/literacy use and language, literacy and other modes and modalities of communicative repertoire. From studies in the 1970s–1980s focused on quantifying or harnessing bilingual teachers' language distributional patterns for academic purposes, and the growing momentum of ethnographic and discourse analytic research in the 1980s–1990s taking more account of multilingual learners' contributions, the sequential flow of classroom discourse and negotiation of meanings moment by moment, we have moved in this century to analyses of the 'agentive ways in which teachers and learners manage the gap between reified institutional monolingualism and the lived multilingual realities of everyday classroom practice' (Saxena & Martin-Jones, 2013: 291).[2] Along the way, there have been increasing calls for educators not only to look at language use in classrooms but also to observe how people use language outside school and base our pedagogy on that, e.g. developing negotiation strategies and a repertoire of codes to shuttle between (García, 2007: xiii, also citing Canagarajah, 2007).

Especially significant for multilingual classroom discourse research, and beyond, was Gumperz' (1982) analysis of bilingual codeswitching as a contextualization cue, shaping and shaped by social context and social identities; a conceptual breakthrough that came within the tradition of research on bilingualism and bilingual pedagogy both before and after, showing the social and cultural meanings of switches and providing empirical evidence for bilinguals' fluid codeswitching as highly context-sensitive, competent but specific language practice (e.g. Grosjean, 1985; Lin, 2006; Martin-Jones & Saxena, 1996; Valdés, 1982; Zentella, 1981). Continuing research by Gumperz and others demonstrated further that bilingual codeswitching is not the only contextualization cue language users deploy in discourse – there are also *other* linguistic and nonlinguistic discursive practices equally shaping/shaped by social context and social identities. This understanding became and remains a mainstay of ethnographic and linguistic anthropological discourse analysis. Study of the actual processes of communicative interaction and co-construction of meanings and identities in multilingual classroom discourse enriched our understanding of codeswitching as fluid, flexible language use and, reciprocally, of fluid, flexible communicative practice as shaping/shaped by social identities and context.

Translanguaging and translanguaging pedagogy – along with a rich terminological terrain of allied concepts applied to pedagogy including bi/multilingual, bi/multidialectal, multidiscoursal, multimodal teaching practices; continua of biliteracy; multilingual literacies; multilingual classroom ecologies; transnational literacies; flexible bilingual pedagogy; bilingual supportive scaffolding (and more) – emerge in this trajectory of research on multilingual classroom discourse, spurred on by experiences of translanguaging pedagogy in Wales and by post-structural understandings of language, the former a specific pedagogical strategy and site of the coining of the term *translanguaging* via the Welsh *trawysieithu* (Baker, 2003; Williams, 1994), the latter a diffuse set of understandings and disciplinary underpinnings for a paradigm shift in how we think about language and language users (García, 2007, 2009; Makoni & Pennycook, 2007).

Most importantly, the emergence and uptake of translanguaging as ideology and pedagogy signaled a shift in educators' and researchers' stance toward pedagogy and social justice for minoritized multilingual/multidialectal learners. Whereas multilingual classroom researchers had for decades recognized and documented the validity and richness of fluid language use in social interaction in and outside schools, pedagogical tradition worldwide remained strict separation of language codes in school. Many of us had for some time been calling for more explicit attention in classrooms to valuing and supporting minoritized language users' ways of speaking, being, thinking and doing, but the hegemonic taboo against mixing languages in school nevertheless prevailed.

This finally began to change with the advent of the 21st century; the proliferation and widespread uptake of translanguaging and allied terms is representative of that shift. Revisiting the CoBi framework in 2000, Ellen Skilton-Sylvester and I explicitly argued for the need to contest traditional power weightings along the continua by paying attention to, granting agency to and making space for actors and practices at the traditionally less powerful ends of the continua (Hornberger & Skilton-Sylvester, 2000: 99). Ofelia García (2007) reflected on the power of Makoni and Pennycook's (2007) proposal for disinventing language and went on to present her tour de force introduction of translanguaging in her influential text on bilingual education in the 21st century (García, 2009). Blackledge and Creese (2010) advocated for flexible bilingualism as an alternative to separate bilingualism in their landmark study of heritage/complementary schools in the UK, arguing that 'flexible bilingualism captures the "heteroglossic" nature of communication in the bilingual context of complementary schools. It leads us away from a focus on "languages" as distinct codes to a focus on the agency of individuals in a school community engaged in using, creating, and interpreting signs to communicate to multilingual audiences' (Blackledge & Creese, 2010: 109). They called for a release from monolingual instructional approaches and an easing of the burden of guilt associated with translanguaging in multilingual educational contexts, asking educators to move beyond acceptance or tolerance of children's languages to developing and cultivating them for teaching and learning.

The prior question and starting point for the exploration of making multiple cultural, linguistic and literate discourse practices available in the classroom is why? why does it matter? – a question I answer in my research and teaching from a social justice standpoint: that is, it matters because of the importance of equal educational opportunity and the persistent concern in the US and elsewhere around minoritized students' academic failure, a concern formulated in US policy and media as 'the achievement gap' and more recently 'the education debt' (Ladson-Billings, 2006), placing responsibility clearly on schools and education rather than assumed or ascribed deficits of learners. Similarly flipping the perspective from why students fail school to why schools fail students, Allan Luke asks the question this way: 'What would a whole-school approach to equity and social justice for linguistic and cultural minority students look like?' (Luke, 2009: 301; see also Varenne & McDermott, 1999).

My research and teaching with CoBi follow in a tradition of holistic approaches to transforming education for social justice for culturally, linguistically and racially diverse student populations in the US and elsewhere, from Freire's (1970) transformative education through Cummins' framework for empowering minority students (Cummins, 1986; see also this volume), Corson's (1990) policymaking at the school level and Bourdieu's model for curriculum and pedagogy, assessment and accountability (Luke, 2009), all of which situate language and linguistic practice as centrally implicated in deficit positionings of minoritized students in schools. Proposals for culturally responsive pedagogy (Cazden & Leggett, 1981), culturally relevant pedagogy (Ladson-Billings, 1995; Osborne, 1996), culturally responsive schooling for Indigenous youth (Castagno & Brayboy, 2008) and culturally sustaining pedagogy (Paris, 2012) address language and linguistic practice as fundamental to the project of reversing and overcoming inequitable educational practices. Flores and Rosa's recent work on raciolinguistic ideologies goes one step further, explicitly theorizing that racialized bodies are ideologically constructed as (not) engaging in appropriately academic linguistic practices, *whether or not their practices actually reflect those norms* (Flores & Rosa, 2015; Rosa & Flores, 2017). Unless and until those ideologies are acknowledged and confronted, little can be accomplished by changing/transforming school or student communicative practices.

In a context of intense debate around decoloniality in South African higher education in recent years, Bassey Antia repurposes the continua of biliteracy as a tool for implementing decolonial pedagogy. In their course on Multilingualism in Education and Society at University of the Western Cape, Bassey and co-lecturer Charlyn Dyers seek to 'de-alienate the academy for our students and [...] heal some of the accruing injuries of coloniality' (Antia & Dyers, 2019: 92, citing Dominguez, 2017: 227). They write:

> Hornberger can be read as arguing that the prospects of educational success, knowledge production, pedagogy and so on are enhanced when orthodoxies of colonial hegemony are subverted, and factors from each end of the power spectrum are allowed to interact. There is a need to challenge a more powerful colonial, Western modelling of the recipes for success in knowledge production and mediation: literacy, texts, monolingualism, writing, colonial languages, decontextualized (i.e. Western) perspectives, abstract styles, keeping distinct different varieties of languages. Hornberger's model creates a third space in which opposites (e.g. of earlier anthropological research) are reconciled. It allows for what has been described as dialogic pedagogy in which Western knowledge and local knowledge are used and mediated to create new and powerful knowledge as well as more rounded and grounded graduates. (Antia & Dyers, 2019: 95)

In terms of applying the CoBi model toward a decolonial pedagogy, they considered it important to 'undermine foundations of coloniality' in the course and to (1) acknowledge students' different cultural backgrounds in exposure to languages and to orate vs. literate practices of knowledge acquisition, (2) make information processing possible across African home/non-home languages and across modes such as visual (reading) and aural (listening), (3) ensure that meanings communicated critically draw on local and non-local sources and are encoded in a mix of abstract and non-abstract formulations and (4) expose students to learning in informal varieties as well as standardized varieties. Inclusion of multilingual course resources and assessments is ongoing since 2013; the authors' analysis of students' essays about their experience in the course yields themes reversing longstanding injuries of coloniality, i.e. (i) decolonializing the context for academic performance, in particular English as the unquestioned *de facto* language of assessment, (ii) decolonializing attitudes toward languages and linguistics knowledge, instead recognizing and valuing African languages and (iii) decolonializing technologies of communication, e.g. enabling students to access course knowledge through oral/aural modes and not only written ones.

How, then, do we teach in linguistically, culturally and racially diverse classrooms? By making multiple cultural, linguistic and literate discourse practices available. Recognizing and incorporating flexible language practices in multilingual/multiethnic classrooms puts the emphasis on speaker voice and agency rather than on language and offers the possibility for teachers and learners to access academic content through the linguistic resources they bring to the classroom while simultaneously acquiring new ones. That, after all, is what learning – and teaching – are all about.

The quest for social justice and equitable education is the foundation of the CoBi framework, as it is for pedagogical translanguaging. Juvonen and Källkvist tell us that their volume aims 'to leverage research in schools and scholarly discussion of inclusive language practices with a view to enhancing social justice in schools and in society at large'. What better aim could there be for educators in this time and place?

Nancy H. Hornberger
Brownsville, Vermont, USA
August 2020

Notes

(1) I am told there is a Swedish proverb that people/items/phenomena we hold very dear tend to have many names: *kärt barn har många namn*, literally meaning 'a dear child has many names'. My thanks to Marie Källkvist for offering this celebratory analogy to the many terms for translanguaging (personal communication, 18 August 2020).

(2) See also Hornberger (1995) and Martin-Jones (1995, 2007) for reviews of this research.

References

Antia, B.E. (2019) Applications of the Continua of Biliteracy Model in Research Projects at a South African University. Presentation at University of Pennsylvania, Philadelphia, USA, 4 September 2019.

Antia, B.E. and Dyers, C. (2019) De-alienating the academy: Multilingual teaching as decolonial pedagogy. *Linguistics and Education* 51, 91–100.

Baker, C. (2003) Biliteracy and transliteracy in Wales: Language planning and the Welsh National Curriculum. In N.H. Hornberger (ed.) *Continua of Biliteracy: An Ecological Framework for Educational Policy, Research, and Practice in Multilingual Settings* (pp. 71–90). Clevedon: Multilingual Matters.

Blackledge, A. and Creese, A. (2010) *Multilingualism: A Critical Perspective*. London: Continuum.

Canagarajah, S. (2007) After disinvention: Possibilities for communication, community and competence. In S. Makoni and A. Pennycook (eds) *Disinventing and Reconstituting Languages* (pp. 233–239). Clevedon: Multilingual Matters.

Castagno, A.E. and Brayboy, B.M.J. (2008) Culturally responsive schooling for Indigenous youth: A review of the literature. *Review of Educational Research* 78 (4), 941-993.

Cazden, C.B. and Leggett, E. (1981) Culturally responsive education: Recommendations for achieving Lau remedies II. In H.T. Trueba, G.P. Guthrie and K.H. Au (eds) *Culture and the Bilingual Classroom: Studies in Classroom Ethnography* (pp. 69–86). Rowley. MA: Newbury House.

Corson, D. (1990) *Language Policy Across the Curriculum*. Clevedon: Multilingual Matters.

Creese, A. and Blackledge, A. (2010) Translanguaging in the bilingual classroom: A pedagogy for learning and teaching? *Modern Language Journal* 94, 103–115.

Cummins, J. (1986) Empowering minority students: A framework for instruction. *Harvard Educational Review* 56, 18–36.

Dominguez, M. (2017) 'Se hace puentes al andar': Decolonial teacher education as a needed bridge to culturally sustaining and revitalizing pedagogies. In D. Paris and H. Samy Alim (eds) *Culturally Sustaining Pedagogies: Teaching and Learning for Justice in a Changing World* (pp. 225–246). New York & London: Teachers College Press, Columbia University.

Flores, N. and Rosa, J. (2015) Undoing appropriateness: Raciolinguistic ideologies and language diversity in education. *Harvard Educational Review* 85 (2), 149–171.

Freire, P. (1970) *Pedagogy of the Oppressed*. New York: Herder & Herder.

García, O. (2007) Foreword. In S. Makoni and A. Pennycook (eds) *Disinventing and Reconstituting Languages* (pp. xi–xv). Clevedon: Multilingual Matters.

García, O. (2009) *Bilingual Education in the 21st Century: A Global Perspective*. Malden, MA: Wiley-Blackwell.

Grosjean, F. (1985) The bilingual as a competent but specific speaker-hearer. *Journal of Multilingual and Multicultural Development* 6 (6), 467–477.

Gumperz, J.J. (1982) *Discourse Strategies*. Cambridge: Cambridge University Press.

Hornberger, N.H. (1989) Continua of biliteracy. *Review of Educational Research* 59 (3), 271–296.

Hornberger, N.H. (1990) Creating successful learning contexts for bilingual literacy. *Teachers College Record* 92 (2), 212–229.

Hornberger, N.H. (1995) Ethnography in linguistic perspective: Understanding school processes. *Language and Education* 9 (4), 233–248.

Hornberger, N.H. (ed.) (2003) *Continua of Biliteracy: An Ecological Framework for Educational Policy, Research, and Practice in Multilingual Settings*. Clevedon: Multilingual Matters.

Hornberger, N.H. (2016) Researching the continua of biliteracy. In K. King, Y. Lai and S.A. May (eds) *Research Methods in Language and Education* (pp. 1–18). Cham: Springer International Publishing.

Hornberger, N.H. and Link, H. (2012) Translanguaging and transnational literacies in multilingual classrooms: A biliteracy lens. *International Journal of Bilingual Education and Bilingualism* 15 (3), 261–278.

Hornberger, N.H. and Skilton-Sylvester, E. (2000) Revisiting the continua of biliteracy: International and critical perspectives. *Language and Education: An International Journal* 14 (2), 96–122.

Ladson-Billings, G. (1995) Towards a theory of culturally relevant pedagogy. *American Educational Research Journal* 32 (3), 465–491.

Ladson-Billings, G. (2006) From the achievement gap to the education debt: Understanding achievement in U.S. Schools. *Educational Researcher* 35 (7), 3–12

Lin, A. (2006) Beyond linguistic purism in language-in-education policy and practice: Exploring bilingual pedagogies in a Hong Kong science classroom. *Language and Education: An International Journal* 20 (4), 287–305.

Luke, A. (2009) Race and language as capital in school: A sociological template for language education reform. In R. Kubota and A. Lin (eds) *Race, Culture, and Identities in Second Language Education*. London: Routledge.

Makoni, S. and Pennycook, A. (eds) (2007) *Disinventing and Reconstituting Languages*. Clevedon: Multilingual Matters.

Martin-Jones, M. (1995) Code-switching in the classroom: Two decades of research. In L. Milroy and P. Muysken (eds) *One Speaker, Two Languages: Cross-disciplinary Perspectives on Code-switching* (pp. 90–111). Cambridge: Cambridge University Press.

Martin-Jones, M. (2007) Bilingualism, education and the regulation of access to language resources. In M. Heller (ed.) *Bilingualism: A Social Approach* (pp. 161–182). Basingstoke: Palgrave MacMillan.

Martin-Jones, M. and Saxena, M. (1996) Turn-taking, power asymmetries, and the positioning of bilingual participants in classroom discourse. *Linguistics and Education* 8 (1), 105–123.

Osborne, A.B. (1996) Practice into theory into practice: Culturally relevant pedagogy for students we have marginalized and normalized. *Anthropology and Education Quarterly* 27 (3), 285–314.

Paris, D. (2012) Culturally sustaining pedagogy: A needed change in stance, terminology, and practice. *Educational Researcher* 41 (3), 93–97.

Rosa, J. and Flores, N. (2017) Unsettling race and language: Toward a raciolinguistic perspective. *Language in Society* 46 (5), 621–647.

Saxena, M. and Martin-Jones, M. (2013) Multilingual resources in classroom interaction: Ethnographic and discourse analytic perspectives. *Language and Education* 27 (4), 285–297.

Valdés, G. (1982) Social interaction and code-switching patterns: A case study of Spanish/English alternation. In J. Amastae and L. Elías-Olivares (eds) *Spanish in the United States* (pp. 209–229). New York: Cambridge University Press.

Varenne, H. and McDermott, R. (1999). *Successful Failure: The School America Builds*. Boulder, CO: Westview Press.

Williams, C. (1994) Arfarniad o ddulliau dysgu ac addysgu yng nghyd-destun addysg uwchradd ddwyieithog. (PhD). University of Wales, Bangor, Wales.

Zentella, A.C. (1981) Tá bien, you could answer me en cualquier idioma: Puerto Rican codeswitching in bilingual classrooms. In R. Durán (ed.) *Latino Language and Communicative Behavior* (pp. 109–131). New Jersey: Ablex.

1 Pedagogical Translanguaging: Theoretical, Methodological and Empirical Perspectives – An Introduction

Päivi Juvonen and Marie Källkvist

Pedagogical Translanguaging

Pedagogical translanguaging is a construct that refers to teaching approaches that involve the intentional and planned use of student multilingual resources in language and content subjects. We take it up from recent translanguaging research (Cenoz, 2017; Cenoz & Gorter, 2020a, 2020b; Ganuza & Hedman, 2017; Probyn, 2015, 2019) as it clearly signals education as the locus of the translanguaging research presented in this volume. Although teaching approaches that use more than one language have a long history in language education (Cook, 2010), pedagogical translanguaging research gained currency as part of the multilingual turn in language learning and language education scholarship (Conteh & Meier, 2014; May, 2014, 2019; Ortega, 2019). This shift in ideology and research focus mirrors the rapidly changing multilingual ecologies worldwide due to technology-assisted globalization and the mobility of people (Blommaert, 2010). Importantly, pedagogical translanguaging research positions students' pre-existing knowledge, such as their prior linguistic and multisemiotic repertoires, as resources and is therefore often underpinned by a social justice agenda, attending to language-minoritized students' needs to gain equitable education and social inclusion in mainstream society.

The concept of translanguaging stems from a school context in Wales, first advanced by Williams (1996), then taken up and translated by Baker

(2001/2011) and subsequently García (2009) and others. García, in particular, has taken the lead in the continued promotion and theorizing of translanguaging. Her early work characterized the act of translanguaging as 'engaging in bilingual or multilingual discourse practices' (García, 2009: 44), later describing it as a 'movement in language education' (García & Kleyn, 2016: 10). It is indeed in education that most translanguaging research to date has been carried out (Cenoz & Gorter, 2020b), using context-sensitive research methodology such as ethnography (Menken & García, 2010).

By now a vibrant field of research worldwide, a profusion of terms in the scholarly literature refers to intentional bi- and multilingual teaching practices. We list some here, without claiming that they denote exactly the same phenomenon. Cummins (2019) uses a total of 10 terms that refer to the same activity, at least on the surface: 'crosslinguistic pedagogy', 'multilingual teaching strategies', 'bilingual teaching strategies', 'teaching through a multilingual lens', 'translanguaging instructional practices', 'translanguaging approaches to teaching', 'crosslingual instructional practice', 'translanguaging pedagogies', 'crosslingual practice' and 'heteroglossic instructional practice'. Further terms used by other researchers include 'the pedagogy of translanguaging' and 'translanguaging pedagogical strategies' (García & Kleyn, 2016), 'dynamic plurilingual pedagogies' (García & Flores, 2012), 'translanguaging as a pedagogy', 'translanguaging for the classroom' and 'translanguaging as pedagogy' (Paulsrud *et al.,* 2017), 'bilingual instructional strategies' and 'bilingual pedagogy' (Creese & Blackledge, 2010), 'translanguaging practice' (Lin, 2020), 'translanguaging practices' (Cenoz & Santos, 2020), 'translanguaging pedagogy' (Seltzer & García, 2020; Tian *et al.,* 2020), 'translanguaging-oriented pedagogy' (Leung & Valdés, 2019) and 'heteroglossic pedagogies' and 'translanguaging approaches' (Probyn, 2019). No doubt there are more that have escaped our eyes.

In a recent Special Issue on Pedagogical Translanguaging, when reflecting backwards in time while planning for future research, Byrnes (2020: 1) calls attention to pedagogical translanguaging and 'the extraordinary situatedness of the kinds of educational practices that it can recommend confidently on the basis of empirical evidence'. In another recent overview of pedagogical translanguaging, Leung and Valdés (2019: 365) conclude that 'we need to develop an ongoing research agenda focusing on translanguaging that can inform instruction for different groups of students'. The work presented in this book, to which we now turn, is one of the many responses needed for this research agenda.

Book Contents: Theoretical, Methodological and Empirical Perspectives

All chapter authors presented their work at The Third Swedish Translanguaging Conference entitled *Translanguaging in the Individual, at School and in Society,* held at Linnæus University, Sweden, in April 2019. As the title suggests, the conference invited presenters to address translanguaging on the scales of the individual, school and society. As in the two prior translanguaging conferences (see Adinolfi *et al.*, 2018; Paulsrud *et al.*, 2017), the majority presented research in pedagogical translanguaging. In this volume, we bring together papers that focus on advancing translanguaging theory, education research methodology and empirical work in multilingual contexts. The educational settings included reflect the location of the conference, i.e. Sweden, and also include research conducted in Italy, Finland and the United States.

This introductory chapter is followed by a chapter on translanguaging theory, Chapter 2, where Jim Cummins critically examines the legitimacy of the theoretical constructs within two alternative theoretical orientations to translanguaging, referred to as *Unitary Translanguaging Theory* (UTT) and *Crosslinguistic Translanguaging Theory* (CTT). He addresses questions about organization, psychological/cognitive reality and the socially constructed nature of languages, additive versus subtractive bilingualism and their ideological underpinnings and (academic) language education – questions that often confound educators and researchers when learning about translanguaging (Adinolfi *et al.*, 2018).

The two chapters that follow, Chapters 3 and 4, address research methodology to do with collecting data involving teachers. In Chapter 3, Marie Källkvist and Päivi Juvonen discuss the practicalities and complexities of initiating and maintaining teacher–researcher collaboration over an extended period of time – a matter that is at the heart of the ethnographic approaches needed to gain an in-depth, context-specific understanding of pedagogical translanguaging. Chapter 4 turns our attention to the gathering of primarily *quantitative* data using an online questionnaire to reach large numbers of teachers. In this chapter, Pia Sundqvist, Henrik Gyllstad, Marie Källkvist and Erica Sandlund present the development of a questionnaire instrument specifically designed to tap teachers' beliefs about multilingualism and their self-reported classroom and school practices.

Sustainable changes in classroom practices require the involvement of different stakeholders, from policymakers to school principals, teachers, other staff, students and parents (see, e.g. Cummins & Early, 2011; García *et al.*, 2017). In Chapters 5 and 6, two school development projects involving teacher–researcher collaboration at the primary school level are presented. In Chapter 5, Gudrun Svensson describes a school-wide, long-term study of the implementation of pedagogical translanguaging in a school that was facing challenges of low goal fulfilment among its students. Chapter 6 takes us to Italy, where Valentina Carbonara and Andrea Scibetta identify tensions between 'emergency approaches' to teaching plurilingual students based on monolingual language ideologies versus pluralistic language ideologies supported by Italian school curricula. Empirically, they focus on several different interactional and multilingual strategies employed in primary-school classrooms, including translation, peer-to-peer mediation, word recall and metalinguistic and cross-linguistic comparison.

Sweden has a long tradition of supporting newly arrived students' learning by offering temporary support in their mother tongues or another prior school language. Chapters 7 and 8 present studies of the upper-secondary school transitional reception education in Sweden for recently arrived students, which is known as the Language Introduction Programme. In Chapter 7, Anne Reath Warren broadens the scope of pedagogical trans-languaging beyond language to study the fluid use of different modes of meaning-making, experienced by different sensory modalities. In the ana-lyzed interactions, pedagogical translanguaging in the form of multimodal semiotic assemblages is taken to contribute to the development of the stu-dents' academic literacies. In Chapter 8, Åsa Wedin presents a study of the negotiation of meaning in two multilingual mathematics classrooms taught by a teacher speaking Farsi, Swedish and English, most of the time in the presence of a Somali-, Arabic- and Swedish-speaking tutor.

The next two chapters relate to Richard Ruiz's (1984) work on lan-guage planning, which has had a profound influence on scholars discuss-ing ideological underpinnings as well as implementation of language policy in the school context (Hornberger, 2017). His orientations to lan-guage (language-as-problem, language-as-right and language-as-resource) function as the backdrop of analyses of language ideologies in educational contexts in Chapters 9 and 10. In Chapter 9, Jessica Sierk discusses the symbolic function of language while examining how two New Latinx Diaspora high schools in the Midwestern United States reacted to their communities' changing demographics using Ruiz's (1984) orientations. In Chapter 10, Jenny Rosén and Berit Lundgren report a study of in-service teacher training in Swedish as a second language education for adult migrants in seven schools. This study problematizes pedagogical translan-guaging practices on grounds that they would never be fair to everyone present, therefore being indexed with the risk of exclusion and inequity.

In Chapter 11, we stay in Swedish adult immigrant language education. Oliver St John analyses the what, the how and to what end of multilingual language assistants' (MLAs) classroom practices in teacher-initiated action-research collaboration with a researcher. This chapter also closes on a criti-cal note, identifying a number of avenues for further developing MLA and teacher collaboration, including educational provisions for MLAs.

In Chapter 12, Anne Pitkänen-Huhta takes us to Finland. She reflects on the past, present and the future by applying concepts of bi- and multi-lingualism to Finnish society, closing with a discussion of 'new multilin-gualism' in present-day classrooms in Finland, where there is little pedagogical translanguaging, although there is frequent spontaneous translanguaging.

All in all, this volume responds to the need and the call to study and shape efficient and effective educational practices in specific language-diverse contexts for different groups of students. We bring together theoretical, methodological and empirical perspectives on pedagogical translanguaging, aiming to leverage research in schools and scholarly discussion of inclusive language practices with a view to enhancing social justice in schools and in society at large.

References

Adinolfi, L., Link, H. and St John, O. (2018) Translanguaging – researchers and practitioners in dialogue. *Translation and Translanguaging in Multilingual Contexts* 4 (3), 331–333.

Baker, C. (2011) *Foundations of Bilingual Education and Bilingualism* (5th edn). Bristol: Multilingual Matters.

Blommaert, J. (2010) *The Sociolinguistics of Globalization*. Cambridge: Cambridge University Press.

Byrnes, H. (2020) Navigating pedagogical translanguaging: Commentary on the special issue. *System* 92.

Cenoz, J. (2017) Translanguaging in school contexts: International perspectives. *Journal of Language, Identity & Education* 16 (4), 193–198.

Cenoz, J. and Gorter, D. (2020a) Pedagogical translanguaging. An introduction. *System* 92.

Cenoz, J. and Gorter, D. (2020b) Teaching English through pedagogical translanguaging. *World Englishes* 39, 300–311.

Cenoz, J. and Santos, A. (2020) Implementing pedagogical translanguaging in trilingual schools. *System* 92.

Conteh, J. and Meier, G. (eds) (2014) *The Multilingual Turn in Languages Education: Opportunities and Challenges*. Bristol: Multilingual Matters.

Cook, G. (2010) *Translation in Language Teaching*. Oxford: Oxford University Press.

Creese, A. and Blackledge, A. (2010) Translanguaging in the bilingual classroom: A pedagogy for learning and teaching? *The Modern Language Journal* 94 (i), 103–115.

Cummins, J. (2019) The emergence of translanguaging pedagogy: A dialogue between theory and practice. *Journal of Multilingual Education Research* 9, 19–36.

Cummins, J. and Early, M. (2011) *Identity Texts: The Collaborative Creation of Power in Multilingual Schools*. Stoke on Trent; Sterling, VA: Trentham.

Ganuza, N. and Hedman, C. (2017) Ideology versus practice: Is there a space for pedagogical translanguaging in mother tongue instruction? In B. Paulsrud, J. Rosén, B. Straszer and Å. Wedin (eds) *New Perspectives on Translanguaging and Education* (pp. 208–225). Bristol: Multilingual Matters.

García, O. (2009) *Bilingual Education in the 21st Century: A Global Perspective*. Oxford: Wiley-Blackwell.

García, O. and Flores, N. (2012) Multilingual pedagogies. In M. Martin-Jones, A. Blackledge and A. Creese (eds) *The Routledge Handbook of Multilingualism* (pp. 232–246). London: Routledge.

García, O., Johnson, S.I. and Seltzer, K. (2017) *The Translanguaging Classroom: Leveraging Student Bilingualism for Learning*. Philadelphia: Caslon.

García, O. and Kleyn, T. (eds) (2016) *Translanguaging with Multilingual Students: Learning from Classroom Moments*. New York: Routledge.

Hornberger, N.H. (ed.) (2017) *Honoring Richard Ruiz and his Work on Language Planning and Bilingual Education*. Bristol: Multilingual Matters.

Leung, C. and Valdés, G. (2019) Translanguaging and the transdisciplinary framework for language teaching and learning in a multilingual world. *The Modern Language Journal* 103 (2), 348–370.

Lin, A.M.Y. (2020) Foreword: Cutting through the monolingual grip of TESOL traditions – the transformative power of the translanguaging lens. In Z. Tian, L. Aghai, P. Sayer and J.L. Schissel (eds) *Envisioning TESOL through a Translanguaging Lens: Global Perspectives* (pp. v–ix). Dordrecht: Springer.

May, S. (ed.) (2014) *The Multilingual Turn: Implications for SLA, TESOL and Bilingual Education*. New York: Routledge/Taylor & Francis.

May, S. (2019) Negotiating the multilingual turn in SLA. *The Modern Language Journal* [Supplement: SLA Across Disciplinary Borders: New Perspectives, Critical Questions, and Research Possibilities] 103 (S1), 122–129.

Menken, K. and García, O. (2010) *Negotiating Language Policies in Schools: Educators as Policymakers*. London: Routledge.

Ortega, L. (2019) SLA and the study of equitable multilingualism. *The Modern Language Journal* [Supplement: SLA Across Disciplinary Borders: New Perspectives, Critical Questions, and Research Possibilities] 103 (S1), 23–38.

Paulsrud, B., Rosén, J., Straszer, B. and Wedin, Å. (eds) (2017) *New Perspectives on Translanguaging and Education*. Bristol: Multilingual Matters.

Probyn, M. (2015) Pedagogical translanguaging: bridging discourses in South African science classrooms. *Language and Education* 29 (3), 218–234.

Probyn, M. (2019) Pedagogical translanguaging and the construction of science knowledge in a multilingual South African classroom: Challenging monoglossic/post-colonial orthodoxies. *Classroom Discourse* 10 (3–4), 216–236.

Ruiz, R. (1984) Orientations in language planning. *NABE Journal* 8 (2), 15–34.

Seltzer, K. and García, O. (2020) Broadening the view: Taking up a translanguaging pedagogy with all language-minoritized students. In Z. Tian, L. Aghai, P. Sayer and J.L. Schissel (eds) *Envisioning TESOL through a Translanguaging Lens: Global Perspectives* (pp. 23–42). Dordrecht: Springer.

Tian, Z., Aghai, L., Sayer, P. and Schissel, J.L. (2020) Envisioning TESOL through a translanguaging lens in the era of post-multilingualism. In Z. Tian, L. Aghai, P. Sayer and J.L. Schissel (eds) *Envisioning TESOL through a Translanguaging Lens: Global Perspectives* (pp. 1–20). Dordrecht: Springer.

Williams, C. (1996) Secondary education: Teaching in the bilingual situation. In C. Williams, G. Lewis and C. Baker (eds) *The Language Policy: Taking Stock* (pp. 39–78). Llangefni: CAI.

2 Translanguaging: A Critical Analysis of Theoretical Claims

Jim Cummins

Introduction

During the past decade, the term *translanguaging* has come to dominate academic discussions regarding pedagogy in bilingual and second language (L2) immersion programs as well as pedagogy for multilingual and immigrant-background students in mainstream programs taught through the dominant societal language (e.g. Leung & Valdés, 2019; Paulsrud *et al.*, 2017). The construct of *translanguaging* was introduced by Williams (1994, 1996, 2000) in the context of Welsh-English bilingual programs that were focused on revitalizing the Welsh language. The term drew attention to the systematic and intentional alternation of input and output languages in bilingual instruction. García (2009) extended the construct of translanguaging to describe the dynamic *heteroglossic* integrated linguistic practices of multilingual individuals and to highlight the legitimacy of bilingual instruction that integrates rather than separates languages. In many subsequent publications, García and colleagues[1] elaborated the theoretical dimensions of translanguaging and also explored with educators how translanguaging pedagogies could be implemented in classroom contexts. The City University of New York (CUNY) New York State Initiative on Emergent Bilinguals (CUNY-NYSIEB) has developed an impressive set of resources and guides to support educators in pursuing translanguaging instructional initiatives (https://www.cuny-nysieb.org/).

Although some scholars (e.g. Edwards, 2012; Grin, 2018) dispute the usefulness and legitimacy of the term *translanguaging*, there is widespread support in the academic literature for the propositions that bi/multilingual individuals draw on the totality of their linguistic resources in communicative interactions and that classroom instruction should encourage students to use their full linguistic repertoire in flexible and strategic ways as a tool for cognitive and academic learning. For example, virtually all theorists and researchers currently endorse some form of *dynamic systems theory* that highlights the transformation of the cognitive and linguistic system brought about by the acquisition of multiple languages (e.g. de Bot *et al.*, 2007; Herdina & Jessner, 2002).

However, the theoretical elaborations proposed by García and colleagues include a variety of propositions that are considerably more controversial. For example, Jaspers (2018) pointed to the problematic nature of stretching the construct of translanguaging to encompass a wide range of disparate theoretical claims:

> In sum, translanguaging can apply to an innate instinct that includes monolinguals; to the performance of fluid language use that mostly pertains to bilinguals; to a bilingual pedagogy; to a theory or approach of language; and to a process of personal and social transformation. By any standard this is a lot for one term. (Jaspers, 2018: 3)

Ballinger *et al.* (2017) similarly point to the vagueness associated with the multiple uses of the term *translanguaging*, which, they claim, encompasses a theory of cognitive processing, societal use of multiple languages in communicative interactions, classroom language use behaviors among emergent bilingual students and teaching practices that attempt to harness students' multilingual repertoires to enhance learning. They propose the umbrella term *crosslinguistic pedagogy* as preferable to translanguaging to refer to pedagogical practices that support and encourage learners to draw on their full linguistic repertoire in the classroom.

These concerns about the multiple meanings and applications of the term *translanguaging* raise the issue of what criteria should be applied to evaluate the extent to which any theoretical construct, proposition or framework is *legitimate*. Translanguaging is clearly non-problematic when viewed as a *descriptive* concept to refer to (a) typical patterns of interpersonal interaction among multilingual individuals where participants draw on their individual and shared linguistic repertoires to communicate without regard to conventional language boundaries and (b) classroom interactions that draw on students' multilingual repertoires in addition to the official or dominant language of instruction. As I argue in a later section, a convincing case can also be made for the *theoretical* claim that these crosslinguistic interactional and instructional practices are legitimate from both ideological and educational perspectives.

As the construct of translanguaging migrated beyond its original formulation in the Welsh context and the core meanings outlined above, it became clear that two very different theoretical positions on translanguaging could be distinguished. According to García and Lin (2017), these theoretical positions can be characterized as *strong* and *weak*:

> On the one hand, there is the strong version of translanguaging, a theory that poses that bilingual people do not speak languages but rather, use their repertoire of linguistic features selectively. On the other hand, there

is a weak version of translanguaging, the one that supports national and state language boundaries and yet calls for softening these boundaries. (García & Lin, 2017: 126)

García and Lin cite the work of Cummins (2007, 2017a) in relation to crosslinguistic interdependence and the importance of teaching for transfer across languages as representative of the so-called weak version of translanguaging. By contrast, they support the so-called strong version of translanguaging as a linguistic theory while at the same time recognizing that bilingual education programs should combine the weak and strong versions of translanguaging theory:

> On the one hand, educators must continue to allocate separate spaces for the named languages although softening the boundaries between them. On the other hand, they must provide an instructional space where translanguaging is nurtured and used critically and creatively without speakers having to select and suppress different linguistic features of their own repertoire. (García & Lin, 2017: 127)

Although this attempt at synthesis between so-called strong and weak versions of translanguaging theory may appear reasonable, I argue in this chapter that it is built on an unstable and problematic theoretical foundation. Specifically, I suggest that as the concept of translanguaging evolved over the past decade, it acquired a considerable amount of what I have termed *extraneous conceptual baggage* that risks undermining its overall credibility (Cummins, 2017a, 2017b).

This extraneous conceptual baggage includes the following interrelated propositions that have been loosely woven together into the theoretical framework elaborated by advocates of the 'strong' version of translanguaging:

- Languages are 'invented' and do not exist as discrete 'countable' entities (Makoni & Pennycook, 2007).
- The multilingual's linguistic system is internally undifferentiated and unitary, reflecting the fact that 'languages' have no linguistic or cognitive reality (García, 2009).
- Codeswitching is an illegitimate monoglossic construct because it assumes the existence of two separate linguistic systems (Otheguy et al., 2015).
- Additive bilingualism is an illegitimate monoglossic construct because it similarly assumes the existence of two separate languages that are added together in bilingual individuals (García, 2009).
- For similar reasons, the notion of a *common underlying proficiency* and teaching for crosslinguistic transfer imply a monoglossic conception of bilingualism (García & Li Wei, 2014).
- *Academic language* is an illegitimate construct, as is the distinction between the language typically used in social and academic contexts (Flores & Rosa, 2015).

- Additive approaches to minoritized students' bilingualism are rooted in raciolinguistic ideologies (Flores & Rosa, 2015).
- Teaching biliteracy involves teaching standardized language norms in a prescriptive way that stigmatizes and suppresses students' authentic varieties of L1 and/or L2 (Flores & Rosa, 2015).[2]

In this chapter, I argue that all of these theoretical propositions are problematic. In varying degrees, they are unsupported by empirical research, they are logically inconsistent, and they detract from the important potential contribution of the construct of translanguaging to effective and equitable pedagogy. Rather than adopting the semantically loaded terms *strong* and *weak*, I use the terms *Unitary Translanguaging Theory* (UTT) and *Crosslinguistic Translanguaging Theory* (CTT) to highlight the distinguishing features of the alternative theoretical orientations identified by García and Lin. MacSwan (2017) has previously used the term *unitary model* to refer to the theoretical propositions advanced by García and colleagues. The UTT claims that languages have no linguistic or cognitive reality, and the bilingual's linguistic system is unitary and undifferentiated. By contrast, the CTT claims that bilinguals actually *do* speak languages, involving multiple registers, and effective teaching promotes translanguaging involving conceptual and linguistic transfer across languages.

The different orientations of UTT and CTT to the legitimacy of the construct of *language* should not obscure the fact that both theoretical perspectives view languages as socially constructed, they reject rigid instructional separation of languages, and they deplore the frequent devaluation of the linguistic practices that many minoritized students bring to school. Both orientations to translanguaging theory also endorse dynamic conceptions of multilingual cognitive functioning. And, finally, both UTT and CTT view translanguaging pedagogy as a central component in the struggle for social justice and equity in education.[3]

In the next section, I propose three criteria for judging the credibility of any theoretical claim relating to language education and then I apply these criteria to an analysis of the credibility both of the core construct of translanguaging (endorsed by advocates of both UTT and CTT) and the additional claims that have been woven into the fabric of the emerging UTT translanguaging theoretical framework.

In the final section, I describe a theoretical framework that is focused on reversing underachievement among minoritized students and that highlights the necessity for educators, both individually and collectively within schools, to implement evidence-based pedagogical approaches that challenge the operation of coercive power structures and ideologies. This framework (derived from Cummins, 1986, 1996/2001, 2000; Cummins & Early, 2011, 2015) incorporates the crosslinguistic version of translanguaging and emphasizes the importance for teachers:

- to engage and valorize students' multilingual repertoires, including their home varieties of L1 and/or L2,
- to promote multilingual literacies involving additive rather than sub-tractive approaches to language learning,
- to reinforce students' grasp of academic language across the curriculum,
- to maximize students' active engagement with literacy (ideally in both home and school languages) and
- to affirm students' emerging identities as cognitively and academically capable bi/multilinguals.

In contrast to the theoretical claims advanced by advocates of the unitary version of translanguaging, this framework affirms the legitimacy of teachers (a) adopting additive approaches to minoritized students' bilingualism and biliteracy, (b) actively and explicitly teaching students how language and languages work in academic contexts and (c) teaching for transfer of concepts, skills and learning strategies across languages.

Criteria for Evaluating Theoretical Claims and Constructs[4]

The literature on scientific inquiry emphasizes the importance of ensuring that claims and supporting arguments are consistent with the entirety of the relevant empirical evidence and are internally coherent and non-contradictory. Britt *et al.* (2014), for example, point out that in evaluating any scientific claim or argument, it is necessary to assess whether the evidence is sufficient to support the claim. This involves 'weighing the extent to which the totality of the support can overcome counterevidence or competing claims […] and considering the degree to which counter arguments and opposing evidence is rebutted, explained, or dismissed' (Britt *et al.*, 2014: 116). Britt and colleagues point out that although completely unqualified assertions often tend to be more persuasive to readers, '[q]ualifiers of scope (e.g. generally, always) and certainty (e.g. probably, suggests) are especially significant in academic and scientific writing' (Britt *et al.*, 2014: 116).

This analytic process is often neglected in popular discussions of scientific concepts (e.g. climate change). von der Mühlen *et al.* (2016), for example, compared the performance of college students and scientists in accurately judging the plausibility of arguments and recognizing common argumentation fallacies. They reported that the superior performance of scientists was mediated by their strategy of evaluating in an analytic manner the internal consistency and empirical foundation of the arguments. In contrast, students often relied on intuitive assertion-based judgments based on the extent to which the claim, and supporting evidence or argumentation, was consistent with their prior attitudes, beliefs and knowledge. In the sections that follow, I will return to this distinction between assertion-based claims that are frequently *evidence-free* and more rigorous analysis-based claims that seriously address the relevant empirical evidence.

In evaluating the legitimacy of theoretical constructs and claims that have been advanced in relation to the construct of translanguaging, I propose three criteria:

(1) *Empirical adequacy* – to what extent is the claim consistent with all the relevant empirical evidence?
(2) *Logical coherence* – to what extent is the claim internally consistent and non-contradictory?
(3) *Consequential validity* – to what extent is the claim useful in promoting effective pedagogy and policies?

These criteria operationally define what is meant by *legitimate* in the current context. The first two criteria reflect the generally accepted analytic processes common to all scientific inquiry. The third criterion was initially articulated in the area of educational testing by Messick (1994) who argued that discussions of the validity of any assessment procedure or test should take into account the consequences, intended or unintended, of applying or implementing this procedure. In a similar way, I argue that theoretical claims and constructs in the area of language education (and education more generally) should be assessed in relation to their implications for both classroom instruction and educational language policies. In other words, such claims should be subjected to a classroom 'reality check' to assess the credibility or usefulness of their instructional implications. These three criteria elaborate earlier discussion of these issues (Cummins, 2000, 2009). In the next section, I use the three criteria to evaluate various theoretical claims in the scholarly literature in relation to translanguaging. In the interests of brevity, I combine several of the claims advanced by advocates of the UTT.

Evaluating Translanguaging Theoretical Claims

Are interpersonal and pedagogical translanguaging legitimate constructs?

Although codeswitching/translanguaging and the use of non-standard varieties of English and/or L1 are still stigmatized in many schools and university contexts, as well as in the job market (Flores & Rosa, 2015; Lippi-Green, 1997/2012), I know of no researcher in recent years who has disputed the legitimacy of these interpersonal language practices. Ever since Labov (1969, 1972) established 'the logic of non-standard English', there has been consensus among researchers and applied linguists that schools should build on the linguistic resources that students bring to school as part of a process of affirming the 'funds of knowledge' that exist in minoritized communities (Moll *et al.*, 1992). In short, there is no academic debate about the legitimacy of interpersonal translanguaging.

With respect to pedagogical translanguaging, the incorporation of students' home languages into instruction and encouraging teachers to promote their continued development is consistent with a broad range of research data showing positive relationships between L1 and L2 literacy-related abilities (for reviews, see Cummins, 1996/2001 and National Academies of Sciences, Engineering, and Medicine, 2017). There are also numerous documented examples of educators mobilizing minoritized students' multilingual resources long before the construct of translanguaging had entered North American educational discourse (Auerbach, 1993, 2016; Chow & Cummins, 2003; Cummins *et al.*, 2005; DeFazio, 1997; Lucas & Katz, 1994). Many of the insights about multilingual instructional strategies we have gained over the past 30 years have been generated by educators who have often worked in collaboration with university researchers to document their initiatives. Documentation of these early instructional initiatives, together with more recent examples (e.g. Carbonara & Scibetta, 2020; Cummins & Persad, 2014; García & Kleyn, 2016; Little & Kirwin, 2019; Prasad, 2016), has demonstrated that multilingual instructional strategies (i.e. pedagogical translanguaging) can scaffold higher levels of academic performance, build critical language awareness, engage students actively with literacy in both their home and school languages and affirm students' identities.

Carbonara and Scibetta's collaborative research project in Italy involving analysis of classroom interaction in 5 primary and 3 middle schools and multiple interviews with almost 20 teachers and 122 students is perhaps the most comprehensive investigation of translanguaging to date. The authors highlight a variety of positive outcomes on students' metalinguistic awareness, academic engagement and attitudes toward multilingualism in general and their home languages/dialects. Similar outcomes were documented by Sierens and Van Avermaet (2014) in a four-year experiment in Flanders. Students developed more positive attitudes toward multiculturalism and their own home languages. However, no impact was noted on students' overall academic performance in Dutch. Jaspers (2018) cautions that these results suggest that researchers should be cautious about making strong causal claims for the transformative power of translanguaging by itself.

In summary, the legitimacy of pedagogical translanguaging is supported by extensive research evidence demonstrating that mobilizing students' multilingual and multimodal repertoires can scaffold students' L2 learning and their understanding of L2 academic content (e.g. Cummins & Early, 2011). These multilingual instructional strategies also serve to connect curriculum to students' lives, affirm their identities and reinforce their knowledge of how language works as an oral and written communicative system. With respect to consequential validity, the recent theoretical focus on translanguaging, together with earlier multilingual instructional initiatives, has resulted in a significant increase in educators' interest in exploring ways in which minoritized students' home languages can be incorporated productively into instruction.

Do languages exist?

A major influence on the elaboration of the construct of translanguaging by García and colleagues was the claim by Makoni and Pennycook (2007) that languages do not exist as real entities in the world but rather are inventions of social, cultural and political movements. They argue that the idea of a *language* is a European invention and a product of colonialism. Advocates of UTT use the term *named languages* to reinforce Makoni and Pennycook's point that languages are socially invented categories. However, García also acknowledged that these 'categories are not imaginary, in the sense that they refer to entities that exist in the societies that have coined the terms and have had real and material effects' (García & Li Wei, 2014: 7). Despite the acknowledgment of so-called named languages as social realities, languages are still presented as somewhat oppressive forces that potentially victimize the fluid linguistic practices of minoritized students. This is evident in the definition of translanguaging as 'the deployment of a speaker's f ull linguistic repertoire without regard for watchful adherence to the socially and politically defined boundaries of named languages' (Otheguy *et al.*, 2015: 281). The phrase 'watchful adherence' suggests that minoritized students' language use is subject to surveillance and devaluation by institutions (e.g. schools) dedicated to enforcing standardized language norms (e.g. through high-stakes testing regimes).

UTT advocates extend the claim that named languages have no objective linguistic or cognitive reality by arguing that the linguistic system of bi/multilinguals is unitary, dynamic and undifferentiated. This *heteroglossic* reality of multilinguals' cognitive system is contrasted with *monoglossic* ideologies that construct named languages as real entities and consequently conceive of multilingualism as the existence of separate monolingualisms within the individual.

Thus, rather than referring to languages as though they actually exist as countable entities or legitimate constructs, advocates of the UTT use the verb forms *languaging* and *translanguaging* in order to position language as a social practice in which learners engage rather than a set of structures and functions that they learn. In other words, they adopt a mutually exclusive (either-or) position with respect to language (noun form) and languaging (verb form). A heteroglossic theoretical orientation, according to this perspective, requires adoption of the verb form (*trans/languaging*) as legitimate and the noun form (*language*) as monoglossic and hence illegitimate. It is not possible to view both verb forms and noun forms as legitimate constructs.

The empirical evidence related to the claim that the bilingual's linguistic system is unitary and undifferentiated will be considered in the next section. Here my concern is with the broader claim that the construct of *a language* is illegitimate. This claim has been disputed on multiple grounds. For example, Grin (2018: 256) pointed to the consensus that bilingualism is not simply the addition of two monolingualisms: 'Nobody denies that languages are the product of human agency and develop historically, and nobody claims that they are watertight compartments'. However, the 'claim seems to be that *since* the users of human language operating in multilingual settings draw on an internal linguistic repertoire, a sort of continuum in which "named languages" blend into each other, *then* it follows that these "named languages" are irrelevant constructs' (Grin, 2018: 255, emphasis original). Grin argued that this is a logically flawed inference. The hybridity of linguistic practices and the complexity of linguistic repertoires 'do not carry the consequence that languages do not exist or that named languages are irrelevant' (Grin, 2018: 257).

Makoni and Pennycook have also pointed to the consequences of the claim that 'discrete languages don't exist' (2007: 2). They acknowledge that, according to this analysis, constructs such as language rights, mother tongues, multilingualism and codeswitching are also illegitimate. Grin highlighted the implications of this claim:

> Very practically, language is a key category in much of human rights law; denying the existence of languages blocks the access of minoritized groups to it. But more fundamentally, if languages in general do not *really* exist, if they are misleading constructs, this is true of small languages as well. Why, then, fight for them? It would be absurd. [...] This is why the advocates of the notion of 'languaging', particularly when they go one step further and deny the existence of languages, are not just making scientifically spurious claims. They are also, willingly or not, the objective allies of linguistic imperialism and linguistic injustice. (Grin, 2018: 260, emphasis original)

Obviously, advocates of the UTT are committed to social and linguistic justice and would dispute this conclusion. However, by adopting counterintuitive positions such as 'bilingual people do not speak languages' (García & Lin, 2017: 126), they have locked themselves into a problematic and unproductive theoretical space. There is clearly something seriously amiss when UTT scholars who advocate for critical multilingual language awareness and for translanguaging as an educationally transformative force are being called to task by credible researchers for promoting theoretical positions that are 'inconsistent with a civil rights orientation on language education policy' (MacSwan, 2020: 1) and as 'the objective allies of linguistic imperialism and linguistic injustice' (Grin, 2018: 260).

Logical inconsistencies are also apparent in the ways UTT scholars contrast their position with so-called weak versions of translanguaging theory. For example, what exactly is meant by García and Lin's (2017: 126) characterization of the 'weak' version of translanguaging as 'one that supports national and state language boundaries, and yet calls for softening these boundaries'? In supporting national and state language boundaries, are we referring to political beliefs, educational policies, cognitive/linguistic processing or all of the above? How does 'supporting national and state language boundaries' differ from García and colleagues' acknowledgment that (a) languages have social reality, (b) '[m]inoritized languages must be protected and developed if that is the wish of people' (García & Lin, 2017: 127) and (c) 'bilingual education must develop bilingual students' ability to use language according to the rules and regulations that have been socially constructed for that particular named language'? (García & Lin, 2017: 126).

The logically problematic nature of the claim that discrete languages do not exist is illustrated in the fact that in multiple publications UTT advocates refer to discrete languages as though they actually *do* exist. For example, García and Kleifgen (2019: 9–10), in discussing a research study by Espinosa and Herrera (2016), talk about how the researchers told students to use their entire linguistic repertoire to state the main idea from their reading. Students drew from all their language resources: 'Some used English, others Spanish, and yet others used both Spanish and English'. There is a clear logical incongruity in using labels such as *Spanish* and *English* as though they actually referred to real conceptual entities while at the same time claiming that these conceptual entities do not exist. How does the claim that 'bilingual people do not speak languages' (García & Lin, 2017: 126) fit with the acknowledgment that some bilingual students 'used English, others Spanish, and yet others used both Spanish and English'?

The most unfortunate aspect of these logical contradictions is that the confusion they are likely to evoke among educators and policymakers is *completely unnecessary*. There is nothing to be gained theoretically or pedagogically from the assertion that 'bilingual people do not speak languages'. There is no difference in the instructional practices that are implied by so-called strong and weak versions of translanguaging (e.g. Cummins, 2007).

In my reading, the basic (and legitimate) point that UTT advocates wish to convey is that the fluid language practices and varieties of all students (bilingual and monolingual) should be affirmed and built upon by schools in all program types. Students' language repertoires should be actively acknowledged as crucial cognitive tools and intrinsic components of their evolving identities. It is also valid to point out that some so-called bilingual programs have failed to connect instruction to students' lives and affirm their linguistic talents and identities – in other words, they have failed to challenge coercive relations of power (Cummins, 1986, 1996/2001). However, affirmation of this perspective is nothing new – similar points have been repeatedly articulated for at least 40 years within the pejoratively labeled *weak* version of translanguaging (e.g. Cummins, 1981a, 1986, 1996/2001).

There is no dispute about the fact that languages are socially constructed with porous boundaries, but languages are also experientially and socially *real* for students, teachers, policymakers, curriculum designers, politicians and most researchers. There is also no conceptual difficulty in reconciling the construct of translanguaging, understood as the integrated process through which multilingual individuals use and learn languages, with the experiential and social reality of different languages, understood as historical, cultural and ideological constructs that have material consequences and determine social action (e.g. language planning, bilingual programs, etc.; cf. Cummins, 2017a). Expressed differently, there is no compelling reason to adopt a binary *either-or* dichotomy between the verb form *trans/languaging* and the noun form *language* rather than a *both-and* position that acknowledges both the legitimacy of the construct of *translanguaging* and the experiential and social legitimacy of languages. Skutnabb-Kangas (2015) has made a similar point, arguing that individuals and groups have the right to claim a language as their own, and there is no contradiction between treating languages as both processes and, at the same time, as concrete entities.

This analysis also challenges the convention of using the term *named languages* to signify that socially constructed languages do not have linguistic reality. Use of this term is no more useful or meaningful than the term *named colors*. For example, it would rightly be considered ridiculous for someone to say: 'I plan to paint my house the named color blue'. Languages and colors are both social constructions that have permeable boundaries but which also have undeniable social and experiential reality (Cummins, 2017a).

In short, the claim that discrete languages do not exist represents a conceptually fragile and profoundly counterintuitive foundation upon which to build an instructional rationale for translanguaging pedagogy.

To what extent is it legitimate to characterize codeswitching, additive bilingualism, the common underlying proficiency and teaching for crosslinguistic transfer as 'monoglossic'?

Advocates of UTT establish a clear binary dichotomy between heteroglossic and monoglossic conceptions of bilingualism. They claim that in contrast to translanguaging and its rootedness in a dynamic, heteroglossic, unitary and undifferentiated conceptual/linguistic system, the constructs of codeswitching, additive bilingualism, the common underlying proficiency and teaching for crosslinguistic transfer reflect a monoglossic orientation that delineates a dual competence model involving separate L1/L2 features that map onto the characteristics of named languages (e.g. García, 2009; García & Li Wei, 2014). I argue in this section that these claims are without empirical foundation, are logically inconsistent and are highly problematic in terms of consequential validity.

With respect to codeswitching, MacSwan (2017: 179) pointed out that the characterization of codeswitching research as monoglossic in orientation is 'merely asserted and not tied to an actual analysis of theoretical proposals in the literature, nor are any actual relevant citations provided'. His detailed analysis of research in the areas of codeswitching and bilingual language development supports what he calls an integrated multilingual model that posits both shared and discrete grammatical and lexical resources rather than the unitary undifferentiated model advocated by UTT scholars. This integrated model of multilingual competence is consistent with the common underlying proficiency construct proposed by Cummins (1981b).

Grin (2018: 256) has likewise disputed the empirical basis for a unitary undifferentiated model, noting that neurolinguistic research shows that 'the very fact of using different languages mobilises different areas of the brain and reflects the need, for bilingual language users switching between languages, to *inhibit* one language in order to speak the other' (emphasis original). In short, serious questions can be raised about the empirical adequacy of the unitary undifferentiated model of bilingual language processing advanced by UTT advocates.

Similar considerations apply to the assertion that additive bilingualism (Lambert, 1974), the common underlying proficiency (Cummins, 1981a, 1981b), and teaching for crosslinguistic transfer reflect monoglossic ideologies. García (2009), for example, argued that the notion of additive bilingualism represents a theoretical framework in which bilingualism is positioned as two separate, isolated languages rather than as an integrated linguistic system. She goes on to argue that this functional compartmentalization of the bilingual's two languages, implied by additive bilingualism, gets translated into separate instructional spaces within bilingual programs. It is important to note that these claims are merely asserted with no supportive evidence or logical argumentation.

García and Li Wei (2014: 69) also questioned the notion of a common underlying proficiency, because, in their estimation, it still constructs students' L1 and L2 as separate: 'Instead, translanguaging validates the fact that bilingual students' language practices are not separated into … home language and school language, instead transcending both'. They also argue that we can now 'shed the concept of transfer … [in favor of] a conceptualization of integration of language practices in the person of the learner' (García & Li Wei, 2014: 80).

In short, UTT advocates conflate notions of additive bilingualism, the common underlying proficiency and teaching for crosslinguistic transfer with monoglossic, dual competence or separate underlying proficiency notions of bilingualism despite the fact that the former constructs have been invoked for more than 40 years to argue *against* separate underlying proficiency (Cummins, 1981a, 1981b) or *two solitudes* (Cummins, 2007) conceptions of bilingualism. No explanation has been provided as to why additive bilingualism (and its opposite *subtractive bilingualism*) is interpreted exclusively as referencing patterns of *linguistic* processing rather than as part of the *social* landscape experienced by students and teachers at school. As Cummins (2017b) pointed out, additive bilingualism emerged largely as a sociopolitical construct to challenge the suppression of minoritized students' home languages in schools. *It implies nothing with respect to how bilinguals process languages.* The conflation of additive bilingualism with monoglossic ideologies derives from the oversimplified dichotomy of heteroglossic/monoglossic and is simply asserted with no empirical evidence or analytic discussion.

The dismissal by García and Li Wei (2014) of the *common underlying proficiency* and *teaching for crosslinguistic transfer* took no account of relevant research consistent with these theoretical constructs. The Report of the National Academies of Sciences, Engineering, and Medicine (NASEM, 2017) summarized more than 40 years of research relevant to these theoretical claims. The following conclusion of this report affirmed the empirical foundation of the common underlying proficiency construct: 'The two languages of bilinguals share a cognitive/conceptual foundation that can facilitate the acquisition and use of more than one language for communication, thinking, and problem solving' (NASEM, 2017: 243). The legitimacy of teaching for crosslinguistic transfer was similarly reinforced in the same report: 'the experimental studies reviewed [...] suggest that instructional routines that draw on students' home language, knowledge, and cultural assets support literacy development in English' (NASEM, 2017: 297).

The categorization of additive bilingualism as monoglossic also ignores the fact that numerous researchers who explicitly endorse dynamic conceptions of bilingual/multilingual cognitive processing also endorse the construct of additive bilingualism, understood as an instructional orientation to build on minoritized students' multilingual repertoires. The originator of the notion of translanguaging, Cen Williams (2000), clearly had no problem in invoking additive bilingualism as a legitimate construct:

> It could be argued that the constant switching from one language to the other, and the fact that sections of the notes were read in English and then explained in Welsh, provided students with opportunities to develop their individual bilingual capabilities; that it was a means of translanguaging and another form of creating an opportunity for additive bilingualism. (Williams, 2000: 139)

Lewis *et al.* (2012: 668) also viewed additive bilingualism as fully compatible with the notion of translanguaging, which, they suggest, shifts perceptions of minority group bi/multilingualism from separate and diglossic to integrated and heteroglossic and 'from ideology that accented the subtractive and negative nature of bilingualism to one that expresses the advantages of additive bilingualism where languages in the brain, classroom, and street act simultaneously and not sequentially, with efficient integration and not separation'.

In summary, there is no basis for UTT advocates to conflate additive bilingualism with monoglossic ideologies. They have cited no research or documentary evidence to support any connection between the construct of additive bilingualism and patterns of bilingual language processing *for the simple reason that there is none*. Rather than ignoring the documentary evidence, it would have been more accurate to acknowledge that educators and researchers who promoted additive bilingualism were challenging the socially imposed hierarchy of languages and language varieties and the coercive power relations that continue to suppress student and community languages in schools (see Cummins, 1986, 1996/2001 for elaboration of this perspective).

With respect to consequential validity, the stigmatization of additive bilingualism as monoglossic and implicated in 'watchful adherence' to standardized language norms raises the question of how this perspective should be communicated to educators who, for many years, have promoted additive bilingualism as a challenge to subtractive ideologies in schools. What are the implications for teachers who are mandated by curriculum policies to help students develop proficiency in the standard academic language, including strong reading and writing skills, in both L1 and L2? García has addressed this issue, but in a way that does little to clear up the confusion:

> Because literacy relies on the standard, the standard language itself is taught explicitly in school, and it *certainly needs to be taught*. [...] We are not questioning the teaching of a standard language in school; without its acquisition, language minority children will continue to fail and will not have equal access to resources and opportunities. But we have to recognize that an *exclusive* focus on the standard variety keeps out other languaging practices that are children's authentic linguistic identity expression. (García, 2009: 36, emphasis original)

Who has argued that the promotion of additive bilingualism involves an *exclusive* focus on the standard language? What García probably intends to communicate here is that the teaching of biliteracy together with L1 and L2 standard language skills should also include affirmation of minoritized students' authentic languaging practices. I completely agree with this sentiment. However, this is not what has been argued in multiple publications by UTT advocates. Additive bilingualism (i.e. biliteracy) is dismissed unequivocally, with no qualifications or exceptions, as monoglossic, and hence stigmatizing of students' integrated heteroglossic language varieties and practices. This may be perceived as a 'strong' and perhaps even superficially persuasive version of translanguaging theory (Britt *et al.*, 2014), but it falls far short of the criteria of empirical adequacy, logical coherence and consequential validity.

To what extent do discourses of appropriateness rooted in raciolinguistic ideologies lie at the core of additive approaches to language education?[5]

This question reflects the claims advanced by Nelson Flores (e.g. Flores, 2019; Flores & Rosa, 2015) and other researchers who have contributed to the emerging 'strong' version of translanguaging theory (e.g. Martin *et al.*, 2019). These researchers argue that 'additive approaches to bilingual education continue to interpret the linguistic practices of bilinguals through a monolingual framework that marginalizes the fluid linguistic practices of these communities' (Flores & Rosa, 2015: 153). They claim that 'notions such as "standard language" or "academic language" and the discourse of appropriateness in which they both are embedded must be conceptualized as racialized ideological perceptions rather than objective linguistic categories' (Flores & Rosa, 2015: 152). According to this interpretation, the teaching of academic language in additive bilingual programs involves the imposition of standardized language norms that are permeated by raciolinguistic discourses of appropriateness focused on molding minoritized students 'into white speaking subjects who have mastered the empirical linguistic practices deemed appropriate for a school context' (Flores & Rosa, 2015: 157).

As noted previously, the use of the term *additive bilingualism* by researchers or educators does not in any way imply the endorsement of a two solitudes conceptualization of bilingual proficiency and bilingual instruction. Furthermore, as Cummins (2017b: 405) pointed out, far from marginalizing bilingual students, 'additive approaches to language education have explicitly challenged historical and current patterns of societal power relations that devalue, disparage, and exclude from schooling the language and cultural accomplishments and practices of minoritized communities'.

The problematic nature of the theoretical claims advanced by Flores and Rosa (2015) can be analyzed with reference to the criteria of empirical adequacy, logical coherence and consequential validity. First, however, it is important to acknowledge the validity and importance of some aspects of their analysis. For example, it is clear that raciolinguistic ideologies *do* exist and that they exert pernicious effects on minoritized students' academic engagement and achievement (e.g. Labov, 1972; Lippi-Green, 1997/2012). It has also been long recognized that ideologies of linguistic purism communicated by teachers to students can undermine bilingual students' confidence and competence in both their home and school languages. Cummins (1981a: 32), for example, noted that '[d]espite the fact that Labov's analysis is universally accepted by linguists and sociolinguists, it is still disturbingly common to find administrators and teachers of language minority students in bilingual education programs disparaging the non-standard version of the primary language (L1) which children bring to school and attempting to teach the standard version through explicit formal instruction'. At this point, despite ongoing discriminatory instructional policies and practices within schools, there is no dispute among educational researchers and applied linguists that 'educators must recognize, validate, and build on the diverse and rich repertoire of language practices that multilingual learners bring with them to school' (Martin *et al.*, 2019: 26). Inspirational educators have been showing for many years how this can be implemented in linguistically diverse classrooms (e.g. Chow & Cummins, 2003; DeFazio, 1997).

Thus, Flores and Rosa's (2015) analysis is a useful reminder of the ongoing reality of both raciolinguistic ideologies and discourses of appropriateness. However, their claim that raciolinguistic ideologies and discourses of appropriateness are *intrinsically and inevitably* implicated in the teaching of academic language and additive approaches to bilingualism and biliteracy is unsupported.

No empirical evidence is cited by Flores and Rosa (2015) to support their conflation of academic language with standardized language and the embeddedness of both of these constructs, together with additive bilingualism, in raciolinguistic discourses of appropriateness. Their views on the teaching of standard language also appear to be at variance with García's (2009: 36) position that the standard language certainly needs to be taught.

Flores and Rosa (2015) do not acknowledge the considerable evidence that *academic language* is a legitimate theoretical construct that can be empirically distinguished from the language typically used in everyday social interactions (for reviews, see Cummins, 2000, 2007b; Heppt *et al.*, 2016; Uccelli *et al.*, 2015). As one example of the research supporting the conceptual reality of academic language, Massaro (2015) reported that the vocabulary in 112 picture books he analyzed contained nearly twice the number of sophisticated or rare words than that found in adult speech directed to children or in speech between adults. Any attempt to dismiss the legitimacy of the construct of academic language that fails to even consider the empirical evidence is unconvincing.

With respect to logical coherence, Cummins (2017b) has pointed to numerous contradictions and inconsistences in the theoretical claims advanced by Flores and Rosa (2015). One inconsistency involves their claim that 'discourses of appropriateness [...] permeate additive approaches to language education' (Flores & Rosa, 2015: 166) and their simultaneous claim that they are 'not suggesting that advocates of additive approaches to language education should abandon all of their efforts to legitimize the linguistic practices of their language-minoritized students' (2015: 167).

The first claim entails a blanket condemnation, without qualification or nuance, of all forms of additive approaches to language education on the grounds that these pedagogical directions are permeated by raciolinguistic discourses of appropriateness. The second claim suggests that under certain unspecified circumstances, additive approaches *can* be mobilized to legitimize the linguistic practices of minoritized students. However, this second claim, which contradicts the initial claim, cries out for clarification and elaboration. Does this second claim mean that teachers should abandon only *some* of their efforts to promote additive bilingualism? If so, which instructional components are problematic, and which are acceptable? Is it acceptable for teachers to promote reading, writing and other academic skills together with additive forms of bilingualism so long as they also 'shift the focus to scrutiny of the white listening subject' (Flores & Rosa, 2015: 167)? If this is in fact the position that Flores and Rosa are advocating, it is unclear why they argue against additive approaches to bilingualism – their argument is against *uncritical* instructional approaches generally that fail to challenge coercive relations of power.

The argument that additive approaches to bilingualism are permeated by discourses of appropriateness and raciolinguistic ideologies invokes the following flawed logic:

Because

some educators who adopt additive approaches to minoritized students' bilingualism in both bilingual and English-medium programs disparage, implicitly or explicitly, students' fluid non-standard language varieties and practices by failing to affirm and build on these language varieties and practices as they teach standard academic language skills,

therefore,

all educators who adopt additive approaches to bilingualism involving the teaching of academic skills in two languages are complicit in the marginalization of students' fluid language varieties and practices.

In addition to failing to meet the criteria of empirical adequacy and logical coherence, Flores and Rosa's (2015) analysis falls short with respect to the criterion of consequential validity. As one example, they critique Olsen's (2010: 33) argument that instruction for long-term English learners should promote their home language literacy skills and focus 'on powerful oral language, explicit literacy development, instruction in the academic uses of English, high-quality writing, extensive reading of relevant texts, and emphasis on academic language and complex vocabulary'. They characterize Olsen's pedagogical recommendations as 'squarely focused on molding [long-term English learners] into white speaking subjects who have mastered the empirical linguistic practices deemed appropriate for a school context' (Flores & Rosa, 2015: 157). They suggest that an alternative pedagogical focus on critical language awareness combined with a heteroglossic rather than a monoglossic perspective has the potential to open up space for unmasking the racism inherent in additive approaches to language education.

A pedagogical focus on critical language awareness that valorizes the home language practices of minoritized students is endorsed by virtually all UTT and CTT advocates who have engaged with the construct of translanguaging (see, for example, Cummins, 1996/2001; García & Kleifgen, 2019; Hélot *et al.*, 2018). But how is this focus in any way inconsistent with Olsen's recommendations that instruction should support students' home language literacies and expand their abilities to use oral and written language in powerful ways? Are Flores and Rosa (2015) suggesting that teachers should *not* encourage the development of powerful oral language, high-quality writing and extensive reading of relevant texts? If it is problematic for teachers to focus on powerful oral language, what should they focus on instead? If extensive reading of relevant texts is a problematic instructional goal, how should teachers expand their students' literacy skills? Are teachers who provide conceptual and linguistic feedback on minoritized students' academic writing complicit with discourses of appropriateness?

In short, Flores and Rosa's critique of additive approaches to biliteracy and of teachers' attempts to expand minoritized students' access to academic language registers has no empirical basis, is logically flawed and is devoid of clear pedagogical directions for teachers. Blanket generalizations simply asserted without qualifications risk undermining the overall credibility of a critical translanguaging approach to teaching minoritized students.

Flores (2019) has recently revisited the construct of additive bilingualism in a way that appears to contradict his earlier analysis. Specifically, despite his earlier claim that discourses of appropriateness permeate additive approaches to language education, he suggests that additive bilingualism is not necessarily infused with raciolinguistic ideologies. The limitation to additive bilingualism resides in the fact that it attributes the educational underachievement of Latinx students to linguistic difficulties rather than to racism:

> In short, from a raciolinguistic perspective, the limitation to additive bilingualism is not that it is 'infused with raciolinguistic ideologies' (Cummins, 2017b: 415) but rather that it offers a purely linguistic analysis of a phenomenon that is highly racialized. Despite nods to structural inequality, at the core of additive bilingualism is a similar theory of change as the one that lies at the core of subtractive bilingualism – that the root of the problems confronted by Latina/o students is linguistic in nature. (Flores, 2019: 56)

To what extent is this claim valid? Obviously, the abstract concept of additive bilingualism is not making any theoretical claims and so the question becomes: To what extent do proponents of additive bilingualism offer a purely linguistic analysis of underachievement among Latinx students rather than identifying the racialized power structures that undermine students' academic engagement and achievement? As one of many proponents for developing minoritized students' biliteracy abilities, I will answer this question with reference to my own academic work.

Evidence-based Frameworks for Promoting Academic Achievement Among Minoritized Students

In multiple publications in the late 1970s and early 1980s, Cummins (1979, 1981a, 1981b, 1986) highlighted the fact that linguistic variables could not, by themselves, explain the underachievement of minoritized students. He argued that the root causes of underachievement lie in sociopolitical and sociocultural realities associated with societal power relations. Cummins (1981a: 39), for example, argued that '[t]here is no evidence for the belief that a switch between the language of the home and that of the school, i.e. "linguistic mismatch", is in itself, a cause of school failure'. Cummins (1986: 20) suggested that the linguistic mismatch hypothesis was 'patently inadequate' and that '[m]inority students are disabled or disempowered by schools in very much the same way that their communities are disempowered by interactions with societal institutions' (1986: 23). An additive orientation toward minoritized students' language and culture was proposed as an essential ingredient to challenge disempowering educational structures. In short, Flores' (2019) claim that proponents of promoting additive bilingualism attribute Latinx students' academic problems, exclusively or primarily, to linguistic factors is without foundation (see Cummins, 1996/2001 for detailed discussion of this issue).

The frameworks outlined in Figures 2.1 and 2.2 sketch the perspectives on the underachievement of minoritized students that, I would argue, are evidence-based, logically coherent and useful in stimulating exploration of classroom and school-based instructional initiatives. The initial framework (Figure 2.1) proposes that relations of power in the wider society, ranging from coercive to collaborative in varying degrees, influence both the ways in which educators define their roles and the types of structures that are established in the educational system. Coercive relations of power refer to the exercise of power by a dominant individual, group or country to the detriment of a subordinated individual, group or country. The assumption is that there is a fixed quantity of power that operates according to a zero-sum or subtractive logic; in other words, the more power one group has, the less is left for other groups.

Collaborative relations of power, by contrast, reflect the sense of the term *power* that refers to *being enabled* or *empowered* to achieve more. Within collaborative relations of power, power is not a fixed quantity but is generated through interaction with others. The more empowered one individual or group becomes, the more is generated for others to share. The process is additive rather than subtractive. Within this context, empowerment can be defined as *the collaborative creation of power*. Schooling amplifies rather than silences minoritized students' power of *self*-expression regardless of their current level of proficiency in the dominant school language.

Educator role definitions refer to the mindset of expectations, assumptions and goals that educators bring to the task of educating linguistically and culturally diverse students. Educational structures refer to the organization of schooling in a broad sense that includes policies, programs, curriculum and assessment. While these structures will generally reflect the values and priorities of dominant groups in society, they are not by any means fixed or static and can be contested by individuals and groups.

SOCIETAL POWER RELATIONS

influence
the ways in which educators define their roles (teacher identity)
and
the structures of schooling (curriculum, funding, assessment, etc.)
which, in turn, influence

the ways in which educators interact
with linguistically and culturally diverse students.

These interactions form
an
INTERPERSONAL SPACE
within which
learning happens
and
identities are negotiated.

These **IDENTITY NEGOTIATIONS**
either
Reinforce coercive relations of power
or
Promote collaborative relations of power

Figure 2.1 Societal power relations, identity negotiation and academic achievement

Note. Adapted from *Negotiating Identities: Education for Empowerment in a Diverse Society* by J. Cummins, 2001, p. 20. Copyright 2001 by J. Cummins. Reprinted with permission.

Student background	Linguistically Diverse	Low-SES	Marginalized Status
Sources of potential disadvantage	-Failure to understand instruction due to home-school language differences;	-Inadequate healthcare and/or nutrition; -Housing segregation; -Lack of cultural and material resources in the home due to poverty; -Limited access to print in home and school;	-Societal discrimination; -Low teacher expectations; -Stereotype threat; -Stigmatization of L1/L2 language varieties; -Identity devaluation;
Evidence-based instructional response	-Scaffold comprehension and production of language across the curriculum; -Engage students' multilingual repertoires; -Reinforce academic language across the curriculum;	-Maximize print access and literacy engagement; -Reinforce academic language across the curriculum;	-Connect instruction to students' lives; -Decolonize curriculum and instruction through linguistically and culturally sustaining pedagogy; -Valorize and build on L1/L2 language varieties; -Affirm student identities in association with academic engagement;

Figure 2.2 Evidence-based instructional responses to sources of potential underachievement

Educational structures, together with educator role definitions, determine the patterns of interactions between educators, students and communities. These interactions form an interpersonal space within which the acquisition of knowledge and formation of identity is negotiated. Power is created and shared within this interpersonal space where minds and identities meet. As such, these teacher–student interactions constitute the most immediate determinant of student academic success or failure. Teacher agency is intrinsic to this framework in the sense that the interactions between educators, students and communities are never neutral; in varying degrees, they either reinforce coercive relations of power or promote collaborative relations of power.

The central tenet of this framework is that effective education for students from minoritized communities *requires* educators to challenge coercive relations of power as they are manifested in the structures and processes of schooling. This obviously includes a challenge to all forms of raciolinguistic ideologies whether manifested through the discourses of appropriateness or some other channel. However, the framework also includes a broader range of discriminatory structures and ideologies than is captured by the construct of raciolinguistic ideologies. For example, deaf students have suffered major discrimination for generations as a result of educational policies that prohibit instructional use of natural sign languages (e.g. Snoddon & Weber, 2021). Similarly, the well-documented and long-term underachievement of White working-class students in the United Kingdom (House of Commons Education Committee, 2014) is not readily captured within discourses of *racial* discrimination.

Figure 2.2 highlights the fact that more than just a critical translanguaging or critical multilingual awareness (García, 2017) approach is required to transform the educational achievement of minoritized students. The international literature on patterns of academic achievement (e.g. OECD, 2010; Van Avermaet *et al.*, 2018) identifies three groups (excluding students with special educational needs) that are commonly seen as potentially educationally disadvantaged: (a) students whose L1 is different from the language of school instruction, (b) students from low-socioeconomic status (SES) backgrounds and (c) students from communities that have been marginalized or excluded from educational and social opportunities as a result of discrimination in the wider society. Figure 2.2 specifies some of the societal conduits through which these potential educational disadvantages operate and also specifies evidence-based educational interventions that respond to these potential disadvantages. It should be noted that *disadvantage* is not a fixed or static construct; the linguistic and social realities of the three groups specified above are transformed into actual educational disadvantages only when the school fails to implement instruction that responds effectively to these realities.

A critical translanguaging or multilingual awareness approach would clearly include the instructional strategies of engaging students' multilingual repertoires, connecting to students' lives, decolonizing curriculum and instruction through linguistically and culturally sustaining pedagogy, valorizing and building on students' varieties of home and school languages and affirming students' identities. However, other instructional strategies such as scaffolding instruction, reinforcing students' grasp of academic language across the curriculum and maximizing literacy engagement have been less emphasized by advocates of UTT (e.g. García, 2017; García & Kleifgen, 2019; Martin *et al.*, 2019). For example, an extremely large body of research demonstrates a causal relationship between literacy engagement and literacy achievement for both native speakers and second-language speakers of the school language (e.g. Guthrie, 2004; Krashen, 2004; Lindsay, 2010), but this research is not highlighted as relevant even in articles focused directly on translanguaging and literacies (e.g. García & Kleifgen, 2019).

Similarly, mixed messages are given about the importance of reinforcing academic language across the curriculum. This instructional strategy is seemingly endorsed by statements such as the following: 'A translanguaging literacies approach also includes strategies such as translation and cross-linguistic study of syntax, vocabulary, word choice, cognates, and discourse structure to advance students' metalinguistic awareness of their own bilingual practices, thus heightening their engagement with texts' (García & Kleifgen, 2019: 13). But at the same time, this message is undermined by arguments that dispute the existence and legitimacy of academic language as well as deny the linguistic reality of languages in general. With reference to the quotation above, educators might well ask questions such as the following: If languages have no linguistic reality, what are we translating between? What does *cross-linguistic* mean if languages do not really exist? If languages are *real* only in a social sense but not a linguistic sense, how should we interpret cognates?

Conclusion

There is probably minimal difference in practice between the instructional strategies promoted by advocates of UTT as compared to those promoted by advocates of CTT. However, I have argued that the *theoretical framing* of these strategies in the scholarly writing of UTT advocates fails to address relevant empirical evidence, incorporates logically inconsistent propositions and communicates unclear and at times confusing messages to educators committed to equitable and effective teaching of minoritized students. Specifically, the theoretical framing proposed by UTT advocates is problematic in light of the following:

- inconsistencies in their depiction of the construct of *language* as (a) illegitimate, (b) socially real, (c) a set of standard conventions that should be taught explicitly in school and (d) potentially oppressive to minoritized students;

- their identification of additive bilingualism, academic language and teaching for crosslinguistic transfer as inherently monoglossic and consequently illegitimate;
- their depiction of additive approaches to minoritized students' bilingualism as permeated with discourses of appropriateness and raciolinguistic ideologies;
- their dismissal of the fact that promotion of additive bilingualism and the teaching of academic language registers have been framed within a detailed analysis of how societal power relations are actualized through patterns of teacher–student identity negotiation in schools;
- the multiple inconsistencies, inaccuracies and contradictions that derive from unqualified assertions and generalizations (e.g. teaching powerful oral language and high-quality writing to minoritized students serves only to mold them into White speaking subjects) and
- their failure to review and evaluate empirical evidence relevant to their theoretical assertions (e.g. research supporting the legitimacy of the common underlying proficiency construct).

The problematic theoretical framing of UTT has resulted in unproductive debates about whether this perspective is inconsistent with the promotion of civil rights (MacSwan, 2020) and an ally of linguistic imperialism and linguistic injustice (Grin, 2018). These debates are, at the very least, a distraction from the main goal of translanguaging theory, namely the transformation of the educational experiences of minoritized students such that their voices are heard in the classroom and beyond.

In contrast to UTT, CTT advocates argue that the interdependence of academic language skills and the integrated nature of bilingual language processing do not require us to relinquish the construct of specific languages nor to banish from the lexicon terms such as home language, school language, L1/L2, etc. A CTT approach also affirms the legitimacy of constructs such as additive bilingualism, common underlying proficiency and teaching for transfer across languages. Additive approaches to bilingualism are conceptualized as committed to challenging coercive relations of power and affirming the fluid linguistic practices of minoritized students. Finally, while cautioning against any form of rigid prescriptivism that devalues minoritized students' linguistic practices and talents, CTT advocates concur with scholars such as Wong Fillmore and Fillmore (2012), García (2009), Olsen (2010) and Delpit (2006) that academic language should be taught explicitly in school in a way that demystifies not only how the language itself works but also how language use intersects with hierarchies of power in all aspects of human society.

This critique of the extraneous theoretical baggage that has accumulated around the construct of translanguaging is not in any way intended to undermine the theoretical and pedagogical value of the core construct. Similarly, the constructs of raciolinguistic ideologies and discourses of appropriateness represent useful tools to conceptualize and guide antiracist teaching (Lee, 1985). My hope is that the credibility and instructional impact of these conceptual tools will benefit from constructive and critical dialogue.

Notes

(1) For ease of expression, I am using the citation 'García and colleagues' to refer to the following publications cited in this chapter which represent a sample of the extensive scholarly output produced by Ofelia García and colleagues over the past decade: Bartlett & García, 2011; Flores, 2019; Flores & Rosa, 2015; García, 2009, 2017, 2018; García & Kleifgen, 2019; García & Kleyn, 2016; García & Li Wei, 2014; García & Otheguy, 2014; Martin et al., 2019; Otheguy et al., 2015.

(2) Cummins (in press) also critiqued an additional theoretical claim regarding the Council of Europe's (2018) notion of *plurilingualism* which, García (2018: 883) argues, ignores power imbalances between speakers of different languages, and 'in today's globalized neoliberal economy, plurilingualism is exalted as a tool for profit making and personal gain'. Cummins pointed out that the conflation of plurilingualism with a neoliberal corporate agenda is simply asserted, without empirical evidence. Furthermore, if knowledge of multiple languages is seen as furthering a neoliberal agenda, the same argument would apply to any educational qualification. Few educators (progressive or non-progressive) would suggest that we should stop educating people because a highly educated workforce promotes corporate profit-making.

(3) It is beyond the scope of this chapter to review other theoretical conceptions of multilingualism that have been proposed during the past decade under the influence of García's (2009) elaboration of the construct of translanguaging. These include Creese and Blackledge's (2010) concept of *flexible bilingualism*, Cenoz and Gorter's (2014) *Focus on Multilingualism*, Slembrouck et al.'s (2018) *Functional Multilingual Learning* and the *Holistic Model for Multilingualism in Education* proposed by Duarte and Günther-van der Meij (2018). All of these approaches, together with Hornberger's (2003) *Continua of Biliteracy*, view the boundaries between languages as permeable and share the goal of 'turning multilingualism into a powerful didactic tool' (Slembrouck et al., 2018: 18). However, unlike UTT, these theoretical proposals do not propose an *either-or* dichotomy between *language* and *languaging* or claim that the notion of *a language* is an illegitimate construct. For example, Cenoz and Gorter (2014: 242) suggest that 'languages can be distinct entities because they are treated as such by social actors in the school context'. In this respect, these theoretical formulations can be seen as consistent with CTT.

(4) In the present chapter, *theory* refers to a principle or set of principles proposed to explain or promote understanding of specific phenomena. To be considered valid, a theory must be capable of accounting for *all* the relevant phenomena that have been credibly established. A *theoretical proposition* or *claim* is a statement that purports to be evidence-based and valid. A *theoretical hypothesis* is a more tentative statement or prediction usually put forward so that its validity can be tested through research. A *theoretical construct* is an abstract explanatory variable or conceptual entity that is not directly observable but which is used to account for observations, behavior or phenomena. Finally, a *theoretical framework* is a more elaborate grouping of inter-related theoretical propositions and constructs designed to account for phenomena, guide research and/or legitimize particular instructional approaches.

(5) Many of the problematic claims in relation to additive approaches to bilingualism and raciolinguistic ideologies discussed in this section relate specifically to the prolific publications of Nelson Flores. I focus primarily on the Flores and Rosa (2015) article

as representative of this work. I also locate this work within the general theoretical framework elaborated by García and colleagues on the grounds that these authors cite Flores' work extensively and have co-published with him. However, it is not clear that García would endorse all of the theoretical claims made by Flores. For example, Flores and Rosa's claim that additive approaches are embedded in discourses of appropriateness would also seem to apply to the book written by Bartlett and García (2011) entitled *Additive Schooling in Subtractive Times: Bilingual Education and Dominican Immigrant Youth in the Heights*.

Similarly, García (2009: 36) does not question the teaching of a standard language in school, whereas Flores and Rosa (2015: 152) view both standard language and academic language as 'racialized ideological perceptions' embedded in discourses of appropriateness. They include no qualifications of scope or certainty (Britt *et al.*, 2014) in relation to this and similar assertions throughout their article. Thus, it is legitimate to interpret their position as claiming that the teaching of standard forms of the school language (and, in bilingual programs, students' home languages) and the expansion of students' ability to use language powerfully in academic contexts are inevitably and invariably rooted in raciolinguistic ideologies.

This position is clearly at variance with García's (2009) perspective. However, at this point, García has not distanced herself from any of the theoretical claims advanced by Flores. Consequently, I feel it is legitimate to include Flores' work as an integral part of the emerging theoretical framework proposed by García and colleagues.

References

Auerbach, E. (1993) Reexamining English only in the ESL classroom. *TESOL Quarterly* 27, 9–32.

Auerbach, E. (2016) Reflections on 'Reexamining English only in the ESL classroom.' *TESOL Quarterly* 50 (4), 936–939. doi: 10.1002/tesq.310

Ballinger, S., Lyster, R., Sterzuk, A. and Genesee, F. (2017) Context-appropriate crosslinguistic pedagogy: Considering the role of language status in immersion education. *Journal of Immersion and Content-Based Language Education* 5 (1), 30–57. doi 10.1075/jicb.5.1.02bal.

Bartlett, L. and García, O. (2011) *Additive Schooling in Subtractive Times: Bilingual Education and Dominican Immigrant Youth in the Heights*. Nashville, TN: Vanderbilt University Press.

Britt, M.A., Richter, T. and Rouet, J.F. (2014) Scientific literacy: The role of goaldirected reading and evaluation in understanding scientific information. *Educational Psychologist* 49 (2), 104–122. doi: 10.1080/00461520.2014.916217

Carbonara, V. and Scibetta, A. (2019) *Imparare Attraverso le Lingue: Il Translanguaging come Pratica Didattica*. Rome: Carocci Editore.

Cenoz, J. and Gorter, D. (2014) Focus on multilingualism as an approach in educational contexts. In A. Creese and A. Blackledge (eds) *Heteroglossia as Practice and Pedagogy* (pp. 239–254). Berlin: Springer.

Chow, P. and Cummins, J. (2003) Valuing multilingual and multicultural approaches to learning. In S.R. Schecter and J. Cummins (eds) *Multilingual Education in Practice: Using Diversity as a Resource* (pp. 32–61). Portsmouth, NH: Heinemann.

Council of Europe (2018) *Common European Framework of Reference for Languages: Learning, Teaching, Assessment. Companion Volume with New Descriptors*. Strasbourg, France: Council of Europe Publishing. Retrieved from https://www.coe.int/en/web/common-european-framework-reference-languages/home.

Creese, A. and Blackledge, A. (2010) Translanguaging in the bilingual classroom: A pedagogy for learning and teaching? *The Modern Language Journal* 94 (1), 103–115.

Cummins, J. (1979) Linguistic interdependence and the educational development of bilingual children. *Review of Educational Research* 49, 222–251.

Cummins, J. (1981a) Four misconceptions about language proficiency in bilingual education. *NABE Journal* 5, 31–45.

Cummins, J. (1981b) The role of primary language development in promoting educational success for language minority students. In California State Department of Education (ed.) *Schooling and Language Minority Students: A Theoretical Framework* (pp. 3–49). Los Angeles: Evaluation, Dissemination and Assessment Center, California State University.

Cummins, J. (1986) Empowering minority students: A framework for intervention. *Harvard Educational Review* 56, 18–36.

Cummins, J. (1996/2001) *Negotiating Identities: Education for Empowerment in a Diverse Society.* Los Angeles: California Association for Bilingual Education.

Cummins, J. (2000) *Language, Power and Pedagogy: Bilingual Children in the Crossfire.* Clevedon: Multilingual Matters.

Cummins, J. (2007) Rethinking monolingual instructional strategies in multilingual classrooms. *The Canadian Journal of Applied Linguistics* 10, 221–240.

Cummins, J. (2009) Transformative multiliteracies pedagogy: School-based strategies for closing the achievement gap. *Multiple Voices for Ethnically Diverse Exceptional Learners* 11, 38–56.

Cummins, J. (2017a) Teaching for transfer in multilingual educational contexts. In O. García and A. Lin (eds) *Bilingual Education: Encyclopedia of Language and Education* (3rd edn) (pp. 103–115). New York: Springer Science+Business Media LLC.

Cummins, J. (2017b) Teaching minoritized students: Are additive approaches legitimate? *Harvard Education Review* 87 (3), 404–425.

Cummins, J. (in press) Teachers as knowledge-generators and agents of language policy: Research, theory and ideology in plurilingual pedagogies. In E. Piccardo, A. Germain-Rutherford and G. Lawrence (eds) *Routledge Handbook of Plurilingual Education*. New York: Routledge.

Cummins, J., Bismilla, V., Chow, P., Cohen, S., Giampapa, F., Leoni, L., Sandhu, P. and Sastri, P. (2005) Affirming identity in multilingual classrooms. *Educational Leadership* 63 (1), 38–43.

Cummins, J. and Early, M. (eds) (2011) *Identity Texts: The Collaborative Creation of Power in Multilingual Schools*. Stoke-on-Trent: Trentham Books.

Cummins, J. and Early, M. (2015) *Big Ideas for Expanding Minds: Teaching English Language Learners across the Curriculum*. Toronto: Rubicon Press/Pearson Canada.

Cummins, J. and Persad, R. (2014) Teaching through a multilingual lens: The evolution of EAL policy and practice in Canada. *Education Matters* 2 (1). Available at: http://em.synergiesprairies.ca/index.php/em/issue/view/7.

de Bot, K., Verspoor, M. and Lowie, W. (2007) A dynamic systems theory approach to second language acquisition. *Bilingualism, Language and Cognition* 10, 7–21. Retrieved from http://www.rug.nl/staff/c.l.j.de.bot/DeBotetal2007-Bilingualism.pdf.

DeFazio, A.J. (1997) Language awareness at The International High School. In L. Van Lier and D. Corson (eds) *Knowledge about Language. Encyclopedia of Language and Education* (pp. 99–107). Dordrecht: Kluwer Academic Publishers, Inc.

Delpit, L. (2006) *Other People's Children: Cultural Conflict in the Classroom*. New York: The New Press.

Duarte, J. and Günther-van der Meij, M. (2018) A holistic model for multilingualism in education. *EuroAmerican Journal of Applied Linguistics and Languages* 5 (2), 24–43. Retrieved from http://dx.doi.org/10.21283/2376905X.9.153.

Edwards, J. (2012) *Multilingualism: Understanding Linguistic Diversity*. London: Continuum.

Espinosa, C. and Herrera, L. (2016) Reclaiming bilingualism: Translanguaging in a science class. In O. García and T. Kleyn (eds) *Translanguaging with Multilingual Students: Learning from Classroom Moments* (pp. 160–178). New York, NY: Routledge.

Flores, N.L. (2019) Translanguaging into raciolinguistic ideologies: A personal reflection on the legacy of Ofelia García. *Journal of Multilingual Education Research*, Vol. 9, Article 5. Available at: https://fordham.bepress.com/jmer/vol9/iss1/5.

Flores, N. and Rosa, J. (2015) Undoing appropriateness: Raciolinguistic ideologies and language diversity in education. *Harvard Educational Review* 85, 149–171.

García, O. (2009) *Bilingual Education in the 21st Century. A Global Perspective.* Boston: Basil Blackwell.

García, O. (2017) Critical multilingual language awareness and teacher education. In J. Cenoz, D. Gorter and S. May (eds) *Language Awareness and Multilingualism, Encyclopedia of Language and Education* (pp. 263–280). doi 10.1007/978-3-319-02240-6_30.

García, O. (2018) The multiplicities of multilingual interaction. *International Journal of Bilingual Education and Bilingualism* 21 (7), 881–891. doi:10.1080/13670050.2018.1474851.

García, O. and Kleifgen, J.A. (2019) Translanguaging and literacies. *Reading Research Quarterly.* Published online, 12 November. doi:10.1002/rrq.286.

García, O. and Kleyn, T. (eds) (2016) *Translanguaging with Multilingual Students.* New York and London: Routledge.

García, O. and Lin, A.M.Y. (2017) Translanguaging in bilingual education. In O. García and A.M.Y. Lin (eds) *Bilingual and Multilingual Education (Encyclopedia of Language and Education, Vol. 5)* (pp. 117–130). Dordrecht: Springer.

García, O. and Li Wei (2014) *Translanguaging: Language, Bilingualism and Education.* New York: Palgrave Macmillan.

García, O. and Otheguy, R. (2014) Spanish and Hispanic bilingualism. In M. Lacorte (ed.) *The Routledge Handbook of Hispanic Applied Linguistics* (pp. 639–658). New York, NY: Routledge.

Grin, F. (2018) On some fashionable terms in multilingualism research: Critical assessment and implications for language policy. In P.A. Kraus and F. Grin (eds) *The Politics of Multilingualism: Europeanisation, Globalization and Linguistic Governance* (pp. 247–273). Amsterdam: John Benjamins Publishing Company.

Guthrie, J.T. (2004) Teaching for literacy engagement. *Journal of Literacy Research* 36, 1–30.

Hélot, C., Frijns, C., VanGorp, K. and Sierens, S. (eds) (2018) *Language Awareness in Multilingual Classrooms in Europe: From Theory to Practice.* Amsterdam: de Gruyter Mouton Publishers.

Heppt, B., Henschel, S. and Haagb, N. (2016) Everyday and academic language comprehension: Investigating their relationships with school success and challenges for language minority learners. *Learning and Individual Differences* 47, 244–251. http://dx.doi.org/10.1016/j.lindif.2016.01.004.

Herdina, P. and Jessner, U. (2002) *A Dynamic Model of Multilingualism: Perspectives of Change in Psycholinguistics.* Clevedon: Multilingual Matters.

Hornberger, N.H. (ed.) (2003) *Continua of Biliteracy: An Ecological Framework for Educational Policy, Research, and Practice in Multilingual Settings.* Clevedon: Multilingual Matters.

House of Commons Education Committee (2014) *Underachievement in Education by White Working Class Children. First Report of Session 2014–15.* London: The Stationery Office Limited.

Jaspers, J. (2018) The transformative limits of translanguaging. *Language and Communication* 58, 1–10.

Krashen, S.D. (2004) *The Power of Reading: Insights from the Research* (2nd edn). Portsmouth, NH: Heinemann.

Labov, W. (1969) *A study of Non-standard English*. Washington, DC: Center for Applied Linguistics. Retrieved from https://files.eric.ed.gov/fulltext/ED024053.pdf.

Labov, W. (1972) *Language in the Inner City*. Philadelphia: University of Pennsylvania Press.

Lambert, W.E. (1974) Culture and language as factors in learning and education. In F.E. Aboud and R.D. Meade (eds) *Cultural Factors in Learning and Education. Proceedings of the Fifth Western Washington Symposium on Learning* (pp. 99–122). Bellingham, WA: Western Washington University.

Lee, M. (1985) *Letters to Marcia: A Teacher's Guide to Anti-Racist Education*. Toronto: Cross Cultural Communication Centre.

Leung, C. and Valdés, G. (2019) Translanguaging and the transdisciplinary framework for language teaching and learning in a multilingual world. *The Modern Language Journal* 103 (2), 348–370. doi: 10.1111/modl.12568

Lewis, G., Jones, B. and Baker, C. (2012) Translanguaging: developing its conceptualisation and contextualisation. *Educational Research and Evaluation* 18 (7), 655–670. http://dx.doi.org/10.1080/13803611.2012.718490

Lindsay, J. (2010) *Children's Access to Print Material and Education-Related Outcomes: Findings from a Meta-analytic Review*. Naperville, IL: Learning Point Associates.

Lippi-Green, R. (1997/2012) *English with an Accent: Language, Ideology and Discrimination in the United States*. New York: Routledge.

Little, D. and Kirwin, D. (2019) *Engaging with Linguistic Diversity*. London: Bloomsbury Academic.

Lucas, T. and Katz, A. (1994) Reframing the debate: The roles of native languages in English-only programs for language minority students. *TESOL Quarterly* 28, 537–562.

MacSwan, J. (2017) A multilingual perspective on translanguaging. *American Educational Research Journal* 54 (1), 167–201. doi: 10.3102/0002831216683935

MacSwan, J. (2020) Translanguaging, language ontology and civil rights. *World Englishes* 1–13. Published online 16 March 2020. https://doi.org/10.1111/weng.12464.

Makoni, S. and Pennycook, A. (2007) Disinventing and reconstituting languages. In S. Makoni and A. Pennycook (eds) *Disinventing and Reconstituting Languages* (pp. 1–41). Clevedon: Multilingual Matters.

Martin, K.M., Aponte, H J. and García, O. (2019) Countering raciolinguistic ideologies: the role of translanguaging in educating bilingual children. *Cahiers Internationaux de Sociolinguistique* 16 (2), 19–41.

Massaro, D.W. (2015) Two different communication genres and implications for vocabulary development and learning to read. *Journal of Literacy Research* 47 (4) 505–527. doi: 10.1177/1086296X15627528.

Messick, S. (1994) The interplay of evidence and consequences in the validation of performance assessments. *Educational Researcher* 23, 13–23.

Moll, L.C., Amanti, C., Neff, D. and Gonzalez, N. (1992) Funds of knowledge for teaching: Using a qualitative approach to connect homes and classrooms. *Theory into Practice* 31 (2), 132–141.

NASEM (National Academies of Sciences, Engineering and Medicine) (2017) *Promoting the Educational Success of Children and Youth Learning English: Promising Futures*. Washington, DC: The National Academies Press. doi: 10.17226/24677.

OECD (2010) *PISA 2009 Results: Learning to Learn—Student Engagement, Strategies and Practices (Volume III)*. Paris: OECD. Retrieved from http://www.oecd.org/dataoecd/11/17/48852630.pdf.

Olsen, L. (2010) *Reparable Harm: Fulfilling the Unkept Promise of Educational Opportunity for California's Long Term English Learners*. Long Beach, CA: Californians Together.

Otheguy, R., García, O. and Reid, W. (2015) Clarifying translanguaging and deconstructing named languages: A perspective from linguistics. *Applied Linguistics Review* 6 (3), 281–307. doi:10.1515/applirev-2015-0014.

Paulsrud, B., Rosén, J., Straszer, B. and Wedin, Å. (2017) (eds) *New Perspectives on Translanguaging and Education*. Bristol: Multilingual Matters.

Prasad, G. (2016) Beyond the mirror towards a plurilingual prism: Exploring the creation of plurilingual 'identity texts' in English and French classrooms in Toronto and Montpellier. *Intercultural Education* 26 (6), 497–514.

Sierens, S. and Van Avermaet, P. (2014) Language diversity in education. In D. Little, C. Leung and P. Van Avermaet (eds) *Managing Diversity in Education: Languages, Policies, Pedagogies* (pp. 204–222). Bristol: Multilingual Matters.

Skutnabb-Kangas, T. (2015) Linguicism. *The Encyclopedia of Applied Linguistics*. Malden, MA: Blackwell. Published Online: 19 June 2015. doi: 10.1002/9781405198431.wbeal1460.

Slembrouck, S., Van Avermaet, P. and Van Gorp, K. (2018) Strategies of multilingualism in education for minority children. In P. Van Avermaet, S. Slembrouck, K. Van Gorp, S. Sierens and K. Maryns (eds) *The Multilingual Edge of Education* (pp. 9–39). London: Palgrave Macmillan.

Snoddon, K. and Weber, J. (2021) (eds) *Critical Perspectives on Plurilingualism in Deaf Education*. Bristol: Multilingual Matters.

Uccelli, P., Barr, C.D., Dobbs, C.L., Galloway, E.P., Meneses, A. and Sanchez, E. (2015) Core academic language skills: An expanded operational construct and a novel instrument to chart school-relevant language proficiency in pre-adolescent and adolescent learners. *Applied Psycholinguistics* 36, 1077–1109. http://dx.doi.org/10.1017/S014271641400006X.

Van Avermaet, P., Slembrouck, S., Van Gorp, K., Sierens, S. and Maryns, K (eds) (2018) *The Multilingual Edge of Education*. London: Palgrave Macmillan.

von der Mühlen, S., Richter, T., Schmid, S., Schmidt, E.M. and Berthold, K. (2016) Judging the plausibility of arguments in scientific texts: A student–scientist comparison. *Thinking and Reasoning* 22 (2), 221–249. doi: 10.1080/13546783.2015.1127289.

Williams, C. (1994) Arfarniad o ddulliau dysgu ac addysgu yng nghyd-destun addysg uwchradd ddwyieithog [An evaluation of teaching and learning methods in the context of bilingual secondary education] (Unpublished PhD thesis). University of Wales, Bangor, UK.

Williams, C. (1996) Secondary education: Teaching in the bilingual situation. In C. Williams, G. Lewis and C. Baker (eds) *The Language Policy: Taking Stock* (pp. 39–78). Llangefni: CAI.

Williams, C. (2000) Welsh-medium and bilingual teaching in the further education sector. *International Journal of Bilingual Education and Bilingualism* 3 (2), 129–148.

Wong Fillmore, L. and Fillmore, C.J. (2012) What does text complexity mean for English learners and language minority students? Stanford University, Graduate School of Education, Understanding Language Project. Retrieved from https://ell.stanford.edu/sites/default/files/pdf/academic-papers/06LWF%20CJF%20Text%20Complexity%20FINAL_0.pdf.

3 Engaging Teachers and Researchers in Classroom Research: Issues of Fluidity and Time in Two Multi-Sited Projects

Marie Källkvist and Päivi Juvonen

Introduction

The need for efficient inclusion of migrants in their new home nations has led to explicit societal demands for more evidence-informed teaching practices, focusing, among other things, on providing equal opportunities and equity for language-minority students (Baker & Wright, 2017; Cummins, 2018, this volume; García, 2009). This calls for more classroom-based research that addresses increasing language diversity in student and teacher populations. This, in turn, presupposes rigorous school and classroom research methodology, which is portrayed as inherently complex, involving multiple social agents such as teachers, students, researchers and sometimes caregivers (Baker & Wright, 2017; Dörnyei, 2007; Mackey & Gass, 2005; Schachter & Gass, 1996; Spada, 2005). School-based research is also described as being time-consuming due to the fluidity of research participants and because schools are providers of education rather than sites to conduct research (Dörnyei, 2007). Mackey and Gass state that 'classroom research is a particularly complex and multifaceted endeavor that must be planned carefully', stressing 'the importance of flexibility' and the need for researchers to be 'patient, flexible, and ready to utilize alternative contingency plans' (2005: 212). According to Baker and Lewis (2015: 119), 'schools and classrooms have complex multi-causality, are ever dynamic and fluid, evolving and ever-changing, sometimes unpredictable and inconsistent'. The 'gold standard' of well-designed experiments that allow for generalisation beyond the sample

37

researched is normally unattainable as any study 'is still dependent on local conditions and is situated within a particular time. Students, teachers and instructional styles cannot be reduced to isolated variables and manipulated as if they were seeds in agricultural experimental research' (Baker & Lewis, 2015: 119).

Classroom research, therefore, tends to rely on qualitative or mixed-method data, which in turn means that participant sampling is 'purposive' (Cohen *et al.*, 2011; Dörnyei, 2007), 'convenient' or 'opportunity' (Dörnyei, 2007). Thus, 'researchers handpick the cases to be included in the sample on the basis of their judgement of their typicality or possession of the particular characteristics being sought [...] they build up a sample that is satisfactory to their specific needs' (Cohen *et al.*, 2011: 156). This is the opposite of random sampling, which is associated with quantitative data collection, often aiming at generalisation beyond the sample studied (Dörnyei, 2007). Given that much classroom research involves qualitative data (Baker & Wright, 2017), purposive/convenient/opportunity sampling can potentially be done in as many ways as there are studies. Referring to Rossiter (2001), Duff and Early (1996) and Schachter and Gass (1996), Dörnyei (2007: 177) points out that research reports and methodology texts underplay the difficulties of collecting data in classrooms. In encouraging more open discussion on 'the inherent difficulties of classroom investigation', Dörnyei (2007: 177) echoes Schachter and Gass, who assert that downplaying challenges is a 'disservice to other researchers, and particularly those with less experience' (Schachter & Gass, 1996: 26). This point from 1996 is still valid; in 2019, Patsy Lightbown and Nina Spada gave a plenary lecture at the American Association for Applied Linguistics, entitled 'In it together: Teachers, researchers and classroom SLA', providing 'illustrations of how the research process is conceptualized and how teachers are engaged in it' (Lightbown & Spada, 2019), elaborating on and illustrating the engagement of teachers in their school research.

In this chapter, we provide data and illustration that address these underdescribed challenges of initiating and sustaining classroom research from the perspectives of two multi-sited linguistic ethnographies carried out in multilingual secondary schools. We focus on the challenging aspects of *participant fluidity* and *time*. The terms *fluid* and *fluidity* are borrowed from Baker and Lewis (2015: 119) and Dörnyei (2007: 188), by which we mean that the participant sample is likely to change through the attrition of some participants and the addition of others. Fluidity is caused by a range of factors: research relies on volunteers, who can withdraw their consent at any time; there is rarely 100% attendance in classrooms as students are away due to, for example, illness and dental and medical appointments; there is mobility among students as they may change schools or classes. The same applies to teachers and researchers, who also catch illnesses, go on leave for a variety of reasons and change jobs. Also, times of financial cutbacks can lead to additional attrition. Our second focus is *time*, discussed in Dörnyei (2007) and Spada (2005), with Spada stating that 'the time-consuming nature of classroom research is not a minor factor' (2005: 336). For the benefit of researchers who are planning classroom research, we illustrate the time needed to secure and sustain the engagement of teacher participants under different circumstances: through inviting both teachers who had been engaged in prior research projects as well as teachers who had not previously been research participants.

As cases, we use our own two linguistic-ethnography projects conducted in secondary schools over a four-year time period. Doing ethnography means engaging with 'a real social environment with real people' (Blommaert & Dong, 2010: 22) over an extended time period. As discussed above, a number of things can go wrong in these scenarios, which warrants a realistic mindset on the part of researchers: '[p]art of this realism, and unfortunately often overlooked, is *to have a Plan B*' (Blommaert & Dong, 2010: 22, emphasis in original). In writing this chapter, we aim to contribute to the methodology literature by sharing details from the realities of conducting multi-sited, longitudinal classroom research. We describe (a) the amount of redundancy in teacher participants that was needed to secure the engagement of a sufficient number of focal teachers for data collection that extended over two and a half years, (b) the impact of *teacher* participant fluidity on the type of data eventually collected, and (c) the impact of *researcher* participant fluidity on the type of data collected and on time.

Both projects are team-based and driven by an inclusive-education agenda, recognising the need for educational practices that engage students' multilingual and multicultural repertoires, manifested as spontaneous translanguaging and/or pedagogical translanguaging (Creese & Blackledge, 2010; García, 2009). We begin by reviewing existing research-methodology publications on participant fluidity, followed by a presentation of the two projects for which we are principal investigators (PIs). In addressing issues of participant fluidity, we describe how we recruited, selected and retained teacher and researcher participants. We conclude by discussing the implications of participant fluidity for the original research designs and schedules, and for researcher and PI flexibility.

Issues of Time and Participant Fluidity in Classroom Research

Several aspects of school-based research combine in making it time-consuming: applying and waiting for ethics approval, setting up meetings with the school management, teachers, their students and sometimes caregivers (Dörnyei, 2007), gaining participant consent and building trust so that participants remain committed (Spada, 2005). Trust is often built over the course of a descriptive research phase, often involving observation, recordings and interviews. In second-language acquisition (SLA) research, the descriptive phase often serves to pave the way for an intervention phase (Spada, 2005). Ethnographic classroom data collection also requires long-term engagement (Barwell, 2019).

When classroom research extends over time, the scene is set for fluidity, not only participant attrition, but also participant *addition* more or less suddenly, for example, when a new student joins the class or when a special-needs teacher shows up in the classroom. As to teacher participation in research, Dörnyei puts that

> [f]or rigorous research we need a well-defined participant sample. This seemingly basic condition can be surprisingly difficult to achieve in school settings if the study involves more than a one-off cross-sectional survey [...] teachers can be very busy and stressed out, and they have their own distinctive beliefs and styles as well as professional and personal agendas. Thus, it may not be easy to bring them on board, and it is a real challenge in almost every case to keep up their commitment. (Dörnyei, 2007: 188f)

In SLA research, questions to do with teacher participant recruitment, selection and long-term commitment in classroom research have been discussed for quite some time. A study by Spada *et al.* (1996) focused specifically on the selection and trust-building of teacher participants in the context of English-as-second language (ESL) primary schools in Canada. Their research focused on the effect of form-focused instruction and error correction on French-speaking primary-school pupils' learning of ESL, using a quasi-experimental design involving three phases: description – correlation – experimental treatment, the latter being delivered by the classroom teachers rather than the researchers. Importantly, for the recruitment of teachers for Spada *et al.*'s study, schools approached the researchers rather than the other way around, and their teacher participants were recruited from the researchers' professional networks, including former students. Following extensive school- and classroom observation (i.e. the descriptive phase), a further selection of focal teachers was then made: '[w]e try to select teachers whose characteristics and previous teaching behaviors match the goals of a particular study' (Spada *et al.*, 1996: 38), almost always following extensive observation. This selection criterion appears particularly suitable in Spada *et al.*'s studies as it was the teachers who delivered the quasi-experimental intervention in the final phase. The publication provides no statistics of the number of teachers recruited and selected for their studies but provides a list of factors that contributed to the successful cooperation with their teacher participants: (a) treating them as colleagues whose knowledge and experience is highly and explicitly valued by the researchers, (b) conducting silent observation, including lunchbreaks and recess to build trust, (c) collaboration with school boards and local ESL teachers' associations, giving workshops as in-service training for teachers, (d) providing teacher-friendly presentations of research results and (e) publishing in professional teaching journals.

In another study focusing on participant attrition in classroom research, Rossiter (2001) describes the fluidity of teacher and student participants in a study of 46 adult ESL students in Canada, all immigrants or refugees, attending a full-time course with planned data collection over 15 weeks. Rossiter lists and discusses a range of challenges encountered, including teacher fluidity. The research schedule spanned the course of one year, and arrangements were initially made so that one and the same teacher was planned to teach the group of students over that year. However, due to a decrease in programme enrollment and a lack of qualified ESL teachers, three different teachers (instead of one) ended up in teaching the group. All three consented to being part of Rossiter's study, but the third teacher showed no interest in the research, which affected the quality of the research in that teaching logs and audio-recordings of classroom activities ended up being incomplete.

In the following, we aim to contribute to the research-methodology literature by elaborating on how we brought secondary school teachers 'on board' (Dörnyei, 2007: 189), how we then made the selection, i.e. reduction, of the teachers to be engaged as focal teachers and the extent to which we managed to 'keep up' (Dörnyei, 2007: 189) their commitment over a data-collection period of two and half years. The fact that both projects involve teams of researchers collecting data in different sites resulted in one of the projects experiencing fluidity not only among participating teachers and students but also in the team of researchers over time. We thus bring in a new category of participant, namely *researcher* in team-based research. We also go beyond the previous research reviewed above by providing statistics on the fluidity of the teacher and researcher participants in the two projects, to which we now turn.

The Two Projects

MultiLingual Spaces

MultiLingual Spaces responds to a need for research in language-diverse English-as-an-additional language (EAL) classrooms and migrant students' learning of EAL in classrooms where monolingual, English-Only practices have been the ideal for a long time (Källkvist *et al.*, 2017). MultiLingual Spaces builds on research in psycholinguistics, bilingualism and additional-language education, which can contribute to explaining the frequent Swedish-English translanguaging found in many EAL classrooms in Sweden (Beers Fägersten, 2012; The Swedish Schools Inspectorate, 2011), despite the English-Only ideal. Launched in 2017, MultiLingual Spaces was funded by the Swedish Research Council for four years, focusing on language practices in multilingual EAL classrooms in school years 7–9 in Sweden, which mark the end of compulsory school.

MultiLingual Spaces engaged four senior researchers in two different, geographically distant sites. Each of the two sites engaged two different secondary schools over a period of two and a half years. Similar to many previous classroom studies (Spada, 2005), MultiLingual Spaces involves two phases: a descriptive, linguistic-ethnographic (Copland & Creese, 2015) phase, followed by an experimental (intervention) phase. The descriptive phase served as an opportunity to collect linguistic-ethnographic data in intact, language-diverse classes taught by experienced EAL teachers and to build trust between researchers, teachers, students and other school staff. On the completion of the descriptive phase, MultiLingual Spaces developed teaching materials for the experimental phase, in which pedagogical translanguaging was introduced as part of quasi-experimental interventions in six purposively selected intact classes, taught by the researchers in the presence of the teachers. Pedagogical translanguaging was introduced by providing vocabulary lists for each minority language represented in the classes involved and by inviting students to translanguage using their full language repertoires. Focusing on vocabulary, qualitative and quantitative data on students' vocabulary learning in EAL were collected along with qualitative data addressing ideologies of language learning and attitudes to classroom language practices.

The Language Introduction Project

The Language Introduction Project (LangIntro) also runs over four years, beginning in 2018, in three research sites, with a main data collection of two and a half years in two of the sites and of one and a half years in one site. The aim of LangIntro is to investigate several (inter)related research questions about recently arrived students' language development, academic development (disciplinary literacy) and social inclusion in the Swedish upper-secondary school Language Introduction Programme (LIP).[1] LangIntro builds on research identifying flexible multilingual practices, including pedagogical translanguaging, in classrooms as beneficial for the development of disciplinary (bi)literacy (García, 2009; Hornberger, 2003; Hornberger & Link, 2012; Schleppegrell, 2004, 2013) and on research on inclusion and inclusive education (Kugelmass, 2006; Nilsson Folke, 2017). LangIntro fills a research gap at the upper-secondary school level and responds simultaneously to a grassroots' call for research to draw on, as LIP rapidly grew to become the fourth largest programme in upper-secondary school in the academic year 2016/2017, following increasing migration flows, especially in 2015 (SNAE, 2018; Swedish Research Council, 2015a: 42–43, 2015b: 52).

LangIntro has a complex interdisciplinary research design, both in terms of researchers and participants as well as in terms of types of data collection for individual studies. Five senior researchers, at three different universities distantly apart, and four PhD students are all conducting individual studies. The common methodological denominator is the combination of linguistic-ethnographic methods such as participant observations, questionnaires and interviews (Copland & Creese, 2015) with the collection and analysis of quantifiable linguistic data (such as student texts, classroom recordings) and assessment data of several kinds (such as data on the students' prior schooling, their individual study plans and their grades). In one of the participating schools, in close collaboration with a teacher, a quasi-experimental intervention study focusing on disciplinary literacy in the social sciences is conducted. Further details regarding LangIntro and MultiLingual Spaces are provided in Table 3.1.

Teachers serve as key participants, with both projects aiming to map experienced teachers' language practices in multilingual classrooms. Below, we describe how we approached schools and teachers in our search

Table 3.1 Description of the MultiLingual Spaces and LangIntro Projects

	MultiLingual Spaces	LangIntro
Sites	Four secondary schools (years 7–9) in two sites distantly apart	Four upper-secondary schools in three different sites distantly apart
Timeframe	2017–2020	2018–2021
Theoretical frames	Linguistic Ethnography Pedagogical translanguaging Nexus Analysis Vocabulary learning	Linguistic Ethnography Inclusive education (including Pedagogical translanguaging) Systemic Functional Linguistics
Aims	Research language practices among experienced EAL teachers and EAL students (age 13–16); Research ideologies underpinning teachers' and students' language practices; Research the effect of monolingual, bilingual and multilingual language practices on teacher–student and student–student classroom interaction and on student learning of English vocabulary.	Research language practices among subject teachers and newly arrived students (age 16–19); Research students' language development, development of disciplinary literacy and assessment; Research ideologies and organisation of education underpinning teachers', principals' and students' language practices; conduct an intervention study with a focus on disciplinary literacy.
Methods	*Descriptive phase:* Questionnaires, ethnographic classroom observation, photography, artifacts, classroom video-recordings and audio-recorded interviews. *Experimental phase:* Quasi-experimental teaching interventions running over three weeks in six intact classes.	Questionnaires, ethnographic classroom observation, photography, artifacts, video- and audio-recordings, interviews, student texts, assessment and grade data, quasi-experimental teaching intervention.
Team	Four associate professors with tenure (at two universities in different parts of Sweden)	Four full professors with tenure, one post-doctoral researcher, four PhD candidates (at three universities in different parts of Sweden)
Funding	The Swedish Research Council	The Swedish Research Council

for suitable research contexts and – in the case of LangIntro – how research participants were recruited.

Recruiting and Selecting Teacher and Researcher Participants

The selection of teacher participants has been elaborated on in the methodology literature reviewed above, with Spada (2005: 333) describing it as 'complicated, particularly when working in intact classrooms'. Both MultiLingual Spaces and LangIntro are based on the epistemology that underpins Linguistic Ethnography (Copland & Creese, 2015), thus involving context-sensitive qualitative data. Therefore, focal schools, teachers, classes and students were purposively selected following 'principled decisions' (Dörnyei, 2007: 126). While Spada *et al.* (1996), reviewed above, describe a context in which teachers approached the researchers to initiate research, both MultiLingual Spaces and LangIntro were offered funding prior to approaching schools. We now turn to describing the decisions made by the research teams and the criteria used for selecting teacher participants, beginning with MultiLingual Spaces.

MultiLingual Spaces

MultiLingual Spaces involved four senior researchers for the full duration of the project, based in two different sites: Site 1 and Site 2. When recruiting and selecting schools and teachers, MultiLingual Spaces made the following principled decisions: (i) To facilitate ethnographic data collection, schools needed to be within commuting distance from the researchers' universities, (ii) to qualify as a *multilingal* class, intact classes should include at least five students who were regular users of a minority language in addition to Swedish (the school language), (iii) teachers should volunteer and express an intention to participate over the course of two and a half years, (iv) teacher participants should preferably involve more than one gender and (v) to address the issue of participant attrition evident in prior, long-term school research, a redundant number of 7 teachers and 14 of their intact classes in 4 different schools were recruited for the descriptive phase. In addition, the principals consented to the schools' participation and committed to participate in case their teachers were to attrite. The target sample for the the experimental phase was four focal teacher participants at four different schools in four different locations, including a total of six intact classes. These were to be evenly distributed across Site 1 and Site 2.

Approaching schools and teachers was done differently in the two sites due to differing profiles of the two universities involved. The university in Site 2 had long had teacher-education programmes and school research, whereas the university in Site 1 did not. The Site-2 researchers therefore had a professional network of secondary school teachers from whom they quickly recruited three teachers at two schools (the aim being to retain two of them for the intervention phase). In the absence of a similar network of EAL teachers, the Site-1 researchers went about their sampling of schools and teachers differently: They wrote to the school authorities in two municipalities, describing the research project and asking for contacts with school leaders in multilingual schools. This resulted in the engagement of a large, urban multilingual and multicultural school where most of the data were collected. In the absence of a response from the second municipality, the second school in Site 1 was in the end recruited through the researchers' private networks, resulting in the engagement of two teachers at an urban school, in which there was less language diversity. As the MultiLingual Spaces team in Site 1 did not know the teachers prior, they engaged greater redundancy than in Site 2: Four volunteer teachers were engaged in Site 1 (the aim being to retain two for the intervention phase), two in each of the two schools so that they could share the experience of having researchers present in some of their classes. Also, this way, the researcher participants (two) matched the number of teacher participants (two) in both schools. Of the seven teachers recruited by MultiLingual Spaces, three were lead teachers (*förstelärare*), in this case meaning that they had been reviewed by school administrators and promoted on the basis of their high-quality teaching skills.

LangIntro

Initially, LangIntro engaged four senior researchers in the research team, employed for the full duration of the project. The plan was also to affiliate a post-doctoral researcher and two PhD students. Once we learnt about the approval of our application, the recruitment of the two PhD students commenced; the post-doctoral recruitment had already started independently. Hence, we planned for an initial recruitment period of research participants, which would enable the project to start with a complete research team of seven researchers in autumn 2018. Below, we recount a somewhat different course of events.

Regarding the recruitment and selection of schools and teachers, the following principled decisions guided LangIntro: (i) Schools should offer LIP, (ii) schools should explicitly state that they offered language-developing education in all subjects, (iii) schools should be within commuting distance of the researchers' home universities, (iv) the principals should express interest in the project and (v) individual teachers should be willing to volunteer over a long period of time (at most two and a half years). These criteria were in the end applied when selecting three of the participating schools – one of the schools did not have a policy offering language-developing education in all subjects (Criterion 2), but as there was established research collaboration between the school and one of the researchers and the other criteria were met, this school was still selected.

The three other schools met all selection criteria. Initially, we approached the local municipality school offices, in order to reach out to all principals in the school districts located in the vicinity of the universities involved. After presenting the project in the municipalities and gaining their approval, all principals in schools offering LIP were approached and asked whether they were interested in participating after talking to their teacher staff. In one of the three research sites, one school meeting the above criteria was identified and selected. In yet another site, several schools expressed an interest in participating, and finally, two schools with different profiles (one reception school mainly focusing on Swedish as a second language and one offering all school subjects) were selected. In line with principles of ethnography, we invited all teachers who wished to participate to begin with. Thus, we had not decided in advance which teachers and classrooms were to become focal. Rather, the individual substudies conducted by the researchers were decided on only after initial analyses of teacher interviews and classroom observation from classrooms taught by the teacher participants. An additional factor guiding these principled decisions was whether the teacher and the researchers believed that the students in the classroom would consent to participate. From initially observing 38 classrooms, we gradually narrowed down the number of focal teacher participants to 10.

Fluidity of Teacher and Researcher Participants Over Time

MultiLingual Spaces: The descriptive phase

In MultiLingual Spaces, the team of four researchers remained intact throughout the duration of the project, so participant fluidity applies to teachers (and student fluidity is beyond the scope of this chapter). Figure 3.1

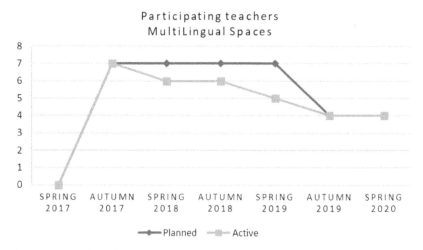

Figure 3.1 Number of teacher participants in MultiLingual Spaces over time

illustrates attrition; there was attrition from seven to six teachers early on. This was due to one of the teachers withdrawing her consent to participate when learning that participation would involve video-recording in the classroom, as she had found video-recording in her classroom to be too obtrusive in a prior research project. At the beginning of data collection, MultiLingual Spaces thus engaged six teacher participants, all of whom were teaching EAL in multilingual schools in four different urban areas. As a token of gratitude and an opportunity for professional development, MultiLingual Spaces invited all six to join the biannual conference of Applied Linguistics organised by the Swedish Association of Applied Linguistics in 2018, which had the suitable theme of *Language(ing) and Classroom Research*.

The next case of attrition was a teacher in Site 1, who moved eight months after data collection began, leading to a long commute to his school. With the current shortage of qualified teachers, he was immediately offered employment in his new hometown. He left MultiLingual Spaces at the end of the descriptive phase (summer 2018). Besides losing a devoted teacher participant, the loss of this particular teacher led to all four teachers engaged during the intervention belonging to one gender (female).

MultiLingual Spaces: The experimental phase

MultiLingual Spaces entered the experimental phase with a retention level of five teachers (three in Site 1 and two in Site 2) while needing to retain four. The fifth teacher remained in the background as a backup should one of the other two Site-1 teacher participants leave.

At the time, there were financial cutbacks, which affected Site 1 in the shape of larger EAL classes in one of the two focal schools. This change was made in the summer break, resulting in one of the intact classes that was targeted for the intervention no longer existing in the autumn semester 2019, which is when the intervention was to take place. This led to the Site-1 researchers, on short notice, needing to involve a new intact class, which was new also to the focal teacher. Engaging the new intact class meant commencing a new descriptive, trust-building phase to collect observation data and pave the way for conducting the intervention. As the experimental phase began, there was no more teacher-participant attrition. The intervention covered six English lessons over three consecutive weeks; it was designed by the research team and was subsequently taught by one of the researchers in the presence of the teacher, and the other researcher, who was in charge of video-cameras and audio-recorders. The length of the intervention (three weeks) caused a further delay in Site 1. We elaborate on this below, but first, we present statistics for researcher and teacher fluidity in LangIntro.

LangIntro: Teacher participant fluidity

Teacher participant fluidity manifested itself mainly in three ways in LangIntro. First, the purposeful selection of focal teachers and classes to engage with in the individual studies had led to a lower number of teacher participants over time, which was according to plan. Second, three of the principals initially participating either changed jobs or delegated the leadership of the LIP to a deputy principal. Support from the principal was an important selection criterion for the participating schools. However, as the new principals expressed their equally strong support of the project, we did not experience any challenges due to these changes in school leadership.

Third, there was attrition among the selected focal teacher participants. At times, they cancelled classroom observations and other appointments with the researcher participants due to illness or changes in their schedules reflecting the realities of classrooms, but this did not interfere with data collection. Two of the 10 focal teachers selected, however, did not participate for the full duration of data-collection phase, thus affecting the implementation of the project in different ways. In the first case, one of the two focal teacher participants in the school where the intervention study was conducted took leave during data collection. Our aim was to be able to select one of the focal teachers as a participant in the intervention study. Hence, the leave just prior to the collaborative planning phase of the intervention commenced affected the data collection directly, resulting in automatically selecting the teacher who did not take leave. In the second case, one of the focal teachers changed jobs. On the whole, however, the purposeful selection of a redundant number of potential focal teacher participants provided the project with rich longitudinal data to analyse according to plan. None of the participating teachers ended their participation on other grounds; they were thus engaged throughout the data-collection phase.

LangIntro: Researcher participant fluidity

In ethnographic studies, researchers play an important role as social agents alongside other participants (Copland & Creese, 2015). The planned number of researchers and PhD students in the LangIntro project was seven: five senior and two junior researchers (PhD students). However, for several reasons, the project can initially be characterised by high *researcher fluidity*. In the first six months (January–June 2018), the PI and one of the senior researchers were, according to plan, actively involved, creating information leaflets, designing questionnaires and interview guides, applying for ethics permission, approaching prospective participants and making calls for PhD student positions, which involved reviewing applications and interviewing candidates. The plan was to create pairwise teams of one senior and one junior researcher, or two senior researchers responsible for one school each, and to start data collection in autumn 2018, immediately following the summer break, with the full number of researcher participants. However,

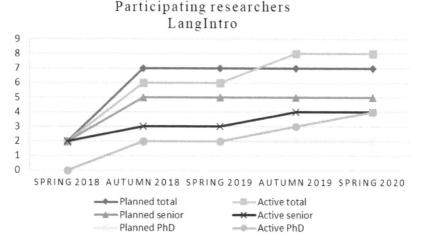

Figure 3.2 Number of researcher participants in LangIntro over time

two of the senior researchers were not able to join the research team as planned. Further, the call for PhD posts rendered only one candidate who could fill the post as project researcher, instead of two. However, the post-doctoral researcher and one additional PhD student were affiliated to the team, which, thus, in autumn 2018, consisted of three operative senior and two junior PhD researchers (see Figure 3.2), commencing data collection in three of the participating four schools.

As shown in the two top lines in Figure 3.2, we planned to have a total of seven researchers (five senior and two junior PhD students) from autumn 2018 but ended up with a total of eight researchers (four senior and four junior PhD students; see also the four bottom lines in Figure 3.2) from autumn 2019. By this time, one of the initially absent senior research-ers joined the team, while the other had retired, and we had successfully recruited two new PhD students as junior researchers and were able to commence data collection also in the fourth school. Thus, the initial fluid-ity of researcher participants in the end resulted in a greater number of active researchers. The data collection in the fourth school was postponed due to the delayed recruitment of the two new PhD students. However, as we were able to recruit not one but two new team members, we were able to intensify data collection in the fourth school, thus reducing the effect on the general data collection in LangIntro to a minimum.

Consequences and Outcomes of Participant Fluidity

MultiLingual Spaces

As explained above, in MultiLingual Spaces, there were delays due to the attrition of one teacher in Site 1 at the end of the descriptive phase. One of his classes was scheduled to participate in the intervention in spring

2019. As the teacher replacing him was a fresh graduate from university, she did not meet the criteria of being qualified *and* experienced in teaching language-diverse EAL classes, so MultiLingual Spaces did not invite her to participate. In the end, the attrition of one teacher at the end of the descriptive phase led to (i) the loss of the only male teacher participant in the intervention phase, (ii) the loss of one intact class that was scheduled to participate in the intervention, which led to a delay of the completion of the intervention by two months and (iii) researcher time was needed for an additional descriptive phase to build trust with students in the new intact class.

The attriting teacher announced his change of jobs well ahead of time (as soon as he knew about it), which enabled the Site-1 researchers to adjust their data-collection schedule by taking the opportunity of designing a case study of the attriting teacher and his students. Case studies are suited to developing the in-depth understanding of complex, dynamic entities in their specific contexts (Duff, 2008) of which language-diverse classrooms are perfect examples (Baker & Wright, 2017; Lin, 2008). The attriting teacher was very successful in explaining the value of research to his students, motivating them to participate in interviews. As part of the case study (Källkvist *et al.*, 2019, 2020), interviews were carried out with the teacher, the team of English teachers at the school and 19 students who were regular users of a minority language and of Swedish.

In Site 2, where the university had a well-established network of teachers, the descriptive and experimental phases involving two focal teachers progressed entirely according to plan, and data collection was complete in December 2019. In Site 1, the experimental phase was also scheduled to end in December 2019 but was delayed until February 2020 due to scheduling clashes; the intervention was to be carried out in six consecutive lessons over three weeks in two different intact classes in November 2019, but as classes were scheduled at the same time in both schools, one of the interventions had to be re-scheduled for December 2019. As December approached, another delay presented itself in that two English lessons were cancelled due to the school's Christmas festivities. This school also had a habit of breaking its normal schedule for theme-based teaching and learning, which made it harder to find the three consecutive weeks of six uninterrupted English lessons that the intervention required. As a result, the sixth and final MultiLingual Spaces intervention was run from mid-January until early February 2020, delayed by six weeks. As is evident in the classroom research-methodology literature, teacher participant attrition as well as delays in data collection were expected and came as no surprise. The adjustments in the data-collection schedule needed were accommodated within the four-year timeframe of the project thanks to Site-1 researchers' flexibility.

LangIntro

Aside from the already mentioned occasional changes in the teacher participants' schedules due to illness or the like, LangIntro experienced only the two cases of teacher participant attrition described above. Fortunately, as there were two potential teachers for the intervention study, it was possible to conduct the intervention. The main effect was, thus, that LangIntro did not actively select one of the teachers for the study; rather, the participating teacher was automatically selected through teacher attrition. Thus, in this case, redundancy in the number of focal teachers proved crucial. Regarding the focal teacher who changed jobs, LangIntro experienced teacher participant attrition that reduced opportunities to conduct data collection according to plan, as the plan was to follow the teacher for a longer period.

In order to retain teacher participants' engagement throughout the project, Lang-Intro researchers visited the schools regularly, participated in staff meetings, had informal conversations during lunch and other breaks, invited some focal teacher participants to conferences and offered the schools in-service education for LIP teachers, as well as had regular email contact with the focal teachers.

Researcher participant fluidity also had an impact on (1) the planned data-collection schedule and (2) the planned pairwise organisation of researchers working in different schools. Most notably, LangIntro started data collection a year later than scheduled in the fourth participating school. However, even though this caused a delay in the project as a whole, there were also some positive outcomes of this delay. For example, as we were able to employ two instead of one PhD student and as the PI had already established contact with the school, we were able to recruit teacher participants rapidly, thus speeding up the otherwise time-consuming process of establishing contacts. LangIntro, thus, also experienced researcher participant reinforcement through the recruitment and affiliation of four rather than two PhD students.

Discussion: Fluidity and Time in MultiLingual Spaces and LangIntro

LangIntro and MultiLingual Spaces are grounded in Linguistic Ethnography, involving multi-sited secondary school classroom research over a period of two and a half years, and were conducted by teams of researchers in different locations. Both recruited school, teacher and student participants following funding approval that was external to the PIs' universities and ethics clearance. LangIntro's design required the recruitment not only of teachers but also junior researchers. We now revisit the aim of this chapter by discussing the amount of redundancy among teacher participants needed and the impact of teacher and researcher fluidity on the data eventually collected and the time needed to collect them.

As to teacher participant attrition, MultiLingual Spaces initially engaged seven teachers for its descriptive (observation) phase, with the target of retaining four focal teachers for its experimental phase. There was attrition of two teachers, one withdrawing her consent as she found classroom video-recording too obtrusive, and the other due to moving to a different town and therefore changing jobs. In LangIntro, there was attrition of two out of the ten focal teachers initially engaged, causing minor adjustments to the data-collection schedule. The recruitment of PhD students (who, in Sweden, have salaried university positions) caused delays in the start-up of LangIntro's data-collection schedule in one of the schools. This required flexibility on the part of the PI, who needed to join the PhD students in three schools.

Measures were taken in order to motivate teachers and junior researchers to remain committed. One key strategy was pairwise constellations of teachers who were new to research. In MultiLingual Spaces Site 1, where the researchers and teachers did not know each other from before, a principled decision was made to engage two teachers at each school. This ensured the redundancy needed, but, equally importantly, teachers could turn to each other for reflection on their roles as research participants as teaching in the presence of researchers may be obtrusive (Sundqvist *et al.,* 2019). In addition, the pairwise constellation created the matched number of two researchers and two teachers in both schools in Site 1. Pairwise work was key in LangIntro as well in providing support for junior researchers, who were all joined by a senior researcher. Another strategy, mentioned in prior research (Spada *et al.,* 1996), was to invite the teacher participants to one or two research conferences over the course of the four years.

When it comes to the effect of teacher participant attrition on the data gathered, previous research (Rossiter, 2001) has shown that attrition can compromise the quality of data in longitudinal studies, in Rossiter's study in the shape of incomplete data. Teacher attrition in LangIntro and MultiLingual Spaces affected data collection in the following ways: LangIntro collected the same amount of data that was initially planned, and in one instance, teacher participant attrition automatically selected which teacher in the end became the focal teacher. In MultiLingual Spaces, attrition led to a larger data set, an additional case study, than originally planned. It also led to Site-1 researchers investing additional time in the descriptive phase when having to engage a new intact focal class for the intervention following budget cuts in one of its schools.

Delays in collecting data were expected in both projects. In LangIntro, the postponed successful recruitment of all the participating PhD students delayed the start of data collection in one of the schools. Having approached the municipality and the school early on, there was a risk of losing the principals' and some of the teachers' interest and commitment to participate. In order to keep up their engagement, the PI was in regular touch with the school throughout the year and invited a couple of teachers to participate in a conference organised by the authors. This is an example of the flexibility required in classroom research (Schachter & Gass, 1996) and the need for a 'plan B' (Blommaert & Dong, 2010: 22, emphasis in original).

In MultiLingual Spaces, flexibility was needed to conduct all six intervention studies, the greatest challenge being the scheduling of the three-week intervention involving six consecutive English lessons in one of the Site-1 schools. The research design involving intervention case studies was important to MultiLingual Spaces as it met calls made in the literature for 'systematic longitudinal, interventionist studies that can work on refining bilingual classroom strategies and pedagogies to achieve the goals deemed worthwhile in specific contexts' (Lin, 2008: 284). In order to ensure the flexibility needed, Site-1 researchers had a Plan B as well as C and D, and the PI had no scheduled teaching at her university over a period of four months, apart from teaching the intervention lessons themselves over the three weeks.

Finally, the opportunity of four-year funding provided time space to conduct classroom research involving both a descriptive and an experimental phase of the kind called for by multilingual-education researchers (Baker & Wright, 2017; Juvonen et al., 2020; Lin, 2008). Preparing for and conducting longitudinal intervention-data collection was particularly time-consuming, as noted by Ortega and Byrnes (2008).

Acknowledgements

We gratefully acknowledge funding from The Swedish Research Council (MultiLingual Spaces: VR-UVK 2016-03469; LangIntro: VR-National Research Programme Migration and Immigration 2017-03566). Our gratitude extends also to our co-researchers, who not only consented to the publication of this chapter and thus became our objects of study, but who also, together with teacher, student and school leader participants, made this team-based school research possible.

Note

(1) In Sweden, almost all students attend upper-secondary school. All adolescent migrants aged 16–19 years, irrespective of their previous school experience, are in Sweden placed in this transitional programme. The aim of LIP is to teach students enough Swedish as well as to obtain grades in at least eight school subjects at the compulsory school level in order to qualify for mainstream upper-secondary school education. LIP, thus, serves a gatekeeping function.

References

Baker, C. and Lewis, G. (2015) A synthesis of research on bilingual and multilingual education. In W.E. Wright, S. Boun and O. García (eds) *Handbook of Bilingual and Multilingual Education* (pp. 109–126). Maldone, MA: Wiley Blackwell.

Baker, C. and Wright, W.E. (2017) *Foundations of Bilingual Education and Bilingualism* (6th edn). Bristol: Multilingual Matters.

Barwell, R. (2019) Language diversity in classroom settings. In K. Tusting (ed.) *The Routledge Handbook of Linguistic Ethnography* (pp. 273–285).

Beers Fägersten, K. (2012) Teacher discourse and code choice in a Swedish EFL classroom. In B. Yoon and H.K. Kim (eds) *Teachers' Roles in Second Language Learning: Classroom Applications of Sociocultural Theory* (pp. 81–98). Hershey, PA: IGI Global.

Blommaert, J. and Dong, J. (2010) *Ethnographic Fieldwork: A Beginner's Guide* (1st edn). Bristol: Multilingual Matters.

Cohen, L., Manion, L. and Morrison, K. (2011) *Research Methods in Education*. London: Routledge.

Copland, F. and Creese A. (2015) *Linguistic Ethnography: Collecting, Analysing and Presenting Data*. London: Sage.

Creese, A. and Blackledge, A. (2010) Translanguaging in the bilingual classroom: a pedagogy for learning and teaching? *The Modern Language Journal* 94 (1), 103–115.

Cummins, J. (2018) Urban multilingualism and educational achievement: Identifying and implementing evidence-based strategies for school improvement. In P. Van Avermaet, S. Slembrouck, K. Van Gorp, S. Sierens and K. Maryns (eds) *The Multilingual Edge of Education* (pp. 67–90). London: Palgrave Macmillan.

Dörnyei, Z. (2007) *Research Methods in Applied Linguistics*. Oxford: Oxford University Press.

Duff, P.A. (2008) *Case Study Research in Applied Linguistics*. London: Routledge.

Duff, P. and Early, M. (1996) Problematics of classroom research across sociopolitical contexts. In J. Schachter and S. Gass (eds) *Second Language Classroom Research: Issues and Opportunities* (pp. 1–30). Mahwah, NJ: Lawrence Erlbaum.

García, O. (2009) *Bilingual Education in the 21st Century: A Global Perspective*. Malden, MA: Wiley-Blackwell.

Hornberger, N.H. (2003) *Continua of Biliteracy an Ecological Framework for Educational Policy, Research, and Practice in Multilingual Settings*. Clevedon: Multilingual Matters.

Hornberger, N.H. and Link, H. (2012) Translanguaging in today's classrooms: A biliteracy lens. *Theory Into Practice* 51 (4), 239–47.

Juvonen, P., Eisenchlas, S.A., Roberts, T. and Schalley, A.C. (2020) Researching social and affective factors in home language maintenance and development: A methodology overview. In S.A. Eisenchlas and A.C. Schalley (eds) *Handbook of Home Language Maintenance and Development* (pp. 38–58). Berlin: De Gruyter Mouton.

Källkvist, M., Gyllstad, H., Sandlund, E. and Sundqvist, P. (2017) English Only in multilingual classrooms? *LMS – Lingua* 4, 27–31.

Källkvist, M., Gyllstad, H., Sandlund, E. and Sundqvist, P. (2019) English Only in multilingual classrooms? A study of students' self-reported practices and attitudes. American Association for Applied Linguistics conference, Atlanta, GA, 9–12 March 2019.

Källkvist, M., Gyllstad, H., Sandlund, E. and Sundqvist, P. (2020) Students and their teacher as language-policy makers in two multilingual, secondary-school English classrooms. *ASLA-symposiet 2020*, The Swedish Association of Applied Linguistics, Gothenburg University, 23–24 April.

Kugelmass, J.W. (2006) Sustaining cultures of inclusion: The value and limitations of cultural analyses. *European Journal of Psychology of Education* XXI (3), 279–292.

Lightbown, P. and Spada, N. (2019) In it together: Teachers, researchers and classroon SLA. Plenary lecture, American Association of Applied Linguistics conference, Atlanta, 9–12 March.

Lin, A.M. (2008) Code-switching in the classroom: Research paradigms and approaches. In N.H. Hornberger and K. King (eds) *Research Methods in Language and Education* (pp. 273–286). New York: Springer.

Mackey, A. and Gass, S. (2005) *Second Language Research: Methodology and Design.* Mahwah, NJ: Lawrence Erlbaum.

Nilsson Folke, J. (2017) *Lived Transitions - Experiences of Learning and Inclusion Among Newly Arrived Students.* Stockholm: Stockholm University.

Ortega, L. and Byrnes, H. (2008) *The Longitudinal Study of Advanced L2 Capacities.* New York: Routledge.

Rossiter, M.J. (2001) The challenges of classroom-based SLA research. *Applied Language Learning* 12 (1), 31–44.

Schachter, J. and Gass, S. (1996) *Second Language Classroom Research: Issues and Opportunities.* Mahwah, NJ: Lawrence Erlbaum.

Schleppegrell, M.J. (2004) *The Language of Schooling: A Functional Linguistics Perspective.* Mahwah, NJ: Lawrence Erlbaum Associates.

Schleppegrell, M.J. (2013) The role of metalanguage in supporting academic language development. *Language Learning* 63 (1), 153–70.

SNAE (2018) *Uppföljning av språkintroduktion. Beskrivande statistik på nationell nivå och nyanlända elevers övergångar till och från språkintroduktion* [Swedish National Agency of Education, Report 46. Follow-up of LIP. Descriptive Statistics on national level and newly arrived students' transfer to and from LIP]. Stockholm: SNAE.

Spada, N. (2005) Conditions and challenges in developing school-based SLA research programs. *The Modern Language Journal* 89 (3), 328–338.

Spada, N., Ranta, L. and Lightbown, P.M. (1996) Working with teachers in Second Language Acquisition research. In J. Schachter and S. Gass (eds) *Second Language Classroom Research* (pp. 31–44). Mahwah, NJ: Lawrence Erlbaum Associates.

Sundqvist, P., Sandlund, E., Källkvist, M., Fredholm, K. and Dahlberg, M. (2019) Ömsesidighet i framtidens praktiknära språkklassrumsforskning: ASLA-symposiets panelsamtal med forskare, lärare och elever [Reciprocity in future practice-oriented classroom research: The Panel Discussion at the ASLA Symposium]. In Ljung Egeland, B., Roberts, T., Sandlund, E. and Sundqvist, P. (eds) *Klassrumsforskning och språkande: Rapport från ASLA-symposiet i Karlstad, 12–13 april 2018 [Classroom Research and Languaging: Report from the ASLA Symposium at Karlstad, 12–13 April],* (pp. 19–42). Karlstad: Karlstad University Press.

Swedish Research Council (2015a) *Forskningens framtid!* Ämnesöversikt 2014 Utbildningsvetenskap [*The Future of Research! Review of Research in Education 2014*]. Stockholm: Swedish Reserach Council.

Swedish Research Council (2015b) *Forskningskvalitet för framtiden.* Redovisning av regeringsuppdrag (U2015/1362/F) [*Research Quality for the Future.* Review Commissioned by the Government]. Stockholm: Swedish Reserach Council.

The Swedish Schools Inspectorate (2011) *Engelska i grundskolans* årskurser 6–9 [*English in Compulsory School Years 6–9*]. Stockholm: The Swedish Schools Inspectorate.

4 Mapping Teacher Beliefs and Practices About Multilingualism: The Development of the MultiBAP Questionnaire

Pia Sundqvist, Henrik Gyllstad,
Marie Källkvist and Erica Sandlund

Introduction and Aims

While language-diverse English classrooms are under-researched in Sweden (Källkvist *et al.*, 2017), teachers are gaining firsthand experience through teaching language-diverse student groups, thus gaining experience and knowledge that warrants documentation. Such knowledge is often conceptualized as beliefs and practices (Borg, 2006), and a suitable instrument for mapping that knowledge among large numbers of teachers quickly is the questionnaire (Dörnyei & Taguchi, 2010; Phakiti, 2015). Questionnaires, like any other instruments, must be capable of yielding reliable data through which valid inferences can be drawn, and scholars have recently called for increased methodological and statistical awareness in Applied Linguistics and Second Language Acquisition (SLA) (Norris *et al.*, 2015; Plonsky, 2015), where the use of questionnaires is widespread (Dörnyei & Taguchi, 2010; Phakiti, 2015). In a similar vein, as pointed out by Borg (2015: 494; our emphasis), in many self-report instruments, there is room for quality enhancement, and 'a first requirement for researchers wanting to use questionnaires […] to study teachers' beliefs is to ensure they understand – theoretically and in practice – *how to design a robust instrument*'. Similarly, Gu (2016) and Valeo and Spada (2016) have called for more attention to how questionnaires are designed, analyzed and validated. Careful reporting of procedures and instruments used also make replication studies possible (Mackey, 2012; Marsden *et al.*, 2018).

Following in the wake of increased mobility, language teachers are experiencing a shift towards greater linguistic diversity in additional language (L2) classrooms (Busse *et al.*, 2020). At the same time, while there is extensive research on teacher beliefs about L2 teaching/learning in general (see, e.g. Borg, 2006, 2015; Pajares, 1992), there is little research on teacher beliefs specifically about the role of multilingualism in L2 classroom contexts (though see Lundberg, 2019). Prior research reveals that the classroom is 'a key site where policies become action' where teachers exercise agency (Hult, 2014: 159; see also Borg, 2006).

In response to the above calls, this chapter provides a detailed description of the methodology behind the development of a new questionnaire instrument called MultiBAP (Multilingualism: Teacher Beliefs And Practices). As part of the school-based research project MultiLingual Spaces (see Källkvist *et al.*, 2017) – in which *multilinguals* are defined as learners of English who use Swedish and one or several additional languages (e.g. Arabic, Finnish or Somali) in their everyday life – MultiBAP was designed to map L2 English teachers' *beliefs* about multilingualism in individuals, in classrooms and schools and in Swedish society at large, and practices in their classrooms and schools. Pajares (1992: 316) suggests *teacher beliefs* be defined as 'an individual's judgment of the truth or falsity of a proposition' and are constructed in everyday practice (van Lier, 2006). Thus, it is relevant to map teacher practices while examining their beliefs, even though beliefs are not always mirrored in their practices (Borg, 2015).

Consequently, the present chapter aims to contribute to developing questionnaire research methodology in L2 language education. In pursuing this aim, we:

(1) describe the development of the instrument MultiBAP,
(2) critically evaluate each step of the development process and
(3) provide a step-wise validation of MultiBAP.

In what follows, we focus on methodological aspects of questionnaire development and then provide an account of the construction and validation of MultiBAP. We end by discussing possible uses of MultiBAP, including the need for further development and validation.

Questionnaires in Research on Beliefs and Practices – Methodological Considerations

Questionnaires have been used extensively in SLA research (e.g. Winke, 2011) and in research on teacher beliefs, although not as frequently. In Borg's (2015) account of 20 studies of L2 teachers' beliefs, half were qualitative, 7 were mixed-method and 3 were quantitative. Of these, 16 investigated the beliefs of in-service teachers. Nine had sample sizes of fewer than 10 participants; three had 11–50 participants; four were composed of 51–100 participants and four > consisted of 100 participants.

Kern (1995), Levine (2003), De Angelis (2011) and Bailey and Marsden (2017) are examples of studies that focus on teacher beliefs, including topics such as comparisons between learner and teacher beliefs, beliefs about target and first language (L1) use and beliefs about anxiety and the role of prior knowledge in learning. Generally speaking, in such studies, validation procedures used are rarely addressed. Furthermore, with relevance to the current study, Norris *et al.* (2015: 472) stress the importance of providing evidence regarding both the consistency of the measurement instruments used and the validity of 'the intended construct interpretations being made in the actual study with the actual population sample'.

Studies discussing reliability and validity in more depth include Graus and Coppen (2016), Loewen *et al.* (2009), Lee and Oxelson (2006), Spada *et al.* (2009) and Winke (2011). Graus and Coppen (2016) investigated the beliefs of student teachers of English as a foreign language ($N = 832$) about grammar teaching. A questionnaire consisting of three parts was developed and validated, and following piloting and revisions, 24 five-point Likert-scale items were retained. Reliability values (Cronbach's alpha) between 0.735 and 0.864 were observed, and items had moderate to large loadings on their respective factors.

Loewen *et al.* (2009) studied learner beliefs about the role of grammar instruction and error correction. University students ($N = 754$) responded to a questionnaire containing 37 Likert-scale items (information about the range of the scale is missing) and 4 prompts (open-ended). The quantitative data were submitted to an Exploratory Factor Analysis (EFA) and '[f]actor loadings of .30 or greater on the obliquely rotated factor matrix were considered significant' (2009: 95), identifying six underlying factors, with a Cronbach'alpha of 0.84 for the questionnaire overall. No reliability values for the subscales are given.

Lee and Oxelson (2006) studied teachers ($N = 67$) responding to 35 questions about their students' heritage language maintenance, 11 about practices and 7 about demographics (plus 3 open-ended questions). A seven-point Likert scale was used. In total, 290 questionnaires were distributed. A rather low return rate (29%) was expected due to timing and an assumed lack of interest in the topic (heritage languages). The questionnaire had eight constructs of which reliability values were satisfactory for six (Cronbach's alpha ranged from 0.76 to 0.85), but low for two (0.51 and 0.53). The researchers used a Varimax principal component factor analysis and report eight underlying factors, highlighting the highest factor loading for each item. Items with a factor loading below 0.40 were excluded from the analysis. There is no further comment on the validity and reliability of the instrument.

Spada *et al.* (2009) centered on developing and validating an instrument for measuring L2 learner preferences for two types of form-focused instruction, 'isolated' or 'integrated', including 294 respondents. Three kinds of validity evidence were gathered: content, reliability and construct. Regarding content validity, 12 expert judges were asked to assess whether items should belong to the 'isolated' or 'integrated' scale. Only items for which there was 70% agreement or higher were kept. To calculate internal consistency reliability, Cronbach's alpha was used, and for construct validity, principal component analysis (PCA) was used. The authors initially created 44 items (5-graded Likert scale), but after several rounds of vetting, the instrument adopted included 20 for practicality reasons. Cronbach's alpha value for 10 items was 0.63 and for the other 10 items was 0.69. With regard to the PCA used for construct validity, 14 items with loadings of 0.30 or above were retained (two subscales, seven items per subscale). These explained 43.35% of the item variance, and the Eigenvalue for the 'integrated' component was 3.77 and for the 'isolated' was 2.30. Even though there were only seven items in each subscale, reliability values around 0.7 were claimed to be 'respectable [...] for a new questionnaire with a small number of items' (Spada *et al.*, 2009: 78).

Winke (2011) included 267 respondents answering a questionnaire about the validity of the English Language Proficiency Assessment (ELPA) test. The questionnaire included three parts corresponding to the social, ethical and consequential dimensions of ELPA test. It had 40 belief statements, asking respondents to mark their answer on a 10-graded Likert scale. Based on the reported figures about the distribution of the questionnaire (Winke, 2011: 637), the response rate appears to have been 15.1% (an initial 2508 questionnaires, minus 585 that bounced back and 156 non-respondents). Internal consistency was 0.94 (Cronbach's alpha) overall based on 134 respondents (due to missing data) and 0.95 when missing values were replaced by the series mean. An EFA resulted in a five-factor solution, explaining 72% of the variance. The Eigenvalues ranged from 1.18 to 11.43. Regarding factor loadings, items with loadings of 0.5 or above were kept.

In sum, it seems that dominating reliability/validity analyses comprise the use of item analysis (item-total correlation, internal consistency reliability and internal vetting), expert judgments (content validity) and various types of factor analysis (underlying constructs). One observation relates to the type of EFA used. Specifically, the use of PCA over a common factor EFA model (e.g. Lee & Oxelson, 2006; Spada *et al.*, 2009) has been questioned (see the section *Item analysis and factor analysis* (p. 66) on the appropriateness of using PCA). Finally, details from piloting rounds are seldom reported, and the response rates are either not reported at all or vary in the way they are reported. In developing MultiBAP, we included item analysis, expert judgments, and an EFA.

Construction and Validation of the MultiBAP Questionnaire

On reviewing prior questionnaire research, it was clear that no extant instrument would capture the type of questions we intended to address. Therefore, we constructed and validated MultiBAP with the purpose of yielding generalizable, quantitative data. The target statistical population was secondary school (Grades 6–9) L2 English teachers in Sweden. A questionnaire cannot possibly cover everything in broad fields, but it may examine some aspects of the fields well, namely the targeted constructs (see below).

The process of creating MultiBAP breaks down into five carefully planned phases, outlined in Table 4.1, in line with important methodological considerations addressed by Wagner (2015). In Phase I, we decided on the parts to be included. In Phase II, we identified the constructs that the instrument was intended to tap into and generated a pool of items for each construct, which was then vetted in the research group. Finally, we asked two raters to link items to the constructs, which led to the final content of the PILOT Questionnaire. Phase III consisted of piloting MultiBAP using a sample of teachers from the same population as the one intended for the FINAL Questionnaire. Based on these data, we analyzed the feedback solicited from the respondents, carried out item analysis and created a Draft FINAL Questionnaire, which an external expert (specialized in multilingualism, L2 learning and translanguaging) was

Table 4.1 Phases and steps in the questionnaire construction and validation

Phase	Steps
Phase I	Deciding on questionnaire parts
Phase II	Theory-driven content specification (constructs)
	Item generation (multi-item scales)
	Internal vetting of items in the research group
	Decision on final content and design of PILOT Questionnaire
	Building of online version of the PILOT Questionnaire
Phase III	Administration of PILOT Questionnaire
	Analysis of teacher feedback on PILOT Questionnaire
	Validation: Item analysis
	Validation: Use of two raters – relating items to constructs
	Validation: Feedback from external expert
	Decision on content and design of FINAL Questionnaire
	Building of online version of FINAL Questionnaire
Phase IV	Administration of FINAL Questionnaire
	Item analysis and EFA of FINAL Questionnaire
Phase V	Content and design of MultiBAP Questionnaire

asked to critique. Following feedback, we decided on the content of the FINAL Questionnaire. In Phase IV, we administered the FINAL Questionnaire, followed by item analysis, an EFA and a reliability analysis. Finally, in Phase V, we decided on the design and content of the MultiBAP Questionnaire.

Phase I: Outlining the questionnaire instrument

Based on best practice for questionnaire design (Dörnyei & Taguchi, 2010; Wagner, 2015), MultiBAP was designed to capture data on beliefs, practices and background information, such as years of teaching experience. Beliefs are essential as they are known to underpin practices (Borg, 2006) of how to teach multilingual groups of students. Such contexts provide opportunities to use pedagogical translanguaging involving teachers' and students' background languages, defined as languages learned prior to classroom exposure to English (Bardel *et al.*, 2013). Demographic background data were deemed important to enable correlation analyses, for example, correlating teachers' experience with their self-reported beliefs and practices.

We used closed-ended items combined with a small number of open-ended items, thereby adopting so-called intramethod mixing (Johnson & Christensen, 2017). For closed-ended items, we used Likert scales with six steps, ranging from 'I fully disagree' to 'I fully agree'. Opinions vary as to whether scales should have an even or odd number of steps; we base our decision on the potential problem of having respondents overusing a middle category (Dörnyei & Taguchi, 2010). Leung (2011) found no clear negative effects of the use of even-numbered scales compared to odd-numbered scales, and by having a six-step scale, we forced respondents to place themselves either to the left or the right of the middle. In Part B, a seventh 'not relevant/don't know' option was included *but separated from the scale*, a procedure in line with Spratt (1999) and recommended by Broca (2015).

Regarding other design aspects, we considered the time needed by respondents to fill in the questionnaire. Dörnyei and Taguchi (2010) suggest that no questionnaire should take more than 30 minutes; knowing of teachers' heavy workload and valuing the need for as high a response rate as possible, our target was 20 minutes. Other considerations concerned starting from a theory-driven list of constructs/concepts/subjects/topics, creating a logical structure, using multi-item scales for constructs and using both positively and negatively worded items.

Phase II: Identifying the constructs and generating questionnaire items

Dörnyei and Taguchi (2010) recommend starting building a questionnaire by identifying critical concepts. This part of our work was guided both by a research problem formulation in the parent study, MultiLingual Spaces, broadly relating to how teachers and students use their linguistic repertoires to facilitate the learning of English, and by research on multilingualism. We now turn to the six constructs that emerged as relevant.

The constructs

The first construct, *Openness towards other cultures*, has bearings on inclusiveness and attitudes towards other cultures other than one's own. Inclusive practices have been identified as fundamental to education (OECD, 2012) and entail using means to meet the range of natural variation among students in a classroom (Swedish National Agency for Education, 2013). In present-day Sweden, this variation in the range of background languages in the same classroom may include, for example, Arabic, Bosnian, Dari, Farsi, Persian, Polish, Serbian, Swedish and Vietnamese (Gunnarsson *et al.*, 2015). Lindberg and Hyltenstam (2013) argue that a resource attitude to diversity and collectively striving for utilizing all students' varied experiences 'is a prerequisite for successfully teaching students with different linguistic and cultural backgrounds than the homogeneous Swedish one' (Lindberg & Hyltenstam, 2013: 126, our translation). Similarly, Edstrom (2006) argues that acknowledging students' L1(s) is teachers' moral obligation; students are then recognized as individuals and treated with respect. On this research background, we generated items aimed at tapping into teachers' attitudes to, *inter alia*, people from other cultures, having contact with them, visiting foreign countries, respecting people with views other than one's own and adapting to other people's habits and needs. This construct was targeted by 10 items in the pilot version (Appendix 1).

The second construct is *Multilingualism in general*, formed against the backdrop of multilingualism being the norm worldwide (Grosjean, 2008). Items were generated asking, for example, whether multilingualism is something positive, whether it is important to be multilingual in today's world and whether multilingual individuals are more likely to succeed in the future. Like the first construct, 10 items target this construct in the pilot version (Appendix 1).

The third construct centers on the current language situation in Sweden, which is characterized as rapidly growing in multilingualism due to refugee migration. Multilingualism researchers Lindberg and Hyltenstam (2013: 122, our translation) suggest that multilingualism be viewed as an asset, whereas in practice, they claim multilingualism involving migrant, minority languages to be commonly 'connected with problems and deficiencies' (our translation).

The fourth (4) and fifth (5) constructs tap into beliefs and practices to do with the use of background languages in learning an additional language. Specifically, whereas Construct 4 deals with learning any additional language, Construct 5 targets English in particular. As to practices, research shows that bi- and multilingualism have a positive effect on the acquisition of additional languages (Cenoz & Genesee, 1998); there is strong evidence that bi-/multilingual users cannot completely deactivate their prior languages when processing information in a target language (see Källkvist *et al.*, 2017). Further, the L1 has been shown to be an effective way 'of communicating meaning' (Nation, 2003: 5).

In terms of beliefs, teachers typically harbor positive beliefs about multilingualism. Research has shown that most teachers are hesitant towards allowing languages that are not known by them in the classroom (De Angelis, 2011; Heyder & Schädlich, 2014). For the beliefs part of MultiBAP, we generated items targeting whether drawing on background languages is good or bad, whether just in general or specifically in the classroom and whether additive multilingualism exists and whether specific language skills (speaking/reading/listening/writing/vocabulary/grammar) may benefit from involvement of background languages. Eleven and 19 items were created for Constructs 4 and 5, respectively, for the pilot version (Appendix 1).

Finally, the sixth construct has to do with monolingual beliefs. Here, it was possible to draw on an existing questionnaire (Pulinx *et al.*, 2015), which focuses on Flanders, Belgium, a region where educational policies are predominantly based on a monolingual ideology. We saw an opportunity of replicating part of Pulinx *et al.* by gathering data from Sweden, where there has been some policy support for multilingualism in that mother-tongue tuition has been offered since 1977. We saw this also as a way of anchoring MultiBAP in an already existing questionnaire.

From constructs to item generation

Our initial goal was for items in Part A (beliefs) to mirror items in Part B (practices). However, it soon became clear that this would only be meaningful for Constructs 1, 2, 5 and 6. Thus, Constructs 3 (the language situation in Sweden) and 4 (using background languages to facilitate learning of an additional language) are included in Part A only.

Next, items were generated aiming to come up with multi-item scales for each construct, that is, 'a cluster of differently worded items that focus on the same target' (Dörnyei & Taguchi, 2010: 24) with no less than 3–4 items be used for each construct. We thus developed 7–10 items for each construct (pilot version) allowing us to, at a later stage, select 3–4 items (final version). Once items had been created, an internal vetting process was carried out, resulting in our PILOT Questionnaire (for all items, see Appendix 1), comprising 64 items in Part A, 40 items in Part B, 19 questions in Part C and 9 questions in Part D. The final step in Phase II was to build an online version of the PILOT using the software Survey&Report (Artologik, n.d.).

Phase III: Administering and evaluating the PILOT Questionnaire

Administration

Prior to its distribution, the PILOT Questionnaire went through 'technical piloting' among colleagues in order to ascertain that it functioned well regardless of the device used when responding. For distributing the PILOT Questionnaire, 45 English teachers from our professional networks were approached, asking them to respond to the extensive pilot version. In total, 23 teachers replied (response rate: 51%). The data collected were exported into statistical software for the analytical work (IBM SPSS 25).

Analysis of teacher feedback in the PILOT Questionnaire

Part D included evaluative questions, including specific questions about each of the six constructs, to find out to what extent the respondents thought they had answered questions about these. The means for the six constructs ranged from 4.39 ($SD = 1.78$) for Construct 3 (*The current language situation in Sweden*) to 5.91 ($SD = 0.29$) for Construct 4 (*Use of background languages when learning an additional language*). In short, the responding teachers stated that they had answered questions about all six constructs. The greatest spread in answers was found for Construct 3 (the language situation in Sweden), with answers scattered across the whole scale. Thus, items in Construct 3 were less salient to the respondents than items belonging to the other constructs.

As expected, the PILOT Questionnaire took a long time to answer, ranging from 15 minutes to more than 40. Thus, several items were deleted when creating the final version.

Item analysis

Item ananlysis was important and entailed analyzing the items in relation to the assumed multi-item scales. Corrected item-total correlations and reliability coefficients were computed in SPSS. The items were then perused in a step-wise process as to their fit into the multi-item scale. The goal was to reach as high a reliability as possible with a scale consisting of 3–5 items. As an example, the items aimed at targeting Construct 3 (*The current language situation in Sweden*) are provided in Table 4.2. The initial scale consisted of six items, and the reliability was 0.574, which is on the low side. The removal of Item A3.2 (see Table 4.2) increased the reliability to 0.735, and reliability was observed at 0.822 through the removal of Item A3.4. As can be seen in Step 3, an even higher reliability could be reached by deleting Item A3.1, but this was felt to have a detrimental effect on the dimension targeted in the construct, as well as bringing the number of items down to three. Therefore, no further deletions were made. The same procedure was subsequently used for all the other scales. The resulting list of items is attached in Appendix 1.

Table 4.2 Cronbach's alpha for items in Construct 3

Item	Cronbach's alpha if item deleted		
	Step 1	Step 2	Step 3
A3.1. In Sweden, it is important that students with another home language than Swedish to keep this language alive	0.547	0.719	0.900
A3.2. In Sweden, in addition to Swedish, it is more important to know English than any other language	0.735	DELETED	DELETED
A3.3. In Sweden, your chances of getting a job increase if you are multilingual	0.405	0.602	0.710
A3.4. I think that the status of the Swedish language is threatened by other languages	0.636	0822	DELETED
A3.5. If you learn English well. your chances of getting a job in Sweden increase	0.403	0.659	0.776
A3.6. If you learn several languages, your chances of getting a good job in Sweden increase	0.352	0.579	0.690
Total Cronbach's alpha	0.574	0.735	0.822

Validation: External raters relating items to constructs

To investigate content validity, data were collected from two external raters. Rater 1 was a senior Humanities researcher, and Rater 2 was a junior scholar in the field of English Linguistics, with expertise in statistics. The raters were presented with all the items in the PILOT Questionnaire, alongside the six constructs, and were asked to categorize each item into these constructs. The external ratings were then compared to that of the research group. According to Altman (1991), pair-wise correlations between 0.60 and 0.80 are considered 'good'. Here, all pair-wise correlations fell within this range (Rater1×ResearchGroup: $r_s = 0.655$; $p < 0.001$; $N = 98$; Rater2×ResearchGroup: $r_s = 0.778$; $p < 0.001$; $N = 102$ and Rater1×Rater2: $r_s = 0.716$; $p < 0.001$; $N = 98$). Using Krippendorff's alpha (Hayes & Krippendorff, 2007), inter-rater reliability for the three ratings reached 0.72, a modest but acceptable result, which was considered satisfactory.

External expert

Another strategy to enhance content validity involved asking a linguist, external to the research group, with expertise in multilingualism to assess the quality of the questionnaire ('external audit', Johnson & Christensen, 2017: 299), leading to further changes. For instance, we streamlined terminology and specified definitions (*multilingualism, background languages*).

Content and design of FINAL Questionnaire

Based on the above analyses and steps, the FINAL Questionnaire consists of 39 items in Part A (64 in PILOT), 38 items in Part B (40 in PILOT) and

19 questions in Part C (19 in PILOT). The FINAL Questionnaire was built in Survey&Report (Artologik, n.d.).

Phase IV: Administering and evaluating the FINAL Questionnaire

Administration

A stratified random sample of L2 English teachers was drawn using statistics from Statistics Sweden coupled with school data from the National Agency for Education. This resulted in the questionnaire being distributed to 441 teachers. It remained open for four weeks, with reminders issued at the end of the first and second weeks. A few automated responses were received from teachers on leave; teachers could also opt out of responding. This lowered the number of respondents to 321. When the questionnaire closed, 139 (43%) teachers had responded, which is a respectable number compared with other studies (e.g. Granfeldt *et al.*, 2019, 35%; Henry *et al.*, 2018, 44%) and higher than rates reported in the studies reviewed above. The sample consisted of 103 women (74.1%), 32 men (23%) and 4 individuals who preferred not to state their gender (2.9%). In sum, it was reasonable to consider the random sample representative of the statistical population (see Appendix 2).

Item analysis and factor analysis

Like the PILOT data, items in the FINAL Questionnaire were subjected to item analysis. As a first step, the scoring of items with a reversed phrasing was corrected as such items, if uncorrected, are known to affect reliability (Field, 2013). Next, a reliability coefficient (Cronbach's alpha) for all the 76 items (Parts A and B) was computed and observed at 0.88. The reliability statistics of the 10 multi-item scales are provided in Table 4.3.

As can be seen, most reliabilities were acceptable, with many values close to or well above 0.7. However, scales for B1 (*Openness towards other cultures*) and B2 (*Multilingualism in general*) were clearly below levels aspired to. A reasonable explanation is that teachers' classroom practices do not necessarily mirror school practices. For MultiBAP, we include items from B5 (*Use of background languages in learning and using English*) and B6 (*Monolingual beliefs in education*), because these scales were reliable.

Table 4.3 Cronbach's alpha reliability for multi-item scales in the FINAL Questionnaire

	Multi-item scales									
	A1	A2	A3	A4	A5	A6	B1	B2	B5	B6
Alpha	0.68	0.58	0.71	0.60	0.88	0.72	0.30	0.46	0.86	0.71

Even though MultiBAP was based on six assumed constructs, we could not be sure whether the items technically mapped onto the constructs. One reason was that most items used had not previously been part of a questionnaire. Therefore, we carried out an EFA rather than a confirmatory factor analysis (CFA).

Factor analysis (FA) comprises 'an array of multivariate statistical methods used to investigate the underlying correlations among a set of observed variables' (Loewen & Gonulal, 2015: 182) and can be divided into EFA and CFA. As we could not ascertain the number and nature of underlying factors, an EFA rather than a CFA was used. Furthermore, EFA can be divided into EFA and PCA. Conceptually, the difference between PCA and EFA has to do with how the models treat variance; PCA analyzes variance, whereas EFA analyzes covariance. In other words, PCA does not differentiate between variance that is shared versus unique among variables, but EFA does. In many cases, PCA and EFA results are very similar, but not always. Conway and Huffcutt (2003) advise that researchers whose purpose it is to understand the underlying structure of a set of variables should decide on a common factor model (EFA) such as principal axis or maximum likelihood factoring, whereas purposes of pure reduction of variables calls for PCA. We therefore opted for an EFA common factor model.

In preparation for running the EFA, we concluded that many Part B items involve reported practice in the respondents' classrooms, but also practices at their schools, and beliefs presumably held by principals. Responses to such disparate items may not necessarily correlate. For this reason, we carried out the EFA only on Part A items.

First, it was necessary to investigate the factorability of the data. A wide range of scholarly advice is given in this regard. In the case of sample size, Loewen and Gonulal (2015) conclude that suggestions for minimum absolute sample sizes vary between 100 and 500. An alternative is to consider the number of respondents per item, where recommendations also vary. Based on their review of the literature, Loewen and Gonulal (2015) report on a range between 3 and 20, and Field (2013) report on a range between 10 and 15. In MultiBAP, Part A (beliefs) included 3.66 respondents per item, thus somewhat low. However, not only absolute sample size matters, and when in doubt, a number of statistical tests should be run. Therefore, the Kaiser–Meyer–Olkin (KMO) measure of sampling adequacy was used. KMO values range from 0 to 1; the higher the value, the better sampling adequacy. Our value was 0.78, which is considered 'good', bordering on 'great' (Loewen & Gonulal, 2015: 187). Furthermore, to test for undesirably low correlations overall, a Bartlett's test was used. The result was significant, with $\chi^2 (703) = 2807.346$, $p < 0.001$, meaning that the variables were sufficiently correlated and suitable for EFA. A related problem involves variables being too highly correlated (multicollinearity), with coefficients of around ±0.90. Only one case of such high correlation was found (Q8 and Q9). Removing one of them did not improve the determinant, but this single case was deemed unproblematic in the light of the high number of items.

As FA seeks to determine 'the fewest number of variables that will still explain a substantial amount of variance in the data' (Loewen & Gonulal, 2015: 182), we employed several criteria to arrive at a decision that would chime well with that aim. One is based on a minimum Eigenvalue cutoff level. According to Kaiser's method, factors with Eigenvalues greater than 1 are retained; Appendix 4 shows that this would leave us with 11 factors. An 11-factor solution was deemed excessive, however, as we observed 1-item factors and factors in which the items were very disparate. Notably, the use of a Eigenvalue >1 in FA is referred to as 'inappropriate' by Pedhazur and Schmelkin (1991: 594), and Field (2013) argues that Kaiser's criterion works well with fewer than 30 items and sample sizes over 250. Another similar method is called Joliffe's criterion, by which factors with Eigenvalues greater than 0.7 would be retained. This would mean keeping even more factors (15); working with these many factors was not deemed feasible. We subsequently tried several analyses with 9, 8 and 7 factors. However, it was still difficult to arrive at satisfactory solutions. An important aspect for deciding on factors to retain is cumulative percentage of variance (CPoV). Plonsky and Gonulal (2015) report that the average CPoV in L2 research is approximately 60%, while Field (2013) suggests a minimum of 55–65%.

Adhering to these guidelines, with a cumulative percentage of 55.11%, six factors can be retained. Next, we checked communalities (h^2) as these can provide an indication of the relationship of each variable to the entire dataset. High communalities are desired, and the mean value for our 38 items after extraction was 0.47 ($SD = 0.21$). A final potential criterion is a scree plot, where the point of inflexion indicates the cutoff point for selecting factors (Figure 4.1). Scree plots are notoriously difficult to interpret and should only be used in light of other selection criteria (Loewen & Gonulal, 2015). In our case, there were many potential cutoff points, and in our interpretation, the plot did not yield a clear picture.

Through a concerted approach, then, drawing on Kaiser's test, Bartlett's test, CPoV and a scree plot, we ultimately decided to retain six factors. This yielded a respectable CPoV of 55% (in line with Field, 2013). As the extraction method, we used maximum likelihood factoring for the analysis of the 38 items in Part A (beliefs). We used oblique rotation, as high correlations were expected for our data (see Loewen & Gonulal, 2015: 197). The rotated factor loadings for the six factors are provided in the form of a pattern matrix in Appendix 3. This type of factor loading matrix is often considered more meaningful and interpretable. As suggested in Loewen and Gonulal (2015), all loadings of < 0.30 have been suppressed. As seen in the matrix, there were deviations from the intended subscales for the 38 items in the sense that the items did not always load

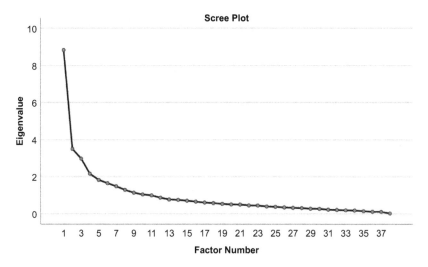

Figure 4.1 Scree plot of components and their associated Eigenvalues

on our six hypothesized constructs. The question code in the left-most column reveals the deviations (items starting with number 1 = *Construct 1*, items starting with number 2 = *Construct 2*, etc.).

As argued by Loewen and Gonulal (2015), when naming a factor, it is important to come up with a descriptive label that represents all items loading onto that particular factor, paying particular heed to items that have the highest load. The four items from the hypothesized Construct 1 (*Openness towards other cultures*) all mapped on Factor 6. In addition, so did one item from Construct 2 (*Multilingualism in general*) and one item from Construct 5 (*Use of background languages in learning and using English*). An analysis of what these items focus on resulted in the factor label *Openness towards other cultures*.

For Factor 5, high loadings from four items from three different hypothesized constructs were observed. These items seemed to focus on the importance of maintaining other languages than the majority language (Swedish). Factor 5 was consequently labeled *Importance of maintaining other languages than the majority language (Swedish)*. Four items from the hypothesized Construct 6 loaded highly on Factor 4. What these items seemed to have in common was *The importance of proficiency in the majority language*.

Regarding Factor 3, four items loaded on this factor, dominated by three from the hypothesized Construct 3 (*The current language situation in Sweden*), and with one item from the hypothesized Construct 2 (*Multilingualism in general*). These items rendered the label *Importance of multilingualism for future employment and success in Sweden*.

For Factor 2, no less than 11 items were observed with high loading: 8 items from the hypothesized Construct 5 (*Monolingual beliefs in education*), 2 items from Construct 4 (*The use of background languages when learning an additional language*) and 1 item from Construct 6. The common denominator was seen as *Positive attitudes to background languages when learning English.*

Finally, for Factor 1, four items were observed to have high loadings. They all came from the hypothesized Construct 5 (*The use of background languages when learning and using English*). An analysis rendered the following label: *Importance of background languages for receptive and productive English skills.*

Phase V: Content and design of MultiBAP questionnaire

The analysis accounted for above resulted in a set of 33 multiscale items for MultiBAP Part A (beliefs). In order to check the reliability of the new subscales, Cronbach's alpha was computed (see Appendix 3). The reliability values observed were 0.84, 0.80, 0.81, 073, 0.68 and 0.75, with a mean of 0.77. This is wholly satisfactory as most guidelines point to 0.7 as a desirable minimal level (Dörnyei & Taguchi, 2010).

As regards Part B (practices), there was no EFA to rely on. However, the multiscale item reliability analysis revealed that two of the 'original' constructs (B5, *Use of background languages in learning and using English*, and B6, *Monolingual beliefs in education*) in the FINAL Questionnaire were reliable, and it was therefore decided to include them in the MultiBAP Instrument (see Appendix 1). Altogether, Part B of the MultiBAP Instrument includes 31 closed items and 1 open question. In sum, then, the MultiBAP Instrument contains two parts: 'Beliefs' (33 closed + 1 open) and 'Practices' (31 closed + 1 open), in total 66 items/questions (64 closed + 2 open). Note that both original constructs B1 (*Openness towards other cultures*) and B2 (*Multilingualism in general*) were unreliable and therefore excluded. However, although excluded as 'scales', individual questions in B1 and B2 may nevertheless be useful in future studies, as answers to the various questions can be informative. For example, in multilingual settings, to what extent do schools view students' cultural backgrounds as resources (see B1.3, Appendix 1)? In addition to the MultiBAP *Instrument*, the full-length MultiBAP *Questionnaire* also contains the items/questions included in B1, B2 and Part C of the FINAL Questionnaire (see Appendix 1).

Discussion

We aimed to account for the development and initial validation of MultiBAP, a questionnaire instrument designed to map teacher beliefs and practices, as well as school practices, about multilingualism. A review of existing instruments revealed a lack of one that served the purposes of our parent study, MultiLingual Spaces (Källkvist *et al.*, 2017). The construction process was guided by best practice advice *inter alia* in Dörnyei and Taguchi (2010), Loewen and Gonulal (2015) and Plonsky and Gonulal (2015). The result is the questionnaire instrument named MultiBAP, included as Appendix 5.

Initial validation of MultiBAP entailed going from *a priori* postulated constructs and pertinent multi-item scales to an evidence-based modification of these. This modification entailed revising the content in Part A in the light of an EFA. Such analysis provided construct-related validity in the sense that we sought to investigate what latent traits our instrument was tapping into. The EFA made us modify the way in which items were linked to assumed constructs. For example, all the items assumed to relate to the *a priori* construct *Openness towards other cultures* clustered together with one item from the *a priori* construct *Multilingualism in general*, and another from *Use of background languages in learning and using English*. There were also some interesting groupings of items, such as the separation of items related to the importance of drawing on background languages for receptive English skills from items related to the importance of drawing on background languages for productive skills. The mean scores of the items linked to those two factors reveal that items targeting receptive skills received higher scores than items targeting productive skills. This could emanate from a belief that receptive skills such as listening and reading may involve an individual's background languages more so than the productive skills.

In terms of reliability, the multi-item scales in MultiBAP Part A rendered respectable coefficients, as did two of the scales in Part B. Thus, this aspect of validity is promising. However, the type of reliability used is sample-dependent, and technically not really a characteristic of the instrument itself, but rather of the sample scores. As suggested by Knoch and McNamara (2015), this can be overcome through the use of Item Response Theory (IRT) approaches, such as extended Rasch models. Consequently, such analyses could provide for further validation of MultiBAP.

Limitations

Some limitations need to be addressed. For example, it was not possible to carry out a factor analysis of Part B items. Thus, only results from reliability analyses of the FINAL Questionnaire are available. Although the overall reliability of Part B was good (0.894), the reliability of constructs B1 (0.3) and B2 (0.465) was unsatisfactory. Thus, if used, this must be kept in mind. In contrast, the reliability values of constructs B5 (0.855) and B6 (0.712) were high, so those constructs can be used. Another potential limitation is the number of respondents. Admittedly, a higher number would have been preferred, but considering the time and effort invested in establishing a random sample, the outcome was satisfactory, in particular in light of multilingualism in Swedish schools being a politically charged topic at the time (and still is). Finally, the number of respondents comes out well in comparison with previous questionnaire studies of teacher beliefs (cf. Borg, 2015), and the response rate is in line with similar studies (Granfeldt *et al.*, 2019; Henry *et al.*, 2018).

Suggested use

The developed and validated questionnaire consists of Parts A, B and C, of which the first two constitutes the MultiBAP Instrument. For example, MultiBAP can be adapted to mapping beliefs and practices about multilingualism in teaching other additional languages by replacing 'English' by another language. MultiBAP can also be used by teachers as a means of raising awareness and initiate professional discussion about prevailing beliefs in specific contexts. Similarly, Part C can be modified. Most likely, nine of the C-items (i.e. C1–C2, C5, C8, C11–C13, C17 and C19) target background variables that are core to many studies.

Conclusion

We have accounted for the construction, development and initial validation of MultiBAP, aimed at mapping teacher beliefs and practices about multilingualism. Care was taken to consider essential methodological procedures, and comprehensive reporting was provided for steps taken. It is hoped that our detailed appendices will aid future similar questionnaire design and validation projects. Suggestions for its use have been offered, outlining straightforward adaptations to contexts. Seeing the pursuit of validity (including reliability) as a perpetual process, initial evidence presented here is promising but may be extended, for example, by using interviews and think-aloud data from respondents while filling out MultiBAP. Finally, it goes without saying that mapping the beliefs and practices among the teachers in our sample is the ultimate aim of this research. These results gained from MultiBAP will be reported in Sundqvist *et al.* (in preparation).

Acknowledgements

The MultiLingual Spaces project was funded by the Swedish Research Council (Reg. No. 2016-03469). Appendices 1–5 are available at Multilingual Matters Resources: https://www.multilingual-matters.com/page/pttmep/

References

Altman, D.G. (1991) *Practical Statistics for Medical Research*. Boca Raton, FL: Chapman & Hall/CRC.

Artologik (n. d.) Survey&Report [computer software]. Retrieved from https://www. artologik.com/en/SurveyAndReport.aspx?pageId=223

Bailey, E.G. and Marsden, E. (2017) Teachers' views on recognising and using home languages in predominantly monolingual primary schools. *Language and Education* 31 (4), 283–306.

Bardel, C., Falk, Y. and Lindqvist, C. (2013) Multilingualism in multicultural Sweden. In D. Singleton and L. Aronin (eds) *Current Multilingualism: A New Linguistic Dispensation* (pp. 247–269). Boston, MA: De Gruyter Mouton.

Borg, S. (2006) *Teacher Cognition and Language Education: Research and Practice.* London: Continuum.

Borg, S. (2015) Researching teachers' beliefs. In B. Paltridge and A. Phakiti (eds) *Research Methods in Applied Linguistics: A Practical Resource* (pp. 487–504). London: Bloomsbury Academic.

Broca, Á. (2015) Questionnaires on L2 learning and teaching practices: Rating responses on frequency and opinions. *TESOL Quarterly* 49 (2), 429–440.

Busse, V., Cenoz, J., Dalmann, N. and Rogge, F. (2020) Addressing linguistic diversity in the language classroom in a resource-oriented way: An intervention study with primary school children. *Language Learning* 70 (2), 382–419.

Cenoz, J. and Genesee, F. (1998) Psycholinguistic perspectives on multilingualism and multilingual education. In J. Cenoz and F. Genesee (eds) *Beyond Bilingualism: Multilingualism and Multilingual Education* (pp. 16–32). Clevedon: Multilingual Matters.

Conway, J.M. and Huffcutt, A.I. (2003) A review and evaluation of exploratory factor analysis practices in organizational research. *Organizational Research Methods* 6, 147–168.

De Angelis, G. (2011) Teachers' beliefs about the role of prior language knowledge in learning and how these influence teaching practices. *International Journal of Multilingualism* 8 (3), 216–234.

Dörnyei, Z. and Taguchi, T. (2010) *Questionnaires in Second Language Research: Construction, Administration, and Processing* (2nd edn). London: Routledge.

Edstrom, A. (2006) L1 use in the L2 classroom: One teacher's self-evaluation. *Canadian Modern Language Review* 63 (2), 275–292.

Field, A. (2013) *Discovering Statistics Using IBM SPSS Statistics: And Sex and Drugs and Rock 'n' Roll* (4th edn). Los Angeles, CA: SAGE.

Granfeldt, J., Sayehli, S. and Ågren, M. (2019) The context of second foreign languages in Swedish secondary schools: Results of a questionnaire to school leaders. *Apples – Journal of Applied Language Studies* 13 (1), 27–48.

Graus, J. and Coppen, P.-A. (2016) Student teacher beliefs on grammar instruction. *Language Teaching Research* 20 (5), 571–599.

Grosjean, F. (2008) *Studying Bilinguals.* Oxford: Oxford University Press.

Gu, Y. (2016) Questionnaires in language teaching research. *Language Teaching Research* 20 (5), 567–570.

Gunnarsson, T., van de Weijer, J., Housen, A. and Källkvist, M. (2015) Multilingual students' self-reported use of their language repertoires when writing in English. *Apples – Journal of Applied Language Studies* 9 (1), 1–21. Retrieved from http://apples.jyu.fi/article/abstract/367

Hayes, A.F. and Krippendorff, K. (2007) Answering the call for a standard reliability measure for coding data. *Communication Methods and Measures* 1 (1), 77–89.

Henry, A., Korp, H., Sundqvist, P. and Thorsen, C. (2018) Motivational strategies and the reframing of English: Activity design and challenges for teachers in contexts of extensive extramural encounters. *TESOL Quarterly* 52 (2), 247–273.

Heyder, K. and Schädlich, B. (2014) Mehrsprachigkeit und Mehrkulturalität–eine Umfrage unter Fremdsprachenlehrkräften in Niedersachsen. *Zeitschrift für Interkulturellen Fremdsprachenunterricht* 19 (1), 183–201.

Hult, F.M. (2014) How does policy influence language in education? In R.E. Silver and S.M. Lwin (eds) *Language in Education: Social Implications* (pp. 159–175). London: Continuum.

Johnson, R.B. and Christensen, L. (2017) *Educational Research: Quantitative, Qualitative, and Mixed Approaches* (6th edn). Thousand Oaks, CA: SAGE Publications.

Källkvist, M., Gyllstad, H., Sandlund, E. and Sundqvist, P. (2017) English only in multilingual classrooms? *LMS Lingua* (4), 27–31.

Kern, R.G. (1995) Students' and teachers' beliefs about language learning. *Foreign Language Annals* 28 (1), 71–92.

Knoch, U. and McNamara, T. (2015) Rasch analysis. In L. Plonsky (ed.) *Advancing Quantitative Methods in Second Language Research* (pp. 275–304). London: Routledge.

Lee, J.S. and Oxelson, E. (2006) 'It's Not My Job': K–12 teacher attitudes toward students' heritage language maintenance. *Bilingual Research Journal* 30 (2), 453–477.

Leung, S.O. (2011) A comparison of psychometric properties and normality in 4-, 5-, 6-, and 11-point Likert scales. *Journal of Social Service Research* 37 (4), 412–421.

Levine, G.S. (2003) Student and instructor beliefs and attitudes about target language use, first language use, and anxiety: Report of a questionnaire study. *The Modern Language Journal* 87 (3), 343–364.

Lindberg, I. and Hyltenstam, K. (2013) Flerspråkiga elevers språkutbildning. In A. Flyman Mattsson and C. Norrby (eds) *Language Acquisition and Use in Multilingual Contexts: Theory and Practice* (Vol. 52, pp. 122–141). Lund: Travaux de l'Institut de linguistique de Lund.

Loewen, S., Fei, S.L., Thompson, A., Nakatsukasa, K., Ahn, S. and Chen, X. (2009) Second language learners' beliefs about grammar instruction and error correction. *The Modern Language Journal* I (1), 91–104.

Loewen, S. and Gonulal, T. (2015) Exploratory factor analysis and principal components analysis. In L. Plonsky (ed.) *Advancing Quantitative Methods in Second Language Research* (pp. 182–212). London: Routledge.

Lundberg, A. (2019) Teachers' beliefs about multilingualism: Findings from Q method research. *Current Issues in Language Planning* 20 (3), 266–283.

Mackey, A. (2012) Why (or why not), when and how to replicate research. In G. Porte (ed.) *Replication Research in Applied Linguistics* (pp. 21–46). Cambridge: Cambridge University Press.

Marsden, E., Morgan-Short, K., Thompson, S. and Abugaber, D. (2018) Replication in second language research: Narrative and systematic reviews and recommendations for the field. *Language Learning* 68 (2), 321–391.

Nation, P. (2003) The role of the first language in foreign language learning. *Asian EFL Journal* 5 (2), 1–8. Retrieved from www.asian-efl-journal.com/june_2003_pn.pdf

Norris, J.M., Plonsky, L., Ross, S.J. and Schoonen, R. (2015) Guidelines for reporting quantitative methods and results in primary research. *Language Learning* 65 (2), 470–476.

OECD (2012) *Equity and Quality in Education*. OECD.org: OECD Publishing.

Pajares, M.F. (1992) Teachers' beliefs and educational research: Cleaning up a messy construct. *Review of Educational Research* 62 (3), 307–332.

Pedhazur, E.J. and Schmelkin, L.P. (1991) *Measurement, Design, and Analysis: An Integrated Approach* (Student edn). Hillsdale, NJ: Lawrence Erlbaum Associates.

Phakiti, A. (2015) Quantitative research and analysis. In B. Paltridge and A. Phakiti (eds) *Research Methods in Applied Linguistics: A Practical Resource* (pp. 27–47). London: Bloomsbury Academic.

Plonsky, L. (2015) Introduction. In L. Plonsky (ed.) *Advancing Quantitative Methods in Second Language Research* (pp. 3–8). London: Routledge.

Plonsky, L. and Gonulal, T. (2015) Methodological synthesis in quantitative L2 research: A review of reviews and a case study of exploratory factor analysis. *Language Learning* 65 (S1), 9–36.

Pulinx, R., Van Avermaet, P. and Agirdag, O. (2015) Silencing linguistic diversity: The extent, the determinants and consequences of the monolingual beliefs of Flemish teachers. *International Journal of Bilingual Education and Bilingualism*, 1–15.

Spada, N., Barkaoui, K., Peters, C., So, M. and Valeo, A. (2009) Developing a questionnaire to investigate second language learners' preferences for two types of form-focused instruction. *System* 37 (1), 70–81.

Spratt, M. (1999) How good are we at knowing what learners like? *System* 27 (2), 141–155.

Sundqvist, P., Gyllstad, H., Källkvist, M. and Sandlund, E. (in preparation) Multilingual classrooms in Sweden: English teachers' beliefs and practices.

Swedish National Agency for Education (2013) *Research for Classrooms: Scientific Knowledge and Proven Experience I Practice*. Stockholm: Swedish National Agency for Education.

Wagner, E. (2015) Survey research. In B. Paltridge and A. Phakiti (eds) *Research Methods in Applied Linguistics: A Practical Resource* (pp. 83–99). London: Bloomsbury Academic.

Valeo, A. and Spada, N. (2016) Is there a better time to focus on form? Teacher and learner views. *TESOL Quarterly* 50 (2), 314–339.

van Lier, L. (2006) Preface. In P. Kalaja and A.M. Ferreira Barcelos (eds) *Beliefs About SLA. New Research Approaches* (pp. vii–viii). New York, NY: Springer Science+Business Media.

Winke, P. (2011) Evaluation the validity of a high-stakes ESL test: Why teachers' perceptions matter. *TESOL Quarterly* 45 (4), 628–660.

5 Developing Pedagogical Translanguaging in a Primary and Middle School

Gudrun Svensson

Introduction

In areas related to multilingualism as a resource, a limited number of studies deal with overall system-changing school projects (but see Carbonara & Scibetta, this volume; García & Kleyn, 2016; Little & Kirwan, 2018a, 2018b; Menken & Sánchez, 2019; Svensson, 2016b). This chapter contributes to this sparsely researched area by showing how a monolingual, Swedish-only teaching norm was gradually replaced by multilingual classroom practices in a primary and middle school in Sweden.

In Tulip School, which is a pseudonym, the roughly 300 students ranging from the age of 6 in preschool class to the age of about 12 in Grade 6 used approximately 30 languages other than Swedish at home. The teachers encountered challenges in teaching and in raising the students' low goal fulfilment (Lindgren *et al.*, 2015; The Swedish National Agency for Education, 2011). When a new principal was appointed to head the school, she turned to the local university to find a senior lecturer in Swedish as a second language, who could provide in-service training concerning teaching practices in multilingual classrooms. The lecturer who was then engaged to fill this position is the author of this chapter and is henceforth in the chapter designated by the pronoun *I*. Relying on a body of research that promotes pedagogy utilising the students' full linguistic repertoire (Baker, 2001; Collier & Thomas, 1999; Creese & Blackledge, 2010; Cummins, 2007, 2008; Cummins & Early, 2011; García, 2009; Hornberger, 2004; Williams, 1996), I emphasised the use of multilingual and cultural experiences as a resource in the classroom to benefit the students' learning. When I introduced pedagogical translanguaging, i.e. 'a planned, deliberate, purposeful and intentional translanguaging to enhance inclusion, social justice and learning among students' (Juvonen & Källkvist, this volume; see also Cummins, this volume), the principal assessed it as a feasible approach to implement at the school. As the school at this time had a decidedly Swedish-only norm, the use of multilingual resources was a new paradigm in teaching, and therefore, the principal engaged me to support the roughly 40 teachers in this endeavour. The implementation of pedagogical translanguaging for the whole school turned out to be a six-year process of learning development, during which I played the role of a coach. During this time, I documented the process for research and published articles about the introduction and use of multilingual teaching in the classrooms in professional journals and edited volumes (Svensson, 2016a; Svensson & Torpsten, 2017; Torpsten & Svensson, 2017), the role of multilingual teachers in the school development process (Svensson, 2016b) and communication with multilingual parents (Svensson & Khalid, 2017). I also published a book on translanguaging at Tulip School for teachers, student teachers and colleagues (Svensson, 2017).

In this chapter, I present a holistic analysis of the six-year development process. The aim of the chapter is to contribute knowledge about how pedagogical translanguaging was collaboratively developed as a recursive learning process by significant actors, that is, principals, teachers and myself (the researcher and coach).

Describing a complex development process lasting several years in a school is an intricate matter, but in this chapter, I focus on ongoing learning processes in the introduction of pedagogical translanguaging. As this process concerns learning as experiencing, reflection, comprehension and experimentation, I use Kolb's Experiential Learning Theory (ELT) (Kolb, 1984; Kolb & Kolb, 2005) to outline how experiences were transformed into knowledge. ELT serves as the structure for qualitative content analysis (Bengtsson, 2016; Berg, 2001; Graneheim *et al.*, 2017; Morse, 2008; Patton, 2002) of contextual themes in the learning process. First, I turn to previous research on overall school development in areas related to multilingualism.

Previous Research on the Implementation of Pedagogical Translanguaging in Schools

Implementation of pedagogical translanguaging in schools has been realised on a large scale in the City University of New York (CUNY)-New York State Initiative on Emergent Bilinguals (NYSIEB)[1] project in New York State. The project, reported by García and Kleyn (2016), was carried out in collaboration between researchers at various universities in 2011, engaging some 50 schools in a number of subjects. The criteria for participation were two non-negotiable conditions: First, that multilingualism should be viewed as a resource in teaching, and second, that the first condition would concern all educational activities in the participating schools. García and Kleyn (2016) assert that teachers cannot develop multilingual teaching strategies on their own, and therefore, an implementation must be done in close collaboration between researchers and teachers. Menken and Sanchez (2019), who also participated in the CUNY-NYSIEB project, describe how supported professional development facilitated a change of mindset among teachers so that they came to view bilingualism as a resource, which disrupted dominant monolingual approaches. The project also provided a guide for educators (Celic & Seltzer, 2011), with theoretical premises and examples to be applied in practice.

Little and Kirwan (2018a, 2018b) report on the development and implementation of teaching practices in a multilingual Irish primary school for girls. In collaboration with parents, teachers and management over the years, the school has developed a multilingual policy, which is now reported to permeate teaching at the institution, particularly multilingual literacy. The teachers' learning about pedagogical multilingual education is developed through the collaboration and support of researchers but also through collegial learning in school.

In the context of Sweden, there is no published research on an extended development process of implementation of pedagogical translanguaging, except for Svensson (2016b), which accounts for multilingual teachers' perceptions of the development process from the Swedish-only norm to the adoption of pedagogical translanguaging at Tulip School. This study shows that the multilingual teachers had adopted the Swedish-only norm of the school but still sometimes used multilingual teaching strategies behind the closed doors of their classrooms. They reported feelings of relief when translanguaging was introduced at the school, and multilingualism gradually came to be perceived as a resource rather than as a deficit. The present chapter goes beyond Svensson (2016b) in presenting research on the school-wide implementation of pedagogical translanguaging at the same school.

In line with prior research mentioned above, I regard professional learning as significant and will in the next section present the theoretical frame, ELT (Kolb, 1994; Kolb & Kolb, 2005), for examining multilingual teaching approaches at Tulip School.

ELT – The Theoretical Frame

ELT, which highlights learning as an experiential and recursive phenomenon, has been used to analyse learning and education in areas such as teacher training, management, health care training and psychology (see references in Kolb & Kolb, 2005). Kolb (1984) founded his theory on Lewin's (1951) and Dewey's (1938) theories of learning as experience; Piaget's (1969) concept of cyclical interaction between the individual and the surrounding world; and Freire's (1974) concept of how reflection and action in the world transform it. In ELT, learning is defined as 'the process whereby knowledge is created through the transformation of experience.

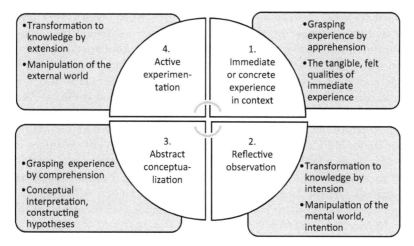

Figure 5.1 The stages in ELT, based on Kolb (1984)

Knowledge results from the combination of grasping and transforming experience' (Kolb, 1984: 41). According to ELT, learning is a holistic and social-constructive adaptation process that includes thinking, emotions, perceptions and actions in relation to the surrounding world. Learning involves a recursive process arising from dialectical tensions between the present and the inflow of new knowledge in a cyclical process whereby experience is transformed into knowledge. ELT is described as a model with two dialectically related ways of capturing experiences, that is, through concrete experience and abstract conceptualisation, and two ways of reshaping experiences into knowledge, that is, through reflective observation and active experimentation.

Figure 5.1 illustrates the ELT process (Kolb, 1984; Kolb & Kolb, 2005) of transforming experience into knowledge in four stages, from observation to action, that is, by grasping experience, reflecting on it, comprehending it and transforming it to knowledge through extension. The process shown in the figure is recursive, which means that Stage 4 is followed by a new stage consisting of concrete experience.

Kolb's model is used in this chapter to highlight phases in a process that is multifaceted and extended over six years. Reality in all its wealth of detail cannot be captured in its entirety in a schematic model, but the model can be used to perceive the stages in the learning process and serve as a basis for further analysis of the contents.

Data, Participants and Ethical Rules

Over the six-year timespan, the following data were collected: field notes and diaries of my observations; PowerPoint presentations; minutes from staff and management meetings; messages as emails and notes from principals to the staff; email correspondence between the principal, teachers and me; a report by the principal and me to the municipal school administration (2015); work instructions; Tulip School activity plans and two questionnaires to all teachers (in 2012 and 2014, respectively). My data also include classroom material and semi-structured video- and audio-recorded interviews with principals, teachers and students. As my intention is to display experiences and learning processes related to pedagogical translanguaging, I have selected data that are illustrative of the four stages in ELT. I have, for instance, used only parts of the interviews for this study. I labelled the teachers as Teacher A, Teacher B, Teacher C, etc. to protect their identities. Other participants in the study are the two principals and me as a lecturer, coach and researcher. All participants signed informed consent forms, in line with guidelines on research ethics by the Swedish Research Council (2019). For analysing the data, I used qualitative content analysis.

Analytical Methods in Qualitative Content Analysis

The ELT model outlined above was employed to reveal different stages in the learning process at Tulip School that were then analysed using qualitative content analysis (Bengtsson, 2016; Berg, 2001), in which data are coded and presented as categories, for instance, things, opinions, experiences or core stories that are interrelated by themes described as a unifying 'red thread' running through several categories (Graneheim *et al.*, 2017; Morse, 2008). The categories were defined using the four stages in ELT. As this chapter illustrates, in the implementation of pedagogical translanguaging, the recurrent theme is *incidents relating to pedagogical translanguaging*. Extracts[2] illuminating this were thus selected from the interviews in the dataset and are analysed like the example in Table 5.1.

In one interview, a teacher says: 'I have noticed that students who are weaker in Swedish can be helped by the others when they use each other and explain # I don't know their language'. The analysis of this sequence according to ELT and qualitative content analysis is illustrated in Table 5.1.

The learning process coded in Table 5.1 illustrates how the teacher verbalises that she has apprehended an experience and then has reflected on it and conceptualised it, which I inferred to mean, in this case, that she has already transformed her reflections into some knowledge and might have formed the hypothesis that it was a good idea to continue this course of action. If she continues to use pedagogical translanguaging, this hypothesis can be confirmed and transformed into a broader knowledge of how to develop pedagogical translanguaging. Using qualitative content analysis, I have thus interpreted the learning processes of the teacher participants in the implementing process first by coding for the ELT categories, second by coding according to 'what is going on' in each category, and then interpreting what this means for the progress of the learning process.

Table 5.1 Coding of learning processes according to ELT content analysis

Teacher Meaning unit	ELT category	Qualitative content analysis, researcher's coding of what is going on
'I have noticed'	1. Immediate and concrete experience (grasping experience by apprehension)	The teacher says that she has gained experience.
'The students who are weaker in Swedish can be helped by the others when they use each other and explain. I don't know their language'	2. Reflective observation (transformation to knowledge by intension)	Perceptible observation of the teacher's statement when she talks about how students are helping each other. Interpretation: Teacher implicitly expresses positive reflections. The final sentence is both a reflective observation and an abstract conceptualisation.
'I don't know their language'	3. Abstract conceptualisation (grasping experience by comprehension)	Inference. As the teacher thinks that students can help each other better than she can, it is a good idea for them to continue to do so.
Continuation of translanguaging in the classroom	4. Active action (transformation to knowledge by extension)	The continuation cannot be directly concluded from this sentence but can be inferred from the context as she continues to promote the use of translanguaging in the classroom.

Source: Interview (11 November 2013).

From Swedish Only to Pedagogical Translanguaging

In this section, I illustrate the development that occurred from late 2012 to spring 2019. I have divided the section into subsections with separate headings depending on the nature of the change in the pedagogical translanguaging context at Tulip School over time.

From Swedish Only

In my in-service training of the teachers in autumn 2012, I started by distributing a questionnaire (Questionnaire 1).[3] The answers to the two questions: 'Mother tongue education has been debated many times. What do you yourself think about the relations between the first and second language?' and 'Does it mean anything in your teaching that your students have a multicultural background?' revealed a common view that the mother tongue was considered significant for learning the second language but that this fact was not relevant to their own lessons. As Teacher A said in a retrospective interview:

> *We have talked to parents # you must sign your children up for mother-tongue tuition so that they get that # because then it's easier to learn Swedish # but we didn't do that in the classroom # that would happen*

only in mother-tongue-tuition classes and through study guidance [...] it never occurred to me that I could stimulate development of the mother tongue in any way. (Teacher A, 11 October 2018)

Against the background of the questionnaire and the students' low goal fulfilment, I decided to highlight the documented advantages of using multilingual resources in the classroom (Collier & Thomas, 1999; Creese & Blackledge, 2010; Cummins, 2007, 2008; Cummins & Early, 2011; García, 2009; Hornberger, 2004; Williams, 1996), but at the end of the spring term, I noticed that the Swedish-only norm was still strong in the mindsets of the teachers (field notes, May–June 2013). From this experience, I learnt that I had to adopt more concrete measures. At the initial staff meeting in August (PowerPoint, 13 August 2013), I introduced García's translanguaging principles of social justice, i.e. equity and tolerance for the students' languages and cultures, and social practice, i.e. a meaningful and long-term implementation of translanguaging (García, 2009: 318). The teachers then had workshops with the task of discussing social justice in relation to their classroom practice. In discussions with the teachers in the workshops, I was met by mixed opinions such as the following: 'Of course, obvious, why haven't I thought about that before?' 'No way! I don't know all these languages and they will say a lot of things I cannot understand', 'Interesting, it's worth trying' and 'This won't work, I haven't got time for it' (field notes, 13 August 2013).

This staff meeting seemed to spark an interest, and three teachers, B, C and D, said that they wanted to try pedagogical translanguaging and asked me for support. In terms of an ELT content analysis, they now started a learning process consisting of 'apprehending the experience' of my lecture and 'reflecting' on it as worth trying, and thereafter 'comprehending' the need for support. The next stage in their learning process was to be the 'transformation to knowledge by extension' to concrete planning and application in the classroom.

At a meeting the next day, the principal appointed the lead teacher in literacy, Teacher A, as the person in charge of implementing pedagogical translanguaging (minutes, 14 August 2013). According to my ELT content analysis, the principal's reflective observation of the concept of translanguaging led her to consider and decide to transform the Swedish-only norm into a multilingualism-as-resource norm, thus initiating pedagogical translanguaging at Tulip School. Thus, she had formed a hypothesis and then transformed her comprehension into an extension by putting Teacher A in charge. An additional point of the extension was that she asked me for a renewal of the in-service training agreement/contact.

When analysing the content of these learning processes – mine, the teachers' and the principal's – a new context was discernible, with two ongoing processes, according to pedagogical translanguaging: one a bottom-up process initiated by interested teachers, and the other a top-down process initiated by the principal. As a coach, I participated in both processes. At the start of the autumn term, the context had thus changed and resulted in emergent pedagogical translanguaging.

Emergent translanguaging

In this section, I first describe the bottom-up processes, followed by the top-down process, and then sum up both. Teacher B had been working as a teacher for several years but had also previously deputised occasionally in study guidance (see Reath Warren, 2017) in her first language, Arabic. She was familiar with working bilingually, and in a retrospective interview, she explained her immediate reaction of recognition and confirmation at the staff meeting in August when I introduced pedagogical translanguaging.

> *I immediately thought # then you brought research # then I just feel like this [waving her hand and looking happy] 'here I am # I've done this' [...] I know myself from experience that when I hear it in my mother tongue it is confirmed more easily # I know from myself [pointing towards her chest] within myself I have known this # but then a researcher comes along and says it # yes I had it confirmed.* (Teacher B, 11 October 2018)

Teacher B thus stressed that she was already familiar with pedagogical translanguaging strategies, which was beneficial to her when, in the autumn term of 2013, she started teaching a preparatory class with 15 newly arrived, preliterate, Somali-speaking students from preschool to Grade 7. She did not speak Somali and did not have the support of study guidance in her classes, so this was a new concrete experience for her. In an interview, she pointed out how she had reflected on the importance of proceeding from her students' experiences to get them involved.

> *So it's not like they were completely blank slates they are able # they have experience somehow as I said and how do I get there # and how do I help them # so that is the way you get the students on board when I teach # that I get them to understand # it's like this # then I want them on board.* (Teacher B, 22 April 2014)

She immediately applied pedagogical translanguaging strategies by starting a blog in order to collaborate bilingually with the students and their parents or guardians. Both Teacher B and the parents could thus observe the students' progress, as the parents were given the opportunity to follow their children's schooling through the blog. Teacher B developed her model by herself without initially cooperating with the other teachers.

Teachers C and D outlined a way to start applying pedagogical translanguaging in their classrooms. As there were no Swedish manuals for teachers on how to apply translanguaging strategies, they had to try to find appropriate methods by themselves in their practice. At this time, I sometimes joined the lessons, assisted in planning and discussed strategies with the teachers, which they transformed into practical action in the classroom (field notes, autumn term 2013).

In an interview a couple of months later, Teacher C spoke of her reflections on the experience of introducing pedagogical translanguaging into the classroom. She had received positive responses from the students and their parents.

> *I notice that they like helping each other very much # they get engaged # Selma [fictional name] who arrived just recently gets lots of help when they talk to each other # I send things home # then they get adult support also about language structure # that must be quicker # indeed it must.* (Teacher C, 11 November 2013)

Teacher C had noticed that the introduction of pedagogical translanguaging influenced her students, who displayed involvement and willingness to cooperate with and support each other. She had also taken the opportunity to receive parental support for her students and concluded that using multilingual resources in the classroom speed up learning.

Teacher D's reflections on pedagogical translanguaging experiences differed from those of her colleague Teacher C. In an interview, she conveyed her reservations, which were caused by both her students' reactions and her own doubts.

> *Many of them have never done it # they don't find it natural # they have never done that at school # well # they think it is embarrassing # maybe their parents don't like it # Swedish is the strongest language for many of them # they are not used to it# they think that they are better at Swedish because at home they speak Swedish with their siblings and the mother tongue with their parents.* (Teacher D, 11 November 2013)

Teacher D seemed to have met opposition from her students when encountering a contradictory Swedish-only norm. In spite of her doubts, she still seemed to perceive pedagogical translanguaging to be advantageous, as a little while later in the interview, she highlighted its benefits for students in need of help.

> *I have noticed that the students who are weaker in Swedish can be helped by the others when they use each other and explain # I don't know their language.* (Teacher D, 11 November 2013)

Teacher D was initially of two minds as to whether to stop or continue, but then she started to cooperate with Teacher C in the parallel class. Together they found strategies to rethink their pedagogical strategies and to experiment, but at times they found making it work very challenging. 'It is a snag', Teacher C said. During the months to come, they tried to implement pedagogical translanguaging in different subjects, sometimes inviting parents to participate by sending the students home with bilingual assignments as homework. They placed multilingual posters with texts and pictures in the corridors, and sometimes when I passed through, I observed students looking at and talking about the posters (field notes, 2013 and 2014).

I have highlighted only the bottom-up processes of Teachers B, C and D to signify the ongoing learning processes, but there were learning processes in pedagogical translanguaging occurring in other classrooms too. I have data (field notes, email conversations, 2013–2014) from one preparatory classroom teacher who posted welcoming texts in many languages on her classroom door and also sent me emails about multilingual 'fruit collections' with the comment: 'One can really see the happiness in their eyes when they notice that we listen to them and are interested in their languages'. I have other annotations from teachers who invited me to visit their lessons at times in order to observe and give advice, and I saw that on the library windows, there were multilingual paintings, and on whiteboards, there were annotations, for example (Figure 5.2; field notes, 2013–2014).

The students' diaries likewise reflected the new multilingual policy, showing that a social justice strategy with equity and tolerance for the students' languages and cultures in line with García (2009: 318) had positively influenced their awareness of language resources, which is illustrated in Figure 5.3.

In terms of ELT content analysis, there were loops of experiential learning processes going on at the end of the school year in tandem with processes of developing knowledge concerning how to handle the new pedagogical translanguaging paradigm. At regular staff meetings, the

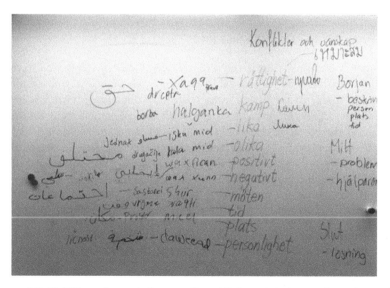

Figure 5.2 Multilingual annotations on the whiteboard during a science lesson in Grade 6

	My languages 12/2 I can speak Kurdish, English, Swedish, a little Persian, a little Arabic, atiny bit of Bosnian and Albanian. I also know Turkish, Spanish, a little Indian.I can understand what others say. If I know more languages.It will be easier to talk to others. I think it is cool that we in the class speak so many

Figure 5.3 A 10-year-old student's notes about her multilingual skills (written in Swedish with my translation into English)

teachers spoke about their experiences and 'transformations to knowledge' (Kolb, 1984) regarding the benefits and challenges of the new approach (field notes, May–June 2014).

That same year, Teacher A had acted upon the mandate that she had received from the principal placing her in charge of implementing pedagogical translanguaging in a top-down process (minutes, 14 August 2013). In a retrospective interview, she pointed out that her reflective observations were initially a combination of contentment because of the existence of research in this area and a concern about her own ignorance of it.

> *This is something new I felt # research # I like research # I thought it was comforting to have some research […] it felt somewhat obvious but it certainly was not obvious in what way we would work # absolutely # I couldn't imagine at first how we would develop it […] no we didn't know that.* (Teacher A, 11 October 2018)

Teacher A had thus been given a mandate she was not prepared to fulfil, and so she turned to me for coaching. We wrote a questionnaire (Questionnaire 2) for discussions with her colleagues, with a focus on social justice. She preferred to speak with her colleagues individually, so it turned out to be a time-consuming assignment that took most of the spring term to complete. In a retrospective interview, Teacher A described this mandate as demanding, as she had to talk to her colleagues and simultaneously learn how to apply pedagogical translanguaging in practice herself:

> *At the same time as I was everywhere trying to reach everyone by going around # talked to everyone […] I was working double there # at the same time as I was supposed to keep it up there I had to develop my own practice.* (Teacher A, 2 June 2019)

From Teacher A's conversation with her colleagues, it emerged that there were teachers who accepted the school's policy and found it consistent with their preferred classroom practices. On the other hand, there was also relatively strong resistance among some colleagues who were not convinced about pedagogical translanguaging as a learning resource. Some said that the approach was detrimental to students' learning and that the method was too demanding in terms of time and the energy needed to effect the change.

When the school year ended in June 2014, there seemed to be a split situation at Tulip School regarding the implementation of pedagogical translanguaging. Some teachers were negative towards translanguaging, while others had adopted García's ideas of social justice, i.e. equity and tolerance for the students, their languages, cultures and communities (García, 2009: 319), and saw the use of their students' linguistic resources as an example of social justice in education, at the same time as they endeavoured to learn how to develop pedagogical translanguaging. Some were finding models of their own, while others, like Teachers C and D, were collaborating. The principal's top-down decision on implementing pedagogical translanguaging had been passed on to all staff by Teacher A, encountering both acceptance and rejection (field notes, 2014). By this time, pedagogical translanguaging was about to become customary for some teachers at Tulip School, but the learning progress was still at a tentative stage.

Collegial development of translanguaging at Tulip School

The autumn term of 2014 commenced with a powerful drive to continue implementing pedagogical translanguaging. The concepts of translanguaging and pedagogical translanguaging were again presented to the staff by experienced teachers and by me. I was contracted to hold regular meetings with the four lead teachers and also to coach any teacher who so desired (field notes, 12 August 2014).

The principal had established a supportive structural organisation for intensified teacher collaboration in teams. Teachers A and B came to play an important role for launching the collaboration in pedagogical translanguaging, which was characterised by increasingly intensive cooperation between some colleagues in the years ahead. In a joint retrospective interview, they described how they tried to find appropriate strategies for a long time.

> It took a whole year for us to develop this practice [...] it's like everything else when it's new # you can't # you don't know how to do it. (Teacher B, 12 October 2018)

> We started rather small # we [= we colleagues] summarized # we were seated in language groups # we started to arrive at # we tried many very many different ways to work on this some went well # we thought # some went well # some did not go well # we were trying to find our feet that whole first year [...] you must feel safe in it. (Teacher A, 12 October 2018)

The development consumed time and was perceived as a challenge among the teachers, who had to try to implement both the Swedish curriculum and the hitherto unfamiliar translanguaging paradigm.

Content analysis revealed that more and more of the development was based on the teachers' own experiences. Through their reflective observations of new concrete experiences of pedagogical translanguaging, the teachers acquired an understanding of how they could be assisted in developing pedagogical translanguaging further, and by trial and error, they laid a foundation for constant change in context through increasing depth of experience (Kolb, 1984). The content analysis of data from this time (field notes, email conversations, 2013–2014) displays alterations in my relations to the teachers. From having been an 'advising' coach, I became a 'receiving' coach, as the teachers developed from asking me about translanguaging in education in practice to displaying it to me. The teachers had thus developed a more independent attitude with regard to me because of their growing experience in practice. Also evident from content analysis is that some teachers applied pedagogical translanguaging in a more advanced way. At first, pedagogical translanguaging was mostly used as a tool for translation of terms and to help the students obtain access to an understanding of texts and topics, but then the multilingual strategies expanded to include various angles of whole themes and fields, as illustrated, for instance, in Figure 5.4, which is part of a series of lessons

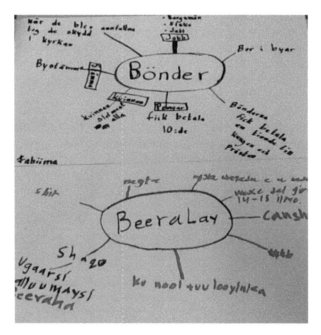

Figure 5.4 Bilingual mind maps in year 5 on the theme of the Middle Ages in Sweden

focusing on history that included multilingual work in the shape of discussions, interviews with parents, texts and, as in this figure, construction of bilingual mind maps.

In late spring 2015, the principal was given different duties, and a new principal was appointed.

In the school year 2015–2016, there was still a discrepancy between the teachers in terms of activities and learning processes. At the end of the year, the principal wanted to know the progress and arranged a meeting for grade teams. My ELT qualitative content analysis of the interviews from this meeting, in which Teacher A and I led the discussions on translanguaging, displays this imbalance (seven focus interviews, 13 June 2016). Although the reflective observations by most of the teachers revealed a positive attitude towards pedagogical translanguaging, some of them did not build hypotheses on how to convert reflections into actions, and so there was no loop by them from apprehending experience to transforming to knowledge regarding translanguaging in educational practice.

Intensified implementation of translanguaging

At the start of the autumn term 2016, the principal appointed Teacher B as lead teacher in translanguaging, with these instructions:

- Follow-up and analyse the students' language development with alignment towards translanguaging.
- Challenge and deepen teachers' knowledge and highlight research and relevant literature in the area (source: lead teacher work instruction 2016, Tulip School).

Here, he additionally stressed the importance of implementing pedagogical translanguaging. He also manifested the implementation in the Tulip School activity plan:

> Translanguaging shall permeate all teaching regardless of subject and the age of the students. (Source: Activity plan 2016, Tulip School)

In the first few years, the question of implementing translanguaging had been an option for teachers, which had led to a confusing situation that Teacher A described in a retrospective interview.

> It's like all other development, 20 per cent are not receptive, 60 per cent are hesitant, and 20 per cent keep going # there's 60 per cent who try now and then and sometimes it doesn't work well # why should we do this when it doesn't work well, they say, and so it is # sometimes it doesn't go well # # not everyone joined when we started # some have left. (Teacher A, 11 October 2018)

By now, the principal was beginning to make demands on teachers and check on whether they were following the school policy in the activity plan.

When we have professional development meetings and when we meet to discuss our salary, he asks us and what's important is an item that he has # how do you use translanguaging # makes sure everyone does it # follows it up. (Teacher B, 11 October 2018)

When employing new teachers, he told them to adhere to the activity plan and to turn to Teacher A or Teacher B if they needed support.

Our principal says when he employs people that this is the way we have to work at our school # that's what he says. (Teacher A, 11 October 2018)

The top-down guidance was thus regulated still more, but from the bottom-up perspective; an extensive knowledge of pedagogical translanguaging was also exercised at the school. In autumn 2017, Teacher A, Teacher B and I decided to establish a joint experience-based idea bank at Tulip School in order to facilitate for all teachers and disseminate knowledge and ideas. The learning processes of increasing knowledge of translanguaging strategies have continued since then as collegial learning. In the last interview for this study, Teacher A emphasised that the approach has become an increasingly natural part of the teaching and gave an example from a professional development day on reading comprehension.

All [the teachers] brought up translanguaging when they were presenting, quite naturally # and I hadn't even told them to think about translanguaging. (Teacher A, 2 June 2019)

An analysis of this excerpt reveals that pedagogical translanguaging seems to be an integrated approach in teaching.

One of the first objectives by the principal for implementing pedagogical translanguaging had been to increase goal fulfilment. Through the years, the students' goal fulfilment had risen, especially in sciences, Swedish and Swedish as a second language, where 80% of students had achieved passing grades. In mathematics, there had been an increase from the previous rate of well below 50% to just more than 50% (interview and email correspondence with the principal, autumn term 2019; see also The Swedish National Agency for Education, 2019). There were many factors influencing students' school success. According to the principal, however, the especially high grades in the sciences were the result of the implementation of pedagogical translanguaging.

Outreach communications

In April 2015, I was asked whether a visit by representatives from the school authority of one of Sweden's major cities was possible, as they had heard about pedagogical translanguaging at Tulip School. Since this first visit from outside the school, Tulip School has had several visits, ranging from media outlets to other schools wishing to learn from what they regard as pioneering work with multilingual students. Teachers A and B accompanied me to conferences, and we have jointly written articles for publication. Teachers A and B give lectures at other schools and municipalities and also involve their students in outreach activities. Through their outreach contacts, they build networks with other schools that are implementing pedagogical translanguaging. In the final interview for the study, they reflected on their experiences, and they recognised that these learning processes were well anchored in research and had led them to acquire empirically proven experience.

> When we have given lectures, we have still had the connection to you [= the researcher] all the time # [...] now we can say for the first time that we have best practice # because now it has turned into best practice # now it's not just one semester # now we've been experimenting for many years [...] we saw that at the translanguaging conference # there's research worldwide on this # this is no longer something new # there is ongoing research all over the world. (Teacher A, 2 June 2019)

A new experience now is the interest from the outside, where the teachers see an opportunity to share their experiences implementing pedagogical translanguaging at Tulip School and 'transform' this into outreach activities that give rise to new recursive processes.

Summary and Conclusions

This study aimed to contribute knowledge about the learning processes involved in the implementation of pedagogical translanguaging in a primary and middle school, focusing on principals, teachers and the researcher. The analysis was framed by the ELT theory (Kolb, 1984) of learning as a recursive process, where experience is transformed to new knowledge, which in this case displayed how experiences of implementing pedagogical translanguaging were transformed to new knowledge about how to develop pedagogical translanguaging in practice and change the context step by step. The content analysis of these experiences and transformations to knowledge reveal a change from a Swedish-only norm to an agenda of equity and tolerance of students' languages and cultures (García, 2009) in teaching. The qualitative content analysis also shows that the educational practice was changed from that of initial ignorance of the students' languages to a substantial experience of pedagogical translanguaging (Juvonen & Källkvist, this volume) in bottom-up processes. Teachers A and B played a prominent role throughout the process when passing on the principals' decisions, working in collaboration with their teacher colleagues in bottom-up processes and disseminating knowledge. The principals played a crucial role by enabling the learning process in top-down activities by contracting me as a lecturer and coach, delegating responsibility to selected teachers, organising and facilitating collegial teamwork, confirming pedagogical translanguaging as the school teaching policy and issuing and following up directives. Initially, I played an important role as the knowledgeable lecturer, initiator and coach but over time came to assume more of a background role. From the perspective of ELT, there were many recursive loops of transforming experience to knowledge as far as the teachers, the principals and I were concerned, but also the changes of the whole school were like a loop from the first tentative attempts to the dynamic and multifaceted applications, aimed inwards at the teachers' own work with collegiality and disseminated outwards for implementation elsewhere.

The project has both similarities to and differences from the CUNY-NYSIEB project (García & Kleyn, 2016) that started a year before. Both projects share the same purpose: to implement pedagogical translanguaging in multilingual schools. The CUNY-NYSIEB project involves several researchers and schools, while this study involves just one researcher and one school; however, both projects involve many teachers. In the two projects, equity and tolerance of the students' languages and cultures were a prerequisite for the opportunity to implement translanguaging. While acceptance of translanguaging strategies was a condition for participation in CUNY-NYSIEB, in this study, the researcher, the principal and the teachers had to develop an agenda of social justice over time, as no such condition existed from the beginning. Unlike the CUNY-NYSIEB project, the teachers at Tulip School had no instruction materials right from the start (Celic & Seltzer, 2011). This could be regarded as a disadvantage for teachers at Tulip School, but for them, this meant that they instead had to devise their own strategies in cooperation and thus built a common bank of materials.

The development did not follow a straight line, partly because of differing opinions and partly because of changes in staff, but the appointment of teachers to lead the implementation created continuity in the process. The learning process at Tulip School is an example showing that working for change is time-consuming but that perseverance pays off in the long run. As Teacher B puts it, 'It took time – but then – whoosh!'

Notes

(1) City University of New York (CUNY)-New York State Initiative on Emergent Bilinguals (NYSIEB).

(2) The transcriptions focus on the content, so there is no marking of hesitation, intonation or extra- and paralinguistic signals. The following transcription key is used (Svensson, 2009):

short pause
longer pause
xxx inaudible speech
[murmurs] brackets to mark metacomments or [...] omitted parts

(3) The questionnaire was in Swedish. The translation into English is mine.

References

Baker, C. (2001) *Foundations of Bilingual Education and Bilingualism* (3rd edn). Clevedon: Multilingual Matters.

Bengtsson, M. (2016) How to plan and perform a qualitative study using content analysis. *Nursing Open Plus* 2, 8–14.

Berg, B.I. (2001) *Qualitative Research Methods for Social Science.* Boston: Allyn and Bacon.

Celic, C. and Seltzer, K. (2011) *Translanguaging: A CUNY-NYSIEB Guide for Educators.* New York: CUNY-NYSIEB, The Graduate Center, The City University of New York.

Collier, V. and Thomas, W. (1999) Making U.S. schools effective for English language learners. Part 1–3. *TESOL Matters* 9, 4–6.

Creese, A. and Blackledge, A. (2010) Translanguaging in the bilingual classroom: A pedagogy for learning and teaching? *The Modern Language Journal* 94 (1), 103–115.

Cummins, J. (2007) Rethinking monolingual instructional strategies in multilingual classrooms. *Canadian Journal of Applied Linguistics* 10 (2), 221–240.

Cummins, J. (2008) Teaching for transfer: Challenging the two solitudes assumption in bilingual education. In J. Cummins (ed.) *Encyclopedia of Language and Education, vol. 5: Bilingual Education* (pp. 65–75). (2nd edn) New York: Springer.

Cummins, J. and Early, M. (2011) *Identity Texts: The Collaborative Creation of Power in Multilingual Schools.* Stoke on Trent: Trentham Books.

Dewey, J. (1938) *Experience and Education.* New York: Macmillan.

Freire, P. (1974) *Education for Critical Consciousness.* London/New York: Continuum.

García, O. (2009) *Bilingual Education in the 21st Century: A Global Perspective.* Malden, MA: Blackwell.

García, O. and Kleyn, T. (2016) *Translanguaging with Multilingual Students: Learning from Classroom Moments.* New York, NY: Routledge.

Graneheim, U.H., Lindgren, B.-M. and Lundman, B. (2017) Methodological challenges in qualitative content analysis: A discussion paper. *Nurse Education Today* 56, 29–34.

Hornberger, N.H. (2004) The continua of biliteracy and the bilingual educator: Educational linguistics in practice. *International Journal of Bilingual Education and Bilingualism* 7 (2 & 3), 155–171.

Kolb, A.Y and Kolb, D.A. (2005) Learning styles and learning spaces: Enhancing experiential learning in higher education. *Academy of Management Learning & Education*, 4 (2), 193–212.

Kolb, D.A. (1984) *Experiential Learning: Experience as the Source of Learning and Development.* Upper Saddle River, NJ: Prentice-Hall.

Lewin, K. (1951) *Field Theory in Social Science.* New York: Harper & Row.

Lindgren, M., Svensson, G. and Zetterholm, E. (eds) (2015) *Forskare bland personal och elever: Forskningssamarbete om språk- och identitetsutveckling på en flerspråkig skola* [Researchers Among Staff and Students: Research Collaboration on Language and Identity Development at a Multilingual School]. Växjö: Linnaeus University Press.

Little, D. and Kirwan D. (2018a) Translanguaging as a key to educational success: The experience of one Irish primary school. In K. Maryns, S. Slembrouck, S. Sierens, P. Van Avermaet and K. Van Gorp (eds) *The Multilingual Edge of Education* (pp. 313–339). Basingstoke: Palgrave Macmillan.

Little, D. and Kirwan, D. (2018b) From plurilingual repertoires to language awareness: developing primary pupils' proficiency in the language of schooling, In C. Frijns, K. Van Gorp, C. Hélot and S. Sierens (eds) *Language Awareness in Multilingual Classrooms in Europe* (pp. 169–200). Berlin: Mouton de Gruyter.

Menken, K. and Sánchez, M.T. (2019) Translanguaging in English-only schools: From pedagogy to stance in the disruption of monolingual policies and practices. *TESOL Quarterly* 53 (3), 741–767.

Morse, J. (2008) Confusing categories and themes. *Qual. Health Res.* 18 (6), 727–728.
Patton, M.Q. (2002) *Qualitative Research and Evaluation Methods: Integrating Theory and Practice.* Thousand Oaks, California: Sage Publications Inc.
Piaget, J. (1969) *Psychology and Pedagogy.* Barcelona: Ariel.
Reath Warren, A. (2017) Developing Multilingual Literacies in Sweden and Australia: Opportunities and Challenges in Mother Tongue Instruction and Multilingual Study Guidance in Sweden and Community Language Education in Australia. PhD thesis Stockholm: Stockholm University.
Svensson, G. (2009) *Diskurspartiklar hos ungdomar i mångspråkiga miljöer i Malmö [Discourse Particles in Youth Talk in Multilingual Settings in Malmö].* PhD thesis. Lund: Lund University Press.
Svensson, G. (2016a) Translanguaging för utveckling av elevers ämneskunskap, språk och identitet [Translanguaging for development of the students' knowledge in subjects, language and identity]. In B. Kindenberg (ed.) *Flerspråkighet som resurs* (pp 31–43). Stockholm: Liber.
Svensson, G. (2016b) Från enspråkig norm till flerspråkighet som resurs: Skola i förändringsprocess [From monolingual norm to multilingualism as a resource: school in a process of change]. In K. Larsson Eriksson (ed.) *Möten och mening* (pp. 209–225). Lund: Nordic Academic Press.
Svensson, G. (2017) *Transspråkande i praktik och teori. [Translanguaging in Practice and Theory]* Stockholm: Natur och Kultur.
Svensson, G. and Khalid, I. (2017) Transspråkande för utveckling av flerspråkighet [Translanguaging for developing multilingualism]. In P. Lahdenperä and E. Sundgren (eds) *Nyanlända, interkulturalitet och flerspråkighet i klassrummet* (pp. 94–115). Stockholm: Liber.
Svensson, G. and Torpsten, A.-C. (2017) Transspråkande för förstärkt tvåspråkighet. [Translanguaging for stronger bilingualism] In Å. Wedin (ed.) *Språklig mångfald i klassrummet* (pp. 37–60) Stockholm: Lärarförlaget.
The Swedish National Agency for Education (2011) Skolutveckling, statistik [School development, statistics] https://www.skolverket.se/skolutveckling/statistik/sok-statistik-om-forskola-skola-och-vuxenutbildning?sok=SokA&kommun=0780&one=92096622&ar=2011&run=1 (Accessed in April 2020)
The Swedish National Agency for Education (2019) Skolutveckling, statistik [School development, statistics]. https://www.skolverket.se/skolutveckling/statistik/sok-statistik-om-forskola-skola-och-vuxenutbildning?sok=SokA&kommun=0780&one=92096622&ar=2019&run=1 (Accessed in April 2020).
The Swedish Research Council (2019) *Good Research Practice.* Stockholm: The Swedish Research Council.
Torpsten, A.-C. and Svensson, G. (2017) Jag tycker det är bra med translanguaging. [I think translanguaging is good]. In Å. Wedin (ed.) *Språklig mångfald i klassrummet* (pp. 61–88). Stockholm: Lärarförlaget.
Williams, C. (1996) Secondary education: Teaching in the bilingual situation. In C. Williams, G. Lewis and C. Baker (eds) *The Language Policy: Taking Stock* (pp. 39–78). Llangefni: Community Associations Institute.

6 '我的…futuro?': Multilingual Practices Shaping Classroom Interaction in Italian Mainstream Education

Valentina Carbonara and Andrea Scibetta

Introduction

This chapter explores translanguaging interactions across the five primary schools included in the project 'L'AltRoparlante', which started in 2016. The aim of the project is to leverage students' multilingual repertoires by embracing translanguaging as a pedagogical resource, with the ultimate goal of transforming school environments in such a manner as to ensure an equal standing for the various languages and cultures in the 'ecology' present there (García & Li Wei, 2014; Hult, 2012).

We begin by providing a review of language policies in Italy with regard to students with a migrant background, mostly focusing on the strain that arises between an emergency approach (Favaro, 2014) based on monolingualism (Italian) and a more inclusive view of students' multilingual repertoires, supported by national curricula. By taking into account the most relevant national investigations and the influence of the pluralistic approaches promoted by the Council of Europe, we suggest pathways towards the integration of translanguaging pedagogy into the Italian mainstream teaching praxis in primary schools.

We then introduce the L'AltRoparlante project and briefly describe the school contexts, showing how City University of New York (CUNY)-New York State Initiative on Emergent Bilinguals (NYSIEB) *Initiatives on Emergent Bilinguals* (García & Sánchez, 2018) was used as a foundation when implementing pedagogical translanguaging in 'L'AltRoparlante'. We also describe the trajectory of an adaptation of this translanguaging model into the Italian education system, considering similarities and differences with other European projects.

We further proceed to analyse translanguaging interactions occurring during classes, aiming at tracing the development of teachers' translanguaging strategies in their interaction with students and researchers. Our data consist of about 53 hours of video-recordings, mainly concerned with multilingual text-based activities (Cummins & Early, 2011), content-based instructions and moments of students' cooperative work. Illustrative excerpts are analysed using conversation analytic methods (Sacks *et al.*, 1974), with the purpose of showing verbal and nonverbal features occurring when negotiating contents of the classese through given translanguaging interactions. We show how both teachers and students may shape classroom interaction through differing interactional and multilingual strategies, such as translation, peer-to-peer mediation, word recall and metalinguistic and cross-linguistic considerations. Our results show that teachers who cannot speak their students' languages tend to employ multimodal support and to reconstruct teacher–student roles, whereas teachers with limited command of one or more of the students' languages use these to prompt translanguaging interactions.

In conclusion, we discuss how researchers and teachers may, by their use of translanguaging, impact the educational and conversational praxis, to develop in a more equitable direction the existing education system and, eventually, thoroughly transform it.

Multilingualism in the Italian School: Opportunities to Trace a Pathway for Pedagogical Translanguaging?

One of the most recent Eurydice Reports on policies and measures promoting the integration of immigrant minority students (European Commission, 2019) discusses several issues concerning the role of migrants' home languages in the education systems across Europe. The Report underlines that students of migrant backgrounds generally have limited access to heritage language instruction in school, even if most of the recommendations, including the Italian ones (MIUR, 2014), recognise the importance of heritage language maintenance in terms of identity formation. Finland, Sweden and Austria have specific curricula for the teaching of home languages; however, according to the Report, such languages are not normally considered as a collective resource for the entire class in policy guidelines, except for Finland (European Commission, 2019: 19). However, intercultural education, which in Italy underpins the whole curriculum, usually concerns *all* students.

Favaro (2014) outlined three different stages in the management of diversity in Italian schools in order to promote a shift from an emergency perspective, based on occasional and autonomous attempts, to well-defined procedures encouraged by top-down educational policy and adapted by each school. The first is the *welcoming stage*, usually based on an essentialist approach to intercultural education (Cole & Meadows, 2013), resulting in activities based on folkloristic views of the so-called 'cultures of origin' of newcomers and first-generation students. The second stage is the period of *integration measures*, founded on compensatory interventions, such as linguistic support in Italian as a second language (L2), intercultural mediation services for families and adaptation of learning materials. Most of the Italian schools have reached this phase. Finally, the third stage, which Favaro (2014) called the *inclusive phase*, should imply dismissing the emergency response and the deficient perception of immigrant minority students, in favour of the promotion of diversity and of the acknowledgement of second-generation students' identities, disregarding assimilationist approaches. As we have argued elsewhere (Scibetta & Carbonara, 2019), in our view, the inclusive stage can be achieved only by adopting a multilingual lens on ordinary teaching and learning practices (Cummins, 2014) and a democratic and transformative approach to the whole education system.

Recently, 'Pluralistic Approaches' promoted by the Council of Europe (Beacco *et al.*, 2016; Candelier *et al.*, 2012) have reached Italian schools, in particular in terms of intercomprehension activities (Canù, 2016) involving European languages and éveil *aux langues* initiatives, in which students are guided in reflecting on how even non-European languages work, with the aim of fostering language awareness and metalinguistic skills (Hawkins, 1999; Sordella & Andorno, 2018). Other projects focus on the home languages of students of migrant backgrounds in order to legitimate multilingual repertoires. The following are two examples worthy of mention: IRIS, 'Identifying and Reconstructing Individual Language Stories' (Favaro, 2018), whose purpose is to analyse language portraits of migrant students for detecting and transferring bi/multilingual competences across languages, and RepertoirePlus (Zanasi & Platzgummer, 2018), which combines a sociolinguistic approach to investigate individual language repertoires with interactive multilingual activities. A few studies have implemented pedagogical translanguaging in class, for example, Coppola and Russo (2019), who explore the use of digital learning tools associated with a multilingual task-based approach, and the L'AltRoparlante project (Carbonara & Scibetta, 2018, 2020a).

The challenge of acknowledging migrant students' language repertoires in Italian schools is twofold: First, there is a need to overcome the sporadic nature of some of the initiatives presented above; second, it is important to promote a shift from the mere identification of linguistic diversity in class to concrete integration of students' language repertoires in mainstream teaching. On one hand, national education policy guidelines promote the whole-child approach and inclusive pedagogy (MIUR, 2012), but on the other hand, migrant students' lower performances and high dropout rates urge scholars and teachers to ponder whether the so-called 'Italian way' ensures equal opportunities for all students (MIUR, 2007; Santagati, 2015). However, comparing European countries with more restrictive language policies towards the educational legitimation of multilingual repertoires (Agirdag, 2010; Hélot & Cavalli, 2017; Kroon & Spotti, 2011; Rosiers, 2017, 2018), the inconsistency of Italian top-down approaches regarding multilingualism eventually results in bottom-up initiatives, mobilised by teachers' agency (Priestley *et al.*, 2012) and encouraged by the Italian constitutional principles of academic freedom and teaching autonomy. These two elements pave the way for inclusive, multilingual teaching practices in Italian schools; however, they may be insufficient without research, such as that pursued in the L'AltRoparlante project.

L'AltRoparlante Project: Theoretical Influences and Practical Steps

The L'AltRoparlante project was developed in response to local and national studies showing that second-generation migrant students tend not to maintain their heritage languages. This may be a result of a belief among educators and even students with migrant backgrounds that 'becoming Italian' is an accomplishment (Carbonara, 2017; Chini & Andorno, 2018). Five schools are currently involved in the L'AltRoparlante project; the number of teachers and students taking part amounts to around 100 and 800 individuals, respectively.

L'AltRoparlante is inspired by CUNY-NYSIEB project (García & Sánchez, 2018) and designed as Transformative Action Research (García & Kleyn, 2016), in which researchers and teachers jointly redefine inclusive educational practices. L'AltRoparlante provides an example of 'monolingual teachers using translanguaging' (García & Li Wei, 2014: 110) as a result of the development and subsequent application of the project. Guidelines set forth by the L'Atroparlante project's team have provided monolingual teachers with an extra tool, the effectiveness of which as a viable example may be judged by reported: (a) good classroom integration of students and (b) some praiseworthy efforts on the teachers' part to acquire the basics of their students' languages (pre-eminently at School 3 where students are, for the most part, Chinese speaking).

The L'AltRoparlante project gradually introduces pedagogical translanguaging (Carbonara & Scibetta, 2020a). Initially, teachers are offered professional development aimed at their acquiring of a 'transformative stance'. As Kleyn and García (2019: 65) underlined, 'translanguaging embedded in instruction cannot be a panacea, but must be part of an overall school and class ecology that is supportive of emergent bilingual students and regards with respect their cultural and linguistic resources'. Subsequently, L'AltRoparlante provides an initial one-year period of tutorship, during which teachers and researchers work together in planning activities and in supporting translanguaging interactions in class. At this stage, most interventions concern the reconstruction of a more ecological schoolscape in various manners: (1) symbolic (multilingual labelling of school areas); (2) instrumental (translation of forms and dissemination of leaflets regarding bilingual advantages) and (3) educational (e.g. word walls and multilingual mind maps). Parents' involvement is also essential at the beginning of the implementation to foster translanguaging communicative practices: They are usually engaged in storytelling, role-plays and multilingual interviews regarding curricular topics. Their participation in school activities provides parents with opportunities to play an educational role – a role that migrant parents in many cases do not feel capable of adopting due to their limited proficiency in Italian and/or to their low socioeconomic status. In later implementation phases, researchers monitor (as mentors, rather) the schools through monthly meetings and classroom observation, and teachers gradually become autonomous in creating materials and applying different strategies, by drawing on the entirety of the students' language repertoire.

The L'AltRoparlante network produced a flexible instructional model combining the US-based *Translanguaging Unit Design* and *Translanguaging Instructional Design Cycle* (García *et al.*, 2017) with a selection of competences and resources described in the Europe-oriented FREPA/CARAP, *Framework of Reference for Pluralistic Approaches to Languages and Cultures* (Candelier *et al.*, 2012) and within the Italian 'Unità di Lavoro/Apprendimento (UdLA, Working/Learning Unit)' (Pona *et al.*, 2018). The latter was selected for its similarities with the CUNY-NYSIEB model in terms of the value conferred to cooperative group work and to specific learning strategies (e.g. building common background knowledge, expanding meaning-making processes through individual research and critical thinking, creating and presenting authentic and meaningful output; see also Carbonara & Martini, 2019). Cummins and Early's (2011) identity texts were used to foster biliteracy engagement across a variety of narrative context-based and multimodal texts, in order to further the cognitive processes in combination with all the intersecting aspects of biliteracy development (Hornberger & Link, 2012) and to enhance the value of students' multilingual identities and of their pre-acquired extra-scholastic knowledge. The resulting synthesis offers a pedagogical approach that responds in practical terms to the principles of 'Democratic Language Education' (De Mauro, 2018), challenges the coercive power relations depicting home languages as a burden for the speakers as well as for the entire class and empowers migrant students to showcase their competences and resources.

In line with other similar groundbreaking European projects (Duarte & van der Meij, 2018; Hélot & Young, 2006), L'AltRoparlante (awarded the European Language Label 2018) promotes language and metalinguistic awareness within mainstream curricular activities and encourages teachers to go beyond the sole acknowledgement of language diversity in the classroom by the integration of minority languages in instructional practices. In order to achieve such a transformation in schools, collaboration between teachers and researchers is crucial; hence, it is important to conduct long-term research.

Research Questions, Data and Data Analysis

In this chapter, we focus on data collected in three schools: School 1 (S1) is a kindergarten, primary and middle school with 35%–85% migrant students, depending on the educational level; School 2 (S2) is a primary and middle school with 30%–50% migrant students and School 3 (S3) is a primary and middle school with 60%–72% migrant students. All data were collected in compliance with legal and research ethical requirements. This applies top rivacy rights: Consent was obtained from all participants prior to the study's commencement. Likewise, privacy authorisation on behalf of minors for video- and/or audio-recordings, for pictures and video reproductions and for the publication of transcripts were formally requested and granted by all those concerned.

Relying on the theoretical background described in the previous section, three research questions were developed:

> Can teachers draw on the multilingual repertoires of their students, when interacting with them, in order to implement pedagogical translanguaging?

> What particular aspects of teachers' conversational performances can encourage situated translanguaging practices?

> Is it possible to identify different degrees of teachers' conversational strategies involving students' multilingual repertoires?

Preliminarily, ethnographic fieldwork data (Blommaert & Dong, 2010), extensively illustrated in other publications (Carbonara & Scibetta, 2018, 2020a, 2020b; Scibetta & Carbonara, 2019), provide information about the different contexts. Sociolinguistic questionnaires (mainly based on language background self-rating scales; see also Extra & Yagmur, 2004) were used to collect information about the multilingual repertoires of the students. We also collected language portraits (Busch, 2012) to gain information about students' individual and collective repertoires, as well as about their perceptions and emotions towards language plurality. A total of 18 teachers in three schools (S1, S2 and S3) and 122 students attending two different schools (S1 and S2) also participated in semistructured interviews (Charmaz & Belgrave, 2012) in different phases of implementation of the project.

To answer the abovementioned research questions, specific translanguaging-based classes, including content-based ones, were video-recorded by both authors of this chapter in S1 (28 hours), in S2 (7 hours) and in S3 (18.5 hours), during a timeframe of several months from December 2018 to June 2019. Selected sequences, reflecting interaction that typically occurred during our observations, were transcribed according to the Jeffersonian transcription system (Jefferson, 1996). Focusing on classroom-interaction data, we intend to shed some light upon the dynamics of translanguaging interaction between teachers and students, as well as among students, during the observed lessons. Such dynamics can be understood as typical (i.e. frequently occurring) indexes of teachers' attitudes towards the functional use of collective multilingual repertoires, supporting their symbolic and educational legitimation within the formal teaching praxis.

The data were analysed using Conversation Analysis (CA; Kasper & Wagner, 2014; Sacks *et al.*, 1974). Specific sequences in the corpus of video-recordings were selected, isolated, transcribed and analysed by taking into account patterns in verbal, paraverbal (e.g. intonation, pauses management, changes in speaking speed) and nonverbal interactions. The duration of talking sequences also was examined, together with the organisation and timing of classroom talk. CA allows us to gain new insights into pedagogical translanguaging practices, focusing on different degrees of teachers' interactional strategies, as will be shown below (Duarte, 2019; Lin & Wu, 2015; Llompart *et al.*, 2019).

Analysis and Preliminary Implications

In this section, we analyse four segments typical of the teacher–student translanguaging interactions observed during data collection. They serve to illustrate the various stages of L'AltRoparlante and to focus on the different strategies adopted by teachers. All four sequences were recorded during curricular classes and reflect a certain degree of heterogeneity in terms of students' age and of topics dealt with by the teachers. In Sequences 1 and 3, a researcher was present in class, actively supporting the teacher (especially in the first case), whereas in Sequences 2 and 4, the researchers had only a nonparticipant observer role.

Sequence 1: The researcher's involvement

Excerpt 6.1 displays the transcription of a segment of video-recording in a fifth-grade primary school class in S1 at an early stage of implementation of the L'AltRoparlante project (October 2018). Languages spoken by the students include Moroccan Arabic, Romanian, French, Polish and a variety of Italian dialects. The researcher (R) actively participates in the lesson by promoting translanguaging interaction during an activity based on a multilingual *wh*-questions grid related to a newspaper article regarding the peace march of Perugia that students had read about in their textbook in the Italian language. Sheets that report different *wh*-questions that are translated into the different languages of the class, including Italian and English, are attached to the blackboard, and R reads the *wh*-questions in an effort to elicit students' answers. In Excerpt 6.1, R is asking the wh-question 'Who?', implying 'Who participated to the peace march?' in Romanian, in Arabic and then in Polish.

Excerpt 6.1 Sequence 1

1	R	Allora GRUPPI (0.4) se dico:: (0.3) [Romanian] <u>cine</u>? *So, if I say… [Romanian]…who?* ((R. points to a multilingual support on the blackboard))
2	Students	[Romanian] cine ↘ *Class: [Romanian] Who…*
3	Student 1	[Romanian] Multa <u>lume</u> .(1.0) >multa lume< . <u>copii</u> stu- denti du <u>liceu</u> major<u>ete</u> batra:n e: adult *[Romanian] Many people…many people, children, high-school students, cheerleaders, old and adult people.* ((R. nods))
4	R	[Arabic] MAN? (3.0) MAN? *[Arabic] Who? Who?* ((R. addresses some students)) ((slight noise))
5	Student 2	Chi <u>è</u> che legge? *Who is going to read?*
6	Student 3	[Arabic] °tul<u>lab</u> (2.0) ua:: atfal° *[Arabic] Students and children.* ((R. nods))
7	Student 4	<u>Io</u> ho fatto diverso. *I did it differently.*
8	R	Non <u>sento</u> J. a voce <u>alta</u> *R.: I can't hear you, J. [Student 3], speak loudly.*
9	Student 3	[Arabic] tullA::B ↖( ) al aleA:md *[Arabic] Students, (?)* ((R. nods))
10	Student 4	Eh? *What?*
11	Student 2	[Arabic] >Umhat< *Mothers.*
12	Student 3	Ah [Arabic] tullA::B (0.5) UmhA:t *Ah, [Arabic] students, mothers.* ((R. nods))
13	Student 2	[Arabic] <u>tullabà</u>! *[Arabic] Students!*
14	Student 3	[Arabic] tullà: (0.5) tula:: *[Arabic] stu..stude..*
15	Student 2	[Arabic] tulla:b (0.5) alhami::d (1.5) [Moroccan Arabic] atfel . *[Arabic] Students, the mayor… [Moroc. Arabic.] children.*

| 16 | R | [Moroccan Arabic] Atfel ok. |
| | | *[Moroccan Arabic] Children, ok.* |

| 17 | Student 2 | [Arabic] atfa:l |
| | | *[Arabic]...children...* |

| 18 | R | [Arabic] atfa:l aftal. |
| | | *[Arabic] Children...children.* |

| 19 | Student 2 | Che sarebbe: bambini. |
| | | *Which means children.* |

20	R	Bambini (.) plurale irregolare. (1.0) e invece tu hai <u>scritto</u>?
		Children...irregular plural. And what did you write?
		((R.addresses another student))

| 21 | Student 4 | [Moroccan Arabic] Sukka:n burgia. |
| | | *[Moroccan Arabic] The inhabitants of the city.* |

| 22 | R | [Moroccan Arabic] Sukka:n burgia. (.) [Ita.] >che vuol dire< tante <u>persone</u>? |
| | | *[Moroccan. Arabic] The inhabitants of the city...[Ita.] which means...many people?* |

| 23 | Student 4 | Si. |
| | | *Yes.* |

| 24 | R | Tante persone. (.) OK |
| | | *Many people, ok.* |

| 25 | Student 4 | NO °cioè° gli abitanti di:: |
| | | *No, I mean the inhabitants of...* |

26	R	Ah <u>no</u> gli <abitanti> di Perugia (.) gli abitanti di Perugia (0.4) e se invece chiedo:: [Polish] <u>kto</u>?
		Ah, no, the inhabitants of Perugia, the inhabitants of Perugia... V: And if I ask [Polish] who?
		((R. first points the blackboard, then turns to the studs.))

| 27 | Student 5 | P. <u>rispondi</u>! |
| | | *P., answer!* |

28	R	<u>Kto</u>?
		Who?
		((R. points a multilingual support on the blackboard))

| 29 | Student 6 | [Polish] <u>Stowarzyszenie</u> |
| | | *[Polish] Associations!* |

| 30 | Student 5 | [Polish] <Stowarzyszenie>. |
| | | *[Polish] Associations...* |

| 31 | Student 7 [P.] | [Polish] marsz dla. |
| | | *[Polish] The march of...* |

32	Student 5	[Polish]: stowarzyszenie.
		[Polish] Associations...
		((Stud. 5 points to a part of the blackboard, where the answer in Polish is written))

33	R	No (.) <u>qua</u> >è quello che stavi scrivendo <u>ora</u>< [Polish] <u>Kto</u>?
		No, here. It is what you have been writing now! [Polish] Who?
		((R. points the blackboard))

| 34 | Student 6 | [Polish] <Stowarzyszenie>. |
| | | *[Polish] Associations...* |

| 35 | R | [Polish] STOWARZYSZENIE:: |
| | | *[Polish] Associations...* |

36   Student 7   [Polish] <stowarzyszenie>. (0.5) chłopców zy <u>liceum</u> (0.5)
              dzieci (.) burmistrzowie.
              [Polish] Associations, high-school students, children, mayors.
                        ((Stud. 7 first corrects a Polish word on the blackboard,
                        then reads from the blackboard))

37   R   <u>Ok</u> (.) WO::W >avete sentito< <u>P.</u> che spettacolo::? ce lo
              rileggi un attimo bene ad alta voce::? (.) <u>fantastico</u>
              sentite.
              Ok, wow, did you hear P., what a performance? Can you read it again loudly?
              Fantastic, listen!
                        ((R. puts a hand on Student 7's head, smiles to him, and hugs him))

38   Student 7   [Polish] <stowarzyszenie>. (.) chłopców zy <u>lice:um</u>↗
              (.) dz<u>ie</u>ci burmistrzowie
              [Polish] Associations, high school students, children, mayors.

39   R   WO:::W >glielo facciamo< un <u>appla:uso</u> a P.?
              Wow, an applause for P.?
                                                              ((Applause))

40   R   R.: Bravo. (0.5) <u>complime:nti</u> >ora finiamo< di scriverlo↗
              Good, congratulations, now we complete the writing of it.

The researcher starts the interactions by addressing groups instead of a single student, by incorporating the Romanian word 'cine' (*who*) in her request. Some students spontaneously repeat the word, and Student 1, who speaks Romanian, self-selects him/herself as the next speaker in Turn 3. The researcher nods and switches to Arabic, but this time students do not self-select, and Student 2, who speaks Arabic, turns to her Arabic-speaking peers, Student 3 and Student 4 and then tries to regulate the order of interaction in Italian in Turn 5. In Turns 6 to 26, it is possible to notice a joint construction of the replies, since Students 2, 3 (J.) and 4 collaborate in the meaning-making process with their varying degrees of linguistic competence in Arabic. The researcher hardly interferes in their interaction except in Turn 8, where she encourages sequential progressivity, and in Turns 16 and 18, where she provides feedback through repetition, and then again in Turn 20, where, drawing on her basic competence in Arabic, she shares a metalinguistic consideration regarding the word 'children', which in Arabic has an irregular plural form. After Student 4 states that she has a different possible answer (Turn 7), Student 3 redesigns the previous utterance (Turn 9) and Student 2 cooperates providing what could, in her view, be considered a more acceptable version of the terms and of their pronunciation (Turns 11 and 13). The interaction ends with utterances in a mixture of different varieties of Arabic (Turn 15) and with a spontaneous translation of the word 'children' in Italian (Turn 19). In Turns 20 to 26, the researcher invites Student 4 to enrich the reply by providing further details. This conversational interchange is based on translation strategies, repetitions (Turn 22) and repairs such as self-corrections (Turn 25) in which the two languages, Moroccan Arabic and Italian, are intertwined in meaning-making.

The sequence from Turn 27 presents similar collaborative interactional exchanges, but with a relevant difference: Students 5 and 6 are Italian-speaking and here support their Polish-speaking peer, Student 7 (P), in several ways (Turns 27–35). Since there is a gap in the transition, in this exchange, both Students 5 and 6 and the researcher encourage the Polish-speaking student (7) in expressing the expected response, which he himself had previously written on the blackboard, by repeatedly prompting the beginning of the answer: 'stowarzyszenie' (*associations*). Finally, in Turn 36, thanks to his peers' verbal and nonverbal support, Student 7 provides the expected response and receives positive feedback from R., who then invites him to reformulate the utterance addressing the class. The researcher then praises the student and his peers clap their hands. In this final section, the researcher does not nominate the next speaker, which allows the students to self-select. The free turn-taking and the researchers' prior translanguaging encourages the students to deploy their whole language repertoires, and even to naturally engage in their peers' languages. The involvement of the researcher in fostering translanguaging pedagogical practices is particularly marked, while the teacher, who is present in the class, is observing the lesson. In the following sequence, we will describe the different degrees of teachers' conversational strategies at the later stages of implementing pedagogical translanguaging.

Sequence 2: The translation perspective

In the following sequence (Excerpt 6.2), T is a Math and Science teacher in a second-grade classroom in S1 primary school. More than 40% of students in this class have a migrant background; their multilingual repertoires include, besides Italian, Romanian, Albanian, Moroccan Arabic, Chinese, Igbo, Sardinian and Italian local and southern dialects. In this lesson, T revises the lexicon regarding the different parts of a tree, taking into account students' languages. She employs a poster showing the drawn sketch of a tree, while children and parents have previously prepared tags displaying the target words in the home languages.

Excerpt 6.2 Sequence 2

1	T	Facciamo la lezione di \<scie::nze> (0.4) pri:ma in \<SA::RDO> (0.5) e poi in albane:se .
		We shall have a science class, in Sardinian first and then in Albanian.
		((T. walks towards the blackboard))
2	Students	O::H!
		Oh!
3	T	Eh. (0.3) però dobbiamo stare molto atte:nti↘(0.4) Allora (0.4) noi abbiamo prepar<u>ato</u> un bel cartellone (0.2) con le varie parti della pianta, giusto?
		Eh, but we really have to pay attention. Well, we have prepared a nice poster, with the different parts of the plant, right?

4	Students	Si! *Yes!*
5	T	Oh↘ <qual<u>cuno</u> ha già fatto la sua lezione> *Oh! Someone has already completed his/her lesson...*
6	Student 1	<u>In rumeno!</u> *In Romanian!*
7	Student 3	Noi due! *Both of us!*
8	T	<La lezione in rumeno> (.) vero? *The lesson in Romanian, right?*
9	Student 1	<u>Si</u> *Yes!*
10	T	E abbiamo anche scritto le <u>paroline</u> (0.3) le paroline in rumeno. (0.5) [<u>Adesso</u>] *And we also wrote some little words... some little words in Romanian... Now...* ((T. points a poster with the little words on the blackboard))
11	Students	[in <u>sardo::</u>] *In Sardinian!*
12	T	Le <sentiamo> e le vediamo scritte(0.2)in <u>sardo</u>? *Shall we listen to them and see how they are written... in Sardinian?* ((T. points Student 3))
13	Student 3	Sì. *Yes.*
14	T	Cominci tu ? >allora< (0.2) ci mettiamo bene da una <u>parte</u> perché dobbiamo <u>indicarle</u>↘, pronuncia:rle <u>bene</u>↘ *Will you start? Well then, but let's stand on one side: we must point them out and pronounce them correctly.* ((T. with the hand, softly pushes Student 3 closer to the blackboard))
15	Student 3	Però albero si dice sempre come in italia:no *But "tree" is the same as in Italian.*
16	T	Ah albero come in italiano va bene . (0.4) allora mettiti bene da una parte ho preparato↘le paroli::ne (0.3) che tu mi hai da:to (0.6) [takes the tags from the desk] così le possiamo <incolla:re> va <u>bene</u>? (0.2) >allora< indichiamo bene la <u>pa:rte</u> della <<u>pianta</u>> (0.4) di cui vuoi <u>parla:re</u> (0.3) e >pronunciamola bene< (0.3) a loro eh! ((T. points the rest of the class)) (0.5) ((Student 3 points the trunk in the drawing)) quello è <u>i:l</u>? *Oh, tree is the same as in Italian, that's right. So, stay aside, I prepared the words you gave me so that we can paste them, ok? Well, let's point out the right parts of the plant you want to talk about, and let's pronounce them well. To them, eh! That's the...*
17	Student 3	Tronco. *Trunk.*
18	T	Si. in sardo? *Yes. but what about Sardinian?*

19	Student 3	[Sardinian] Matta. *[Sardinian] trunk.*
20	Student 4	[Sardinian] <MATTA> *[Sardinian] trunk!*
21	T	[Sardinian] <MATTA> (.) il tro:nco in sa:rdo_si dice:: *[Sardinian] trunk, trunk in Sardinian is...*
22	Students	[Sardinian] <Matta>! *[Sardinian] trunk!*
23	T	Ma::tta . benissimo. allo:ra .(0.3) eccola qua . ((shows a piece of paper with the Sardinian word 'matta')) Si scrive cosi. io l'ho scritto come me lo hai scritto tu. ma:tta. (0.6) matta poi ↑ (0.5) la incollia:mo (0.8) eh si la mettia:mo al posto giusto *[Sardinian] Trunk, [Ita.] very well, so, here it is. We write it this way. I wrote it same way as you. [Sardinian] Trunk. Trunk. [Ita.] Then let's paste it. Yes, and let's put it in its right place.*

In Turn 1, the teacher introduces the topic of the day, emphasising that the class will learn new words in two specific languages, Sardinian and Albanian. In Turn 5, she hints that other peers may be giving lectures in their different languages; then, at this transition-relevance point, Students 1 and 2 self-select to confirm that they have used Romanian in the previous lesson (Turns 6 and 7). The distribution of turns across the entire interactional segment, the use of the inclusive first-person plural personal pronouns (see, e.g. Turns 1, 3 and 10) and the covert entrustment of a teaching role to the students suggest that the teacher is sharing her status with the emergent bilingual students, whose languages and knowledge have become essential in the co-construction of the lesson. Transitions between Turns 10, 11 and 12 present a slight overlap, since the students are enthusiastically waiting for the lesson in Sardinian, but the teacher, in Turn 13, selects Student 3, who speaks Sardinian and is standing next to the poster. The teacher scaffolds the activity, by explaining to him the strategies he should employ for an effective lesson such as pointing to the right part of the plant, pronouncing the word and addressing the class and not the teacher only, while at the same time she takes the tags from the desk (Turns 14 and 16). Student 3 performs a nonverbal response, by indicating the trunk of the plant in the poster and expressing the word initially in Italian (Turn 17) and then, after the teacher's request, in Sardinian. When Student 3 introduces the new word *matta* in Turn 19, the next turn is allocated by self-selection of Student 4, who repeats the word. The teacher reinforces the word repetition strategy with a voluntarily interrupted request act with free turn-taking, addressing all the students (Turn 21), who repeat the target word again (Turn 22). Afterwards, she helps Student 3 to pick the right tag and to paste it in the right place on the poster. It is possible to notice that the usual ternary scheme of class-room interaction (Fele, 2007) based on Request (by the teacher), Reply (by the student) and Evaluative feedback (again by the teacher) is not completely relevant in this context. In correspondence with Turn 16, Student 3 points to the trunk of the plant in the poster, thus initiating the interaction; then, the teacher asks for the translation; Student 3 answers, but the teacher cannot evaluate the answer but only confirms and repeats it (Turn 21), by involving all the students in a fourth inter-actional turn. It is also important to underline that strategies such as repetition and translation that usually belong to second language les-sons have been integrated in the classroom interaction through peda-gogical translanguaging, which enhances teachers' awareness of the language dimension of learning subject-specific content (Beacco *et al.*, 2015). Even if the degree of teacher interactional strategies is mostly based on a translation perspective of individual lexical items, still the teacher takes the risk of repeating words in another language, while the visual/written resources previously arranged support her and facilitate non-Sardinian speakers' comprehension.

Sequence 3: Towards a dynamic perspective

The following sequence (Excerpt 6.3) is related to a translanguaging-based activity conducted in a second-grade classroom in primary school S2 in April 2019. Almost half of the class have a migrant background; among them, a high percentage is Chinese speaking, but there are also Albanian, Romanian, Moroccan Arabic, Sardinian speakers and speakers of several Italian dialects. When the video was recorded, the children had already been exposed to pedagogical translanguaging since the beginning of the first grade. This lesson was part of a multimodal activity, starting with a story about the Brother Grimms' tale 'The wolf and the seven little goats', performed in Chinese by a Mandarin-speaking mother with the help of the researcher (R), who acted as a mediator, translating Chinese into Italian. Following the storytelling, the teacher (T) carried out activi-ties in the languages spoken by her students, first by use of multilingual vocabulary for the tale and, afterwards, by focusing the main text sequences, both at receptively and productively. The students, working in small groups, which were heterogeneous in terms of languages, were able to produce short summaries of the story in different languages. Following this, the researcher (R) visited the class and carried out a collective oral reflection activity on the contents of the tale, in collaboration with the teacher. The sequence below shows that the researcher starts asking the class for the translation of a few words of Chinese; after that, the teacher manages the conversation, stimulating students' translanguaging (Chinese–Italian) feedback.

Excerpt 6.3 Sequence 3

1	R	Ce lo <u>dite</u> un po' come si dice in cinese il lu:po e i sette capretti? *Can you tell us how do we say 'the wolf and and the seven little goats'?* ((a few seconds of silence))
2	T	[Chinese]狼::[lá::ng] *[Chinese] Wolf*
3	Student 1	[Chinese]狼:和七个小羊↘[lá:ng hé qī gè xiǎo yáng↘] *[Chinese] The wolf and the seven little goats*
4	R	[Chinese]狼:和七个小羊↘[lá:ng hé qī gè xiǎo yáng↘] (0,5) vi ricordate 狼↘[lá:ng] chi era? *[Chinese] The wolf and the seven little goats, [Ita.] do you remember? What was [Chinese] láng?*
5	Students	IL LUPO *The wolf!*
6	R	[Chinese] 小羊? [xiǎo yáng?] *[Chinese] Little goats?*
7	Students	CAPRETTI *Little goats!*
8	R	<i capretti> (0.4) perfetto. *Little goats, perfect.*
9	T	Poi (0.5) la:: <u>mamma</u> di Luca invece. ha parla:to *Then, Luca's mother has talked (about)...*
10	Students	Dei segni <u>zodiaca::li</u> *About zodiac signs!*
11	T	I segni zodiacali. (.) e i segni quanti sono? *The zodiac signs. How many are these signs?* ((T. points some students))
12	Students	DODICI *Twelve!*
13	T	Dodici. (1.0) eh e sono rappresentati da che cosa? *Twelve. And what are they represented by?*
14	Students	ANIMALI *Animals!*
15	T	Eh animali. (0.3) provia:mo a dire almeno il nome di un animale in cinese. *Eh animals. Let's try to say at least the name of an animal in Chinese.* ((T. starts counting with the fingers))
16	Student 2	[Chinese] 龙:: [ló::ng] *[Chinese] Dragon!*
17	T	[Chinese] <u>龙::</u> [<u>ló::ng</u>] (0.5) che cos'è 龙::? [ló::ng?] *[Chinese] Dragon! [Ita.] What is [Chinese] Dragon?*
18	Student 2	<u>Dra::go</u> *Dragon.*
19	T	Drago. (0.5) poi? *Dragon, and then?* ((T. points student2 and smiles to him))

20	Student 3	[Chinese] 狗 [gǒu] *[Chinese] Dog!*
21	T	[Chinese] 狗 [gǒu] (.) che cos'è 狗 ? [gǒu?] *[Chinese] Dog! [Ita.] What is [Chinese] Dog!*
22	Student 3	il ca:ne *The dog.*
23	T	poi? *Then?* ((T. points to student4))
24	Student 4	[Chinese] 老鼠 [lǎoshǔ] (0.3) topo. *[Chinese] Mouse, [Ita.] mouse.*
25	T	[Chinese] 老鼠:: [lǎoshǔ::] (0.3) topo . (0.5) poi [Chinese] 马? [mǎ?] 马 ? [mǎ?] *[Chinese] Mouse, [Ita.] mouse. Then? [Chinese] Horse, horse?* ((T. imitates a horse))
26	Student 5	CAVALLO *Horse!*
27	T	cavallo. (0.5) poi? il mio segno zodiaca::le ? (0.5) come si dice? *Horse. Then? What about my zodiac sign? How do we say it?*
28	Student 3	[Chinese] 兔子 [Tùzǐ] *[Chinese] Rabbit* ((Stud. 3 indicates herself with the fingers))
29	T	[Chinese] 兔子 [Tùzǐ](.) bravissima. *[Chinese] Rabbit, [Ita.] very good!*
30	R	E il mio invece? *What about mine?*
31	Student 6	Qual era? *What was it?*
32	R	Drago *Dragon!*
33	Student 6	Drago (0.5) allora [Chinese] 龙:: [ló::ng] *Dragon. So it's [Chinese] dragon.*
34	R	[Chinese] 龙:: [ló::ng] (0.5) bravo. *[Chinese] Dragon, [Ita.] good.*

Both the researcher and the teacher perform short turns, by facilitating students' interaction in co-constructing room for students to self-nominate themselves as the next speaker. The usual tripartite interactional structure (teacher's request + students' reply + researcher's or teacher's verbal feedback) implies a high degree of classroom involvement, even if the conversation flow is controlled by the teacher and, as a consequence, is potentially predominated by teacher talk. The use of nonverbal communication does not appear to be as widespread as in the previous sequence, whereas that of paralinguistic communication (intonation, pauses and decelerations of speaking speed), as in the other cases, is crucial in order to facilitate the co-construction of meaning.

The extract starts with the researcher's input through a request for translation (Turn 1). In the following turn, the teacher hints at the answer in Chinese. Following the researcher's management of the initial conversational interchanges, the teacher starts taking the initiative. First, she contextualises in Italian the main topic of the interaction (Turns 9, 11, 13 and 15). After that, she provides questions and feedback using Chinese lexical items also: The strategies underlying her use of Chinese are aimed, on one hand, at consolidating students' recall of Chinese words through repetition (as in the first parts of Turns 17, 21 and 25) and, on the other, at performing request acts by alternately using Italian and Chinese (as in the last parts of Turns 17 and 21). Moreover, in the following segment, in Turns 25 to 29, the teacher starts to adopt Chinese not only as a support for the construction of a translanguaging utterance but also (see last part of Turn 25) as if it were the only language through which she could try to make a request. Despite being rudimentary in the use of Chinese, such a request appears to be clear and to have a high degree of illocutionary force, since it immediately produces a translation-based reply. It is also interesting to note how the teacher structures the triple structure, that is, Turn 27 (request) – 28 (reply) – 29 (feedback): The request, formulated in Italian, is aimed at obtaining a reply in Chinese, which actually occurs, and the feedback is provided directly in Chinese, by avoiding the use of Italian (first part of Turn 29). The result is that the sequence composed by Turns 27–28–29 reflects a naturally alternated use of Chinese and Italian, since mutual understanding and classroom co-construction of meaning is reached through both Italian and Chinese. Subsequently, the researcher carries on the conversation by again adopting a translation strategy.

In this case, the researcher facilitates pedagogical translanguaging practices. The teacher seems to manage the conversation with a high degree of autonomy, by making meaningful use of Chinese and integrating it in meaning-making processes. Moreover, from the teacher's interactional behaviour, we can detect a co-occurrence of a translation-oriented perspective with a fairly dynamic use of translanguaging interaction, which, however, is still limited to the level of lexical items or short, single utterances.

Sequence 4: The achievement of a fluid translanguaging conversational behaviour

The last sequence (Excerpt 6.4) refers to a translanguaging-based activity on migrations across the Mediterranean Sea conducted in a fifth-grade classroom in school S3 in January 2019. Almost the entire class were of immigrant background: Students' home languages were Mandarin Chinese, the Wenzhou dialect (a variety spoken in the area of origin of most of Chinese immigrants in Italy), Albanian, Moroccan Arabic, Urdu, Tagalog, Spanish, Georgian, English, Italian and Italian dialects. At the time of the video-recording, the class had already been involved in the 'L'AltRoparlante' project for more than two years. The excerpt reported below refers to the teacher's (T) oral introduction of the activity, in which the Italian title of the text that the class is going to read is explained. Since there is no exact translation of the title, the teacher tries to make use of two more languages, English (the foreign language studied at school) and Chinese, with the aim of implicitly drawing students' attention to meta-linguistic considerations about the syntactic order of elements in a clause.

Excerpt 6.4 Sequence 4

1	T	Una <u>cosa</u> che in italiano si può fare:: (0.3) NON in tutte le lingue si può fare.(0.3) >in italiano si può dire< il <u>futuro</u> dei miei. (1.0) >per esempio< in <u>inglese</u> non si potrebbe. (0.5) >perché< in <u>inglese</u> si dice (.)[English] my (0.2) blablabla <u>fu</u>:ture (1.0) my <u>parents</u>' future (0.5) my:: <u>grandparents</u>' future (0,5) my <u>friends</u>' future (.) my:: <u>relatives</u>' future (0.4) ok? si mette prima . (0.5) <u>esattamente</u> come in cinese. (0.4) giusto? (1.0) [Chinese] 我的:: [Wǒ de:::] (1.0) mmmm (0.4) futuro?

[Ita.] Something we can do in Italian, may not be equally done in other languages… in Italian, we can say 'il futuro dei miei'… – for example – but in English, we cannot because the English form is [English]'my blah blah blah future', my parents' future, my friends' future, my relatives' future, ok? [Italian] we put it at the beginning, exactly as we do in Chinese, right? [Chinese]'my'… [Italian] mmmm, future?

((T. makes gestures with her hands while speaking, and then addresses a Chinese-speaking student with her head))

2	Student 1	[Chinese] 未来 [wèilái]

[Chinese] Future.

3	T	[Chinese] 未来 [wèilái] (.) 未来 [wèilái] . (0.5) ok siete pronti adesso per conoscere il testo?

[Chinese] Future, future, ok. [Italian] Are you ready to know the text now?

4	Student 2	[English] Yes!

[English] Yes!

5	T	Be::ne.

Good.

The teacher starts performing a long turn (1), which may imply the potential risk of not co-constructing the interaction together with the students. Notwithstanding this, the relevant length of the turn allows her to introduce an argumentation using different languages, by enhancing metalinguistic considerations (mainly related to the translation of the Italian expression *il futuro dei miei*) through a cross-linguistic comparison. The turn appears to be transparent, both from the point of view of verbal communication and from that of paralinguistic communication (e.g. intentional pauses, emphasis on key elements of the utterances). Moreover, from a translanguaging perspective, we can observe that the teacher integrates three languages in her turn, namely Italian, English and Chinese. After introducing the main topic of her argumentation, which relates to the difficulty of translating an Italian expression into other languages, she starts making examples of possible, albeit not perfectly correct, translations in English. In this way, she suggests a metalinguistic consideration about the syntactic order of determiner and determined elements in Italian, English and Chinese. She then focuses on the similarities between English and Chinese in realising such kinds of structures, by formulating a few examples in English and trying to come up with a sentence in Chinese. The interactional cooperation with the rest of the class is constructed through the transition relevance place between Turn 1 and Turn 2: The teacher seeks the students' collaboration in order to complete the Chinese sentence she has started and therefore asks for the translation of the word 'future'. Once the translation is provided by a student, she reinforces the reply by providing feedback through repetition in Chinese (Turn 3).

We argue that in this final excerpt, the teacher is able to adopt a highly dynamic strategy of translanguaging interaction, which results in certain flexibility in drawing, in Turn 1, on her multilingual repertoire, that includes also a basic competence in Chinese. Through such conversational behaviour, she is able to shift from a perspective based on translation of lexical items or short expressions to more spontaneous fluidity in using multiple languages and, thus, breaking language boundaries. Such an ability might be due to the teacher's general disposition towards the use of several languages in her conversational interchanges with the students; at the same time, however, it can be a reflection of the critical use of pedagogical translanguaging in her ordinary teaching praxis (Scibetta & Carbonara, 2019).

Conclusion

In this chapter, by applying CA, we have focused on four interactional sequences drawing from a corpus of translanguaging-based activities, video-recorded in classes affiliated to the 'L'AltRoparlante' network. The analysis shows that, at an early stage of implementation of pedagogical translanguaging, the researchers' involvement plays a significant role in scaffolding the co-construction of translanguaging interactions (Sequence 1), enabling teachers to gradually integrate the multilingual repertoires of their classes in their instructional practices and to expand the boundaries of meaning-making processes. This progressive achievement of autonomy from the guiding role of the researcher can be distinguished in three different main stages.

First, we detected translation strategies (Sequence 2) whereby the teacher starts 'taking risks' by including lexical items in students' languages in her conversational interchanges, although she still relies mostly on requests for translations of words and of short chunks of phrases. However, the translation perspective represents a starting point in order to promote de-hierarchisation processes of teachers' and students' roles, as emerged also from results of qualitative analyses of interviews described in previous publications (Carbonara & Scibetta, 2020b; Scibetta & Carbonara, 2019). This de-hierarchisation results in an educational legitimation of language diversity, as can be observed also in students' active engagement in minority languages and dialects.

The second stage of teachers' conversational strategies (Sequence 3) is represented by a shift towards more dynamic translanguaging instructional practices, where translation-based requests and feedback between students and teachers are understood as a springboard to a multilingual cooperative development of knowledge.

Finally, teachers achieve a fluid translanguaging approach in their classroom interaction (Sequence 4), by stimulating metalinguistic awareness and cross-linguistic comparisons, and going beyond the level of the single utterance. By doing so, it is possible to weaken language boundaries and hierarchies, in particular in a condition in which the teacher is able to spontaneously and autonomously recall multilingual chunks of phrases that previously emerged from classroom translanguaging activities.

In terms of CA, turn-allocation techniques mainly based on self-selection, short-size turns and paralinguistic traits such as deceleration of speed and intentional pauses, which do not tend to be ordinary in content-based instruction (Fele, 2007), contribute to support a meaningful and efficient translanguaging interaction.

The L'AltRoparlante project, in line with CUNY-NYSIEB *Initiative on Emergent Bilinguals* and other European experiences, confirms that pedagogical translanguaging is possible, even in mainstream education and on a regular basis. The dismantlement of the monolingual view and the process of implementing translanguaging in instructional practices are slow. The latter, however, would provide some of the very best means of achieving a well-thought-out, durable, and democratic language education approach. It might not, of course, be fulfilled without some degree of negotiation between teachers, parents and researchers in order to obtain their respective full cooperation, but, granted that, they would be able to mutually contribute to their own and their students' linguistic, educational, emotional and scientific scaffolding, by leveraging their repertoires and competences. As Paulo Freire affirmed in 1992, 'Without a minimum of hope, we cannot so much as start the struggle. But without the struggle, hope, as an ontological need, dissipates, loses its bearing, and turns into hopelessness' (Freire, 2004: 3). As researchers, our scope is to nurture hope in educators and to sustain the struggle with research outcomes.

Acknowledgements

We thank all the schools involved in the project L'AltRoparlante and Kio Barnato, who edited our text for English.

This chapter is the result of a research initiative conducted by both authors jointly. Valentina Carbonara collected data in S1, Andrea Scibetta in S2. In S3, data have been collected jointly.

Valentina Carbonara wrote the following sections: 'Multilingualism in the Italian School: Opportunities to Trace a Pathway for Pedagogical Translanguaging?'; 'L'AltRoparlante Project: Theoretical Influences and Practical Steps'; 'Sequence 1: The researcher's involvement' and 'Sequence 2: The translation perspective'.

Andrea Scibetta wrote the following sections: 'Data Collection, Methods of Analysis and Research Questions'; 'Sequence 3: Towards a dynamic perspective' and 'Sequence 4: The achievement of a fluid translanguaging conversational behaviour'. Where not indicated, the paragraphs were written together.

The transcription and the translation of all the sequences have been provided by both authors.

References

Agirdag, O. (2010) Exploring bilingualism in a monolingual school system: Insights from Turkish and native students from Belgian schools. *British Journal of Sociology of Education* 31 (3), 307–321.

Beacco, J.C., Byram, M., Cavalli, M., Coste, D., Cuenat, M.E., Gouillier, F. and Panthier, J. (2016) *Guide for the Development and Implementation of Curricula for Plurilingual and Intercultural Education*. Strasbourg: Council of Europe Publishing.

Beacco, J.C., Fleming, M., Goullier, F., Thürmann, E., Vollmer, H. (2015) *Les dimensions linguistiques de toutes les matieres scolaires. Guide pour l'élaboration des curriculums et pour la formation des enseignants*. Strasbourg: Council of Europe Publishing.

Blommaert, J. and Dong, J. (2010) *Ethnographic Fieldwork: A Beginner's Guide* (1st edn). Bristol: Multilingual Matters.

Busch, B. (2012) The linguistic repertoire revisited. *Applied Linguistics* 33 (5), 503–523.

Candelier, M., Camilleri-Grima, A., Castellotti, V., De Pietro, J.F., Lőrincz, I., Meißner, F.J., Noguerol, A., Schröder-Sura, A. and Molinié, M. (2012) *FREPA/CARAP, A Framework of Reference for Pluralistic Approaches to Languages and Cultures*. Strasbourg and Graz: Council of Europe Publishing.

Canù, S. (2016) Intercomprensione nella scuola primaria: cominciamo dall'oralità. In E. Bonvino and M.C. Jamet (eds) *Intercomprensione: Lingue, Processi e Percorsi* (pp. 113–128). Venezia: Edizioni Ca'Foscari.

Carbonara, V. (2017) Contatto linguistico, percezione linguistica e pratiche didattiche nelle scuole secondarie di primo grado della provincia di Alessandria. Il caso di Serravalle Scrivia. In M. Vedovelli (ed.) *L'italiano dei Nuovi Italiani* (pp. 227–245). Roma: Aracne.

Carbonara, V. and Martini, S. (2019) Un modello operativo per l'approccio pedagogico del translanguaging? Esempi di applicazione in una Unità di Lavoro/Apprendimento (UdLA). *Lend, Lingua e Nuova Didattica* 4, 18–36.

Carbonara, V. and Scibetta A. (2018) Il translanguaging come strumento efficace per la gestione delle classi plurilingui: il progetto 'L'AltRoparlante'. *Rassegna Italiana di Linguistica Applicata (RILA)* 1, 65–83.

Carbonara, V. and Scibetta, A. (2020a) *Imparare attraverso le lingue. Il translanguaging come pratica didattica* (with a Preface by Jim Cummins). Roma: Carocci.

Carbonara, V. and Scibetta, A. (2020b) Integrating translanguaging pedagogy into Italian primary schools: Implications for language practices and children's empowerment. *International Journal of Bilingual Education and Bilingualism* 1–21, https://doi.org/10.1080/13670050.2020.1742648 (accessed April 2020).

Charmaz, K. and Belgrave, L.L. (2012) Qualitative interviewing and grounded theory analysis. In F. Jaber, J. Gubrium, A. Holstein, A.B. Marvasti and K.D. McKinney (eds) *The SAGE Handbook of Interview Research: The Complexity of the Craft* (pp. 347–366). Thousand Oaks: SAGE Publications.

Chini, M. and Andorno, C.M. (eds) (2018) *Repertori e usi linguistici nell'immigrazione. Una indagine su minori alloglotti dieci anni dopo.* Milano: Franco Angeli.

Cole, D. and Meadows, B. (2013) Avoiding the essentialist trap in intercultural education. In F. Dervin and A.J. Liddicoat (eds) *Linguistics for Intercultural Education* (pp. 29–47). Amsterdam/Philadelphia: John Benjamins Publishing Company.

Coppola, D. and Russo I. (2019) Risorse digitali per il translanguaging e lo sviluppo di competenze lessicali e metalinguistiche. In V. Carbonara, L. Cosenza, P. Masillo, L. Salvati and A. Scibetta (eds) *Il parlato e lo scritto, aspetti teorici e didattici* (pp. 269–280). Pisa: Pacini Editore.

Cummins, J. (2014) Teaching through a multilingual lens: Classroom resources for global education. In K. Broad, M. Evans, D. Montemurro and M. Gambhir (eds) *Inquiry into Practice: Learning Global Matters in Local Classrooms* (pp. 12–15). Toronto: Ontario Institute for Studies in Education.

Cummins, J. and Early, M. (2011) *Identity Texts: The Collaborative Creation of Power in Multilingual Schools.* Stoke-on-Trent: Trentham Books.

De Mauro, T. (2018) *L'educazione linguistica democratica.* Bari: Laterza.

Duarte, J. (2019) Translanguaging in mainstream education: A sociocultural approach. *International Journal of Bilingual Education and Bilingualism* 22 (2), 150–164.

Duarte, J. and Günther-Van Der Meij, M. (2018) A holistic model for multilingualism in education. *E-JournALL, EuroAmerican Journal of Applied Linguistics and Languages* 5 (2), 24–43.

European Commission (2019) *Integrating Students from Migrant Backgrounds into schools in Europe. National Policies and Measures. Eurydice Report.* See https://eacea.ec.europa.eu/national-policies/eurydice/sites/eurydice/files/integrating_students_from_migrant_backgrounds_into_schools_in_europe_national_policies_and_measures.pdf (accessed January 2020).

Extra, G. and Yagmur, K. (2004) *Urban Multilingualism in Europe: Immigrant Minority Languages at Home and School.* Clevedon: Multilingual Matters.

Favaro, G. (2014) Per una scuola dell'inclusione. In G. Favaro (ed) *A scuola nessuno è straniero* (pp. 22–29). Firenze: Giunti.

Favaro, G. (2018) Le lingue, le norme, le pratiche. Il contesto, i dati, i riferimenti della scuola multiculturale e plurilingue. *Italiano Lingua Due* 10 (2), 1–41.

Fele, G. (2007) *L'analisi della conversazione.* Bologna: Il Mulino.

Freire, P. (2004) *Pedagogy of Hope: Reliving Pedagogy of the Oppressed.* London and New York: Continuum.

García, O., Johnson, S.I. and Seltzer, K. (2017) *The Translanguaging Classroom: Leveraging Student Bilingualism for Learning.* Philadelphia: Caslon.

García, O. and Kleyn, T. (eds) (2016) *Translanguaging with Multilingual Students: Learning from Classroom Moments*. New York: Routledge.

García, O. and Li Wei (2014) *Translanguaging: Language, Bilingualism and Education*. Basingstoke: Palgrave Macmillan.

García, O. and Sánchez, M.T. (2018) Transformando la educación de bilingües emergentes en el estado de Nueva York. *Language, Education, and Multilingualism* 1, 138–156.

Hawkins, E.W. (1999) Foreign language study and language awareness. *Language Awareness* 8 (3–4), 124–142.

Hélot, C. and Cavalli, M. (2017) Bilingual education in Europe: Dominant languages. In O. García, A. Lin and S. May (eds) *Bilingual and Multilingual Education. Encyclopedia of Language and Education* (3rd edn) (pp. 1–18). Cham: Springer.

Hélot, C. and Young, A. (2006) Imagining multilingual education in France: A language and cultural awareness project at primary level. In O. García, T. Skutnabb-Kangas and M.E. Torres Guzmán (eds) *Imagining Multilingual Schools: Languages in Education and Glocalization* (pp. 69–90). Clevedon: Multilingual Matters.

Hornberger, N. and Link, H. (2012) Translanguaging and transnational literacies in multilingual classrooms: A biliteracy lens. *International Journal of Bilingual Education and Bilingualism* 15 (3), 261–278.

Hult F. (2012) Ecology and multilingual education. In C. Chapelle (ed.) *Encyclopedia of Applied Linguistics* (pp. 1835–1840). Malden, MA and Oxford: Wiley-Blackwell.

Jefferson, G. (1996) A case of transcriptional stereotyping. *Journal of Pragmatics* 26 (2), 159–170.

Kasper, G. and Wagner, J. (2014) Conversation Analysis in Applied Linguistics. *Annual Review of Applied Linguistics* 34, 171–212.

Kleyn, T. and García, O. (2019) Translanguaging as an act of transformation: Restructuring teaching and learning for emergent bilingual students. In L. de Oliveira (ed.) *Handbook of TESOL in K-12* (pp. 69–82). Malden: Wiley.

Kroon, S. and Spotti, M. (2011) Immigrant minority language teaching policies and practices in The Netherlands: Policing dangerous multilingualism. In V. Domovic, S. Gehrmann, M. Krüger-Potratz and A. Petravic (eds) *Europsko obrazovanje: Koncepti i perspektive iz pet zemalja* (pp. 80–95). Zagreb: Skolska Knjiga.

Lin, A.M.Y. and Wu, Y. (2015) 'May I speak Cantonese?' – Co-constructing a scientific proof in an EFL junior secondary science classroom. *International Journal of Bilingual Education and Bilingualism* 18 (3), 289–305.

Little, D. and Kirwin, D. (2019) *Engaging with Linguistic Diversity*. London: Bloomsbury Academic.

Llompart, J., Masats, D., Moore, E. and Nussbaum, L. (2019) 'Mézclalo un poquito': plurilingual practices in multilingual educational milieus. *International Journal of Bilingual Education and Bilingualism* 23 (1), 98–112.

MIUR (Italian Minister of Education, University and Research) (2007) *La Via Italiana per la scuola interculturale e l'integrazione degli alunni stranieri*. See https://archivio.pubblica.istruzione.it/news/2007/allegati/pubblicazione_intercultura.pdf (accessed January 2020).

MIUR (2012) *Indicazioni Nazionali per il curricolo verticale della scuola dell'infanzia e del primo ciclo d'istruzione*. http://www.indicazioninazionali.it/2018/08/26/indicazioni-2012/ (accessed January 2020).

MIUR (2014) *Linee Guida per l'accoglienza e l'integrazione degli alunni stranieri*. https://www.istruzione.it/allegati/2014/linee_guida_integrazione_alunni_stranieri.pdf (accessed January 2020).

Paulsrud, B., Rosén, J., Straszer, B. and Wedin, Å. (2017) *New Perspectives on Translanguaging and Education*. Bristol: Multilingual Matters.

Pona, A., Cencetti, S. and Troiano, G. (2018) *Fare grammatica valenziale nella scuola delle competenze*. Napoli: Tecnodid.

Priestley, M., Edwards, R., Priestley, A. and Miller, K. (2012) Teacher agency in curriculum making: Agents of change and spaces for manoeuvre. *Curriculum Inquiry* 42 (2), 191–214.

Rosiers, K. (2017) Unravelling translanguaging: The potential of translanguaging as a scaffold among teachers and pupils in superdiverse classrooms in Flemish education. In B. Paulsrud, J. Rosén, B. Straszer and Å. Wedin (eds) *New Perspectives on Translanguaging and Education* (pp. 148–169). Bristol: Multilingual Matters.

Rosiers, K. (2018) Translanguaging revisited challenges for research, policy and pedagogy based on an inquiry in two Belgian classrooms. *Translation and Translanguaging in Multilingual Contexts* 4 (3), 361–383.

Sacks, H., Schegloff, E.A. and Jefferson, G. (1974) A simplest systematics for the organization of turn-taking for conversation. *Language* 50 (4), 696–735.

Santagati, M. (2015) Researching integration in multiethnic Italian schools. A sociological review on educational inequalities. *Italian Journal of Sociology of Education* 7 (3), 294–334.

Scibetta, A. and Carbonara, V. (2019) Translanguaging as a pedagogical resource in Italian primary schools: Making visible the ordinariness of multilingualism. In J. Won Lee and S. Dovchin (eds) *The Ordinariness of Translinguistics* (pp. 115–129). London: Routledge.

Sordella, S. and Andorno, C.M. (2018) Esplorare le lingue in classe. Strumenti e risorse per un laboratorio di éveil aux langues nella scuola primaria. *Italiano Lingua Due* 2, 162–228.

Won Lee, J. and Dovchin, S. (eds) (2019) *The Ordinariness of Translinguistics*. London: Routledge.

Zanasi, L. and Platzgummer, V. (2018) Repertori linguistici in contesti di plurilinguismo. In M. Hepp and M. Nied Curcio (eds) *Educazione plurilingue. Ricerca, didattica e politiche linguistiche* (pp. 51–64). Roma: Istituto Italiano Studi Germanici.

7 Semiotic Assemblages in Study Guidance in the Mother Tongue

Anne Reath Warren

Introduction

Addressing the complex educational needs of newcomers who are in the process of developing knowledge of a new language is an ongoing, crucial issue for schools and researchers. All new students benefit from mentorship and need a settling-in period. However, these needs are amplified when students need to learn a new language to access knowledge and bring different forms of linguistic, sociocultural and subject knowledge to school with them. Moreover, these newcomers are expected not only to learn a new language, including academic genres, but also to pass high-stakes tests identical to those taken by all students, for example, national tests in core subjects.

The value of multimodal resources, including visual imagery and embodied responses, for making meaning in educational contexts, is well established (Kress, 2000). Recognition of the value of languages other than the socially dominant language, however, has been slow to arrive in many school contexts, although researchers have long promoted strategies (Cummins, 1986, this volume; García & Li Wei, 2014; Skutnabb-Kangas & Toukomaa, 1976; Thomas & Collier, 2002).

Research on multimodality often has a monolingual perspective, and research on translanguaging has a stronger focus on linguistic than multimodal resources (Kusters *et al.*, 2017). This study brings multimodal and multilingual perspectives together to investigate semiotic assemblages, or 'how different trajectories of people, semiotic resources and objects meet at particular moments and places' (Pennycook, 2017: 280) in a form of multilingual support available to newcomers in the Swedish education system.

'Study guidance [tutoring] in the mother tongue' (Swe. *studiehandledning på modersmålet*), hereafter SGMT, formally recognises the benefits of using students' strongest languages as resources for learning. SGMT aims to help newcomers reach the learning goals of subjects in the Swedish curriculum (taught in Swedish), by providing tutoring in their mother tongue or strongest school language. SGMT is provided on a temporary basis if the students' level of Swedish prevents them from achieving learning goals (The Compulsory School Ordinance, 2011: Chapter. 5§ 4; The Upper-Secondary School Ordinance, 2010: Chapter 9§ 9).

Good-quality SGMT has been identified as the single most important educational measure for newcomers, as it addresses head-on the biggest obstacle to their school achievement, namely, understanding of academic content in Swedish (Ministry of Education and Research, 2019). Little is known about how SGMT is practiced, which limits our capacity to make recommendations for providing good-quality SGMT. By analysing interactions during SGMT, this study contributes to filling that gap in our knowledge.

Audio and video recordings of SGMT, field notes and photographs collected during a one-year linguistic ethnographic study in classrooms at an upper-secondary school where SGMT is conducted are analysed in this study. The following questions are in focus: (1) What kinds of semiotic assemblages emerge during SGMT in practice? (2) How do the semiotic assemblages contribute to learning in the context?

Learning, Translanguaging and Semiotic Assemblages

Learning is not about 'piecemeal migration of meanings to the inside of the learner's head' (van Lier, 2000: 46), but it is rather a process during which increasingly efficient ways of dealing with the world and its meanings are developed. The environment that surrounds learners is full of potential meanings, providing a semiotic budget from which resources for interaction and learning (affordances) can be harnessed, or ignored or left unnoticed (van Lier, 2000: 46). These resources are verbal, aural, visual and embodied. Explicit work with the potentials and constraints offered in the environment that surrounds the learner has impacts on their opportunities for communication and learning. Investigation of the potentials and constraints can show 'the emergence of learning, the location of learning opportunities, the pedagogical value of various interactional contexts and processes and the effectiveness of pedagogical strategies' (van Lier, 2000: 250).

This study is grounded in theories of translanguaging and focuses on how different combinations of semiotic resources are harnessed as resources for learning, or not, during SGMT. From its origins as a methodological approach in the context of bilingual education in Wales, researchers now reason that translanguaging extends beyond the classroom into the daily lives of multilingual individuals who translanguage to 'include and facilitate communication with others, but also to construct deeper understandings and make sense of their bilingual worlds' (García, 2009: 45). Translanguaging is thus associated with meaning-making, inclusion and identity as well as language learning and development.

Studies of multimodality consider body language (including gesture and gaze) and visual images as equally integral to communication as spoken and written words (Kress, 2000). Modes are 'socially and culturally shaped resources for meaning making (image, writing, speech, moving image, action, artifacts)' (Bezemer & Kress, 2008: 6). Our senses, particularly touch, taste and smell, also play an important role in communication (Mondada, 2016: 362). Pennycook (2017) argues for incorporating the multisensory, including touch, sight, smell, movement and material artefacts, with the multimodal and multilingual, when analysing interactions. This focus on what he calls semiotic assemblages is important in order to 'redress an historical imbalance that has placed language and cognition in the head, while relegating the body and the senses to the physical'. The affordances that semiotic resources offer for meaning-making are closely connected to their specific, individual characteristics, the sociocultural and sociohistorical environments in which they are used (Kress & van Leeuwen, 1996) and the relationships between them (Danielsson, 2016; Pennycook, 2017: 279).

The semiotic repertoire includes both the multimodal and multilingual resources that are drawn on in communication (Kusters *et al.*, 2017: 219). This enriches purely linguistic conceptualisations of translanguaging and expands monolingual understandings of multimodality, providing a more holistic focus on the communication resources in circulation in multilingual contexts. In classrooms where SGMT is conducted, broadening the focus from linguistic to semiotic repertoire enables a more fine-grained analysis of translanguaging, departing from the notion that languages are bounded systems and insisting that repertoires are multimodal and embodied interactions (Kusters *et al.*, 2017: 228).

Translanguaging in this study is thus conceptualised as the fluid use of all modes of meaning-making (García & Li Wei, 2014: 29), including spoken and written forms of different languages, touch, sight, smells, movements, material artefacts and visual images. These modes cluster together in certain places and at certain times, forming semiotic assemblages that facilitate meaning-making specific to that place and time. Analysing the relationships between linguistic resources, the body, objects, trajectories of people and space for meaning-making in this study clarifies how different combinations of these modes during SGMT takes the learning further. Moreover, it extends understandings and applications of pedagogical translanguaging (see Juvonen & Källkvist, this volume) during SGMT and contributes to better understanding of how it can be conducted.

Education for Newcomers in Upper-Secondary Schools

Newcomers who enter schools midway through their educational career face educational, emotional and social pressures (Jaffe-Walter & Lee, 2018; Suárez-Orozco & Suárez-Orozco, 2009). These pressures are entwined with students' identities as second language learners, lack of power and the delays they face in pursuing their preferred study path (Rawal & Da Costa, 2019). Moreover, gaining communicative competence in the new language is insufficient to succeed at the upper-secondary level (Fránquiz & Salinas, 2013); rather, students must gain academic literacies in different subjects that express content- and knowledge-specific ways (Schleppegrell, 2004).

The effectiveness of monolingual approaches in educating multilingual and newcomer students has been questioned, leading to the development of alternative approaches that build on newcomers' existent linguistic, cultural and knowledge resources (García, 2009; García & Sylvan, 2011; García & Li Wei, 2014). These include identification of students' incoming literacy and academic skills, second language instruction, support in the form of tutoring, collaboration, translanguaging and learner-centred classroom approaches (García & Sylvan, 2011; Hornberger & Link, 2012). Bilingual and bicultural mentors are also key in supporting newcomers' learning: by helping to bridge old and new cultures, heal ruptures in relationships caused by migration and reunification and, for college-educated mentors, providing academic tutoring and advice about progress through academic systems (Suárez-Orozco & Suárez-Orozco, 2009: 338).

Combining translanguaging and multimodal resources can improve adolescent newcomers' vocabularies and metalinguistic and metasemantic awareness and can also enhance literacy engagement by offering embodied experiences of literacy development (Ollerhead, 2019: 14). Translanguaging practices can also enhance conceptual and linguistic understanding and raise levels of participation and investment in tasks (Martin-Beltrán, 2014: 39).

In Sweden, newcomers between 16 and 19 years of age, after initial assessment of their language and knowledge development, are usually enrolled in Language Introduction Programmes (hereafter, LIPs) where they undertake intensive education in Swedish as a second language and study subjects from the lower- and sometimes upper-secondary curriculum. LIPs prepare the students for continuing studies in national programmes at the upper-secondary level or other educational pathways. A passing grade in 8 subjects is required for admission to vocational programmes and 12 subjects for academic programmes. Meeting the learning goals of these subjects in a new language is challenging, requiring carefully chosen and intensive support from schools, and immense commitment from students. LIPs have been described by students as uncomfortable places, cut off from the rest of the Swedish school and society (Hagström, 2018) where Swedish is the 'hard currency', necessary to succeed (Sharif, 2017: 176).

Swedish Research on SGMT

There is a lack of research on SGMT in the Swedish context (Ministry of Education and Research, 2019). Most are interview studies of perceptions of SGMT. Tutors describe an overarching tension between conceptualisations of their roles as simultaneously pivotal but peripheral (Thorstensson Dávila, 2016: 961). The peripheral role is emphasised when tutors are utilised as general resources in schools rather than for their specialised pedagogical competence (Straszer *et al.*, 2019). In interviews with 20 tutors, Dávila and Bunar (2020) identified a pressing need for advocacy for tutors in a system that accepts newcomer youths on a rhetorical and procedural level, 'without authentic consideration for how policies influence individual teachers and students' (Dávila & Bunar, 2020: 14). They argue for showcasing the work that tutors do and the establishment of structures and processes that strengthen the collaboration between tutors and teachers (Dávila & Bunar, 2020). Teachers are key in creating conditions for collaboration with tutors (Straszer *et al.*, 2019: 6).

Teachers in the compulsory school report that SGMT facilitates learning (Juvonen, 2015), and students in both the compulsory school (Jepson Wigg, 2016; Nilsson Folke, 2015) and the upper-secondary school (Sharif, 2016) say that SGMT helps them learn Swedish and other subjects as well as better understand how the Swedish school and society works.

There is still only a limited number of studies that focus on interactions during SGMT. In these studies, SGMT has been found to provide opportunities for interactional scaffolding (Uddling, 2013) and create a temporary space for translanguaging (Reath Warren, 2016). Tutors have been identified as important adults in schools who help students to communicate their thoughts to the teacher (Winlund, 2019).

Implementational and organisational challenges constrain the potential of SGMT, as does the lack of tutors and a general lack of knowledge about SGMT in schools (Avery, 2016). While it is possible to study subjects at university that prepare SGMT tutors for their work with newcomers, no formal qualifications are required for the position. This situation does little to improve knowledge about SGMT or impact positively on tutors' status in schools.

Methodology and Data

The data analysed in this chapter come from a larger linguistic ethnographic study. Linguistic ethnography combines close analysis of linguistic features with in-depth knowledge of the context gained through extensive time spent there (Copland & Creese, 2015). I spent two days a week over a period of six months (October 2018 to March 2019), at an upper-secondary school, interacting with teachers, tutors and students in the LIP during SGMT and outside the classroom. Approximately 1000 students attend the school, which is located in a medium-sized Swedish town (population 172,000) and has offered the LIP for more than 20 years. Ninety students, mostly newcomers, were enrolled in the LIP when fieldwork was conducted. There are three levels that students advance through in LIP, as they improve their Swedish and subject knowledge.

The school provides SGMT primarily for students enrolled in LIP, and in many but not all of the languages spoken by newcomers. SGMT is organised either as a group tutorial or during lessons. Group tutorials are organised according to the language of the majority of the students in that group. Subject teachers also attend the group tutorials, giving students the possibility of getting subject-specific help in their mother tongue, strongest school language, Swedish and any other languages that the subject teachers speak (in this study, Arabic, Armenian, English and Farsi).

SGMT is organised during lessons when teachers indicate that students need extra support. After an initial presentation of the subject matter in Swedish, the tutor assists students in their strongest language and Swedish as they work through tasks.

During fieldwork, I observed audio- and video-recorded SGMT sessions, took field notes and photographs, conducted interviews with teachers, the tutor and the principal and distributed a questionnaire to get background information on students in the LIP. In this chapter, analysis of the observations of SGMT with students who speak Dari is in focus. I observed both group tutorials and SGMT during mathematics, social science and Swedish as a second language (hereafter, SSL).

Participants

The SGMT tutor I observed in this study is given the pseudonym of Hassan.[1] Hassan migrated from Iran in his teens and studied at the same upper-secondary school where fieldwork was conducted. He speaks Dari, Farsi, Swedish and English and has worked as an SGMT tutor at several different schools for the past six years.

I observed many students during the initial unrecorded observations of SGMT. Twenty-two students gave their written consent to be audio-recorded and filmed; however, when filming began, several withdrew their permission. Five students in total were filmed during SGMT.

Data

The data analysed for this chapter comprise audio/video recordings taken during four sessions of SGMT and field notes and photographs taken

Table 7.1 Data: Analysed and contextual

Material	Subject	Description
Analysed data		
Audio/Video recordings SGMT (4)	Group (2) Math (1) SSL (1)	83 min 51 min 69 min
Photographs	Classroom/school environments Classroom artefacts	>200 photographs
Field notes	Group SGMT (13) SGMT during lessons (15)	Taken over 12 days of classroom observations over 6 months
Contextual data		
Interviews (6)	2 teachers (2 interviews) 1 tutor (3 interviews) 1 principal (1 interview)	65 min 105 min 70 min

during observations of 28 sessions. Transcripts of interviews with the tutor provide contextual information which informs the discussion of the results (see Table 7.1).

One of the strengths of a linguistic ethnographic method is that the same phenomenon can be captured and interrogated from different perspectives and through different means. This triangulation in combination with the length of time spent in the school strengthens the validity of the conclusions (Yin, 2011: 79). Approval to conduct research at the school, in accordance with The Ethical Review Act (2003: 460), was gained before fieldwork commenced.

Data collection and analysis

Before fieldwork formally began, I met the principal, teachers and Hassan and visited classrooms, where I met students. In the initial unrecorded observations of SGMT group tutorials, I first sat at the back of the room writing field notes, then moved around the classroom, observing and, with students' permission, taking photographs of their work. In field notes and photographs, I attempted to capture both the whole classroom environment and moments where different semiotic resources were drawn on in interactions. During observation of subject lessons, the semiotic resources drawn on by the teachers as well as Hassan and the students were included in analysis.

During the later sessions, I filmed only the students who had given their consent. Hassan carried a small digital audio-recorder to record the conversations that he had with the students who had given their consent to participate.

Audio and video recordings of the observed tutorials, field notes and photographs were analysed qualitatively, following principles of compilation, disassemblage and reassemblage (Yin, 2011). All data were uploaded to a software program on a password-protected server at the university (compilation). Disassemblage was done in several stages and ways with different data. Field notes and audio recordings were coded into categories representing different semiotic resources observed in relation to learning among newcomers, for example, 'spoken languages other than Swedish'; 'gesture' and 'written texts in Swedish'. Examples of semiotic assemblages (highly multimodal and multilingual interactions) were identified in the video recordings of SGMT, focusing thus on practices in place rather than on identifying patterns of linguistic use (Pennycook, 2017: 280).

The audio recordings of these interactions were transcribed in Dari and translated into Swedish by an authorised translator. The data have been reassembled by providing thick descriptions (Geertz, 1973) of the semiotic assemblages, comprising:

- multilingual extracts from transcriptions;
- screen shots from the video recordings illustrating gesture, bodily positions and other semiotic resources;
- photographs of resources used during the interactions.

Extracts from the interviews contextualise the discussion and analysis of the observed classroom interactions.

These thick descriptions address the first question and underpin the discussion where the second question, relating to affordances for meaning-making in the interactions, is in focus. Conclusions and implications are drawn in the final section of the chapter.

Semiotic Assemblages in SGMT

SGMT during group tutorials

Thirteen of the 28 observed sessions of SGMT were group tutorials, where students worked independently or in small groups, raising their hand if they needed help. Group tutorials were held in the same large room, every Friday morning. Attendance varied, and as tutorials were not compulsory, students came and left. On days when 20 or more students attended, it became quite noisy. A large aerial view of the town where the school was located, a small picture of a Swedish queen from the 1800s and two faded abstract paintings hung on the walls of the classroom.

Hassan usually came first, to unlock the room. As the students arrived with their computers, textbooks, pens, papers and smartphones, they exchanged the Dari greeting *salaam alaikum* ('peace be upon you') with Hassan and each other, accompanied by a handclasp, hug or back thump. Figure 7.1 captures a brief interaction between students, who briefly clasp hands, at the beginning of a lesson. The student on the right has raised his left hand to his heart.

Figure 7.1 Gestures, touch and spoken Dari

Figure 7.2 Neck hug

When students approached each other during the tutorial, there was often a show of play fighting, shoulder rubbing and back thumping (see Figure 7.2).

After students took their seats and opened their books and computers, they worked either independently or together, speaking Dari and Swedish, calling on Hassan, if they needed help in Dari, or teachers, if they wanted help in Swedish. If no hands were raised, Hassan and the teachers circulated, asking the students if they needed assistance.

During a group tutorial with the LIP Level 3, two students, Azad and Bidar, were completing a geography worksheet with questions about population density, using a world map. Three questions were in focus in the discussion between the students:

- Circle at least two regions in the world with a low or no population. What do you call these regions?
- Circle at least two regions with a high population density. What name do you give to these regions?
- Think about the reasons behind the uneven distribution of human populations. Choose one of the regions you circled in Exercise 1a. Explain why people choose not to live there. What reasons are there?

Azad appeared unsure about the exercise and asked Bidar if he had done it (Extract 7.1).[2]

Extract 7.1 Population density

( ) صدای های نامشخص)

- جواب این را تو چه دادی؟

- " شینا" که هسته که مردم خودش زیاد است, بیشتر که هست "مرکنداس اکونومی" است "

- (صدای نامشخص)

- "اومروده" گفته, نه گفته بسته "لنده"

- منطقه را گفته

- اینالی شینا که هست بزرگه و یک قسمت شی که هسته تحت (صدای نامشخص) و باز هم (صدای نامشخص)

- Sedan finns det delar som människorna inte väljer för att besöka (ohörbar)

- Välj ett område

Azad: Have you answered this one?
Bidar: China [inaudible] which is a land with many inhabitants [and] which mostly has a market economy [inaudible]
        'Region' it says not the whole 'country'
        It says region.
        It's like this, China is big, one area is under [inaudible] and then
        Then there are areas that people choose not to live in. Choose a region.

During the interaction in Extract 7.1, the students pointed at the Swedish questions in the worksheets (see Figure 7.3). Responding to Azad's question, Bidar (on the right) first used Dari to describe China. Still using Dari, he then distinguished between the words 'region' and 'country' before reading aloud the Swedish words on the worksheet.[3]

In this interaction, spoken linguistic resources from Dari, spoken and written linguistic resources from Swedish, images (the world map) and gestures were combined as Bidar attempted to help Azad. Azad repeated the Swedish words on the worksheet in the final exchange, including the request to 'Choose a region', repeating one of the Swedish

Figure 7.3 Gestures and spoken Dari and Swedish to identify and discuss

words, the meaning of which he previously explained in Dari. After the interaction, Azad used an application on his smartphone to translate, and then he returned to the worksheet, writing in the margins of the worksheet in Dari. Bidar, meanwhile, continued to fill in answers on the worksheet using the Swedish textbook as a reference (see Figure 7.4).

Azad used Bidar's spoken Dari and Swedish and written Dari (accessed through the dictionary application) as resources to complete the exercise in written Swedish. He did not ask for help from Hassan or the Swedish teacher who was at the tutorial, and unlike Bidar, he did not consult the textbook, which contained written Swedish and images.

Another exercise that Azad and Bidar worked on during this tutorial required them to link subject-specific terminology that describes physical features of landscapes with students' personal experiences. Bidar requested help, first by leaning towards Azad, calling him 'my

Figure 7.4 Written Dari and Swedish in smartphones, textbooks and worksheets

brother' in English, and then by raising his hand to attract Hassan's attention. Hassan came over, and they started discussing the task.

Extract 7.2 What is oasis?

ـ چه میخواهی از جانم؟

ـ اینجا نموره, اینجا که اصلن نموره

ـ (صدای نامشخص)

ـ استاد, چه می خواهی از جانم؟

ـ (صدای نامشخص)

ـ اینجا که نموره, (صدای نامشخص)

- Vad är det här?
- Oasen, torr öken
- Vad är oas?

Hassan:	What do you want from me?
Bidar:	I can't do this. I can't this at all.
	Lord, what you want from me?
	I can't do this at all.
	What is this?
Hassan:	*Oasis, arid desert, oasis* [turns to the researcher]. *What is 'oasis'?*

Bidar's response, initially in Dari, indicated that he was frustrated and felt unable to answer the question. Bidar then pointed to the question ('What attracts humans?') and the alternative answers that students were asked to tick or not (for example, oasis, arid desert) and then asked Hassan in Swedish what it meant. Hassan read through two of the words given and then turned to me and asked what an oasis is. I explained it briefly in Swedish, and the discussion between Hassan and the students continued.

This question about 'attraction' related to the issue of population density (see also Extract 7.1). The geography textbook used similar words, for example, 'Certain areas are more attractive to live in than others' (Thorstensson *et al.*, 2013: 311). Hassan did not refer to the textbook, although it was on Bidar's desk. The students and Hassan together decided that an oasis would attract humans, and they continued going through the list of terms in the worksheet together. Hassan translated and explained terms such as 'volcano', 'rainforest', 'heavy rainfall' and 'large conifer forest'. Hassan also helped with pronunciation when Bidar stumbled over the word 'bördiga' (*fertile*). As the discussion continued, the word 'delta' came up, and Azad joined in (Extract 7.3, Figure 7.5).

Figure 7.5 What is a river delta? Gestures and spoken Dari

Extract 7.3 What is a river delta? Gestures and spoken Dari

- (صدای نامشخص) Stor floddelta

- این چی؟

- flod که میشه رودخانه

- فکر کنم که Stor floddelta

- delta یکجای میگه که دوشاخه میشه

- یک دریاچه اش

- آ, اینهم Det kan vara faktiskt

Hassan: (inaudible) *Big River delta*
Bidar: What is that?
Hassan: *River* is river
Bidar: I think *big river delta* is
Azad: *Delta* is a place where the water branches out (gestures with hands). A sea.
Bidar: *That could actually be right*

There was a photograph of the Ganges river delta in the geography text-book (Thorstensson *et al.*, 2013: 424) (Figure 7.6), but this was not referred to in the discussions.

Azad used a very clear gesture to demonstrate what he thought a delta looked liked while speaking in Dari. For approximately one minute of time, Azad talked about Egypt and the Nile with Hassan. Bidar continued working through the wordlist, reading aloud in Swedish the expressions such as 'mountainous region', 'small island' and 'big ocean' and

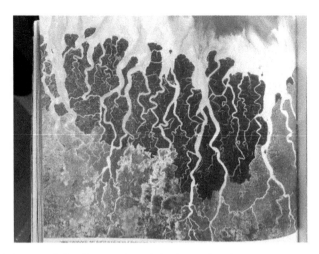

Figure 7.6 Image of the Ganges river delta in textbook

intermittently sighing with exasperation, saying in English, 'Are you kidding me?' and in Swedish, 'Don't understand it'.

SGMT as a group tutorial ran on the assumption that students themselves identified a need for help, and asked for it, in either Dari or Swedish or any of the other languages spoken by the teachers who attended. It was, however, quite common for students to work on their own, interacting principally with a text in Swedish, a smartphone or computer with a multilingual dictionary application and a notebook to write translations. Figure 7.7 illustrates this kind of semiotic assemblage.

Figure 7.7 A Swedish novel: Written Swedish and Dari on paper and on smartphone

Cirus, the student in Figure 7.7, was reading a novel in Swedish, on his own, using his smartphone to look up new Swedish words, and writing them in Dari. He did not raise his hand to ask for assistance, and Hassan, who was continually helping others, did not ask if he needed help.

The semiotic resources that Cirus used during this tutorial comprised written Swedish (the novel and words that he writes in his list) and Dari (translations of words that he does not understand in the novel; Figure 7.8). He did not interact with Hassan, other students or the teachers but is afforded and made use of the time and space that the tutorial provided to use Dari as a resource in reading a Swedish novel.

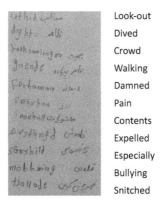

	Look-out
	Dived
	Crowd
	Walking
	Damned
	Pain
	Contents
	Expelled
	Especially
	Bullying
	Snitched

Figure 7.8 Hand-written wordlist: Written Swedish and Dari (translated to English by the author)

Semiotic assemblages in tutoring during lessons

Fifteen of the 28 observed sessions of SGMT were conducted during lessons. In this form, Hassan attended the lesson with the students, and after the teacher introduced the content, he assisted the students with the task at hand.

The semiotic assemblages that contextualised SGMT during subject lessons were shaped by the individual teachers' use of multimodal resources, and how often students and teachers asked Hassan for support in Dari. Most lessons observed began with an introduction to the topic, often accompanied by a digital presentation and, once in social science, a short film in Swedish.

Figures 7.9 and 7.10 show an SSL teacher introducing a lesson during which students started writing an essay about the influence of social norms and patriarchal structures on individual expression. The SSL teacher focused on referencing procedures in this lesson. Hassan sat in the classroom, listening, but not participating, in the teaching.

Figure 7.9 Spoken/written Swedish, image, colours and gestures

The teacher began by explaining the importance of referencing in essays and asked the class what word described taking another writer's idea without acknowledging the source. 'Plagiarism', responded a student. The teacher confirmed this response and then indicated the words *Referat-och citatteknik* ('Reference and citation techniques') on the slide and asked if the students knew what the words meant (Figure 7.9).

As the SSL teacher explained how to write references, she pointed to the examples on the slide, which was written in Swedish. Her gaze shifted between the screen and the students. In Figure 7.10, she pointed to the

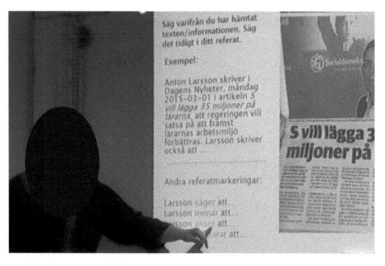

Figure 7.10 Spoken/written Swedish, and gestures

reporting verbs that students are encouraged to use: *säger* ('says'), *menar* ('means'), *anser* ('considers') and *förklarar* ('explains'), written in green.

The teacher drew on a rich but entirely monolingual palette of written and spoken linguistic resources in Swedish. The written words varied in size, font, colour and style. She also used pictures, gestures and gaze to introduce this complex task to the students. When she finished, she said 'finished' in Swedish, repeated it in Dari (*kharij*) and finished in Swedish 'Now it's time for questions'.

The students had many questions and appeared to find the task challenging. My field notes record that:

> Students don't know where to begin. The teacher gives examples on the whiteboard. One student asks, 'Are we supposed to write a whole book?' After several comments, the teacher told him, 'Du gör en höna av en fjäder' ('You are making a mountain out of a molehill'; [literally, 'You are making a hen out of a feather']). (Field notes, 12 December 2018)

Some time was then spent discussing what that Swedish idiom meant, in a good-natured and supportive atmosphere. The teacher also wrote some example sentences on the whiteboard, modelling for students how the introduction could be written while frequently turning back to the class to ask for suggestions for formulations (see Figure 7.11).

Students started on the writing task, and Hassan and the SSL teacher circulated, responding when students raised their hands and assisting in Dari and in Swedish. The students being filmed (Daana and Bihar) had brought biscuits and energy drinks to the class. They ate, drank and asked many questions as they started on the task (see Figure 7.12).

The title of the essay was 'The individual and society'. Hassan, using Dari, encouraged the students to take photographs of the model sentences written on the whiteboard and read through the essay question with them, prompting them to write first an introduction and then the main body of

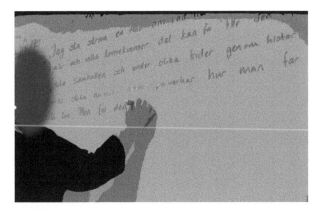

Figure 7.11 Modelling written Swedish, spoken Swedish

Figure 7.12 Spoken/written Swedish, spoken Dari, biscuits and drinks

the text. He explained that the question asked what was required for individuals to choose their own path and the potential consequences of doing so. Daana asked what *individen* ('the individual') meant, and Hassan explained it in Dari. The conversation continued:

Extract 7.4 Being oneself: Written and spoken Swedish and spoken Dari

- مه هیچ نفهمیدم درباره چه نوشته کنم این تکست را؟! -

- این درباره -

Det finns olika sätt att gå sin väg -

- میگه در قانون های مختلف است که آدم راه خود را پیش ببره و هر کسی هر رقم که میخواهد باشه olika samhällen -

- mod یعنی جرأت -

Samhället, släkten och vänner har förväntningar på hur man kan leva -

Många väljer att gå sin egen väg och vara sig själv, trots att det kan väcka reaktioner -

- ولی بعضی ها میگه نه من راه خود را میرم باوجودیکه مثلا عکس العمل است -

- مه راه خوده میرم و به هیچ کسی دیگر مربوط نیست -

Skriv en text om vad det innebär att vara sig själv och varför det kan vara svårt -

- att vara sig själv؟ چیه -

- اگه این راه را که تو انتخاب کردی بری چی است؟ -

- این راه را که تو انتخاب کردی چه مشکلات داره -

Daana:	I don't understand anything, what should I write this text about?
Hassan:	It's about *There are different ways of living life*. It says that there are different rules in *different societies* which means that one can choose one's own path and be who one wants to be. It requires *courage*.
Daana:	What does *courage* mean?
Hassan:	*Society, family, relatives and friends have expectations about how one should live. Many choose their own path and dare to be themselves, even though it causes reactions.* But then there are those who say that I am choosing my own path, regardless of the reactions. I'm choosing my own path, and it's no one else's business. *Write a text about what it means to be yourself.* What does *to be yourself* mean? *And why it can be difficult?* What are the implications of choosing the path you have chosen? What problems will you meet if you follow the path you have chosen?
Daana:	And what advantages?
Hassan:	Yes, what advantages?

In Extract 7.4, Daana expressed in Dari that he did not understand the task. Hassan read through the essay question, in Swedish, translating and explaining in Dari section by section.

Neither images nor gestures were used to clarify this relatively high-level and abstract task, nor are the texts that students have read in preparation referred to directly. The discussion between Daana and Hassan focused purely on the meaning of the words and the writing task. They did not mention the referencing system that the SSL teacher spent more than 30 multimodal minutes for explaining. Daana simply did not understand what he was supposed to write about.

Field notes record what the teacher told me at the beginning of that lesson, namely that the students had come directly to her lesson after a reading comprehension test and were very tired. The written assignment in focus in Extract 7.4 was part of a cross-curricula project, so students would have further opportunities in their social science lesson to ask questions, read relevant texts and work on their own texts, but whether or not Hassan would attend these lessons was unclear.

The semiotic assemblages that comprised interactions during the teacher's presentation included her slides in Swedish and pictures, accompanied by gestures and spoken Swedish. When the focus of the lesson changed to students' writing, interactions between Hassan and individual students, as illustrated in Extract 7.4, comprised written and spoken Swedish and spoken Dari.

Semiotic assemblages in SGMT during mathematics lessons consisted of similar resources. The mathematics teacher introduced the unit (graphs) using a digital presentation, with visual images and diagrams in Swedish. He used gestures to draw students' attention to particular phrases or features on the graph and asked questions in Swedish to the whole class (see Figure 7.13).

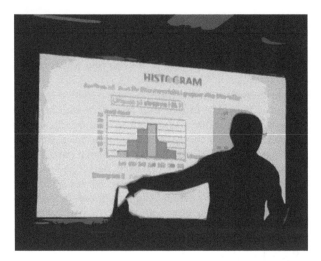

Figure 7.13 Spoken/written Swedish, images

Hassan sat in the classroom and listened to the presentation. After the digital presentation, students worked independently, while the teacher and Hassan moved around, helping them individually. As the students worked, they used the mathematics book, with words in Swedish, and those who spoke Dari discussed with Hassan.

One aspect of the semiotic assemblages during SGMT in mathematics that differed from those observed in SGMT during SSL was that the mathematics teacher, a speaker of Arabic, orally translated a few of the subject-specific words in the Swedish digital presentation into Arabic for the benefit of those students who spoke Arabic. The students in the mathematics lesson did not want their voices recorded, so there are no recordings of Hassan's interactions with students to analyse in this context.

Semiotic resources across all forms of SGMT

Common to all SGMT sessions, regardless of whether they were arranged as group tutorials or took place during subject teaching, were the students' digital resources. Computers and smartphones were used during SGMT to look up words, write texts, access teachers' instructions on the school's learning platform and access information, both in Swedish and other languages as well as through pictures (Figure 7.14). During group tutorials, there was more freedom for students to access information in their own language, for example, watching a physics tutorial in Dari (see Figure 7.15).

Also omnipresent were A4 papers entitled *Veckans ord* ('Weekly words'), a list of academic words that were common across subject areas, compiled by the SSL teacher and the mathematics teacher. Students were frequently observed writing translations and practicing these words during SGMT.

Figure 7.14 Written Swedish and Dari, still images

Figure 7.15 Written and spoken Dari, moving images

There were more opportunities to use Dari during group tutorials and more time spent on Swedish during subject instruction. However, both languages were present regardless of how SGMT was arranged. The kind of digital presentations in Swedish observed during SGMT during lessons was not present during group tutorials. Students did not always use the visual images in textbooks when they were working with worksheets, and the the tutor did not appear to refer textbooks unless students were actively working from them.

The Learning Affordances of Translanguaging and Semiotic Assemblages in SGMT

Analysing the above interactions as semiotic assemblages provides insights into the 'dynamic relations among objects, places and linguistic resources' (Pennycook, 2017: 279) and the localised nature of interactions. The resources available to and drawn on by the students during SGMT, and the relationships between the resources, vary dynamically, depending on the way the SGMT is organised, the tasks that students are working on, the individual needs of the students at that particular moment and the ability to use or awareness of what resources are available and are beneficial for learning. The affordances they offer for learning thus also vary.

When Hassan interacts with students, regardless of whether it is during group tutorials or in a subject classroom setting, he combines written and spoken Dari, written and spoken Swedish, gestures and touch as he responds to students' questions. The embodied nature of the greetings and interactions between the students and Hassan is distinctly different from the students' interactions with their other teachers, hinting at the similarities in their cultural background and migration trajectories. In an interview, Hassan mentioned that he often took it easy with the students, as they did not always feel good. This reflects other research highlighting the emotional and social pressures that the adolescent newcomers face (Jaffe-Walter & Lee, 2018; Rawal & Da Costa, 2019; Suárez-Orozco & Suárez-Orozco, 2009). Hassan said that it was important to 'create a relationship so that they feel secure, so that they can talk about anything'. This indicates that Hassan positions himself as a kind of bicultural mentor (Suárez-Orozco & Suárez-Orozco, 2009: 338) who can help students understand their new environment (cf. Reath Warren, 2016; Sharif, 2016), which is an essential pre-condition for learning.

The use of resources from different languages (Dari, Swedish and English) in different combinations during SGMT also helps students understand concepts and perform tasks presented in Swedish, reflecting other studies in Sweden (Ministry of Education and Research, 2019; Reath Warren, 2016; Uddling, 2013; Winlund, 2019) and internationally (García, 2009; García & Sylvan, 2011; Hornberger & Link, 2012; Martin-Beltrán, 2014; Ollerhead, 2019). Moreover, this study illustrates how translanguaging during SGMT is also embodied and multimodal (Bezemer & Kress, 2008; García & Li Wei, 2014; Kress, 2000; Kress & van Leeuwen, 1996; Kusters *et al.*, 2017; Mondada, 2016; Pennycook, 2017).

The embodied greetings that are familiar to students from other contexts (Figures 7.1 and 7.2) can help them feel more at home in a space which may otherwise feel unfamiliar and uncomfortable (Hagström, 2018). The interactions between students and Hassan in Extracts 7.1, 7.2 and 7.3 illustrate how multilingual resources, objects, the space, the people in the space and gestures intertwine and help the students understand subject-specific language and, to some extent, the task. Translanguaging in these interactions can thus contribute to the development of academic literacies (Fránquiz & Salinas, 2013; Schleppegrell, 2004). It can also be noted, however, that the visual images and the Swedish textbook are not drawn on by Hassan. These potential affordances for learning are, in these examples, left unnoticed or ignored (cf. van Lier, 2000).

Multilingual glossaries (Figure 7.8) can offer affordances for learning; however, in Reath Warren's (2016) study, the tutor actively checked the words, ensuring that the students had understood. I did not see whether Hassan actively checked Cirus's translations and therefore cannot verify whether they supported his learning or not. The fact that Hassan was often extremely busy, trying to help a room full of students working on different tasks, and that he did not always have time to help everyone undoubtedly restricts the potential that SGMT has for learning, when organised as a group tutorial. This reflects the Swedish literature pointing out organisational and implementational problems with SGMT (Avery, 2016) and the need for the establishment of structures and processes to strengthened collaboration with teachers (Dávila & Bunar, 2020).

Semiotic assemblages during SGMT in subject teaching were impacted by teachers' individual approaches to teaching, as it was during the initial presentations that students received the information that would be further worked on with Hassan's assistance. In Figures 7.9–7.11, the rich palette of multimodal but monolingual resources that the teacher presents appears to offer opportunities for learning. However, field notes and the interaction in Extract 7.4 reveal that students have not understood the task itself. Hassan, through use of Dari and Swedish together, gives his interpretation of the question but does not draw on the texts that students have read to prepare for this task, nor is he asked to help with presentation that the SSL teacher gave. This indicates that the potential affordances for learning are again left unnoticed or ignored (van Lier, 2000) and that the opportunities for collaboration are missed (Avery, 2016).

The use of multilingual and multimodal resources with adolescent newcomers in other contexts resulted in improvements in writing and individual and collaborative learning (Martin-Beltrán, 2014; Ollerhead, 2019). These studies, however, describe one-off, carefully designed intervention studies where researchers and teachers collaborate closely to create the best possible opportunities for learning, while SGMT is an established but largely unregulated form of support for newcomers, which has existed since the 1960s in Sweden. It has been pointed out that the collaboration is key to providing good-quality SGMT (Straszer *et al.*, 2019), yet opportunities for collaboration and formal education for SGMT tutors or about SGMT, through which knowledge about the importance of collaboration might be spread, are still extremely limited (Dávila & Bunar, 2020; Ministry of Education and Research, 2019). This significantly limits the potential affordances for learning that this and other studies show that SGMT withholds.

Analysing translanguaging practices in SGMT as semiotic assemblages also sheds light on the multiple competencies required for the job. Hassan was available to the students in this study for a limited number of hours each week. Both he and the teachers indicated in interviews that they did not plan SGMT together, nor did Hassan receive material in advance. His job was to try to support as many students as possible, during a limited period of time, with minimal preparation for the task. Hassan's largely *ad hoc* support was, however, praised by the teachers and the principal, indicating that Hassan is positioned as both peripheral and as pivotal (Thorstensson Dávila, 2016).

This study indicates a need for an emphasis on the pivotal role of tutors. As well as showcasing the work, they do so that teachers and principals better understand it; there is a pressing need to develop strategies for collaboration (Dávila & Bunar, 2020). Moreover, without formal education, there is a significant risk that tutors and teachers will remain unaware of the affordances for learning that semiotic assemblages, through connecting languages that students understand, Swedish, images, gestures, objects and spaces, can offer in SGMT.

Notes

(1) All research participants have been given pseudonyms to protect their anonymity.
(2) **Transcription conventions:**
    In the extracts in this paper, I have retained words in Dari as they were transcribed and translated using Arabic script, with the Swedish words that were used transcribed using Latin letters. The original transcription, being mostly in Dari (written in Arabic letters), was written from right to left. However, Swedish sentences or phrases embedded in utterances that are otherwise in Dari are written from left to right.
    The names of the people speaking are only given in the English translation.

لغت	original words in Dari
ord	original words in Swedish
word	words translated from Dari to English
word	words translated from Swedish to English
?	rising intonation
,	short pause
.	longer pause

(3) In the final comment in the transcription, there is a Swedish word that is incorrectly transcribed: 'besöka' (*to visit*). The sentence spoken by Bidar is 'bosätta' (*to live*). I corrected this in the English translation.

References

Avery, H. (2016) At the bridging point: Tutoring newly arrived students in Sweden. *International Journal of Inclusive Education* 21, 404–415. https://doi.org/10.1080/1 3603116.2016.1197325

Bezemer, J. and Kress, G. (2008) Writing in multimodal texts: A social semiotic account of designs for learning. *Written Communication* 25 (2), 166–195.

Copland, F. and Creese, A. (2015) *Linguistic Ethnography –EEE Collecting, Analysing and Presenting Data*. London: Sage.

Cummins, J. (1986) Empowering minority students: A framework for intervention. *Harvard Educational Review* 56 (1), 18–37.

Danielsson, K. (2016) Modes and meaning in the classroom – The role of different semiotic resources to convey meaning in science classrooms. *Linguistics and Education* 35, 88–99. https://doi.org/10.1016/j.linged.2016.07.005

Dávila, L.T. and Bunar, N. (2020) Translanguaging through an advocacy lens: The roles of multilingual classroom assistants in Sweden. *European Journal of Applied Linguistics* (8), 107–126.

Fránquiz, M.E. and Salinas, C. (2013) Knowing English is not enough! Cultivating academic literacies among high school newcomers. *The High School Journal* 96 (4), 339–357.

García, O. (2009) *Bilingual Education in the 21st Century*. Malden, MA: Wiley-Blackwell.

García, O. and Li Wei (2014) *Translanguaging: Language, Bilingualism and Education*. Basingstoke: Palgrave Macmillan.

García, O. and Sylvan, C.E. (2011) Pedagogies and practices in multilingual classrooms: Singularities in pluralities. *Modern Language Journal* 95 (3), 385–400. https://doi. org/10.1111/j.1540–4781.2011.01208.x

Geertz, C. (1973) *The Interpretation of Cultures*. New York, NY: Basic Books.

Hagström, M. (2018) Raka spår, sidospår, stopp [straight ahead, sidetrack, stop]. PhD thesis, Linköping University.

Hornberger, N.H. and Link, H. (2012) Translanguaging in today's classrooms: A biliteracy lens. *Theory Into Practice* 51 (4), 239–247. https://doi.org/10.1080/00405841.2 012.726051

Jaffe-Walter, R. and Lee, S.J. (2018) Engaging the transnational lives of immigrant youth in public schooling: Toward a culturally sustaining pedagogy for newcomer immigrant youth. *American Journal of Education* 124 (3), 257–283. https://doi. org/10.1086/697070

Jepson Wigg, U. (2016) Betydelsefulla skeden: Från introducerande till ordinarie undervisning [Significant phases: From introductory to mainstream education]. In P. Lahdenperä and E. Sundgren (eds) *Skolans möte med nyanlända [The Reception of Newcomers in Schools]* (pp. 65–91). Stockholm: Liber.

Juvonen, P. (2015) Lärarröster om direktplacering av nyanlända elever [Teacher voices on the direct placement of newcomers]. In N. Bunar (ed.) *Nyanlända och Lärande – mottagande och inkludering [Newcomers and Learning – Reception and Inclusion]* (pp. 139–176). Stockholm: Natur och Kultur.

Kress, G. (2000) Multimodality: Challenges to thinking about language. *TESOL Quarterly* 34 (2), 337. https://doi.org/10.2307/3587959

Kress, G. and van Leeuwen, T. (1996) *Reading Images: The Grammar of Visual Design*. London: Routledge.

Kusters, A., Spotti, M., Swanwick, R. and Tapio, E. (2017) Beyond languages, beyond modalities: Transforming the study of semiotic repertoires. *International Journal of Multilingualism* 14 (3), 219–232. https://doi.org/10.1080/14790718.2017.132165

Martin-Beltrán, M. (2014) 'What do you want to say?' How adolescents use translanguaging to expand learning opportunities. *International Multilingual Research Journal* 8 (3), 208–230. https://doi.org/10.1080/19313152.2014.914372

Ministry of Education and Research (2019) *För flerspråkighet, kunskapsutveckling och inkludering. Modersmålsundervisning och studiehandledning på modersmål [For Multilingualism, Learning and Inclusion. Mother Tongue Instruction and Study Guidance in the Mother Tongue]* (SOU 2019:18). Stockholm: Ministry of Education and Research. See https://www.gov.se/rattsliga-dokument/statens-offentliga-utredningar/2019/05/sou-201918/ (accessed 3 May 2021).

Mondada, L. (2016) Challenges of multimodality: Language and the body in social interaction. *Journal of Sociolingusitics* 20 (3), 336–366.

Nilsson Folke, J. (2015) Från inkluderande exkludering till exkluderande inkludering? [From inclusive exclusion to excluding inclusion?] In N. Bunar (ed.) *Nyanlända och Lärande – Mottagande och inkludering [Newcomers and Learning – Reception and Inclusion]* (pp. 37–80). Stockholm: Natur och Kultur.

Ollerhead, S. (2019) Teaching across semiotic modes with multilingual learners: Translanguaging in an Australian classroom. *Language and Education* 33 (2) 106–122.

Pennycook, A. (2017) Translanguaging and semiotic assemblages. *International Journal of Multilingualism* 14 (3), 269–282. https://doi.org/10.1080/14790718.2017.1315810

Rawal, H. and De Costa, P.I. (2019) 'You are different and not mainstream': An emotion-based case study of two south Asian English language learners. *International Multilingual Research Journal* 0 (0), 1–13. https://doi.org/10.1080/19313152.2019.1 590906

Reath Warren, A. (2016) Multilingual study guidance in the Swedish compulsory school and the development of multilingual literacies. *Nordand* 11 (2), 115–142.

Schleppegrell, M.J. (2004) *The Language of Schooling. A Functional Linguistic Perspective.* New York, NY and London: Routledge.

Sharif, H. (2016) Ungdomarnas beskrivningar av mötet med introduktionsutbildningen för nyanlända. 'Inte på riktigt, men jätteviktigt för oss.' In P. Lahdenperä and E. Sundgren (eds) *Skolans möte med nyanlända* (pp. 92–110). Stockholm: Liber.

Sharif, H. (2017) 'Här i Sverige måste man gå i skolan för att få respekt'. Nyanlända ungdomar i den svenska gymnasieskolans introduktionsutbildning ['Here in Sweden you have to go to school to get respect.' Adolescent newcomers in the Swedish upper-secondary language introduction programme]. PhD thesis, Uppsala University.

Skutnabb-Kangas, T. and Toukomaa, P. (1976) *Teaching Migrant Children Mother Tongue and Learning the Language of the Host Country in the Context of the Socio-cultural Situation of the Migrant Family.* Tampere. Finland: Tukimuksia Research Reports.

Straszer, B., Rosén, J. and Wedin, Å. (2019) Studiehandledning på modersmål. *Educare – Vetenskapliga Skrifter* 3, 49–61. https://doi.org/10.24834/educare.2019.3.4

Suárez-Orozco, C. and Suárez-Orozco, M. (2009) Educating Latino immigrant students in the twenty-first century: Principles for the Obama Administration. *Harvard Educational Review* 79 (2), 327–340. https://doi.org/10.17763/haer.79.2.231151762p82213u

The Compulsory School Ordinance (SFS 2011: 185) See https://www.riksdagen.se/sv/dokument-lagar/dokument/svensk-forfattningssamling/skolforordning-2011185_sfs-2011-185 (accessed 3 May 2021).

The Upper Secondary School Ordinance (SFS 2010: 2039) See https://www.riksdagen.se/sv/dokument-lagar/dokument/svensk-forfattningssamling/gymnasieforordning-20102039_sfs-2010-2039 (accessed 3 May 2021).

The Ethical Review Act (2003: 460) *Om etikprövning av forskning som avser människor.* See http://rkrattsbaser.gov.se/sfst?bet=2003:460 (accessed 3 May 2021).

Thomas, W.P. and Collier, V.P. (2002) *A National Study of School Effectiveness for Language Minority Students' Long-Term Academic Achievement.* Santa Cruz: University of California. See https://escholarship.org/uc/crede_finalrpts (accessed 25 May 2021).

Thorstensson, P., Thorstensson, A-B., Jonasson, C. and Myrenberg, L. (2013) *Geografi 9* *[Geography 9]*. Stockholm: Natur & Kultur.

Thorstensson Dávila, L. (2016) The pivotal and peripheral roles of bilingual classroom assistants at a Swedish elementary school. *International Journal of Bilingual Education and Bilingualism* 0050, 1–12. https://doi.org/10.1080/13670050.2016.1224224

Uddling, J. (2013) Direktintegrerade elevers möjligheter till lärande i ämnesundervisningen [Subject learning opportunities for directly integrated pupils]. Master's thesis, Stockholm University.

van Lier, L. (2000) From input to affordance: Social-interactive learning from an ecological perspective. In J.P. Lantolf (ed.) *Sociocultural Theory and Second Language Learning* (pp. 245–259). Oxford: Oxford University Press.

Winlund, A. (2019) 'Man kan tänka men inte säga' ['You can think, but not say']. *Nordand* 14 (2), 142–157.

Yin, R.K. (2011) *Qualitative Research From Start to Finish*. New York, NY: The Guilford Press.

8 (Trans)languaging Mathematics as a Source of Meaning in Upper-Secondary School in Sweden

Åsa Wedin

Introduction

There is a growing body of research that focuses on the role of linguistic repertoires and students' use of material, linguistic and social resources in meaning-making in mathematics classrooms. However, research has seldom taken a linguistic perspective on the use of language in the negotiation of knowledge of mathematics. In this chapter, the focus is on language, or rather languaging, in a mathematics classroom for recently arrived students (RAS) in upper-secondary school in Sweden where multiple languages were used. Barwell's (2018) concept *language as a source of meaning* will be used for the analysis by distinguishing three dimensions: multiple languages, multiple discourses and multiple voices. This means that students and teachers will be understood as languaging mathematics rather than as using mathematical language, which is in line with Barwell (2018). Thus, the aim of this chapter is to investigate languaging in the negotiation of meaning in a multilingual mathematics classroom in an upper-secondary school in Sweden.

Language Introduction for RASs in Sweden

RASs who migrated to Sweden as adolescents face the challenge of having to learn a new language, Swedish, and using it to learn new content. Almost all students in Sweden who finish compulsory school, i.e. Year 9, continue to nonmandatory upper-secondary school. RASs who do not have the entry requirements to one of the mainstream programs in upper-secondary school before the age of 16 are instead admitted to the Language Introduction Program (*språkintroduktionsprogrammet*, here LIP), where they take Swedish as a Second Language and other content subjects to meet the entry requirements. The challenge of attaining the required level of Swedish is in itself demanding, and both international (Cummins, 2000; Thomas & Collier, 1997) and national research (Axelsson, 2013) show that this can take several years. In addition to learning Swedish, most students need to complete courses in other subjects in order to meet the entry requirements. Current regulations stipulate that they need to do so by the age of 19. LIP is thus a transitional program, and students try to transfer to mainstream programs as quickly as possible.

According to the Education Act (2010:800: Chapter 6), LIP courses should be planned individually for each student following careful mapping procedures. Students also have the right (Ordinance for Upper-Secondary School 2010:2039: Chapter 9 §9) to mother tongue tuition and study guidance in the mother tongue (SGMT). Students who need SGMT should be given support in a language that they master (not Swedish, however).

In a situation that is demanding for schools as well as students (there being a high number of students who need SGMT and a considerable number of languages involved), there is a need for qualified SGMT tutors as well as teachers who are proficient in some of the languages used by students. In the classroom selected for this study, the teacher, here named Khaled, had himself emigrated from Iran and had a sound command of Farsi and English, as well as Swedish. As some of his students were of Afghani origin and spoke Dari, a language that is close to Farsi, Khaled used all three languages – Swedish, English and Farsi – in class. An SGMT tutor who was present for parts of the lessons spoke Somali and some Arabic. In the two classes selected for this chapter, most students understood one or two of the languages mentioned here.

From Using Language in Mathematics to Languaging Mathematics

The main body of research on languaging in mathematics among second language (L2) students focuses on their use of mathematical language. Mathematics is a challenging subject for L2 students as it requires language development from everyday ways of talking about mathematical phenomena to a more technical register, which Halliday (1975) calls *the mathematics register*. According to Prediger *et al.* (2018: 1), 'language proficiency is the background factor with the strongest connection to mathematics achievement among all social and linguistic background factors'. Schleppegrell (2007: 139) describes challenges as including 'the multi-semiotic formations of mathematics, its dense noun phrases that participate in relational processes, the precise meanings of conjunctions and implicit logical relationships that link elements in mathematics discourse'. Developing language skills in mathematics includes learning not only new vocabulary but also new 'styles of meanings and modes of argument [...] and of combining existing elements into new combinations' (Halliday, 1978: 195–196). It is widely known that academic language is explicit and precise, and this is specifically the case when we consider the natural sciences (see, for example, Lemke, 1989, 2003; Wedin & Bomström Aho, 2019). However, Schleppegrell (2007) stresses that in mathematics, the precision lies not in language itself but in the way it is used and that mathematical knowledge is constructed through language in ways that differ from what is the case with other academic subjects.

Mathematics is often talked about as being a language in itself, and through the multisemiotic systems that mathematics draws on to construe knowledge, features such as order, position, relative size and orientation are used (Pimm, 1987). These multisemiotic and meaning-creating systems include symbols, oral language, written language, graphs and diagrams. Thus, through mathematical language, meanings may be expressed beyond what ordinary verbal language can express (Schleppegrell, 2007). The following characteristics are suggested by Halliday (1975, in Cuevas, 1984: 136) for the mathematics register:

- Natural language words reinterpreted in the context of mathematics, such as *set, point, field, column, sum, even* (number) and *random*.
- Locutions, such as *square on the hypotenuse* and *least common multiple*.
- Terms created from combinations of natural language words, such as *feedback* and *output*.
- Terms formed from combining elements of Greek and Latin vocabulary, such as *parabola, denominator, coefficient* and *asymptotic*.

According to Meaney *et al.* (2011), the register of mathematics includes styles of meaning and ways of presenting arguments that require language structures that are often borrowed from specialized forms in what they call natural language. They exemplify this with the phrase *the area under the given curve*. Lemke (2003) too stresses the importance of teaching mathematics in parallel with language while also highlighting the role of visual representation.

Two key features in the mathematics register are highlighted by Schleppegrell (2007):

- Multiple semiotic systems (mathematics symbolic notations, oral language, written language, graphs and visual displays) and
- Grammatical patterns (technical vocabulary, dense noun phrases, *being* and *having* verbs, conjunctions with technical meanings and implicit logical relationships).

The multiple characteristics of the mathematics register make the concept of translanguaging particularly relevant for the use of multiple languages in mathematics classrooms. Among common grammatical features in mathematics language, Schleppegrell (2007) mentions verbs, conjunctions and nouns. The verbs *be* and *have* (and related verbs such as *equals*, *means*) are types of vocabulary whose functions vary between languages. The verb *be* is often a function word, as is the Swedish copula verb *vara*. As such, they are not easily translated between languages. Schleppegrell describes a type of noun phrase that is common in mathematics, consisting of three components: a pre-numerative phrase, the head noun and a qualifier. The pre-numerative phrase may be an abstract, quantifiable mathematical attribute of the head noun, such as *the volume of, the difference between, the angle of*, while the noun may be, for example, a geometrical form such as *a cube* or *a rhomboid*, and the qualifier may be a qualifying phrase (*which can be divided by 3*). Examples of such noun phrases are *the volume of a cube with the sides 4 cm, the square of 5*. Schleppegrell also shows that conjunctions have specific, technical meanings in the register of mathematics, such as *if, when* and *therefore*. Other verb forms that are used in a register-specific sense include *given* and *assume*.

Schleppegrell (2007) also highlights the fact that mathematics problems express processes but become 'a thing' when represented through language. She exemplifies this with an equation, which in mathematics is expressed as a process, such as $(1 + x)^2 + x^2 = 25$, but is represented in language as a noun: The sum of the square of one plus x and the square of x is 25. Thus, the student needs to understand the relation between 'the things' of grammar and the processes of reasoning in mathematics.

For science, Gibbons (2003) describes students' linguistic development as a mode continuum, where students move from visual contextualization through everyday language to formal, scientific language. She also reveals the important role that teachers have in guiding students in this development. Furthermore, she stresses that teachers' spoken language is an important link between symbolic and visual representations in mathematics, with its multisemiotic nature, as support for students to draw on different meaning-making modes for understanding. However, Hansson (2012) has shown in her research that mathematics education in Sweden is characterized by a low level of teacher instruction, and as a result, a great deal of responsibility for their own understanding is placed onto the students themselves. According to Hansson, this is even more, so the case in classes with a high proportion of migrant students or a high rate of students from homes with low socioeconomic status, which, she claims, results in pedagogical segregation in Sweden when it comes to mathematics education.

The importance of building on and including students' prior linguistic repertoires, as well as their prior subject knowledge, has been stressed by researchers such as Thomas and Collier (1997), Cummins (2000), Gibbons (2006) and García (2009). As shown in other chapters in this volume, this includes translanguaging, which Lindahl (2015), from her studies in science classrooms that are based on sign language, describes as 'seamless shuttling' between different linguistic resources.

In research on mathematics education, Gwee and Saravanan (2018) studied code-switching between Singapore Colloquial English and Standard English among teachers in Singapore classrooms, finding that the former was used mainly for curriculum access. Dahm and de Angelis (2019) also found mother tongue literacy to have a positive impact on mathematics learning among students with multilingual backgrounds in Grade 9 in France. In a study of mathematics education in Grade 8 in Los Angeles, Abedi and Lord (2001) showed that linguistic modification had a positive impact on the performance of students in tests. They found that students who especially benefited were English language learners, students from low socioeconomic backgrounds and students at a low level and in average-level mathematics classes. For L2 students, it is important to remember that not all languages have developed mathematics terminology. In Arabic, for example, there is highly specific mathematical terminology. Thus, Arabic or concepts in Arabic are often used in the teaching of mathematics in the Middle East. However, for students who have limited education, these concepts may be unknown, and there may not be translation equivalents in their mother tongues. Thus, they may be encountering this terminology in Swedish for the first time ever.

In Sweden, Norén and Svensson Källberg (2018) argue that RASs are constructed in official policy documents as mathematics learners in need of rescue while lacking the asset that is most valued, namely the Swedish language. Mother tongues other than Swedish are, according to Norén and Svensson Källberg, seen as assets by teachers, while these students are at the same time thought of as having deficiencies and needing to improve their skills in Swedish and to progress in mathematics if they are to become desirable citizens. They found that when the mapping of students' prior knowledge is carried out with the Swedish curriculum as the norm, some of the earlier mathematical knowledge of the students is made invisible or at least not valued. As in other studies, they found a strong focus on the need to have a command of Swedish, the highest valued language.

Moschkovich (2015) argues for more complex perspectives on multilingualism and mathematics, and for viewing language as a resource, based on Ruiz's (1984) categorization of language as a problem, right or resource. Also, Planas and Setati-Phakeng (2014) draw on Ruiz in their study from Catalonia (Spain) and South Africa when analyzing monolingual norms and multilingual classroom practices. Barwell (2018), however, argues that this reasoning has its limitations. First, he finds the categorization made by Ruiz imprecise, as right and resource work together and are used in parallel. Second, he argues that language as a resource is of limited analytic value as it lacks a definition of resource. Thus, he sees a risk that the concept of language as resource may contribute to a pedagogical approach that supports existing language ideologies rather than challenging them. He also argues that language as a resource carries implicit assumptions about the nature of language as a neutral substance.

Referring to students' use of multiple material, linguistic and social resources, Barwell (2018) draws on the shift in sociolinguistics from describing languages, varieties, dialects and registers to a more complex view of language as fluid and changing, a shift that is the result of the work of researchers such as Hornberger (1989, 2003), García (2009), Blackledge and Creese (2010), Blommaert (2010) and Blommaert and Rampton (2011). Based on a view of language as socially loaded linguistic resources (Blommaert, 2005), Barwell proposes *sources of meaning* as an analytic concept. He argues for a need to consider participants' repertoires of multiple sources of meaning, organized along three dimensions: languages, discourses and voices. Thus, he argues that this 'framework involves several principles: Mathematical meaning-making is relational, language is agentive, language is diverse and involves multiple languages, multiple discourses and multiple voices, and language is stratified and stratifying' (Barwell, 2018: 166). Language is thus perceived as being in constant tension, between a centripetal force (uniformity) and an opposing tendency toward novelty and variation (a centrifugal force). In mathematics, this means that some forms of mathematical expression are seen as less desirable, such as those that are closer to everyday language, while others are seen as better, namely those that conform to what has been called the mathematics register.

Thus, classroom practices that are in focus in this chapter will be studied with a focus on the development from informal language resources about mathematics to the register of mathematics, which construes more technical and precise meanings, with attention paid to multiple discourses, multiple voices and multiple languages, which is referred to here as (trans)languaging in mathematics. In this case, for some of the students who had not studied mathematics at higher levels, this also included developing varied types of mathematical thinking.

Methodology

The data that are analyzed in this chapter was created as part of a research project on RASs in upper-secondary school in Sweden[1]. Linguistic ethnography has been used as the methodological frame (Creese, 2008; Copland & Creese, 2015; Martin-Jones & Martin, 2017). Linguistic ethnography links 'the micro to the macro, the small to the large, the varied to the routine, the individual to the social, the creative to the constraining, and the historical to the present and to the future' (Copland & Creese,

2015: 26). In this case, the use of linguistic ethnography is particularly relevant when a complex phenomenon is being analyzed such as how language is used in meaning-making in multilingual classrooms.

The data were created in two classes, A at the beginner level and B at the advanced level, consisting of 10–15 students each, taught by the same teacher. However, only four to nine students were present during the observed lessons. Due to the vulnerability of these students, ethical issues were carefully considered throughout, and the students and teacher were carefully informed about the study prior to their consent being requested. Pseudonyms are used, and presentations are such that recognition is avoided.

The data consist of fieldnotes; photographs and audio recordings; artifacts such as handouts and textbooks from eight 60-minute lessons, two of which are analyzed here and formal and informal teacher interviews. The content of the lessons may be understood as corresponding to Grade 4 and Grade 9 in Swedish compulsory school. The languages used by students were Dari, Somali, Arabic, Tigrinya, Kurdish (Kurmanji), English and Swedish. As I myself master only a few of these, the analysis is based on what may be understood from the interaction as a whole, with features such as body language, gaze, engagement and the solutions to the mathematical tasks as important.

To identify situations where (multiple) language(s) is (are) used as a source(s) of meaning, a modification of Gibbons' (2006) model of episode summary (see Figure 8.1) was used to create analytic units. The theoretical base for Gibbons' model is a combination of Sociocultural Theory and Systemic Functional Linguistics, with field (what is the topic and content), tenor (who are involved) and mode (which modalities are used). Here, tenor will include multiple discourses; interaction pattern will include multiple voices and mode will include multiple languages. Thus, the three dimensions of Barwell's language as sources of meaning – multiple languages, multiple discourses and multiple voices – were combined with Gibbons' episode summaries.

How (*Tenor*, interaction, relation) discourses			What (*Field*, representation)		
Teaching and learning processes	Dominant participant and interaction structures voices	*Mode*, degree of context–embedding languages	Knowledge constructed about the subject	Knowledge constructed about language	Knowledge constructed about being a student

Figure 8.1 Episode summary modified from Gibbons (2006: 96) including Barwell's sources of meaning

The analytic unit *episode* is defined by Gibbons as 'a bonded unit that roughly correlates with a single teaching activity' (2006: 96). Gibbons' episode builds on Lemke (1990) and is linguistically marked by 'realizations of frames and markers', such as 'well' and 'now', and its opening and closing is marked by three nonlinguistic features: (1) participant structure is likely to change, as are (2) physical seating arrangements, and (3) each episode has its own particular purpose or function. The analysis involves the kinds of meanings created within and across episodes and the intertextual relationships that exist between them. In this case, this means that the sequences of activities in the lessons, the episodes, were analyzed with a focus on languaging in the negotiation of meaning in mathematics. Thus, understanding was constructed as part of what goes on in the classroom to contextualize what 'being in the classroom was like: what sorts of things that were said and done' (Gibbons, 2006: 97). Thus, a thick description was created in the form of an analysis of the episodes in the cultural and linguistic context of the classroom by analyzing aspects of discourse, voice and language in the learning of the second language and acquisition of subject knowledge to show language patterns of negotiation of meaning. The main focus was on language, while voice was used in relation to who gets to talk and who is listened to, and discourse was here mainly used for the roles that individuals had in classroom interaction.

Different episodes are linked to each other, not only during a particular lesson but also between lessons, for example, by having related a topic. The teacher may link a certain episode to an earlier one through repetition or reference ('Do you remember X?') or to a future lesson by referring to a next step or an upcoming test. Thus, individual episodes are linked to and nested in each other.

Observations of eight lessons revealed a three-stage pattern in the organization of each lesson: (I) Opening of lesson, (II) Mathematical meaning-making and (III) Termination of lesson. For this chapter, two of the eight lessons were selected, one from Group A and one from Group B, to represent the eight lessons. The range of oral interaction varies between the groups with students in the more advanced group (Group B) working mainly on their own on exercises.

Negotiation of Meaning in Group A

In the first lesson, with Group A, the teacher (Khaled) has five students in the classroom, here called Gulan, Maxamed, Osman, Sarwar and Hani. All five had received very little schooling prior to arriving in Sweden. During the first half of the lesson, Suleymaan, who works as an SGMT tutor in Somali, is also present. The five students speak different languages (as well as Swedish): Gulan speaks Kurdish (Kormanji); Maxamed, Osman and Hani speak Somali and Sarwar speaks Dari. Suleymaan, the SGMT tutor, speaks Somali and Arabic. This means that while Hani,

Maxamed, Osman and Sarwar may receive support in both Swedish and another language (Somali and Farsi/Dari), Gulan is helped only in Swedish. Maxamed and Osman are brothers, and as Maxamed has difficulties with mathematics, his brother helps him in the lessons, also correcting his mistakes.

In the lesson, seven episodes were identified in Stage I: (1) Welcome, (2) Take out the book and (3) Organize work; in Stage II: (4) Repetition and individual work and (5) Handout and in Stage III: (6) Termination of the lesson. Stage I, including the first three episodes, Introduction, Take out the book and Organize work, covers the first 11 minutes of the lesson. The teacher starts by welcoming the students and asking them how they are. He introduces the lesson by saying that two of them, Hani and Sarwar, are to work on their own using their books, while he will go through fractions and decimal numbers with the other three, Gulan, Osman and Maxamed. He then asks all students to take out their books and makes sure that Hani and Sarwar know what they are expected to do. Hani says that she forgot her book at home, so Khaled gives her his book. Khaled shows concern for students' well-being and says to Gulan,[2] for example, 'If you are not tired and if you feel well enough, you can answer the questions'. His interest in his students' well-being is obvious in the other lessons as well, and in interviews with him, he explains that he is aware that some of them have a tough time outside school. In the third episode, Khaled divides the class by asking Gulan to move to where Maxamed and Osman are sitting, close to the whiteboard. While Gulan is moving, Hani asks Suleymaan in Somali for help, so he sits down at her desk and starts helping her.

At this first stage, the discourse is that of a traditional classroom, with interaction dominated by the teacher's directives, while the students' role is to listen and do as they are told. Khaled is the one holding the floor and students listen, as does Suleymaan, the SGMT tutor. Khaled uses mainly Swedish at this initial stage and exchanges only a few words in Dari with Sarwar but tells him in Swedish that the reason why he is to work on his own is that he has studied geometry before and that the other students are to work with fractions and decimal numbers. The focus is on why individual students should do particular activities rather than on learning mathematics. At this stage, social relations play an important role, and Khaled demonstrates his interest in ensuring that students are at ease.

At Stage II, and Episodes 4 and 5, Khaled turns his focus to the group of Gulan, Maxamed and Osman. In Episode 4, he is involved with these three students, and when Suleymaan is not helping Hani, he is also involved with this group and sometimes provides explanations to Maxamed and Osman in Somali. Khaled starts by revising the decimal system from earlier lessons about units, tens, hundreds and thousands. He takes out a sack of teaching material and empties its contents onto the desks in front of the three students. The teaching material consists of fake money and magnetic figures resembling units, tens, hundreds and thousands. He uses these artifacts, mainly the magnetic figures that he arranges on the whiteboard (pictures), to talk about the decimal system. He starts by demonstrating the use. On one occasion, he pretends to make a mistake and questions the students (nonitalics is said in Swedish).

Excerpt 8.1

Khaled:	Är det rätt?
	Is this right?
Gulan:	Ja
	Yes
Osman:	Nej, det är fel
	No, it's wrong
Khaled:	Efter tusental kommer …
	After thousand comes …
Students:	Tiotusental
	Ten thousands
Khaled:	efter tiotusental
	After ten thousands
Osman:	Miljoner
	Millions
Khaled:	Aaa innan miljoner … hundratusental eller hur? Sen som Osman säger miljon.
	Ahh before millions … hundred thousands, right? Then, as Osman says, million.
Osman:	Därför att jag gillar mycket pengar (skrattar)
	Because I like a lot of money (laughs)

Here, Khaled invites students to correct him and to perform the role of expert while he himself takes on the role of novice. He uses pause (…) to encourage students to fill in, and when they do not do so, he gives the answer himself. Khaled then hands out the fake money and says: 'A lot of money here' and laughs, 'but not real money, this helps us to understand', thus connecting to Omar's statement that he likes money. He then writes '2785' on the whiteboard and invites students to help him show this by using the material. He asks: 'How many tens? Eight or five?' He starts to arrange tens on the board and has students help him. Then, he asks:

Excerpt 8.2

Khaled:	Hur många hundratal?
	How many hundreds?
Osman:	Nästan tio
	Nearly ten
Khaled:	(points to the Figure, 7)
Osman:	Sju
	Seven

He asks the three students to show numbers individually on the desk using the fake money. While they are trying to work out the correct way to represent the numbers, he and Suleymaan help them individually. They continue to represent numbers, led by Khaled, using numbers and magnetic figures on the whiteboard, money on the desks and talk. When Maxamed has problems completing the task to represent a number in magnetic figures on the bench, Osman explains to him, mainly in Somali, and provides corrective feedback on what he has done. He asks Khaled to also explain to Maxamed, making sure that what he said to Maxamed was correct. Khaled then asks each of the students to represent a four-digit number on the whiteboard in magnetic figures.

In Figure 8.2, we can see how meaning is negotiated through interaction in collaboration between the teacher and students using digits, material and oral number-naming. The pictures visualize how the body is part of the negotiation, particularly through pointing (Picture 1) and gaze (Picture 3). Picture 2 shows how Osman (to the right) monitors the work of his brother (in black at the whiteboard) and walks up to help him represent the number correctly using the material. In Episode 4, knowledge is negotiated in terms of the relation between numbers in digits (2785), oral number names in Swedish 'tvåtusensjuhundraåttiofem' (*two thousand seven hundred and eighty-five*) and their representation mainly in magnetic figures as well as to some extent in fake money. For Maxamed and Osman, this is also expressed in Somali in their interaction with each other and with Suleymaan.

In Episode 5, Khaled hands out exercises on the decimal system to these three students. At this point, Suleymaan leaves the room. Khaled tells them to read the instructions carefully, and as they start working, Sarwan asks for help, and Khaled goes to his desk and explains to him in Farsi, reading his text in Swedish, translating and explaining. When Khaled returns from Sarwan, Gulan, who is working on exercises in the handout where she is required to write a row of numbers in order of magnitude, addresses him: 'I don't understand order of magnitude'. Khaled starts explaining to Gulan, while Osman explains in Somali to Maxamed what Khaled is saying, but soon Khaled includes the whole class in his explanations (the words in bold are said in English):

Figure 8.2 Pictures 1, 2 and 3

Excerpt 8.3

K:	Kolla på mig, jag tror han har förklarat (hänvisar till Osman) men störst, mindre, minst förklara störst, minst, vilken är minst? *Look at me, I think he has explained (referring to Osman) but biggest, smaller, smallest explain biggest, smallest, which one is smallest?*
Gulan:	Ental *Units*
K:	Vi pratar inte om ental, vi pratar om vilken är minst (vänder sig mot Maxamed) förstår du? *We are not talking about units, we're talking about which is smallest (he turns toward Maxamed): do you understand?*
Maxamed:	(nods)
K:	Storleksordning betyder den kommer först sen den sen den eller hur? (visar med kroppen) **Size small** eller **large** eller (tittar i Gulans uppgiftspapper) Gulan börja med minst … men här började vi med störst *Order of magnitude, means this is first then this, then this, doesn't it? (demonstrates with his body)* **Size small** *or* **large** *or (looks in Gulan's hand out) Gulan, start with smallest … but here we started with biggest*
Osman:	Till exempel **Large, X Large, Small** på kläder *For example,* **Large, X Large, Small** *in clothes*
K:	(laughs and starts to show on his own shirt in the neck where the marking for size is, and turns to Osman) **Large, X Large** kanske din pappa **är X Large** jag vet inte (vänder sig till Gulan) du måste skriva ett tal ett belopp **Large, X Large** *perhaps your father is* **X Large** *I don't know (turns toward Gulan) you have to write a number a sum*

In this example, Khaled talks about size order, and his comment on Gulan's suggested answer 'Units' is that they are not talking about units but about which is smallest. By way of negotiation, initiated by Osman, exemplifying with L, XL and so on, he turns to the task of selecting the greatest sum. Pictures 4, 5 and 6 in Figure 8.3 show how the body is part of the negotiation of mathematical meaning. Here, Khaled's explanation is initiated by Gulan's question from the handout with exercises, but he turns to explain the words *biggest/smaller/smallest*, while Osman turns to size in clothes, and Khaled uses his shirt to demonstrate. After his explanation to everyone in Swedish, he turns toward Sarwan and explains in Farsi, while Osman explains to his brother, Maxamed, in Somali. Students then continue to work on their exercises for another 20 minutes with Khaled walking around assisting those who ask for help and with Osman helping Maxamed while also working on his own questions.

In Episodes 4 and 5, mathematical knowledge is negotiated by the teacher, Khaled, and mainly the three students in the small group, Gulan, Maxamed and Osman, while Sarwan and Hani (to a lesser extent) are included in the last part about size order. In Episode 4, Suleymaan, the SGMT tutor, is also included in the interaction. The main topic for Gulan, Maxamad and Osman is the decimal system, which they work on through talk, digits and objects in the form of fake

Figure 8.3 Pictures 4, 5 and 6

money and magnetic figures, and order of magnitude. Negotiation involves shuttling between different modes (orality, mathematics numbers on the whiteboard, textbooks and handouts, gestures and materials including the inside collar of the teacher's shirt) and different languages (Swedish, Somali, Farsi and Dari). For students, different modes and languages are important when negotiating meaning, and collaboration is important for the meaning-making. During these episodes, Gibbons' (2006) mode continuum regarding science, where students start with visual contextualization moving through everyday language to formal scientific language, is not reconstructed. Rather, Khaled moves between written numbers, oral expressions and the material, starting and ending with the written representation, using written mathematics language, anchored in everyday language and thinking using gestures and materials. As in Gibbons' mode continuum, this includes going between varied language registers (mathematics register and everyday language) and varied ways of reasoning (mathematical reasoning and everyday thinking about mathematical matters).

Finally, at Stage III, Episode 6, when about 10 minutes of the lesson remain, Khaled ends the lesson. He addresses all five students, saying: 'Bra jobbat, mitt förslag, på kvällen fortsätt jobba, under helgen. Jag känner mig lugn, alla' (*Well done, my suggestion, continue to work in the evening, over the weekend. I feel calm, everybody.*) Just like at the beginning of the lesson, he talks about being a student and working at home and expresses confidence in the students' performance.

To sum up, at the beginning and closing stages, the teacher addresses issues of being a student, making sure that they are feeling confident and also encouraging them to study at home. At the second stage, meaning-making, which constitutes the main part of the lesson, the focus is on negotiation of meaning – in this lesson with the teacher focusing on three students and the topic of the decimal system and the student-initiated topic of size. Swedish is the main language used here, particularly at the start and end of the lesson, but for the negotiation of meaning, various linguistic resources are used – both oral and written – together with embodied expressions. Written digits are combined with written text in handouts and textbooks, and some students write comments in different languages. Swedish is combined with Somali, Farsi and Dari, which makes the fluidity of languaging visible. It is interesting to note how Osman takes on the role of mediator between the teacher and his brother, checking with the teacher that he is right. This process includes translanguaging between mainly Swedish and Somali, including the multiple semiotic systems of mathematics. In the negotiation of mathematical meaning, the teacher and students use the linguistic resources that are at hand without visible borders or restrictions. While Swedish is used more than other languages, the fluidity and 'seamlessness' (Lindahl, 2015) of their translanguaging is obvious. Thus, the analysis shows that the teacher's talk dominates, as he initiates activities, addresses students and poses questions to them, while the students answer questions and ask for clarification or explanation. Swedish predominates along with mathematical expressions, while other languages are used as sources of meaning through translanguaging.

Intensive Work in Group B

The characteristics of the selected lesson in Group B differ from the previous lesson. Group B includes students who are close to meeting the requirements of mainstream programs at upper-secondary school, and as the lesson takes place at the end of the term, the national tests are approaching, only a week way. In this lesson too, only five students are present, and these are the five who are confident they will pass the test: Kifle, who speaks Tigrinya, English and Arabic, and Mehran, Ali, Baqer and Hamid, who are all speakers of Dari. As Khaled speaks Farsi (as well as Swedish and English), he uses Farsi with the Dari-speaking students, while Suleymaan, the SGMT tutor who is present, places himself close to Kifle as they share Arabic. During the lesson, a teaching assistant, who speaks English and Swedish, is also present. It is his first day at the school, and in the first part of the lesson, he sits down at an empty desk.

As in the other lesson, this lesson involves three stages: (I) Introduction, Episode 1, (II) Meaning-making, Episodes 2 and 3 and (III) Termination, Episode 4. The first stage is only about 5 minutes long, with one episode where Khaled welcomes the students and introduces the lesson. As the national tests are approaching, the plan is that students will work on a topic that he finds important and relevant, the equation of a line. He starts the next stage, meaning-making, and Episode 2, preparation for the national test, by walking up to the whiteboard and drawing a coordinate system (Figure 8.4). He briefly repeats the rules for the relation between different equations and their graphs, focusing on the slope of the line and where it cuts the y-axis.

Thus, the topic itself includes going between different representations of the same mathematical knowledge, something that Khaled demonstrates by pointing to the equations and their corresponding lines, explaining their relations. Khaled speaks mainly Swedish, with

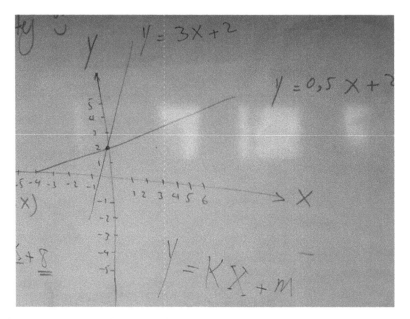

Figure 8.4 Picture 7, illustrations for the equation of a line

translations into Farsi, while Suleymaan makes sure that Kifle has understood. As Kifle's mathematical skills are good (he passed the test the week after), Suleymaan does not have to explain much and mainly makes sure that he understands Khaled's Swedish. Khaled does not ask many questions, and although students listen attentively, it is not possible to tell from the interaction whether they all understand. When Khaled says in Swedish, 'Linjen skär y-axeln' (*the line cuts the y-axis*), Baqer comments, 'Ibland på dari det betyder åsna' (*Sometimes in Dari it means donkey*). Then, Khaled laughs and comments that it is true because 'خر', which is pronounced similar to the Swedish *skär* (pronounced like *share* in English) means donkey in Dari as well as in Farsi. This short comment makes students' navigation between languages in their meaning-making visible. This episode is the short introduction and during the next episode (Episode 3), students work individually with assigned pages in their books for the most part of the lesson, more than 40 minutes. Some students find the exercises difficult, and both Khaled and Suleymaan help the students individually. Because Kifle manages to complete the exercises well, Suleymaan mainly helps the other students who are using Swedish. The teaching assistant, who is new to the position, sits close to two students and tells them in Swedish and English how to complete the exercises, but after a while, Khaled asks him to let the students think on their own. The students work through the whole lesson until 5 minutes remain, at which point Khaled ends the lesson by telling them to work on exercises at home in preparation for the test.

While this lesson includes less talk and less work with materials than the previous lesson, it follows the same pattern, with an introduction and end mainly focused on social relations and on what the students are expected to do. At Stage II, the meaning-making part, the teacher and students negotiate meaning focusing on the mathematics topic for the lesson, going between the representations. In this lesson, the teacher's instructions are shorter than in the previous lesson, and he does not involve many modalities except for drawings and writing on the whiteboard to illustrate the relation between equations and the coordinate system with relevant lines and explanations in everyday language with few questions to students. Nonetheless, several languages are involved, mainly Swedish, Farsi, Dari and Arabic, and the one student's comment on the similarities between Dari and Swedish is an example of the role of multiple languages in student engagement.

Languages as Sources of Meaning

The combination of Barwell's languages as sources of meaning with its focus on languages, discourses and voices, and Gibbons' episode summaries provided analytical tools for these lessons, to reveal patterns of discourse, voice and language. The discourse may be understood as a discourse of mathematics education. The shuttling between modes is common in mathematics classrooms, although here this includes different verbal linguistic resources. The teacher's three-stage plan for the lessons included mainly social relations in the first and last stages, where he opened and closed the lesson by making sure that students were well and urging them to study outside school, while Stage II, the meaning-making, constituted the part where the main part of the negotiation of meaning in mathematics took place. In both lessons, the teacher, the students and the SGMT tutor made use of varied resources for meaning-making, navigating between linguistic resources. Particularly in the first lesson, varied resources were at play, and the negotiation of meaning took place using oral and written language in combination with illustrations, body language and objects such as fake money and magnetic figures. Furthermore, in the other lesson, in Group B, the teacher's strategy may be characterized as anchoring mathematical knowledge, this time starting with a mathematical expression in the form of an equation related to the coordinate system drawn on the whiteboard, followed by an explanation using everyday language in combination with body language and the representations on the board, and ending with the expected answer.

That mathematical knowledge represented through various modes in Group A is relevant, as students had not yet developed advanced mathematical knowledge and were still at a basic level. The strategy used by the teacher (negotiating mathematical knowledge by starting and ending with the most typical form of representing knowledge in mathematics, written digits, explaining in between by using materials and oral talk) is common in mathematics education. This does not straightforwardly represent what Gibbons calls a mode continuum referring to science, but for mathematics, this could be explained as *anchoring* mathematics language and thinking in everyday talk and thinking through material while shuttling between languages and modalities. The anchoring may be exemplified by Khaled writing '2785', pronouncing it and supporting students to represent it using teaching material, and then finally referring back to the digits. He thus anchored the language of mathematics not only in everyday language but also in everyday ways of thinking mathematically. Another example is the student-initiated topic order of magnitude that Khaled related to clothes sizes, and his use of his own clothes and body, starting and finishing with the given mathematics task. Thus, this became a link between students' living sense and mathematical thinking. In this process, language played a central part, and Khaled and the students negotiated mathematical meaning by shuttling between diverse modalities and languages.

In Group B, where content and students' thinking were at a higher, more abstract mathematical level, Khaled and the students built on students' prior knowledge, and as a result, much more took place invisibly in their minds, and what could be observed (and recorded) was more fragmented, and consisted mainly of talk in relation to mathematical constructs, such as the coordinate system and relations between lines with varying slopes and equations. The talk was close to the task in the textbook, and the focus was on solving given problems.

In the lessons, students' prior knowledge was linked to different languages, and in the case of students who had already mastered the mathematics content, such as Kifle, their main task was to learn how these relations are expressed in Swedish. Thus, the task for the participants in both lessons may be understood as being a combination of negotiating knowledge (about the equation of a line and the decimal system) and developing Swedish mathematics language. This is an abstract process, taking place in the minds of individual students and being difficult to capture, but the case of the comparison between Dari and Swedish is one example of how the negotiation of meaning in mathematics included navigation between languages. Thus, the shuttling between different modalities commonly used to express mathematical meaning, using numbers and formula in combination with material and oral expressions in these two classrooms, also included navigation between varied linguistic resources.

Through the analysis, varied aspects of languages, discourses and voices were made visible. While the discourse in the first lesson included more visible shuttling between languages and modalities, and meaning was more openly negotiated in collaboration between the participants, in the second lesson, students worked hard and most work took place in silence and visibly through writing. With a high-stakes test approaching, it is not surprising that the students were quiet in this lesson. The teacher–student roles were mainly traditional, although there were exceptions: for example, the change in roles initiated by the teacher pretending to be ignorant and several student initiatives, such as when one student related the Swedish *skär* to dari چ, and when Osman changed roles in his mediating. One example of pragmatic language use was when Suleymaan, whose official task was to support students through Somali, found there was no Somali-speaking student present. His first choice was to support Kifle because they both knew Arabic, and when he realized that Kifle was managing on his own, his next choice was to support other students whose only language they had in common was Swedish.

Discussion

In these two lessons, translanguaging plays an important role as a source of meaning in ways where language is not fixed but is negotiated. Similar to Gibbons' mode continuum from science classrooms, this classroom also shows a shuttling between registers, modes and languages in the negotiation of meaning and anchoring mathematical knowledge and mathematical language, in written and oral form, through everyday language and in relation to students' everyday experiences and thinking.

The analysis of these two lessons shows that there is much more going on than simply the negotiation of meaning in mathematics. The patterns of translanguaging show the importance of making mathematics teachers aware of the role of (trans)languaging in mathematics education. The teacher's anchoring of knowledge through translanguaging in this case gives the impression of it taking place without deliberate planning by the teacher but rather gives a spontaneous impression. This shows the importance of considering not only the negotiation of mathematical knowledge but also aspects of (trans)languaging in mathematics teacher education and research on mathematics education. Using an explicit translanguaging pedagogy, the development of both knowledge and language may be more deliberately planned. Teachers need to be able to assess students' mathematical understanding, for which language is crucial. While students need to be given space to express process and product in mathematical knowledge, teachers need to understand the role of (trans)languaging as a source of meaning in mathematics.

Notes

(1) The project *Recently arrived students in Swedish upper-secondary school – a multidisciplinary study on language development, disciplinary literacy and social inclusion,* 2018–2021 – was financed by the Swedish Research Council, Grant No. 2017-03566.
(2) Transcripts were translated from Swedish by the author.

References

Abedi, J. and Lord, C. (2001) The language factor in mathematics tests. *Applied Measurement in Education* 14 (3), 219–234.

Axelsson, M. (2013) Flerspråkiga barn utvecklar litteracitet. In H.P. Laursen (ed.) *Literacy og sproglig diversitet.* [Literacy and Linguistic Diversity] (pp. 249–274). Århus: Aarhus Universitetsforlag.

Barwell, R. (2018) From language as a resource to sources of meaning in multilingual mathematics classrooms. *Journal of Mathematical Behavior* 50, 155–168.

Blackledge, A. and Creese, A. (2010) *Multilingualism: A Critical Perspective.* London: Continuum.

Blommaert, J. (2005) Situating language rights: English and Swahili in Tanzania revisited. *Journal of Sociolinguistics* 9 (3), 390–417.

Blommaert, J. (2010) *The Sociolinguistics of Globalization.* Cambridge: Cambridge University Press.

Blommaert, J. and Rampton, B. (2011) Language and superdiversity. *Diversities* 13 (2), 1–21.

Compulsory School Ordinance (2011) Svensk författningssamling. [Swedish Code of Statutes] 2011:185. Available at: https://www.riksdagen.se/sv/dokument-lagar/dokument/svensk-forfattningssamling/skollag-2010800_sfs-2010-800

Copland, F. and Creese, A. (2015) *Linguistic Ethnography: Collecting Analysing and Presenting Data.* Los Angeles: SAGE.

Creese, A. (2008) Linguistic ethnography. In K. King and N. Hornberger (eds) *Encyclopedia of Language and Education* (2nd edn) (pp. 229–241). New York: Springer.

Cuevas, G.J. (1984) Mathematics learning in English as a second language. *Journal for Research in Mathematics Education* 15 (2), 134–144.

Cummins, J. (2000) *Language, Power and Pedagogy: Bilingual Children in the Crossfire.* Clevedon: Multilingual Matters.

Dahm, R. and De Angelis, G. (2019) The role of mother tongue literacy in language learning and mathematical learning: Is there a multilingual benefit for both? *International Journal of Multilingualism* 15 (2), 194–213.

Education Act (2010) 2010:800. Stockholm: Skolverket.

Eikset, A. and Meaney, T. (2018) When does a difference make a difference? Teaching about language diversity in mathematics teacher education. *Nordic Studies in Mathematics Education* 23 (3–4), 225–246.

García, O. (2009) *Bilingual Education in the 21st Century: A Global Perspective.* Oxford: Wiley-Blackwell.

Gibbons, P. (2003) Mediating language learning: Teacher interactions with ESL students in a content-based classroom. *TESOL Quarterly* 37 (2), 247–73.

Gibbons, P. (2006) *Bridging Discourses in the ESL Classroom: Students, Teachers and Researchers.* London: Continuum.

Gweea, S. and Saravanan, V. (2018) Use of code-switching in multilingual content subject and language classrooms. *International Journal of Multilingualism* 15 (2), 117–134.

Halliday, M.A.K. (1975) Some aspects of sociolinguistics. In E. Jacobsen (ed.) *Interactions Between Linguistics and Mathematical Education: Final Report of the Symposium Sponsored UNESCO, CEDO and ICMI, Nairobi, Kenya, September 1–11, 1974* (UNESCO ED-74/CONF.808, pp. 64–73). Paris: UNESCO.

Halliday, M.A.K. (1978) *Language as Social Semiotic*. London: Edward Arnold.

Hansson, Å. (2012) The meaning of mathematics instruction in multilingual classrooms: analyzing the importance of responsibility for learning. *Educational Studies in Mathematics* 81, 103–125.

Hornberger, N.H. (1989) Continua of biliteracy. *Review of Educational Research* 59 (3), 271–296.

Hornberger, N.H. (ed.) (2003) *Continua of Biliteracy: An Ecological Framework for Educational Policy, Research, and Practice in Multilingual Settings*. Clevedon: Multilingual Matters.

Lemke, J.L. (1989) Making text talk. *Theory into Practice* 28 (2), 136–141. https://www.jstor.org/stable/1477000

Lemke, J.L. (1990) *Talking Science: Language, Learning, and Values*. Norwood: NJ: Ablex.

Lemke, J.L. (2003) Mathematics in the middle: Measure, picture, gesture, sign, and word. In M. Anderson, A. Sáenz-Ludlow, S. Zellweger and V.V. Cifarelli (eds) *Educational Perspectives on Mathematics as Semiosis: From Thinking to Interpreting to Knowing* (pp. 215–234). Brooklyn, NY, and Ottawa, Ontario: Legas.

Lindahl, C. (2015) *Tecken av betydelse: En studie av dialog i ett multimodalt, teckenspråkigt tvåspråkigt NO-klassrum*. [Signs with Meaning: A Study of Dialogue in a Multimodal Sign Language natural Sciences Classroom.] PhD Thesis, Stockholm: Stockholms universitet.

Martin-Jones, M. and Martin, D. (2017) *Researching Multilingualism: Critical and Ethnographic Perspectives*. London: Routledge.

Meaney, T., Trinick, T. and Fairhall, U. (2011) Teaching Mathematics in a Second Language. Charles Sturt University, University of Auckland, Te Kura o Te Koutu Conference paper.

Moschkovich, J.N. (2015) Academic literacy in mathematics for English learners. *The Journal of Mathematical Behavior* 40, 43–62.

Norén, E. and Svensson Källberg, P. (2018) Fabrication of newly-arrived students as mathematical learners. *Nordic Studies in Mathematics Education* 23 (3–4), 15–37.

Petersson, J. and Norén, E. (2017) To halve a fraction: An issue for second language learners. *Education Inquiry* 8 (3), 173–191.

Pimm, D. (1987) *Speaking Mathematically: Communication in Mathematics Classrooms*. London: Routledge & Kegan Paul.

Planas, N. and Setati-Phakeng, M. (2014) On the process of gaining language as a resource in mathematics education. *ZDM The International Journal of Mathematics Education* 46 (6), 883–893.

Prediger, S., Wilhelm, N., Büchter, A., Gürsoy, E. and Benholz, C. (2018) Language proficiency and mathematics achievement: Empirical study of language-induced obstacles in a high stakes test, the central exam ZP10. *Journal für Mathematik-Didaktik* 39 (3). doi: 10.1007/s13138-018-0126-3

Ordinance for Upper-Secondary School (2010) 2010:2039. Available at https://www.riksdagen.se/sv/dokument-lagar/dokument/svensk-forfattningssamling/gymnasieforordning-20102039_sfs-2010-2039

Ruiz, R. (1984) Orientations in language planning. *NABE Journal* 8 (2), 15–34.

Schleppegrell, M.J. (2007) The linguistic challenges of mathematics teaching and learning: A research review. *Reading & Writing Quarterly* 23, 139–159.

Svensson, P., Meaney, T. and Norén, E. (2014) Immigrant students' perceptions of their possibilities to learn mathematics: The case of homework. *For the Learning of Mathematics* 34 (3), 32–37.

The School Inspectorate (2014) *Utbildningen för nyanlända elever.* [The Education for Recently Arrived Students] Rapport 2014:03. Stockholm: Skolinspektionen.

The School Inspectorate (2017) Skolhuvudmäns mottagande av nyanlända elever i grundskolan. [Reception among school authorities of recently arrived students in primary school]. Stockholm: Skolinspektionen.

Thomas, W.P. and Collier, V.P. (1997) *School Effectiveness for Language Minority Students.* Washington: National Clearinghouse for Bilingual Education.

Wedin, Å. and Bomström Aho, E. (2019) Agency in science learning in a second language setting: Multimodal and multilingual strategies and practices among recently arrived students in upper-secondary school in Sweden. *International Electronic Journal of Elementary Education* 12 (1), 67–74. DOI: 10.26822/iejee.2019553339

9 Language 'Barriers' or Barriers to Translanguaging? Language as a 'Problem' in the New Latinx Diaspora

Jessica Sierk

Introduction

English language acquisition is an assimilative task of education which is related specifically to immigrant students in US schools. Language is often used as a symbol of how well an immigrant group has assimilated. According to Valdés (2001), difficulties in learning English are sometimes misinterpreted as a lack of commitment to becoming American. English-only policies and xenophobic attitudes can have many deleterious effects on immigrant youth:

> These messages reach the ears of [immigrant] youths, who then swallow and internalize these policies, inevitably feeling as though they do not belong in the United States. The language policy frames bilingualism as a liability, a socioeconomic noose promising to strangle youth. (Bejarano, 2005: 34)

Both difficulties in language learning and attempts to maintain one's first language (L1)[1] may be seen as acts of resistance to assimilation. Rosaldo (1993: 198) explains the inverse relationship between attaining full citizenship and maintaining one's culture, stating 'full citizenship and cultural visibility appear to be inversely related. When one increases, the other decreases. Full citizens lack culture, and those most culturally endowed lack full citizenship'. Since language is a component of culture, full citizenship and linguistic visibility also tend to be inversely related. While 'Latino' is considered an ethnicity in the United States, as opposed to a race, Latinos continue to be racialized through immigration policies that detain and profile Latino citizens and non-citizens alike due to their 'Brown' skin tone and other phenotypical characteristics. Thus, it is in newcomers' 'best interest' to learn English at the expense of their L1, lest they be seen as un-American in a political climate that features the mass deportation/detention of Brown bodies, especially when those bodies are accompanied by the linguistic markers of multilingualism.

Given this context, it is of the utmost importance to understand how schools, who are often tasked with enforcing the aforementioned assimilation, perpetuate and contribute to the construction of language ideologies. Ruiz (1984) discusses three orientations to language planning: language-as-problem, language-as-right and language-as-resource. These orientations 'constitute the framework in which attitudes are formed; they help to delimit the range of acceptable attitudes toward language, and to make certain attitudes legitimate' (Ruiz, 1984: 16). Language planning is not a neutral domain of inquiry; as such, these orientations are important to consider when examining how linguistic assimilation coincides with schooling. This chapter uses Ruiz's (1984) language orientations to examine how two New Latinx Diaspora (NLD) high schools (Springvale and Stockbridge – both pseudonyms) in the Midwestern United States reacted to their communities' changing demographics.

Generally, when one hears the term *policy*, legislators, administrators or government officials come to mind. However, Menken and García (2010: 1) contest, 'it is ultimately educators – particularly classroom teachers – who are the final arbiters of language policy implementation'. Thus, observing enacted language ideologies in schools and classrooms offers one way of seeing how policies are being implemented at the local level. This chapter examines linguistic ideologies through the lenses of the lived experiences of students and school personnel from Springvale and Stockbridge.

Language-as-Problem

The language-as-problem orientation is at the heart of the debate about whether or not to include multilingualism as a goal of schooling. One of the most common arguments against bilingual education programs is that 'multilingualism leads ultimately to a lack of social cohesiveness' (Ruiz, 1984: 21). Within the language-as-problem orientation, monolingualism is the norm and language learning is subtractive. Therefore, when language-as-problem is the dominant orientation toward language planning, bilingual programming will likely take on a transitional approach; in the case of the US, favoring English. Transitional bilingual and one-way immersion programs – which frequently border on submersion or sink-or-swim approaches – see students' L1s as useful only in helping them gain access to English language instruction. 'The use of the native language in the classroom is phased out [...due to] the belief that students should not be too reliant on their native language throughout formal schooling or they will not become fully proficient in English' (Kim *et al.*, 2015: 238).

While schools tend to conceptualize newcomers as monolingual, Brisk (2006: 4) asserts, 'most recent arrivals indeed are in the very early states of bilingualism'. Similarly, Agnihotri (2014: 365) discusses multilinguality, pushing back against the multiple monolingual view of multilingualism and resisting the notion that 'there is always a dominant language of the community and that there is a target language toward which children must progress'. This kind of dichotomous thinking surrounding language learning promotes the view that you either are or are not bilingual, presenting the concept as either/or. As a result, language is often seen as a problem to be solved rather than a resource to be leveraged.

Language-as-Resource

Language-as-resource views language as a skill and an asset. The logic goes that the more languages you know, the better you are able to communicate and with more people. When language is conceptualized this way, minoritized language communities are seen as important sources of expertise. Ideally, when language is viewed as a resource, plurilingualism is the norm, and language learning is additive. One example of how this may play out in practice is through the utilization of translanguaging:

> Translanguaging tries to draw on all the linguistic resources of the child to maximise understanding and achievement. Thus, both languages are used in a dynamic and functionally integrated manner to organise and mediate mental processes in understanding, speaking, literacy, and, not least, learning. (Lewis *et al.*, 2012: 655)

Thus, translanguaging uses a student's entire linguistic repertoire toward the desired end of academic success. Rather than seeing a student's L1 as a problem to overcome, translanguaging uses students' L1s as resources they can draw on to make sense of new material.

However, the language-as-resource orientation is often enacted in a way that is more consistent with language-as-commodity, which 'perpetuate[s] a view of language as instrument – as opposed to language as identity marker – and, by doing so, seeks to garner support for the teaching and learning of heritage languages by de-linking language from ethnicity or race' (Ricento, 2005: 357). This is evident in the contrast between how language learning is conceived for English learners (ELs) versus how it is envisioned in 'foreign' language departments.[2] In terms of the former, linguistic assimilation usually calls on a language-as-problem orientation. In the latter, language-as-commodity reigns supreme, often focusing on the 'most acceptable' variety of a language (e.g. Castilian Spanish). Leeman (2005) calls this 'linguistic subordination', whereby the variety of language a native speaker uses is seen as lesser than the 'standard' variety of that same language. While not all US states require foreign language for high school graduation, most students who plan to continue on to a four-year college or university take at least two years of foreign language in high school per college entrance requirements. As such, the foundation for resource pedagogies is there, but only for a portion of the students and only for certain languages and language varieties.

Language-as-Right

Language-as-right promotes language as a basic human right. When one is not included in the linguistic realm, one cannot fully participate in society, acquire new skills or better their lot in life. Students' linguistic rights have continually been a matter of debate in the United States, and this is exemplified in language policy. For example, the plantiffs in the 1974 *Lau v. Nichols* case asserted that the San Francisco school district was excluding their children from participation due to limited English proficiency. The US Supreme Court ruled that the school district was in fact violating students' rights under Title VI of the Civil Rights Act of 1964, which guarantees that no person can be excluded on the basis of race, color or national origin. As a result of this case, all US public schools are required to identify and make academic accommodations for identified ELs. This decision drew on the precedent of *Brown v. Board of Education*, the landmark decision that ruled that racial segregation of children in schools is unconstitutional. *Lau* invoked the 14th Amendment's constitutional promise of 'equal protection under the law' and extended the ruling in *Brown* to include those whose skills in English were not yet sufficient for them to succeed in an unsupported mainstream classroom (Hamann & Reeves, 2013). However, in general, this decision has meant that students have a right to acquire English, not necessarily a right to maintain their L1.

In 1965, US Congress passed the Elementary and Secondary Education Act (ESEA). This act funds elementary and secondary education while emphasizing high standards and accountability. Since it was signed into law, the ESEA has been amended several times. In 1968, an amendment to ESEA, the Bilingual Education Act (also known as Title VII), was added. This presented bilingual education as a viable instructional model; however, it did not make bilingual education mandatory. More recently, in 2001, ESEA was reauthorized; this reauthorization was referred to as No Child Left Behind (NCLB). Under NCLB, concerns about bilingual education were classified under Title III of the Act, which deals directly with how to ensure that ELs attain the English language and meet state standards. This reauthorization created a system of accountability that includes measurement of students' English language proficiency. As part of NCLB, the Bilingual Education Act was renamed the English Language

Acquisition, Language Enhancement and Academic Achievement Act. This signaled a commitment to English over students' L1s at the federal level. In the recent past, some states have gone so far as to pass propositions abolishing more progressive forms of bilingual education (e.g. the 1998 Proposition 227 in California, which significantly shortened the length of time that ELs could spend in classes aimed at language proficiency and required that those classes be taught nearly all in English). However, the fight for students' linguistic rights has continued in these states with some success (e.g. the 2016 Proposition 58 in California, which repealed Proposition 227 and authorized schools to once again establish bilingual programs, such as dual-language immersion).

It is important to note that under the International Covenant on Civil and Political Rights, a multilateral treaty adopted by the United Nations of which the United States is a member, linguistic minorities are free to use their own language in community with the other members of their group, according to Article 27. As such, it is reasonable to assume that this right extends into the educational realm, thereby protecting language as a right.

Methods

This chapter, which examines how two Midwestern NLD high schools reacted to their communities' changing demographics, is part of a larger study (Sierk, 2016). This qualitative research used ethnographic methods to answer the following questions:

- How do students view themselves, their home communities and their aspirations as they transition from high school to their postsecondary plans?
- How does being *of* a particular NLD community influence students' identities and worldviews?
- How are race and whiteness understood in these two NLD high schools?
- How do race and whiteness manifest themselves in the context of these two particular NLD high schools?
- How do school personnel and students conceptualize the growing linguistic diversity of their school and community?

Researcher's positionality

I identify as a White, native English-speaking female who was raised in a lower-middle class family by a single mother. I was born in the United States, automatically making me a US citizen. I have studied Spanish as my second language since 2002 and am currently auditing intermediate Spanish at the higher education institution at which I work.

My interest in schooling dynamics within the NLD is personal; I grew up in a community that transitioned from being a majority-White community to one that is majority-Latinx while I was living and attending school there. When I began attending kindergarten in 1992, there were only a few Latino families living in my hometown. By the time I graduated high school in 2005, my school district was around 50% Latinx, becoming majority-Latinx the following year. Many communities experiencing demographic shifts experience forms of White flight or White avoidance. Clotfelter (2004: 66–67) defines White flight as 'the movement of Whites to rural or suburban areas and to private schools'. White avoidance, on the other hand, is shown by 'changes in interracial contact in schools followed by abnormally large declines in white enrollment' due to 'whites [preferring] to avoid racially mixed schools' (Clotfelter, 2004: 91).

For some White families, staying is an economic necessity. My mother, however, chose to stay because she saw value in her daughter being raised and attending school in a diverse environment. As Spradley (1980: 57) suggests, 'Doing ethnographic fieldwork involves alternating between the insider and outsider experience, and having both simultaneously'. Therefore, while I have my own experiences with this topic, it was important for me to remain as objective as possible, to allow my participants' stories to come through unadulterated by my 'insider' knowledge.

Site selection

The two communities in which this research took place were purposefully selected due to their location in two NLD communities in the state of Nebraska. Both communities have experienced significant demographic change in the past 10–20 years. Compared to the approximately 11% of the Nebraska population that identifies as Hispanic (US Census Bureau, 2018), these two school districts are significantly more Hispanic[3] than the state of Nebraska writ large.

While neither of these two communities is located within an urbanized area – a Census classification for a place with more than 50,000 people – they do have sizeable differences in population. The larger of the two, Stockbridge, is designated as an urban cluster (i.e. a place with a population between 2500 and 50,000). The smaller of the two, Springvale, is a rural community – a Census designation for a place with fewer than 2500 people. To put it concisely, Springvale's population is about a tenth of the size of Stockbridge.

These two communities also differ in their racial and ethnic makeup. Stockbridge has a school enrollment that is about two-thirds of Hispanic and a quarter of White, with a modest and growing – approximately 5% during the 2014–2015 academic year – Black population that includes more African refugees from Somalia and Sudan than African Americans.

However, Springvale has a school enrollment that is almost half of Hispanic and very little other racial diversity.

Another contextual difference between the communities has to do with ELs. In Stockbridge, the percentage of students identified as ELs has been steadily decreasing in the past five years. In contrast, between 2010 and 2014, Springvale's EL population remained relatively steady; however, during the 2014–2015 school year, the school saw a spike in the number of EL-identified students, as this population more than doubled.

Prior to the present study, I had already conducted research in both communities. I began my role as a researcher in Stockbridge in 2008 as an undergraduate student conducting thesis research. In 2013, my role as a researcher continued in Stockbridge and simultaneously began in Springvale when I was contacted by the Nebraska Department of Education to conduct research on the 10 most proportionally Latinx high schools in the state. My previous experiences at both schools afforded me access to gatekeepers, through whom I began the recruitment process.

Participants and recruitment

During the fall of 2014, I began the entry process for this research, including submitting a research proposal through the University's Institutional Review Board (IRB). After acquiring school district permission from both Stockbridge and Springvale, I was granted IRB approval and began the recruitment process. Since this research was specifically targeted at students in the 12th grade, I recruited student participants in classes that were required for all 12th graders to take (American government and economics).

Fourteen students (aged 17–19 at the beginning of the study) from Springvale and seven students from Stockbridge volunteered to participate (see Table 9.1). The racial and ethnic identities of these participants roughly mirror that of the school population.

Throughout the semester, I also recruited school personnel (e.g. teachers, guidance counselors and administrators) who regularly interacted with my student participants by having one-on-one conversations with them at a mutually convenient time (e.g. before/after school or during their plan period). Thirty-one school personnel including 24 teachers (9 from Springvale and 15 from Stockbridge), 5 guidance counselors (1 from Springvale and 4 from Stockbridge) and 2 administrators (1 from each school) agreed to participate. All of the school personnel self-identified as racially/ethnically White, which is fairly representative of all school personnel at the two schools (i.e. 100% White at Springvale, 93% White at Stockbridge). Three school personnel (all from Stockbridge) indicated that they were second-language Spanish speakers.

Student participants under the age of 19 were required to have a parent/guardian sign their informed consent form, and they were also

Table 9.1 Student participants

Pseudonym	School	Race/ethnicity self-identification	Languages spoken (in the order the participant listed them)
Alexis	Springvale	White	English
Cassandra	Springvale	White	English
Cecilia	Springvale	Mexican	English, Spanish
Chloe	Springvale	White	English
Eddie	Springvale	Hispanic	Spanish, English, Q'anjob'al
Elizabeth	Springvale	Caucasian	English
Grace	Springvale	Caucasian	English
Javier	Springvale	Hispanic	Spanish, English
Michael	Springvale	White	English
Olivia	Springvale	Guatemalan	Spanish, English
Sergio	Springvale	Mexican	English, some Spanish
Tiffany	Springvale	Caucasian	English, some Spanish
Tomas	Springvale	Guatemalan	Spanish, English
Will	Springvale	White	English
Brad	Stockbridge	White	English
Daniel	Stockbridge	Asian	Vietnamese, English
Gerardo	Stockbridge	Mexican	Spanish, English
Isabel	Stockbridge	Mexican	Spanish, English
Jenny	Stockbridge	White Hispanic	Spanish, English
Joseph	Stockbridge	Hispanic	Spanish, English
Luis	Stockbridge	American of Mexican descent	English, Spanish

required to sign a student assent form. School personnel and student participants who were 19 or older were given an informed consent form to sign. All participants were given pseudonyms to protect their anonymity.

Data collection and analysis

I conducted participant observations (Spradley, 1980) for 27 non-consecutive days during spring 2015 (14 at Springvale and 13 at Stockbridge), for a total of approximately 102 hours of observation. I observed on various days of the week and in different settings (e.g. Stockbridge's 'grand march' before prom, assemblies, school hallways, homeroom periods and classrooms), as well as in 40 different classes (23 at Springvale and 17 at Stockbridge), representing a variety of subject areas, both core and elective. I also conducted ethnographic interviews (Spradley, 1979) with all 52 participants (21 students and 31 school personnel) during April and May 2015. I designed interview questions to be open-ended, and interviews were semistructured. I did follow-up interviews with 13 student participants (10 from Springvale and 3 from Stockbridge) on a voluntary basis in October and November 2015.

To analyze the data, I used a qualitative content analysis approach, as well as following Fasching-Varner's twofold approach to analyzing data about whiteness. According to Williamson *et al.* (2018: 464), 'Qualitative content analysis is an approach that focuses on interpreting and describing, meaningfully, the topics and themes that are evident in the contents of communications when framed against the research objectives of the study'. To do so, I first constructed a detailed description of each individual participant drawing from multiple data sources (i.e. observations, interviews and collected artifacts). Once codes were developed individually, cross-case comparisons were made. Fasching-Varner asserts, 'An individual's manifestation of something is important, but seeing how the manifestations remain across participants within a study is significant' (2014: 164). Codes from the analysis of individual participants' datasets were validated through the interconnectivity of participants' narratives when patterns of behavior emerged during the cross-case comparison phase of data analysis. The juxtaposition of the micro (i.e. individual cases) and macro (i.e. cross-case comparisons) allowed me to see the interconnectivity of my participants' narratives.

Findings

While analyzing the data according to Ruiz's (1984) three language orientations – language-as-problem, language-as-resource and language-as-right – and Ricento's (2005) addition of language-as-commodity, there was a glaring lack of examples of language-as-resource and language-as-right. In these two schools, language was seen as a problem for newcomer ELs and as a commodity for White monolingual English speakers. In the next two sections, I outline how these two views of language were demonstrated in the schooling environment.

Language-as-problem: 'That's going to be something to deal with'

White school personnel and students framed newcomers' linguistic identities according to the language 'barrier', they presented in the English-only school environment. In describing Stockbridge, a guidance counselor GC1 said:

Excerpt 9.1

It's a community that I think has constantly worked to knock down barriers between cultures, between languages, so that we can obviously live together and cohabitate the same area and same school district and same businesses. (GC1, 15 May 2015)

The word 'constantly' suggests that this barrier is something that is not easily eradicated. Thus, language and the barriers that it presents are seen as a persistent burr with which the community has to contend. Despite the negative connotation of a barrier, however, this striving is presented as having a positive outcome that both groups can coexist in the same spaces. The barrier evoked in this description of the community takes on an almost tangible feeling with his use of the phrase 'knock down'. One can imagine a wall or fence separating the two groups.

When asked what people who are coming to Springvale for the first time should know, Michael, a White student, warned:

Excerpt 9.2

Be ready for a language barrier at certain points. (Michael, 27 April 2015)

Similarly, Teacher 1 (T1) at Springvale reacted to the school's new Guatemalan students, saying:

Excerpt 9.3

It's a whole different group of people. It's a whole different language barrier to deal with. And then trying to understand a whole different culture. Here everybody just assumes, well they're the same, and they're not. And so that's going to be something to deal with, too.... When you have another cultural group of people come in whose language is different, dialect is different, and you're already trying to handle and help this group and now you've got another group. (T1, 14 May 2015)

As previously mentioned, the EL population at Springvale had more than doubled the year prior to this study. In Excerpt 9.3, T1 contrasts the extant Latinx population (mostly Mexican) with the new Latinx population (mostly Guatemalan). He references the assumption that these two groups of students are the same and refutes this by emphasizing the difference in culture, language and dialect. On top of the already deficit-oriented use of the word 'barrier', also 'deal with' and 'handle' are used. The phrase 'deal with' evokes having to cope with a difficult situation, likewise, the word 'handle' is mostly used in situations that are problematic and require management. Thus, the use of this type of language in conjunction with the metaphor of a language barrier invokes a language-as-problem ideology.

Students (both White and Hispanic) referenced that the United States is an 'English-speaking country' and that the school (Springvale, specifically) was an 'English-speaking school', policing their peers' language use within this monolingual expectation:

Excerpt 9.4

I think they should be able to communicate with us... with Hispanics. I think it's a good thing that they're coming here because they get the education that [Eddie] got and now he knows how to speak English. So that'll really help them throughout the future. If you can't really speak English in an English-speaking country, then it's not really good. (Javier, 5 May 2015)

Rather than acknowledging the rich linguistic diversity and lack of an official language of the United States, Javier reduces it to a monolingual country, one where English is the only language that matters. Education is equated with knowing how to speak English, not with being multilingual and able to translanguage; this is evident as Javier brings up Eddie as an example. Prior to learning English, Eddie was already bilingual, speaking Spanish and Q'anjob'al. However, English, not multilingualism, is seen as a tool for future success. Furthermore, *not* speaking English is seen as detrimental, whereas the same is not said for not speaking Spanish. In Javier's statement, the internalized dominance of English experienced by bilingual students educated in Springvale since kindergarten, such as Javier, becomes evident. Chloe also referenced Eddie as an example of the power of learning English:

Excerpt 9.5

[Eddie] came here and he wanted to conform, he wanted to learn English, he wanted to get into sports. And they're just like no, you have to learn our language. And we're just like this is America. Yeah, there's different languages, but learn English, we're an English-speaking school. (Chloe, 12 October 2015)

In Chloe's statement, English correlates with assimilation. She contrasts Eddie's willingness to assimilate with the newer Guatemalan students ('they') continuing to speak their L1s. Her statement also uses the pronouns *our* and *we* showing ownership of languages.

Similarly, school personnel framed speaking Spanish as the 'downfall' of the community and something that made communication 'difficult'. The 'language barrier' associated with the newcomer students was cited as a reason for minimal interaction between ESL and non-ESL students:

Excerpt 9.6

I feel like then they're still in that habit of their dialect, their own language. They need to learn some [English], especially if they're going to be here, just for their own benefit… About three-fourths of our population doesn't speak English, so that's going to be the downfall. (T2, 6 May 2015)

While T2 (Springvale) frames learning English as beneficial, the onus for making communication easier falls completely on those who speak Spanish. Little to no responsibility is taken by their monolingual, English-speaking counterparts, making it the Spanish speakers' responsibility to assimilate to the English norm of the community rather than that of the

English speakers to adapt to the changing linguistic landscape of the town and nation.

The emphasis of a language 'barrier' further solidified the boundaries between 'mainstream' and ESL students. According to T3 (Stockbridge), one outcome of this type of English-only mindset is language loss:

Excerpt 9.7

Kids speaking Spanish in class is rare. When I first came, you heard groups speaking Spanish in the hallways more. Now I would say it's more rare [sic], or it's a lot more like Spanglish where they go in and out. So I've found that interesting over the years, how in 13 years it's seemed to have really changed, which in some ways is sad because I feel like they're losing some of their cultural identity. (T3, 15 May 2015)

While language loss is often a real consequence of transitional bilingual programs, the use of Spanglish is also indicative of a cultural shift. It is probable that students in assimilative schooling contexts do lose some of their cultural identities, as indicated in Excerpt 9.7; however, if we view culture as more of a verb than a noun, as something students *do* instead of something they *have*, then it is more accurate to say that their cultural identities are shifting, as are their linguistic identities and repertoires.

Furthermore, what T3 refers to as Spanglish or 'where they go in and out' could otherwise be described as translanguaging. This is different than code-switching, which would entail students seeing the classroom as an English-only space and the hallways or cafeteria as a space where it is appropriate for them to speak Spanish. Rather, the fluidity with which they are utilizing both languages shows their ability to conceptualize communication as a sum of their linguistic abilities instead of an either/or dichotomy. However, the way in which T3 discusses this phenomenon renders Spanglish, or translanguaging, as inferior to speaking 'pure' Spanish or 'pure' English, describing it as something that is sad instead of an asset.

In contrast to Stockbridge, Springvale is at an earlier stage of demographic change; thus, school personnel and students relate to language loss differently:

Excerpt 9.8

We have a generation who just speaks Spanish still so for them to relate to us that just speak English is hard. That's changing as these kids grow up and they speak English... just like it would've been when our ancestors came and they spoke German or Swedish or whatever. I think it's a pretty accepting town for diversity though. I think some people struggle with it, which I would guess again happened when our ancestors came and they started to mix and people weren't sure if they wanted to mix or didn't want to mix. I see it as the same thing. (T4, 11 May 2015)

Implicit in T4's (Springvale) statement in Excerpt 9.8 is that immigration and language maintenance are mutually exclusive. Since there are not many examples of prior immigrant communities retaining their language – or learning to translanguage – in a robust, nationwide way, the assumption is that it cannot happen. Language loss, then, becomes an almost retaliatory, ritualistic initiation for modern-day immigrants. In the same way that German and other immigrant populations gave up parts of their cultures for the privileges of whiteness, so too do Hispanic newcomers when they hide their Hispanic-ness and insist that their Hispanic peers do the same.

Another outcome of the English-only expectations is that teachers become 'language-blind', akin to color blindness. This was at play when T5 at Stockbridge, relayed the following story:

Excerpt 9.9

Somebody asked me, 'How many of your students are Hispanic?' I was like, 'I don't know. I'll go tomorrow and I'll let you know'. I came to school and I remember looking around thinking, 'I don't have one Caucasian kid in here'. But I didn't notice that. Kids like [Isabel], she's just [Isabel]. It wasn't until one day when she started speaking Spanish, and I was like '[Isabel]! What?' I guess I don't see it as much. I see it if they speak Spanish or if they've got a thick accent like a lot of the Somalian kids do. I don't see it like a lot of people do. (T5, 1 May 2015)

Similar to how T5's statement in Excerpt 9.9 illustrated colorblindness, as she feigned ignorance that her entire class was Hispanic before having her attention explicitly drawn to the demographics of her students, she was also language-blind, acting surprised when Isabel, a bilingual Latina, started speaking Spanish.

When the norm of the school is English-only, one might expect teachers to be surprised to hear other languages in their classrooms. However, the school is a social micro-context within a multilingual macro-context. Expecting students to only use a portion of their skillset is putting them at a disadvantage. Imagine this applied to anything else: Please come to math class and do these division problems, but whatever you do, do *not* use your multiplication skills. Just as mathematics builds upon itself, so too does language. If teachers act in this way, students miss out on pedagogical translanguaging, which may facilitate their academic success.

Language-as-commodity: 'I stayed average in it, like low A'

Tiffany and Brad, White students at Springvale and Stockbridge, respectively, both took Spanish all four years of high school but had different motivations for doing so and different views of their own emergent bilingualism after graduating. Brad took a fourth year of Spanish in high school because it was a weighted class, and he was trying to be valedictorian. In our follow-up interview, he told me that he did not remember any Spanish even though it had only been six months since he was in the class (24 November 2015).

Stockbridge, like Springvale, did not offer any Spanish for Native Speakers classes, although they had in the past. However, unlike Springvale, Stockbridge's higher-level Spanish classes were taken mostly by Hispanic students. Therefore, Brad was one of the six White students in his 24-person Spanish IV class. Judging from class presentations, most, but not all, of the Hispanic students in the class had native-like fluency in Spanish (field notes, 11 March 2015). While observing, I noted that the six White students were clustered together at the back of the room. According to T6, the White Spanish teacher, the students self-selected their seats. However, she assured me that the White students did interact with their Hispanic peers in the class. In my observations, this interaction was limited.

In terms of school personnel, Stockbridge was dissimilar to Springvale in that some of the staff at Stockbridge High were bilingual to varying degrees and varying confidence levels as shown in Excerpts 9.10 and 9.11:

Excerpt 9.10

It's where my Spanish really developed the most. That's where I got over the hump of the speaking part because we talked to so many parents. (T6, 4 May 2015)

Excerpt 9.11

I can still understand what people are saying, but it takes me a little longer to spit it back out. If I have a parent here with an intense situation, then I will bring somebody else in just to make sure I'm not missing something. Sometimes I get nervous, too, because we do have some Guatemalan students here and their parents' dialect is a little different. So I struggle with that because it does have a little bit of the native Indian, Inca Maya, with it. (GC2, 1 May 2015)

Since her time as a Spanish teacher, GC2 had lost some of her proficiency in speaking and listening comprehension. Since leaving the classroom, she had less opportunity to practice these skills. Furthermore, while GC2 acknowledges in Excerpt 9.11 that there are different dialects of Spanish present in the community, she then reduces Spanish to a monolithic entity. In general, while school personnel did acknowledge the presence of Latinx indigeneity, it is evident that this knowledge is only surface level.

Similarly, Brad, having not developed close relationships with any of his Spanish-speaking classmates from Stockbridge and attending a university with a smaller Hispanic population, reports losing most of the Spanish fluency he had gained in his four years of taking Spanish. Similar to Springvale, Spanish language classes were seen as a commodity to

White students like Brad in Stockbridge. However, the ability to speak Spanish fluently was not the commodified entity; rather, the class's weighted status made it an appealing course to take to boost one's grade point average.

Tiffany's motivation for enrolling in Spanish classes during high school was more interpersonal, as she sought to better understand her Hispanic classmates:

Excerpt 9.12

Half my class is Hispanic, and looking at the elementary [school], there's a lot more Hispanic cultured people. I think it'd just be nice to understand them a little bit more. I just find that their culture is unique. I love their food, so it's like make me something! I think they really did influence where I'm going today. It also makes me not as... I know some people can be more racial toward them. I feel like sometimes my grandparents are like that. (27 April 2015)

In Excerpt 9.12, Tiffany contrasted her level of acceptance to that of her grandparents and attributes this difference, in part, to learning the language. While I was unable to observe Spanish classes at Springvale due to lack of consent from the teacher, Tiffany's focus on things like her love of Mexican food shows that these language classes may have taken on more of a 'Heroes and Holidays' approach, neglecting to address the language-power nexus present in the juxtaposition of language-as-problem for native Spanish speakers and language-as-commodity for monolingual English speakers.

While in her first semester of college, Tiffany reflected back on her high school Spanish class, nothing that the variety of Spanish taught by Springvale's Spanish teacher was different than the varieties of Spanish spoken by her Hispanic classmates, possibly accounting for the lack of Hispanic students taking upper-level Spanish classes in Springvale.

Excerpt 9.13

I stayed average in it, like low A. (12 October 2015)

In Excerpt 9.13, Tiffany provides another motivation for taking Spanish, highlighting that it was an easy class for her. However, she also acknowledged that the actual speaking portions of the class were difficult for her.

Discussion

Neither school viewed the Spanish spoken by many (but not all) of the schools' Hispanic students as an academic resource worth further developing or utilizing in the classroom through pedagogical translanguaging. Students' L1s were seen as divorced from schooling, which impacted their experiences not only with the schools' ESL programs but also with how Spanish language classes were taught.

Language-as-problem is most evident in three of the excerpts shared throughout the findings (i.e. Excerpts 9.1, 9.2 and 9.3), where the word 'barrier' is used. In analyzing the data according to Ruiz's (1984) language orientations, this type of discourse made language ideologies more outwardly apparent. Furthermore, this is an example of how Fasching-Varner's (2014) approach was helpful in seeing how individual manifestations of language ideologies were bigger than a personal bias. Rather, participants from both sites and in different positions were all referencing a 'barrier' when discussing language, indexing its relevance to these communities and their collective sense-making around demographic change and linguistic landscape shifts.

Similarly, comparing Chloe and Javier's statements (Excerpts 9.4 and 9.5) with T2's (Excerpt 9.6), we see individual deficit orientations and English superiority coalescing into a collective attitude toward languages other than English. This challenges the view that linguicism is merely present in individual prejudices, moving toward a realization that linguistic discrimination is rooted in societal norms and reproduced in institutions by individuals. Hence, institutions can have a role in dismantling prejudice.

The assimilative attitude toward language exemplified by this study's participants promotes the idea that students' L1s are something they must give up in order to be successful. Bilingualism 'is seen as working against the grain of American history, which has been an assimilating, acculturating history in which immigrants forget their pasts, repudiate any foreign allegiances, and become Americans' (Glazer, 1993: 321). Moreover, the idea of Spanglish is brought up with a negative connotation, consistent with García and Li Wei:

> Monolingual communities and the elite often refer to the fluid ways in which non-dominant communities speak with terms that are stigmatized such as *Spanglish* [...] it disparages ways of speaking of Latinos, focusing on what is seen as structural mixing and unusual hybridity. (García & Li Wei, 2014: 41–42)

This reinforces the idea that English is superior by seeking to purify and standardize the way students draw on their linguistic repertoires. This makes translanguaging difficult to promote as it necessitates the utilization of all language resources, which cannot be done if English is seen as the only language with academic utility.

However, as exemplified above, this is not just a matter of language; it is also an issue of race and racialization. Rosa (2019: 3) explains raciolinguistics by stating, 'Regardless of perceived phenotypic heterogeneity, semiotic ideologies recruit linguistic practices and various signs of difference to homogenize Latinxs as racial Others'. In the same way that color blindness protects those with racial privilege from encountering their own racist tendencies, 'language-blindness' provides a way to preserve *linguistic* privilege while disavowing linguicism. Thus, students and school personnel can uphold harmful English-only rhetoric and policies as long as they see language as a problem to be solved.

However, language *was* seen as a resource for the schools' White students. This presents another example of how Fasching-Varner's (2014) approach to data analysis was used, this time to contrast individual narratives. This helps us understand the differences between language-as-resource and language-as-commodity ideologies in Brad and Tiffany's understandings of language's utility in their lives. Embracing language as a resource can create solidarity within schools and communities, as well as in society writ large, something that we see potential for in Tiffany's approach to language learning. Even so, the advantages of multilingualism are often used to amplify the privilege of an already advantaged group, as we see in Brad's use of language as a commodified entity for personal gain.

Conclusion: Moving Toward Language-as-Resource and Language-as-Right

The language-as-problem orientation observed in these schools could be challenged by employing a 'linguistic addition' approach (Leeman, 2005) in a dual-language or two-way immersion (TWI) program, critically examining the language-power nexus. To make language a resource for all students, the forced separation of languages (e.g. Spanish versus English versus indigenous languages) and the multiple monolingual view of plurilingualism (Agnihotri, 2014) must be dismantled. Instead, students should be reframed as emergent plurilinguals and encouraged to use all languages in their repertoire to learn through pedagogical translanguaging. This would involve intentionally supporting ELs' maintenance of their L1 while adding English and simultaneously helping native English speakers form a new identity – moving away from the idea that Spanish should solely be a commodity used for upward mobility and toward the idea that multilingualism is a way of achieving unity and solidarity.

Given the raciolinguistic power dynamics that are already present in society, TWIs must work to ensure that the multilingualism they foster does not unequally advantage certain students (e.g. White previously monolingual students) over others (e.g. Latinx students who were already bilingual) by allowing the language-as-commodity orientation to reify multilingualism as a type of property. Furthermore, critical consciousness is not something that automatically develops under laissez-faire conditions; it must be deliberately fostered through the educational policies and teaching methods used in TWI programs. This includes giving students explicit permission, encouragement and guidance to strategically use their entire linguistic repertoire through translanguaging.

TWI programs have the power to move us away from the assimilative, subtractive status quo. However, this requires a shift from language-as-problem and multiple monolingual ideologies in favor of seeing language as a resource and right, and students as emergent polyglots. While TWI programs are not without their issues, thoughtful language planning that includes attention to power dynamics and the benefits of translanguaging may help us actualize the benefits of bilingual education.

Notes

(1) I am using the term *L1* to mean a language that a person has been exposed to from birth or early childhood; however, I recognize that some of my participants have used multiple languages from a young age. For example, when I say L1 in reference to Eddie, I am talking about both Spanish and Q'anjob'al.

(2) Given that roughly 13% of the United States population (five years and older) speak Spanish at home (US Census Bureau, 2015), the term *foreign* has been placed in quotes to emphasize Spanish's role as the second most prevalent language spoken in the country.

(3) I recognize the complex nature of the debate between using 'Hispanic' versus 'Latin@/Latinx'; however, as a result of this study's students exclusively using the term *Hispanic* in their self-identifications, I have opted to use their terminology throughout this paper when discussing my sites and participants. I will, however, use Latinx when describing the NLD.

References

Agnihotri, R.K. (2014) Multilinguality, education and harmony. *International Journal of Multilingualism* 11 (3), 364–379.

Bejarano, C.L. (2005) *¿Qué onda? Urban Youth Culture and Border Identity.* Tucson, AZ: The University of Arizona Press.

Brisk, M.E. (2006) *Bilingual Education: From Compensatory to Quality Schooling* (2nd edn). Mahwah, NJ: Lawrence Erlbaum Associates.

Clotfelter, C.T. (2004) *After Brown: The Rise and Retreat of School Desegregation.* Princeton, NJ: Princeton University Press.

Fasching-Varner, K.J. (2014) (Re)searching whiteness: New considerations in studying and researching whiteness. In A.D. Dixson (ed.) *Researching Race in Education: Policy, Practice, and Qualitative Research* (pp. 153–168). Charlotte, NC: Information Age Publishing, Inc.

García, O. and Li Wei (2014) *Translanguaging: Language, Bilingualism and Ducation.* New York, NY: Palgrave.

Glazer, N. (1993) Where is multiculturalism leading us? *Phi Delta Kappan* 75 (4), 319–323.

Hamann, E.T. and Reeves, J. (2012) ICE raids, children, media, and making sense of Latino newcomers in flyover country. *Anthropology & Education Quarterly* 43 (1), 24–40.

Kim, Y.K., Hutchison, L.A. and Winsler, A. (2015) Bilingual education in the United States: An historical overview and examination of two-way immersion. *Educational Review* 67 (2), 236–252.

Leeman, J. (2005) Engaging critical pedagogy: Spanish for native speakers. *Foreign Language Annals* 38 (1), 35–45.

Lewis, G., Jones, B. and Baker, C. (2012) Translanguaging: Origins and development from school to street and beyond. *Educational Research and Evaluation* 18 (7), 641–654.

Menken, K. and García, O. (2010) Introduction. In K. Menken and O. García (eds) *Negotiation Language Policies in Schools: Educators as Policymakers* (pp. 1–10). New York, NY: Routledge.

Ricento, T. (2005) Problems with the 'language-as-resource' discourse in the promotion of heritage languages in the U.S.A. *Journal of Sociolinguistics* 9 (3), 348–368.

Rosa, J. (2019) *Looking Like a Llanguage, Sounding Like a Race: Raciolinguistic Ideologies and the Learning of Latinidad.* New York, NY: Oxford University Press.

Rosaldo, R. (1993) *Culture & Truth: The Remaking of Social Analysis.* Boston, MA: Beacon Press.

Ruiz, R. (1984) Orientations in language planning. *Journal of the National Association for Bilingual Education* 8 (2), 15–34.

Sierk, J.L. (2016) Coming of Age in the New Latino Diaspora: An Ethnographic Study of High School Seniors in Nebraska. Unpublished PhD thesis: University of Nebraska.

Spradley, J.P. (1979) *The Ethnographic Interview.* Belmont, CA: Wadsworth.

Spradley, J.P. (1980) *Participant Observation.* New York, NY: Holt, Rinehart and Winston.

US Census Bureau (2015) Detailed Languages Spoken at Home and Ability to Speak English for the Population 5 Years and Over: 2009–2013. See www.census.gov/data/tables/2013/demo/2009-2013-lang-tables.html (accessed April 2020).

US Census Bureau (2018) Nebraska QuickFacts. *U.S. Census Bureau.* See www.census.gov/quickfacts/NE (accessed April 2020).

Valdés, G. (2001) *Learning and Not Learning English: Latino Students in American Schools.* New York, NY: Teachers College Press.

Williamson, K., Given, L.M. and Scifleet, P. (2018) Qualitative data analysis. In K. Williamson and G. Johanson (eds) *Research Methods: Information, Systems and Contexts* (pp. 453–476). Cambridge, MA: Chandos Publishing.

10 Challenging Monolingual Norms through Pedagogical Translanguaging in Adult Education for Immigrants in Sweden?

Jenny Rosén and Berit Lundgren

Introduction

In this chapter, we shed light on translanguaging pedagogy for adult immigrants learning Swedish from a teacher perspective. Our main focus of interest is in teachers' recognition of the spontaneous translanguaging taking place in their classroom, the negotiation of language norms and how translanguaging pedagogy may be enacted in their classrooms.

Over the past 10 years, immigration to Sweden has increased, peaking in 2016 with 163,000 individuals having immigrated to Sweden (Statistics Sweden, 2020). Adult immigrants who have received residency in Sweden but lack skills in Swedish are given the opportunity to learn Swedish through the program Swedish for Immigrants (SFI), provided by municipal adult education. This is in line with the Swedish Language Act (SFS, 2009: 600), which stipulates that Swedish is the principal language in Sweden and that all residents of Sweden are to be given the opportunity to learn, develop and use Swedish.

Over the past decade, the translanguaging approach has spread among both researchers and educators in diverse contexts (see, for example, Juvonen & Källkvist, this volume; Paulsrud *et al.*, 2017), often presented as an alternative to upholding the monolingual norm in additional language education. Li Wei suggests that a translanguaging perspective challenges the validity of conventional views of language (Li Wei, 2016: 1). Translanguaging has developed both as a theoretical approach and a pedagogy as part of the multilingual turn (Conteh & Meier, 2014; May,

2014; cf. also Cummins, this volume), which questions the monolingual bias in second language acquisition and bilingual education.

The aim of this chapter is to examine how teachers in language education for adult migrants perceived translanguaging pedagogy in relation to their teaching practices. Furthermore, it aims to find out whether language norms were made visible as well as partly challenged in the process. The educational setting for the study was the program explained above: Swedish for Immigrants (SFI). Our point of departure is to explore whether and how instruction that is inclusive of students' various experiences, focusing on their language background and language use in everyday and work life as resources for learning, can be developed for adult migrants in Sweden. Thus, the study highlights teachers' views and their experiences of teaching practices, in order to develop a pedagogical approach that builds upon students' experiences and language use in their everyday and work life.

However, as Canagarajah argues, scholars should not fall into the dichotomy of multilingual versus monolingual but rather 'adopt a critical attitude towards the resources/limitations and prospects/challenges of translanguaging' (Canagarajah, 2011: 3). Regarding translanguaging in an educational context, studies have mainly focused on spontaneous practices that are not initiated by the teacher (Canagarajah, 2011). Already in 2011, Creese and Blackledge (2010: 113) called for 'further research to explore what "teachable" pedagogic resources are available in flexible, concurrent approaches to learning and teaching languages bilingually' which is supported by Cummins (this volume). Since 2011, a number of studies on translanguaging have been published, suggesting the development of a pedagogical approach that involves translanguaging (Juvonen & Källkvist, this volume). However, many of these previous studies have focused on education for children and adolescents, and hence, the need to explore the potential of pedagogical translanguaging in adult education is now more critical than before.

SFI – Framing the Educational Context

Sweden has a long tradition of providing formalized language education in Swedish for adult migrants. Since the 1960s, instruction has been provided for adult migrants lacking basic competence in Swedish. The curriculum for adult education and the syllabus for the SFI program are regulated by the Swedish Education Act. The syllabus states that

> Municipal adult education in Swedish for Immigrants (SFI) is an advanced language instruction that is intended to give adult immigrants a basic knowledge of the Swedish language. This tuition gives students with a mother tongue other than Swedish the opportunity to learn and develop a functional knowledge of a second language. (SNAE, 2018)

Everyone older than the age of 16 who has residence in Sweden and lacks basic skills in Swedish has the right to participate in SFI. The program is organized in three tracks: The first targets students who have no or limited previous formal education; the second track targets students with between 6 and 12 years of previous education and the third track targets students with an academic background. Students may study SFI up to B1/B1+ according to the Common European Framework of Reference for Languages (CEFR), and national language tests are provided throughout the program. In 2018, 159,127 students were enrolled in SFI, and, despite a long tradition of providing language education for adult immigrants (Lindberg & Sandwall, 2007, 2012; Rosén, 2013), research concerned with the pedagogical aspects of the program has been limited (Lundgren *et al.*, 2017).

Pedagogical Translanguaging in Adult Education

Translanguaging has developed as a pedagogical approach in diverse contexts (e.g. Juvonen & Källkvist, this volume; Paulsrud *et al.*, 2017) and as a pedagogical theory emphasizing dual language use as a strategy to retain and develop bilingualism (García, 2009). Mazak (2017) suggests that translanguaging as pedagogy involves the flexible use of linguistic and semiotic resources among students and teachers. Studies of translanguaging in higher education illustrate how teachers adopt a pedagogical stance of allowing and implementing translanguaging in different educational contexts that are often dominated by monolingual ideologies (Mazak & Carroll, 2017). As suggested by Carroll (2017), it is by implementing such a pedagogical stance that 'translanguaging becomes a set of practices whereby educators build on and use their students' linguistic resources and background knowledge to convey meaningful content' (Carroll, 2017: 181).

Moreover, Mazak *et al.* (2017) show, in their study of three university teachers, that translanguaging pedagogy may include spontaneous practices even when intentionally planned. They argue that translanguaging pedagogy could be seen to be 'more of an attitude or stance that sees the value of using all of students' linguistic resources and takes steps (sometimes more deliberate than others) to use and develop those resources' (Mazak *et al.*, 2017: 72). Furthermore, they question whether translanguaging pedagogy should involve teachers giving up their authority in the classroom. Instead, their study shows that although teachers become learners in a translanguaging pedagogy, this does not force them to give up their authority but rather, by using translanguaging, to 'enact an identity as authorities who can successfully apprentice college students in the discourses of their respective disciplines' (Mazak *et al.*, 2017: 73). Questions of intentionality as well as authority are shown to be relevant in the present study.

García (2017) argues that the linguistic integration of adult migrants needs to involve meaningful participation in society rather than focus on acquiring a grammatically correct national language. García (2017) suggests five guiding principles for translanguaging pedagogy for adult migrants:

- Give migrants 'voice' and help them to develop it.
- Build on their strengths and interests.
- Make sure that students are 'doing' language, performing genuine and authentic tasks, not just that they 'have' language structures.
- Recognize the entanglements of migrants' worlds and words and use them in the process of finalizing the product that you intend to.
- Ensure that migrants appropriate new features into an expanded repertoire that is their own, and not just that of a nation state or specific national group.

These principles make explicit a strong connection between translanguaging pedagogy, social justice and social change. Jaspers (2019) addresses concerns with scholars arguing for translanguaging as real and natural or/ and in terms of effectiveness and argues that education is not only about facts but also about values, and researchers need to 'reclaim language-in-education-policy from positivist discourse and reconstruct them as sites for jointly envisioning what types of language we find desirable and wish to pursue' (Jaspers, 2019: 101).

Ruiz (1984) had already in the 1980s identified three orientations in language planning: language-as-problem, language-as-right and language-as-resource. Whereas the language-as-right orientation focused the question of linguistic minorities using and maintaining their language as a human and civil right of the group or the individual, language-as-resource emphasized the importance of linguistic diversity for society as a whole, and language-as-problem denotes to a deficit view of a language(s) (Hornberger, 1990: 24). In the context of education, a language-as-right orientation recognizes students' right to use and maintain their linguistic repertoires, whereas a language-as-resource orientation acknowledges and encourages students to use, maintain and develop their linguistic repertoires as resources for learning (Paulsrud & Rosén, 2019). A language-as-problem orientation centers on monolingual majority education and language diversity is devalued. In line with the criticism by Jaspers (2019), translanguaging pedagogy needs to address the fact that a language-in-education policy involves questions about the values of education in society rather than just effectiveness in learning. The language-as-resource orientation has been important in challenging a deficit perspective of students based on monolingual norms. Therefore, Flores (2017) argues that the institutionalizing of a language-as-resource orientation has separated it from the community struggle against racial inequalities and hence reinforced the racial status quo. Thus, 'in a society with racial hierarchies between language-majoritized and language-minoritized communities, language as a resource for all is likely to benefit the language-majoritized community more than the language-minoritized community' (Flores, 2017: 75).

Moving toward a language-as-struggle orientation as an alternative to language-as-resource, Flores (2017) suggests that this orientation can be founded on the principles of (i) embedded notions of language proficiency in the context of the racial inequalities exacerbated by neoliberalism, (ii) situated calls for bilingual education within calls for larger social transformations, (iii) connection with community organizations that are working to address racial inequalities and (iv) bringing language struggle into the classroom which has been questioned by Cummins (this volume).

Previous research on the SFI program in general is limited, especially focusing on pedagogy and translanguaging (Lundgren *et al.*, 2017). In a study based on nexus analysis, Rosén and Bagga-Gupta (2015) studied how the principle of Swedish as the main and uniting language variety in the political space of Sweden was transformed and contested through the actions taking place in two SFI classrooms. A study by Rydell (2015: 542) showed how SFI students, based on 27 videotaped pair dialogues in a test situation, 'expressed their beliefs on language use and language learning'. It was found that the students oriented themselves toward the dominant Swedish-only discourse in the classroom. Furthermore, the study also showed how the test situation oriented the students toward a monolingual ideology. In a report from a development project at a Swedish folk high school, Mörnerud (2010) describes how students' prior language experiences and resources were used in the classroom. With parallel instructions in the students' mother tongue and Swedish, both languages and literacies developed, and the students' identities as competent people were confirmed according to the teachers (Mörnerud, 2010). Colliander (2019) studied the SFI context with a focus on teachers' identity. Her study shows that processes of migration, marketization and streamlining as well as digitalization has had effects on teacher identity as they changed their work practices and challenged their position in the local school communities. Even though teacher identity was transformed by these external processes, the teachers were also active agents in these transformations.

Material and Method

The study presented in this chapter was part of a research and development program (2018–2020) with the overall objective of developing SFI education in collaboration with teachers and school leaders in seven schools in Sweden. Participating schools were assigned by the municipalities or outsourced to private providers, so the researchers were not involved in the selection process. The participating schools were located in different parts of Sweden.

The study was based on a collaborative approach to professional development (Carpenter, 2015; Lieberman, 1986). The particpating teachers were informed of the study and provided written consent. Before audio-recordings, the participants were informed that they could ask for the recorder to be turned off if they so desired. The empirical data analyzed consist of interviews with the teachers at five schools. All teachers interviewed were eligible to teach in the SFI program, which means that they had completed a teaching degree (for any age-group) and at least 30 ECTS credits (European Credit Transfer Accumulation System) of Swedish as a second language. Most of the teachers were teaching students in Tracks 2 and 3, teaching the courses B-D[1]. Since there are no teacher-education courses specifically devoted to the SFI program, the teachers had diverse educational backgrounds and professional experiences. Since most of the teachers are women, feminine pronouns will be used for all participants in the study to protect anonymity. Schools and teachers have been anonymized, and certain information that could make identification of specific teachers possible has not been included in the chapter, for example, the language repertoires of the teachers.

The data were collected in the first few months of the program, consisting of group interviews with the teachers. Interviews focused on two activities: photographs and mind maps that the teachers were working with in order to reflect multilingualism in relation to their teaching. Hence, the interviews centered on descriptions and reflections on the activities rather than questions asked by the researchers. In the following section, we describe the activities in the program leading up to the group interviews.

The teachers and school leaders were introduced to Ruiz's (1984, 1990) orientations of language as problem, as right and as resource and to Hornberger's (2003) continua of biliteracy through a short lecture given by the researchers. The teachers were then asked to discuss the concept of multilingualism and to consider how multilingualism could be used as a resource in their classrooms using photographs reflecting the linguistic diversity of the school and through a student activity in which they were making mind maps about the concept of multilingualism in a school context. The photographs were taken by the teachers in the classrooms, and they were asked not to include students or other individuals in the school. A limited number of photographs were then selected by the teachers to be discussed in the interview.

The group interviews were conducted in Swedish and hence the citations have been translated by the authors. The researchers had an eclectic approach to the interviews. A focus-group interview was deemed too formal. Group interviews are more informal (Morgan, 1997). The nature of this study depended on the participants' retelling and interaction with each other and the researcher. Therefore, group interviews were chosen in order to reveal the participants' views, knowledge and experiences. Furthermore, the researcher's role as moderator was toned down. The aim was for an open discussion that provided space for the teachers to interact with each other, so a few open-ended questions, the same used for all groups, were formulated. While one researcher moderated the interview, the other researcher silently observed while taking notes. Hence, group interviews were chosen in this study to reveal the participants' views, knowledge and experiences as the method provides opportunities to gain multi-dimensional data.

During the interviews, the teachers were asked to present and reflect upon multilingualism in relation to the photos and the mind maps. The interviews lasted about 120 minutes for each group. They were audio-recorded and transcribed. The transcribed interviews were analyzed using Ruiz's three orientations to reflect multilingualism in the schools. During the analysis, the interviews were approached as interactions taking place between researcher and teachers, in some schools also a school leader. In other words, what is expressed by teachers was analyzed in relation to the wider context of the activities in the program as well as in relation to what the researchers and other teachers said during the interviews.

The analysis is presented using Ruiz's three orientations for language planning: language-as-problem, language-as-right and language-as-resource. As a further step, we problematize whether and how the teachers were developing translanguaging pedagogy. We begin by describing an awareness of the linguistic diversity of the classroom from different points of view.

Language-as-Problem

The use of photographs and mind maps in the group interviews helped to make visible a multi-faceted view of multilingualism and linguistic diversity in general as well as to show the use of languages other than Swedish in the teaching practices of the teachers. The material produced by the participants included both expressions that in the analysis were coded as a language-as-problem as well as a language-as-resource orientation. Hence, the three orientations suggested by Ruiz should not be seen as exclusive of one another since these orientations often exist in parallel. The linguistic diversity of the classroom was, on one hand, perceived by the teachers as a resource, as it forced students to use Swedish when they did not share another common language and, on the other hand, as a problem, since students did not use Swedish in the classroom if they shared other languages. The analysis of the teacher interviews revealed a view of two co-existing language norms.

Another dilemma raised by the teachers concerned disorder, respect and exclusion in the classroom. An ambivalent view toward the use of languages other than Swedish was expressed by one of the teachers.

[M]en vi kom faktiskt ganska mycket in på det där att är det bra eller dåligt och där var det just många som sa att, att det är ju jättebra att det är många olika språk det är positivt. Men att det kanske skulle vara bättre om det skulle vara en balans så att det inte är som nu att femtio procent pratar arabiska. Och sen är det då tio, tolv andra språk. Just det här som vi pratade om tidigare att dom kan ha lite svårt att dämpa, dämpa sig och att det upplevs som lite störande. Ah men vi diskuterade eller kom överens om att det där är nånting vi måste jobba kring. (T2A²)

We talked a lot about whether it is good or bad and many said that it is really good that we have many languages. It is positive but it would be better if there was a balance so that not fifty percent speak Arabic and then there are twelve other languages. That was what we talked about earlier, that they are having a hard time lowering their voices and it was perceived as a bit disturbing. But we discussed or agreed upon that it is something we need to work on. (T2A)

As shown in the excerpt, teacher (T2A) uses 'we', referring to herself and the students in her class, first stating what could be regarded, in relation to the overall theme of the program and the presence of the researchers, as the legitimate discourse: that linguistic diversity is something positive. The group interview with the researchers and other colleagues present constructed discursive boundaries of what was the preferred discourse. However, the teachers also negotiated this discourse, as shown in the transcript above, where this teacher first expresses the idea that multilingualism can be viewed as being positive. She then adds a *but*, explaining that it would be better if there was a balance instead of one dominating language among the students. Another teacher in the same group interview reported on similar experiences from her teaching practice, framing the question of a language policy in the classroom as complex:

[S]å är det nog ganska komplicerat för å ena sidan om vi säger finns att, fördelar med flerspråkigheten vilket vi har understrukit här med jättemånga exempel. Fördelar med flerspråkighet samtidigt så så får vi ju inte glömma bort att vi är här för att träna svenska. Den den balansen att att formulera det för sig själv och i klassrummet det är det är inte helt lätt. (T4A)

It is pretty complex because, on the one hand we say that there are advantages of multilingualism which we have underlined with many examples, advantages with multilingualism but at the same time we shouldn't forget that we are here to practice using Swedish. This balance, to formulate it for yourself and for the classroom, it is not so easy. (T4A)

Similar to teacher T2A, this teacher describes a dilemma with regard to the balance between Swedish and other languages in the classroom. Questions of balance and the status of languages in the classroom were also discussed among the teachers in relation to the use of English. Whether to use English or not when teaching was a point of discussion among the teachers. Some expressed great concern about the injustice of using a language that some, but not all students, understand, while others used English to initiate chains of translations by the students.

The status of English in Swedish schools and in higher education has been examined by several scholars (Hult, 2012; Salö, 2010; Toth, 2018; Yoxsimer Paulsrud, 2014). The role and status of English was also debated in the language policy work leading up to the Swedish Language Act in 2009 (SFS, 2009: 600), where the risk of English taking over academic domains was addressed. However, English could be positioned as a second language for many, especially for adolescent students. In the Swedish school system, students start classroom instruction in English already in primary school, and English is one of the core subjects in the Swedish schools. In this context, English is a language known by the teachers and is therefore a legitimate choice to use in the Swedish school context and in society in general.

In the interviews, the teachers expressed ambivalent approaches toward the use of English in order to scaffold students' learning of Swedish. Using English was often positioned as a problem or a less adequate choice than trying to teach and explain vocabulary and grammar using Swedish. One teacher expressed laughingly that she had committed a 'sin' by using English in her beginner class. The teacher explained that she had started out using Swedish only but that students had told her that they did not understand and so she started to provide her explanations in both English and Swedish in the first week.

The dilemma of using English was also voiced by teacher T7:

> Ja men jag tycker att det är viktigt det här men engelskan för att man tänker ibland så att, ja men dom flesta kan ju engelska, men så är det ju inte riktigt för när man förklara något på svenska så dom som kan engelska säger: Ja det är det på engelska. Och då får man säga, ja du kan engelska och det är rätt på engelska men alla kan ju inte engelska så här måste vi se till att alla förstår på alla språk. (T7)

> *Yes, but I think it is important with English because you sometimes think that most students know English. But it is not really like that, because when you explain something in Swedish the ones who know English say, Ah it is that in English, and then you have to say, yes you know English and its correct in English but everyone doesn't know English, so we have to make sure everyone understands regardless of the language background. (T7)*

To sum up, the question of English being positioned as a problem or a resource illustrates many of the dilemmas addressed by teachers in terms of social justice, the status of different named languages (Otheguy *et al.*, 2015) in the classroom as well as in society and the limitations of the teachers in regard to their linguistic repertoires. The role of English further highlights how the three orientations often intersect in the negotiations of language norms among the teachers. Thus, the discussion about English as well as the balance between languages also concerns the next orientation, language-as-right.

Language-as-Right

Expressions of the language-as-right orientation were not common in the data analyzed. In Ruiz's work, the language-as-right orientation involves the right of minorities to maintain and develop their languages. However, the teachers in this study approached language rights in terms of the right to study the majority language (in this case, Swedish) in order to be able to participate in society. Thus, they oriented toward the right to study Swedish rather than the right to maintain and recognize other languages. One teacher noted that discussing and writing in the classroom made it more visible how multilingualism was a question of democracy; it is only by comprehending the language that you can fully participate in society and make your voice heard, be understood and understand others. Thus, teachers claimed that developing skills in the majority language, in this case, Swedish, was important in order to become independent.

Another question, related to the language-as-right orientation, was about the injustice that arose when one language group was supported, either through specific material translated only into a limited number of languages or by the teacher while other groups were not provided similar support. Thus, questions regarding the right of students to use their linguistic repertoires in the classroom were in conflict with the value of equity and the right to equal education. Teachers argued that the use of languages other than Swedish could be unjust and that equality was a question of democracy. In another interview, one teacher expressed the view that even though students should be able to use 'their language', Swedish should be used 'with respect for the class' to include everyone in the classroom activities. Thus, the teacher argued in favor of a monolingual Swedish norm in the classroom, motivated by equity and equal rights to participate.

To sum up, language-as-right was approached by the teachers in terms of the right of learning Swedish to participate in society and to become independent language users. The right for individuals to use and to learn Swedish is also stipulated in the Swedish Language Act (2009: 600). Moreover, teachers recognized students' right to use their linguistic repertoires but also indicated that doing so in the classroom was not always compatible with the right to equal education and the inclusion of all students in the classroom as a safe space.

Language-as-Resource

The language-as-resource orientation originally referred to language as a resource for a nation or society (Ruiz, 1984). In our analysis, the orientation included both languages as a resource for the individual, such as assisting in finding a job, making it easier to travel, facilitating meeting new people and finding friends. In other words, being multilingual was formulated as potentially providing cultural, social and economic capital.

Recognizing the linguistic diversity of the classroom, some teachers described how they were already acknowledging and using it as a resource:

Men sen den här diskussionen, om fler, att prata modersmål i klassrummet, det jag jag tänker att jag frågar ofta, vad heter det på ditt modersmål när vi pratar i klassen, i gruppen, i helklass. Vad heter det, på svenska säger vi så här, hur säger man på arabiska? Hur säger man på tigrinja? Hur säger man på franska eller vad det nu är för språk vi har, så där brukar vi prata också. (T5)

This discussion about using the mother tongue [referring in the Swedish context to all languages other than Swedish] in the classroom, I think that I often ask: What is this called in your mother tongue when we talk in class, in groups, in the whole class. What is this called? In Swedish we say like this. How do you say it in Arabic? How do you say it in Tigrinja? How do you say it in French or whatever language we have, that is how we usually also speak. (T5)

As shown in this excerpt, teacher T5 encouraged student translanguaging in the classroom even though it was not an intentional pedagogy for her (see also Mazak *et al.*, 2017). In a similar way, another teacher expressed how translanguaging was used spontaneously in her classroom.

In the interviews, some of the teachers described how the attitude toward multilingualism had changed since they first started as SFI teachers. One teacher explained that multilingualism was somewhat of a 'taboo' when she started teaching, but added that:

Jag tycker att även om det var lite tabu när jag började här flerspråkighet men eh jag tycker att det är en bra resurs i vissa fall, men jag tänker i vissa fall när jag behöver förklara ett ord oftast en abstrakt koncept, till exempel så jag kan inte använda kroppsspråk till att för att förklara hopp eller fred eller nånting sånt eh och ibland tar det fem minuter för att förklara på svenska. (T4B)

Even though it was a bit of a taboo when I started here, multilingualism, eh, I think that it is a good resource in some cases, I think sometimes I need to explain a word, often an abstract concept. When I can't use body language to explain, like hope or peace or something. Sometimes it takes five minutes to explain it in Swedish. (T4B)

As noted in the extract above, this teacher suggests that using translation can be a strategy to explain the meaning of a word in order to stay focused on the task rather than devoting time to explain it in Swedish. In response to one school leader addressing the issue of not all students having a shared language with the teacher apart from Swedish, and therefore may not receive equal support, the teachers discussed the issue of justice.

T4B: Men när jag säger, det är inte att jag översätter på Språk A[3] och engelska som jag kan, jag försöker att några elever hjälper mig att översätta

[…]

T4B: Jag försöker alltid täcka alla språk som finns i gruppen i alla fall, för jag tycker att det är lite, det kan kännas orättvist

T5: Ja å andra sidan så hjälper vi ju dom att komma vidare, vi kan inte, vi har ju inte alla språk men många kan få hjälp så det är jättesvårt

T4B: *But when I say it, it is not like I translate into Language A or English which I understand, I try to get students to help me translate*

[…]

T4B: *I always try to include all the languages in the group because I think it could feel a bit unfair.*

T5: *Yes, but on the other hand, we help them to move forward, we cannot, we don't have all the languages, but many can get help, so it is very hard.*

Rather than agreeing with the problem raised by the school leader, the teachers (T4B and T5) give voice to a dilemma in their teaching involving questions of equal rights and social justice regarding translanguaging. Another teacher (T3) argued that the translation in itself was empowering for the students as 'you can also perceive pride among the students, I think when I see that they are allowed to translate and they can see that yes I can I help another person here'. So, on one hand, translation could scaffold the learning of Swedish in addition to empowering students. But on the other hand, teachers face the dilemma of how to include the linguistic repertoires of all students. This example also highlights the linguistic repertoires of the teachers. Due to the linguistic diversity in the classroom, teachers were seldom able to use all languages that were used by the students. One way of approaching this dilemma was for teachers to ask students to translate for each other, as pointed out by teacher T4B, thus creating 'language chains' in the classroom, often initiated by a translation into English by the teacher: 'then this student knows English and Turkish and can translate into Turkish for the student who doesn't know English' (Teacher T3). However, teachers also expressed concerns as to whether these chains reached everyone in the classroom using all the linguistic resources at hand.

To sum up, the analysis shows that the teachers experienced a shift with regard to language norms from a monolingual Swedish-only norm toward a more pluralistic norm where students as well as teachers could use their linguistic repertoires in the classroom. The teachers oriented toward using the linguistic repertoires as resources mainly in terms of translations.

Working Toward Translanguaging Pedagogy

The aim of this chapter was to find out how teachers in the SFI program perceived translanguaging pedagogy in relation to their teaching practices and how language norms were made visible as well as were partly challenged in the process. In order to explore how teachers' language norms were negotiated, Ruiz's (1984, 1990) three orientations were used as a framework. The analysis showed that rather than leaning toward one single orientation, teachers were navigating, as well as taking ambivalent positions toward translanguaging pedagogy. All teachers reproduced views of multilingualism as something positive in general as well as support for the right of their students to maintain their linguistic repertoires. However, they also stressed the importance of learning Swedish, which was the overall aim of the SFI program.

Previous studies of translanguaging in school contexts involving children and adolescents have highlighted the potential of translanguaging for content learning as well as for developing the weaker language (Baker, 2011). In the context of language education for adult migrants, students were expected to learn the majority language as fast as possible in order to independently be able to engage in everyday activities and find work. No teacher gave voice to a view that students should use only Swedish to the exclusion of their other linguistic resources.

Regarding the language-as-right orientation, the SFI context could be interpreted as an arena for adult migrants to learn basic Swedish in accordance with the Swedish Language Act (SFS, 2009: 600). Learning Swedish was positioned as essential in order to participate not only in workplaces but also in society at large, which raises the question of democracy. While translanguaging originally meant the use of two named languages, more recent understandings of the concept of translanguaging refer to a flexible approach involving a wider range of linguistic resources (Mazak, 2017). SFI classrooms are characterized by linguistic heterogeneity, and the teachers were concerned both with balancing different languages as well as Swedish vis-à-vis other languages.

Teachers expressed the view that translanguaging practices were taking place in their classrooms but were seldom intentionally planned by the teacher. Mazak *et al.* (2017) question intentionality in translanguaging pedagogy, but this study revealed that translanguaging was not only taking place unintentionally but also, in some cases, it was used as a last resort or a less valued option than using Swedish only.

As shown in the examples above, some teachers felt that the use of languages (often English) other than Swedish might raise questions about them being professional. Thus, the dominating language norm in the classrooms represented in this study was of Swedish or Swedish as the preferred language for teachers in the SFI classroom. This illustrates the ambivalence of teachers who, at the same time, recognized the value of multilingualism.

Other languages were used in the classroom with the objective of translating and explaining texts, tasks or provide instructions by the teacher. Students often used online dictionaries or translated among themselves. Some teachers also explained that they encouraged these practices by asking questions about what certain vocabulary was in other languages or by creating chains of translations. Teachers expressed that they accepted or encouraged these practices, recognizing language-as-resource, but if students were too loud, dominating the classroom, this could be a problem of order rather than of language.

The question of balance between different named languages, and the use of English was often positioned as a problem of injustice when not all students were given equal support for learning Swedish. Thus, teachers acknowledged that the aim of education was to expand the students' linguistic repertoires in order to include Swedish and that using prior knowledge among the students as a resource would facilitate their learning of Swedish. Hence, the question of how such support could be organized as an integrated part of the instruction rather than just spontaneous practices in the classroom remained. In other words, the teachers were hesitant to move beyond a kind of pedagogical translanguaging that could support students' learning of Swedish toward a translanguaging pedagogy that, in line with the principles presented by García (2017), would give students a voice and help teachers to build upon and include students' strengths and interests in their teaching. Such a critical pedagogy has the aim of not only supporting the learning of the majority language (Swedish) but also facilitating social justice and social change in society at large.

As suggested by Jaspers (2018), translanguaging is not empowering or transformative by default. The use of English, a high-status language in Sweden, as a lingua franca in the classroom shows that opening up the classroom for translanguaging does not automatically mean that all languages are made visible. As noted by some teachers, the use of English could actually lead to exclusion of some students. Thus, using English could be effective scaffolding for some students but may not challenge language norms and hierarchies in the classroom or in society. A translanguaging pedagogy for adult migrants, with regard to social change and social justice, needs to move beyond the classroom in order to address inequality and marginalization in society.

In line with the language-as-struggle orientation presented by Flores (2017), it is essential to connect language struggle with the struggle against racial inequality. In SFI education, teachers were concerned that, since the classroom was the only space for many students to use and develop Swedish, diminishing the use of Swedish in the classroom would not facilitate students' learning. Due to segregation, many migrants lack opportunities to use Swedish outside of school, and learning Swedish as fast as possible is often indexed with opportunities of employment or other benefits that may put students in a stressful situation. Still, the activities and discussions initiated by the researchers made the teachers more aware of the language norms in their classrooms and how they, as teachers, had an active role in how they reproduce or transform those norms.

Notes

(1) Course B represents A1/A2, Course C represents A2/A2+ and Course D represents B1/B1+ according to the Common European Framework of Reference for Languages (CEFR).
(2) All participants in the study have been given codes that are displayed in the citations.
(3) The language is not named here in order to protect the anonymity of the teacher.

References

Baker, C. (2011) *Foundations of Bilingual Education and Bilingualism* (5th edn). Bristol: Multilingual Matters.

Canagarajah, S. (2011) Translanguaging in the classroom: Emerging issues for research and pedagogy. *Applied Linguistics Review* 2, 1–28.

Carroll, K.S. (2017) Concluding remarks: Prestige planning and translanguaging in higher education. In C.M. Mazak and K.S. Carroll (eds) *Translanguaging in Higher Education: Beyond Monolingual Ideologies* (pp. 177–185). Bristol: Multilingual Matters

Carpenter, D. (2015) School culture and leadership of professional learning communities. *International Journal of Educational Management* 29 (5), 682–69.

Colliander, H. (2019) Being transformed and transforming oneself in a time of change: A study of teacher identity in second language education for adults. *Studies in the Education of Adults* 51 (1), 55–73.

Conteh, J. and Meier, G. (eds) (2014) *The Multilingual Turn in Languages Education: Opportunities and Challenges*. Bristol: Multilingual Matters.

Creese, A. and Blackledge, A. (2010) Translanguaging in the bilingual classroom: A pedagogy for learning and teaching? *The Modern Language Journal* 94 (i), 103–115.

Flores, N. (2017) From language-as-resource to language-as-struggle: Resisting the Coke-ification of bilingual education. In M.-C. Flubacher and A. Del Percio (eds) *Language, Education and Neoliberalism: Critical Studies in Sociolinguistics* (pp. 62–81). Bristol: Multilingual Matters.

Gall, M.D., Gall, J.P. and Borg, W.R. (2003) *Educational Research: An Introduction* (7th edn). Boston: Allyn & Bacon.

García, O. (2009) *Bilingual Education in the 21st Century: A Global Perspective*. Malden, MA: Blackwell.

García, O. (2017) Problematizing linguistic integration of migrants: The role of translanguaging and language teachers. In J.-C. Beacco, H.-J. Krumm, D. Little and P. Thagott (eds) *The Linguistic Integration of Adult Migrants/L'intégration linguistique des migrants adultes: Some Lessons from Research/ Les enseignments de la recherché* (pp.11–26). Berlin: De Gruyter Mouton.

Hornberger, N.H. (1990) Bilingual education and English-only: A language-planning framework. *The Annals of the American Academy of Political and Social Science* 508, 12–26.

Hornberger, N.H. (ed.) (2003) *Continua of Biliteracy: An Ecological Framework for Educational Policy, Research, and Practice in Multilingual Settings*. Clevedon: Multilingual Matters.

Hult, F.M. (2012) English as a transcultural language in Swedish policy and practice. *TESOL Quarterly* 46 (2), 230–257.

Jaspers, J. (2018) The transformative limits of translanguaging. *Language & Communication* 58, 1–10.

Jaspers, J. (2019) Authority and morality in advocating heteroglossia. *Language, Culture and Society* 1 (1), 83–105.

Li Wei (2016) New Chinglish and the post-multilingualism challenge: Translanguaging ELF in China. *Journal of English as a Lingua Franca* 5 (1), 1–25.

Li Wei (2017) Translanguaging as a practical theory of language. *Applied Linguistics* 39 (1), 9–30. https://doi-org.www.bibproxy.du.se/10.1093/applin/amx039

Lieberman, A. (1986) Collaborative research: Working with, not working on. *Educational Leadership* 43 (5), 28–32.

Lindberg, I. and Sandwall, K. (2007) Nobody's darling? Swedish for adult immigrants: A critical perspective. *Prospect* 22 (3), 79–95.

Lindberg, I. and Sandwall, K. (2012) Samhälls- och undervisningsperspektiv på svenska som andraspråk för vuxna invandrare [On perspectives of society and education on Swedish as a second language for adult migrants]. In K. Hyltenstam, M. Axelsson and I. Lindberg (eds) *Flerspråkighet: En forskningsöversikt* [Multilingualism. A Reserach Overview] (pp. 368–502). Stockholm: Vetenskapsrådet.

Lundgren, B., Rosén, J. and Janke, A. (2017) *15 års forskning om sfi: en överblick – förstudie inför ett Ifous FoU-program.* [15 Years of Reserach on Sfi: An Overview for an Ifous R & D Program] Stockholm: Ifous.

Mazak, C.M. (2017) Introduction: Theorizing translanguaging practices in higher education. In C.M. Mazak and K.S. Carroll (eds) *Translanguaging in Higher Education: Beyond Monolingual Ideologies* (pp. 1–10). Bristol: Multilingual Matters.

Mazak, C.M. and Carroll, K.S (eds) (2017) *Translanguaging in Higher Education: Beyond Monolingual Ideologies*. Bristol: Multilingual Matters.

Mazak, C.M., Mendoza, F. and Pérez Mangonéz, L. (2017) Professors translanguaging in practice: Three cases from a bilingual university. In C.M. Mazak and K.S. Carroll (eds) *Translanguaging in Higher Education: Beyond Monolingual Ideologies* (pp. 70–90). Bristol: Multilingual Matters.

May, S. (2014) Introducing the 'Multilingual Turn'. In S. May (ed.) *The Multilingual Turn. Implications for SLA, TESOL and Bilingual Education* (pp. 1–6). New York: Routledge.

Morgan, D.L. (1997) *Focus Groups as Qualitative Research* (2nd edn). Thousand Oaks, California: Sage Publications.

Mörnerud, E. (2010) *Modersmålsbaserad svenskundervisning för invandrare.* [Mother Tougue Based Instruction in Swedish for Immigrants]. Malmö: Fou Malmö/ Utbildning, Avdelningen barn och ungdom, Malmö stad.

Norton, B. and Toohey, K. (2004) Critical pedagogies and language learning: An introduction. In B. Norton and K. Toohey (eds) *Critical Pedagogies and Language Learning* (pp. 1–17). Cambridge: Cambridge University Press.

Otheguy, R., García, O. and Reid, W. (2015) Clarifying translanguaging and deconstructing named languages: A perspective from linguistics. *Applied Linguistics Review* 6 (3), 281–307.

Paulsrud, B., Rosén, J., Straszer, B. and Wedin, Å. (eds) (2017) *New Perspectives on Translanguaging and Education*. Bristol: Multilingual Matters.

Paulsrud, B. and Rosén, J. (2019) Translanguaging and language ideologies in education: Northern and Southern perspectives. In S. Brunn and R. Kehrein (eds) *Handbook of the Changing World Language Map*. Springer, Cham. https://doi. org/10.1007/978-3-319-73400-2_124-1

Rosén, J. (2013) *Svenska för invandrarskap? Språk, kategorisering och identitet inom utbildningsformen Svenska* för invandrare. [Swedish for Immigrantness? Language, Categorization and Identity in the Education Swedish for Immigrant] Örebro Studies in Education 38. PhD thesis. Örebro: Örebro universitet.

Rosén, J. and Bagga-Gupta, S. (2015) Prata svenska vi är i Sverige! [Talk Swedish we are in Sweden!]. A study of practiced language policy in adult language learning. *Linguistics and Education* 31, 59–73.

Ruiz, R. (1984) Orientations in language planning. *NABE Journal* 8 (2), 15–34.

Ruiz, R. ([1990] 2016) Official languages and language planning. In N. Hornberger (ed.) *Honoring Richard Ruiz and his Work on Language Planning and Bilingual Education* (pp. 33–58). Bristol: Multilingual Matters.

Rydell, M. (2015) Performance and ideology in speaking tests for adult migrants. *Journal of Sociolinguistics* 19 (4), 535–558.

Salö, L. (2010) *Engelska eller svenska? En kartläggning av språksituationen inom högre utbildning och forskning*. [English or Swedish? Mapping the Language Situation in Higher Education and Eesearch]. Rapporter från Språkrådet 1. Stockholm: Språkrådet.

Statistics Sweden. SCB https://www.scb.se/hitta-statistik/sverige-i-siffror/manniskorna-i-sverige/invandring-till-sverige/).

SFS 2009:600 SFS 2009:600. Språklag. [Language Act] Accessed: http://www.riksdagen. se/sv/Dokument-Lagar/Lagar/Svenskforfattningssam.

SNAE 2018 *Syllabus for municipal adult education in Swedish tuition for immigrants (SFI)*. https://www.skolverket.se/download/18.472714ce16b70ab982719b8/ 1570018131726/Kursplan%20sfi%20engelska%201.pdf

Toth, J. (2018) English-medium instruction for young learners in Sweden: A longitudinal case study of a primary school class in a bilingual English-Swedish school. PhD thesis. Stockholm: Stockholm University.

Yoxsimer Paulsrud, B. (2014) English-medium instruction in Sweden: Perspectives and practices in two upper secondary schools. PhD thesis. Stockholm: Stockholm University.

11 Doing Multilingual Language Assistance in *Swedish for Immigrants* Classrooms

Oliver St John

Introduction

The present study focuses on the classroom practice of *multilingual language assistants* (MLAs) who, as the term suggests, assist adult immigrants in acquiring Swedish as a second language by means of their multilingual knowledge and competence. In terms of research results, very little is known about this kind of second language support person who works alongside the class language teacher. Therefore, to gain background for this study, it is necessary to turn to other kinds of supplementary educational assistants who share a common *para*-educator position. Nordic and international studies of *school subject-oriented* practitioners have highlighted their marginalized and precarious work conditions (Baker, 2014; Dávila, 2018; Martin-Jones & Saxena, 2003).

A further challenge in relation to multilingual assistance has to do with the necessary conditions for learning new language both common and school subject oriented. The pedagogical use of students' language backgrounds is heralded as significantly advantageous in learning an additional language and achieving academic success (Baker, 2011; Cummins, 2018; García, 2009). At the same time, second language acquisition (SLA) research has clarified that plenty of meaningful 'target language' experience is a prerequisite for mastering it (Flyman Mattsson, 2018; Swain, 2000; Swain & Deters, 2007). Both these findings raise the important question of how different language resources in plurilingual settings should be brought into pedagogical play and coordinated to optimize learning conditions for second language development. They also point to the vital importance of generating knowledge about 'when' and 'how' use of students' primary languages is advantageous in a context where there is a strong commitment to valorize students' home languages and a con-current overriding educational goal to teach the majority language.

The above issues are particularly important for newly arrived adult immigrants for whom learning the host language is at a premium for resettlement and social cohesion (Abdulla, 2017; Beiser & Hou, 2001). Yet, despite motivation and ambition (Nilsson & Bunar, 2016), language acquisition among adult newcomers, especially those with little or mini-mal school background, is generally a frustratingly slow business (Lindberg, 2008). Adult language learning difficulties are reflected in the educational results of the *Swedish for Immigrants* (SFI) language program – Sweden's national state-funded school form for teaching newcomers foun-dational skills in Swedish. Inspired by the prospects of learners using their strongest language to acquire another language and concerned about the slow progress of the students on their courses, a team of SFI teachers recruited MLAs as instructional assistants for their classes. The MLAs were employed as educational partners to stimulate language learning among adult immigrants with little or severely interrupted previous schooling and with varying degrees of literacy. Class teachers together with MLAs thus configure the multilingual SFI classrooms in which this study is set. From the start of the MLA project, the teachers have been aware that the task of developing new roles and practices was going to be formidable not least because the MLAs lack the pedagogical expertise and experience teachers rely on. As several researchers point out (Dávila & Bunar, 2020; Straszer *et al.*, 2019), uncertainty about the qualification required to work as an assistant alongside the inevitable instructional responsibility the role entails within education for newly arrived students creates an educational dilemma.

Against this background, the present study aims to investigate what MLAs actually do and how they deploy language in SFI settings as a basis for drawing conclusions about their role and multilingual assistance. The study relies on direct observation and video recordings of classroom inter-action to describe and analyze their multilingual performances. It seeks to answer the following three research questions: (1) What kind of assis-tance do MLA's provide? (2) How do they deploy their language resources to realize this assistance? (3) What are the noticeable effects of MLA assis-tance on student classroom conduct?

Multilingual Language Assistance

With the dramatic displacement of peoples and their transnational move-ment around the world today (García, 2017), many pupils and adult learn-ers are forced to make sense of language education and school teaching in a communicative medium they do not fully understand. International research has shown convincingly that when opportunity to use and learn in both 'first' and 'second' languages is provided, multilingual pupils

develop language skills in both varieties and, regarding academic achievement, outperform pupils who work in exclusively target language learning
environments (Cummins, 1996/2001). New knowledge is more effectively
and easily acquired in and through a well-known language one can think
clearly with (Official Inquiry, 2019: 18). However, the extent to which use
of a learner's first language (L1) is advantageous to additional language
learning and its effect on learning conditions or even learner attitudes are
currently still open-ended questions (Macaro *et al.*, 2014). The cost of L1
use in terms of reducing the *beneficial* opportunity for learners to engage
constructively with unmodified messages in a second language (L2)
(Turnbull & Dailey-O'Cain, 2009), to express themselves strategically so
that their current L2 competence is challenged (Swain *et al.*, 2009) and to
negotiate L2 meanings interactionally for comprehension (Long, 1996) is
a particularly thorny question (see Littlewood & Yu, 2011).

Research into MLAs with an orientation to school curricular subject
learning is scarce but reveals that while their educational services are valo-
rized by policy documents and school personnel, contradiction and con-
straint surround their roles. On the valorization side, studies find that
bilingual support staff are well equipped to counter the educational
inequalities of linguistically vulnerable learners by supporting their learning (Baker, 2014), fostering the social and emotional aspects of children's
learning and developing links between home and school-based learning
environments (Cable, 2004; Dávila, 2018). Contradicting these advantages, bilingual assistants were marginalized by low status, precarious
positions, overtly transitional educational policy (Bourne, 2001; Kenner
et al., 2008; Martin-Jones & Saxena, 2003), the power of the class teacher
over classroom activity and turn-taking (Martin-Jones & Saxena, 1996)
and by a lack of training among teachers for working in pedagogic partnership with another adult (Dávila, 2018).

In Sweden, the provision of *study guidance in the mother tongue*
(SGMT) is a legal right for multilingual pupils and students assessed as in
need of it because they risk failing to meet minimum curricular course
requirements without it (Swedish Education Act, 2010: 800; see Reath
Warren, this volume; Wedin, this volume). While the Swedish National
Agency for Education (SNAE) outlines an array of competences that affect
the quality of SGMT positively including pedagogical skill, no formal
qualifications are required to work as an SGMT tutor (SNAE, 2019).
Moreover, a tutor's position is cast as temporary and dispensable by a transitional educational policy (SNAE, 2019). At the same time, research has
pointed to the devaluing effects of sporadic and superficial cooperation
between tutors and other teachers (Avery, 2017) and the critical importance of joint planning for tutor professionalism (Straszer *et al.*, 2019).

The thrust of available research indicates that when SGMT is available, both students and teachers perceive it as creating conditions for multilingual learners to follow Swedish-medium instruction and to attain

subject learning goals (Official Inquiry, 2019: 18). Forging links between students' experience of their previous schooling and Swedish school subject learning (Nilsson & Bunar, 2016), student advocacy (Dávila & Bunar, 2020) and boosting the self-confidence and engagement of newly arrived pupils (Rosén, 2018) are foregrounded as key aspects of a SGMT role. Regarding language choice, several studies report a tutor's translanguaging practice (Dávila & Bunar, 2020; Reath Warren, 2016; Rosén, 2017) in which students' mother tongues are used to translate instructional content orally, explain, discuss and raise pupils' metalinguistic awareness. Rosén (2018) and St John (2018) describe the tutor task of mediating two-way communication. By pivoting between home language and Swedish, the tutor can make divergent communication between teacher and pupils comprehensible as well as support the latter's engagement in classroom meaning-making.

In the context of Japanese first-year university students learning English as a foreign language in the UK, Macaro *et al.* (2014) report that, according to the students, the participation of a bilingual language assistant alongside a main teacher enabled them to tune in to the monolingual teacher talk, to produce the complex contributions they would not have been able to make on their own and to transfer culturally-specific concepts and expressions to communication in English. On the other hand, the study cautions that L1 may be used excessively and can undermine efforts to develop goal-related language skills.

The SFI Context

The municipal adult education in *Swedish for immigrants* (SFI) is a state-funded and steered part of the Swedish education system. According to the National Curriculum for SFI, the purpose of this language program is to:

> give adult immigrants a basic knowledge of the Swedish language. This tuition gives students with a mother tongue other than Swedish the opportunity to learn and develop a functional knowledge of a second language. The tuition shall provide the language tools for communication and enable active participation in everyday life, in society, at work and in pursuing further study. (SNAE, 2018: 7)

The aim of SFI is also to 'give adult immigrants who lack basic reading and writing skills the opportunity to acquire these skills' (SNAE, 2018: 7). SFI education is organized into three study paths that all provide courses for beginners in Swedish but target students with different educational backgrounds, learner characteristics and ambitions (Official Inquiry, 2019). This study focuses on MLA work alongside SFI teachers on Study Path 1 geared to students with little or interrupted formal education whose literacy skills and language proficiency vary extensively.

While SFI is a segregated educational setting (St John & Liubinienè, 2021), it aspires to be 'a qualified language education' (Lindberg & Sandwall, 2012) as an integral part of the national school system (Official Inquiry, 2019). According to the education act, the local municipality is responsible for offering study and career guidance for those at foundational levels of adult education courses and, with students who are beginners in Swedish, for providing this support in a student's mother tongue or in another language a student is proficient in (Official Inquiry, 2019; Swedish Education Act, 2010:800).

SFI has been the target of persistent criticism such as low flow-through rates, poor course achievements and inappropriate pedagogical approaches (Hyltenstam & Milani, 2012). Areas identified as deficient include inadequate measures to tailor teaching to the experiences, pre-existing knowledge and needs of the individual learners, teaching characterized by an insufficient level of challenge and passive learning, low relevance content, a lack of an adult oriented pedagogy and few opportunities for oral communication as critical issues to address (Official Inquiry, 2019; School Inspectorate, 2018). At the same time, SFI classes tend to be excessively linguistically and culturally diverse, making the task of adapting teaching to student circumstances particularly challenging (Hyltenstam & Milani, 2012).

Theoretical Framework

In SLA, engaging in conversational interaction (Long, 1983, 1996) and verbal production which challenges learners' existing communicative capacities (Swain & Deters, 2007; Swain *et al.*, 2009) is highlighted as important, if not essential, in language learning processes. Translanguaging has its roots in classroom practice (Baker, 2011) but has been developed into a theoretical approach and a pedagogy (García, 2009; Li Wei, 2018). In this study, the concept of translanguaging *corriente* proves fruitful for perspective on multilingual practice as pedagogical resource (García *et al.*, 2017). Translanguaging corriente describes the dynamic flow of bilingual communication through classrooms or other school settings that supports sense-making. With teachers in focus, the corriente assumes a translanguaging *stance* (core convictions), *design* (instructional specifications) and *shifts* (teacher flexibility) for a translanguaging *pedagogy*. Like the three strands of a rope, these aspects intertwine to form a classroom pedagogy permeated by the following four translanguaging purposes:

(1) To support student engagement with complex content and texts.
(2) To provide opportunities for students to develop linguistic practices for academic contexts.
(3) To make space for students' bilingualism and ways of knowing.
(4) To support students' socioemotional development and bilingual identities (Garcia *et al.*, 2017: 29).

Bakhtin's insights into understanding add theoretical dimension to the framework. Bakhtin (1981: 282) interrogates the monologic view that understanding an utterance is a pre-condition for replying to it by asserting that 'understanding comes to fruition only in the response'. From a dialogic perspective, it is in *achieving a response* that communicative means turn into *meanings* and recognition transforms into *understanding*.

Research Methodology

This study is part of an action research project (Bailey, 2001) in which a team of SFI, Study Path 1 teachers, in collaboration with a university researcher, have investigated their current practices with MLAs in the classroom as a basis for bringing about change that enhances learning conditions for the students. Early in the project, the teachers became aware that they needed to learn more specifically about how they could develop their cooperative work with the MLAs in and outside the classroom to attain their goal of facilitating and simplifying the students' language learning. In the absence of research into MLA-mediated language education, action research has enabled these teachers to take charge of their own competence development by analyzing their classroom interaction with MLAs and applying the findings strategically.

Participants and Research Ethics

There were four MLA participants in this study: Yasmin, Samireh, Latisha and Waris. *Yasmin* was from Syria and described herself as having two mother tongues: Syrian and Arabic. She had completed two years of a degree in agricultural engineering when her university studies were interrupted by the civil war. At the time of the study, she had lived in Sweden for four years. She was studying on the SFI Study Path 3 for students with academic backgrounds when she applied to the local municipality for the job of MLA.

Samireh was born and raised in Iran. In her homeland, she attended university for a year and, having studied English at a private school, worked as a teacher of English with children between the ages of 5 and 15. On arrival in Sweden, Samireh landed the job of MLA while studying Swedish on an advanced SFI course having been in the country for a year and half. As an MLA, she assisted in Dari.

Latisha was from Syria and studied law at the university in Damascus. Before applying for the job of MLA, she had taken a course in truck driving, worked as an Arabic teacher at a culture association and taken courses in Swedish as a second language. She applied for the post of MLA through the job center. She assisted with Arabic.

Waris came from Somalia where she completed a university teacher training course. In Sweden, she took a series of SFI language courses and became an MLA through the job center personnel who matched her work experience with the MLA role. She had been in Sweden five years at the time of the study and assisted the Somali-speaking students.

Regarding research ethics, use of pseudonyms and alteration of recognizable references have anonymized the participants and de-identified the research site. Given the sensitivities of working with immigrants in a research project, care has been taken to gain the consent of both MLAs and their students without exploiting a position of authority or immigrant vulnerability. Since this action research was jointly conducted by the SFI teachers and researcher, obtaining the consent of the teachers was not an ethical issue.

Data Production and Analysis

The study data claim to capture the multilingual moves and voices of MLAs in SFI classrooms and focus group arenas. To investigate MLA work, data were generated by video recordings of MLA-mediated classroom instruction, focus groups and classroom observations. The 10 video sequences, recorded by the teachers, of SFI whole-class and group work interaction used in this study amount to approximately four and a half hours of recorded material. Professional translators were used to transcribe and translate the multilingual classroom interaction. Three focus groups were conducted with all MLAs at the beginning, in the middle and at the end of the study providing six hours of interview data. Nine half-days of classroom observations spread over the study period yielded a fund of field notes. In view of the incongruity that can arise between what people say they do and what they do in practice (Patton, 2002), the analytic procedure was to first look closely at the MLAs' practices before drawing on their perceptions as a strategy for producing an account of the kind of assistance MLAs provide. Accordingly, qualitative content analysis (Hjerm *et al.*, 2014) was conducted on the transcripts of classroom interaction in relation to field notes, and then these findings were correlated with the interview material. Triangulation, participant validation checks and the collaborative affordances of the action research model are likely to enhance the transferability value of study results to similar contexts. With the research questions ringing in relevance, this analytic process yielded four outstanding themes, namely *transposing* teacher performance, multilingual *linking*, *contextualizing* instructional content and *thresholding* student performance.

Doing Multilingual Language Assistance

With the aim of answering the study's three research questions, this section profiles several salient aspects of MLA practice when doing multilingual assistance in SFI learning settings. These *multilingual moves* or *interacts* link critical communicative relations in the classroom to realize pedagogical projects. While these multilingual moves flow into each other and form integral aspects of an MLA-mediated approach to teaching and supporting students, they exhibit distinction in terms of what they accomplish *in situ*.

Transposing teacher performance

With their capacity to mediate teacher meanings in terms intelligible to students, MLAs do not reproduce what the teachers do and say but routinely *transpose* teacher performance to bring it into student communicative range. That is, they regularly modify classroom interaction by attuning teacher talk to student 'wavelengths'. Extract 11.1 comes from a lesson opening introducing group work on the theme of 'It's burning' and illustrates MLA *treatment* of teacher instructional performance. The teacher has projected a picture of a burning saucepan as an aid to elicit the students' previous experiences of fires in the home and identify words they would like to learn in Swedish related to the theme (Figure 11.1). In this extract, the teacher (T) speaks Swedish, the students (S1/2) answer in Arabic and the MLA (A) uses Somali (see 'Key to transcript symbols' at the end of the text). English translations are provided under the speakers' utterances in the transcript.

Extract 11.1 On fire.[1]

1 **T:** Alla tänker (2) vad se- vad händer på bilden? ((T adopts questioning pose))
   Everyone think   what's happening in the picture?

2   Vad händer? ((T gestures combustion and flames))
   What's happening?

3 **S1:** حريق(2)
   There's a fire

4 **S2:** حريق
   Ah there's a fire

5 **T:** (13) ((T moves to computer and full-screens picture))

6   Vad händer på bilden? ((T fingers number 1))
   What's happening in the picture?

7 **S2:** حريق
   There's a fire

8 **T:** Vilka ord kan jag saga? ((T fingers 2 and encircles picture with her hands))
   Which words do I know?

9   Vad kan jag- ((T mimes words coming out of her mouth))
   What can I-

10   Vilka ord vill jag lära mig? Vad vill jag lära mig?
   Which words do I want to learn? What do I want to learn?

11 **A:** *maxaad doonaysaa inaad ka baratid?*
   What do you want to learn?

Figure 11.1 Visual aid

In this extract, the teacher introduces two tasks – to talk about the picture (Lines 1, 2 and 6) and to share the Swedish words the students already know related to the theme as a basis for identifying those words that they would like to learn (Lines 8–10). Coherent student response in Arabic signals that at least some students have understood her questions accompanied by rich nonverbal representation (Lines 3, 4 and 7). In the four questions explaining the second task (Lines 8–10), the teacher adopts a rhetorical device by using *I*, and only the first two utterances are supported gesturally. It is the last two potentially less comprehensible questions (Line 10) that the Somali-speaking MLA attends to by transposing them into a single, more direct and accessible question in Somali (Line 11).

Research on SGMT tutors has identified oral translation as an integral part of a tutor practice (e.g. Dávila, 2018; Rosén, 2018; Straszer *et al.*, 2019). While MLAs regularly turn Swedish into language students can comprehend, study data illustrated by Extract 11.1 indicate that any description of the multilingual moves MLAs make needs to consider two important features. First, MLA's oral translation of teacher performance from one kind of language to another is highly *selective* practice and seems to be governed by situated judgments of student need and understanding in the throes of classroom interaction. Second, when MLAs do multilingual assistance, they tend not to replicate the teacher's words or other actions but rework them analytically into student-attuned performance. In other words, their representation of teacher communication entails *transposing* – altering and adapting language kind and key – rather than translating teacher performance into another language as exactly as possible.

Furthermore, the extract also illustrates that legitimized use of the learners' linguistic repertoires enables the students to engage constructively with the teacher's instructions (Lines 3, 4 and 7). However, the teacher does not acknowledge these student responses because she does not understand them (later on in this lesson two students try to teach her the Arabic for 'There's a fire'). In this divergent language scenario, unless the MLA transposes the Arabic utterances into Swedish, the teacher is not able to take up these students' answers meaningfully. Rosén (2018) reports that two-way communication between teachers and students mediated by SGMT tutors means that newcomer pupils can participate in classroom discussion. In the absence of the MLA's intervention to forward these Arabic answers in Swedish, the students' contributions are marginalized and their attempts to participate are frustrated.

An important finding in the data is that, in making teacher talk transparent to students, MLA's use of Swedish can be as communicatively significant for student understanding as their language work across language boundaries. When MLAs were asked in a focus group interview about their own views on their role and contribution, they agreed that their way of explaining in Swedish was frequently easier for students to understand than the teachers' talk in Swedish because 'we know exactly what can reach [the students] and what cannot'. Alluding to the teacher talk with a class he was currently working with, one MLA explained:

> The teachers' explanations are in difficult language. There are easy and difficult synonyms. The teacher was not able to focus on her use of the difficult synonyms. Use the easiest synonyms [...]. Use Swedish in an easy way to be sure that students understand both teachers and the assistants.

The following two fragments, documented during classroom observation, illustrate MLA transposing work in Swedish for the sake of easy language access:

Extract 11.2 Transposing a question

1 T: Vad betyder hyresgäst?
       What does tenant mean?
2 A: Vem är hyresgäster?
       Who are tenants?

Extract 11.3 Transposing an instruction

1 T: Jag ställer en fråga och ni svarar
       I'll ask a question and you answer
2 A: Fråga ((MLA points to T)) Svar ((MLA indicates Ss))
       Question   Answer

In the interview data, simpler and more straightforward MLA use of Swedish is explained in terms of MLAs' own emergent language development ('Because we aren't fluent at Swedish') and associated to MLA *approachability* ('Students are not afraid of explaining their particular problems to the assistants in Swedish but dare not to teachers'). Their highly accessible use of Swedish is also linked to their articulatory affinity with the students ('For we have Arabic ears').

Multilingual linking

A significant amount of multilingual assistance in the data is geared to linking students and teachers communicatively in the classroom for meaningful pedagogical participation. Multilingual linking most involved clarifying the meaning of language students did not comprehend so that they could follow and contribute to Swedish-medium instruction. Data show that MLA moves to illuminate sometimes small but troublesome pieces of language regularly made significant differences to students' level of engagement. Here, the classroom interaction features Swedish (Normal) and *Somali* (in *italics*).

Extract 11. 4 Linking students to teachers

```
1   T:    igår så pratade vi om fyra årstider. Vi pratade om vinter, höst, sommar och vår.
          Yesterday we talked about the four seasons. We talked about winter, autumn, summer and
          spring
2   S1:   maxey tiri?
          What did she say?
3   A:    [dhaxantii, somarkii, qaboowgii, deyrtii.
          Autumn,    summer,    winter,    spring
4   T:    [Det kan man säga i en mening.  Om det är vår, de:t ä:r vå:r.
          We can put these into a sentence If it is spring It   is spring
5   S2:   Det är vår
          It is spring
6   T:    Det är vår
          It is spring
7   S2:   Det är vår
          It is spring
8   T:    Höst? ((shakes head))
          Autumn?
9   S1:   Det är [inte höst inte höst
          It is not autumn  not autumn
10  T:           [Det är inte höst
                 It    is not autumn
11        Vår hö:st (2.5) Vår hö:st
          Spring autumn Spring autumn
12  S1:   Sommar=
          Summer
13  T:    =sommar ja >hur säger man det<
          Summer yes how do you say that?
14  S1:   De:t [ä:r inte ((gestures no)) so:mmar
          It    is not                    summer
15  T:         [de:t ä:r i:nte so:mmar
               It is not summer
    [...]
```

16	T:	Vinter
		Winter
17	S1:	De:t ä:r [inte so:mm-
		It is not summer
18	T:	[De:t ä:r i:inte
		It is not
19	A:	**Vinter**=
		Winter
20	S1:	=vinter=
21	T:	=vinter

This extract documents the way a student's ability to respond successfully to instructional challenge is mediated by MLA clarification of the Swedish words for the four seasons (Line 3) she did not initially understand (Line 2). As soon as the teacher has prompted 'negative' constructions with the different seasons (Lines 8, 13 and 16), the student takes a leading role in formulating the target sentences correctly in Swedish (Lines 9, 14, 17 and 20) and displaying her understanding. Her confident and eager performance is 'first off the mark', ahead of the teacher and other students whose answers trail and confirm what she has already accomplished.

In linguistically diverse classrooms in which teachers strive to attune their teaching to the performance levels and needs of the learners, teachers also need to be linked to students. Analysis shows that, without access to what the students have achieved or struggled with in MLA-mediated group work, teachers are prevented from building pedagogically on students' emerging language competence. The consequences are that teachers cannot engage with their students' language learning efforts, and ongoing teaching may not 'scratch where students are itching'. The following extract represents interaction between an MLA, student and a teacher at the end of group work in which the teacher gains access to the student's answer to what she would do if a fire broke out in her kitchen. The teacher has probed understanding in the group and the MLA attempts to report in Swedish what the student has said in Arabic. The sequence is launched by the MLA question 'What is the first thing we must do?'

Extract 11.5 Linking teachers to students

1	S:	أول شي بدنا ندق للأمبولانص
		First we should ring for the ambulance
2	A:	لأ, إزا أنتي شفتي الزيت شاعل بتتصلي بالأمبولانص ولا بتحاولي إنتي
		But if you see oil burning, would you ring the ambulance or try yourself?
3	S:	ديركت, بحاول, الطفاية اللي بالبيت. بطفي الغاز, بشيل الطنجرة. والطفاية بطفيا. إزا
		First, I'd try to use the fire-extinguisher in the house. I'd turn off the stove, take off the pot and use the fire- extinguisher
4		شفتا ولعت كتير بطالع ولادي و بدق للأمبولانص.
		If the fire gets bigger, I'd take out my children and ring for the ambulance
5	A:	först (.) Salma säger (.) först hon (3) <try>=
		first Salma says first she try
6	T:	=försöker=

```
            tries
7    A:   =försöker att s=
            tries to e-
8.   T:   =släcka (.5)  släcka Det  när   man stoppar (.5) släcka=
            extinguish  extinguish  what you do to stop     extinguish
9    A:   =brinnet först (.) men om brinnet är större (.5) Hon ska ringa ambulans
            the fire first     but if the fire is bigger       she's going to call the ambulance
10   T:   Precis
            Exactly
11   A:   och ta hennes barn och gå ut direkt.
            and take her children and get out immediately
12   L:   Precis
            Exactly
13   S:   Direkt!
            Immediately
```

This extract shows the teacher scaffolding the MLA's reporting efforts cooperatively with her (Lines 5–11) to connect with Salma's current knowledge and previous experience of dealing with home fire emergencies (Lines 1–4). When the MLA pauses in search of Swedish verbs to describe Salma's actions (Lines 5 and 7), the teacher immediately supplies the target words (Lines 6 and 8) that the MLA then uses as stepping stones to get her meaning across (Lines 7 and 9). Lines 5–11 also reveal that one significant obstacle to the practice of MLAs reporting back group work activity or interpreting student contributions for teachers in whole-class arrangements is *linguistic* challenge. Thus, as this teacher demonstrates, teachers may need to make special linguistic provision for MLAs to reciprocate a flow of information and meaning about learner performance and knowledge levels so that their ensuing instruction can meet students where they are and enable them to orient to ongoing instructional content.

In the interviews, the notion of linking is used by the MLAs to describe their role as language assistants as in the following:

> We are the link that connects the students and the teachers. That's the role. Some students need a little push and we are the link between teachers and those who hardly dare to say a word, to motivate them, engage them.

Contextualizing instructional content

A recurring multilingual move is to enable multilingual students to make sense of instructional content by setting it in a personally relevant context. MLAs make particular contexts communicatively relevant so that students can apprehend and orient to new Swedish language. Such contextual resources include personal experiences and participants' knowledge about focal events related to the language. The following extract demonstrates the power of contextualizing targeted language in immediately meaningful student circumstances and experiences for igniting student understanding. It is taken from a lesson in which one student's written description in Swedish of an outing the whole class had been on the previous week is used by the teacher as a platform for language learning. While the main teaching focus was on past tenses, other language challenges featured in the text that warranted attention, one of which was the *definite plural form* in Swedish. The sequence presents the way this Swedish structure was explained by the teacher and the MLA.

Extract 11.6 Who are the teachers?

1   T: var det en eller två lärare (1) lärare en (.5) lärarna flera (1) varför lärarna
         was it one or two teachers   teacher <u>one</u> the teachers <u>several</u> (1) why <u>the</u> teachers

2   S1: tre
         three

3   T: studenterna? (.) många studenter
         the students   many students

4   A: varför <u>na</u> (.5) vem är läraren (.5) bestämd form (.5)
         why <u>na</u>   who are the teachers definite form

5   ليش / لماذا المعلمين أو المعلمون؟ مين المعلم)الأستاذ(المعرف ب ال ..
         why al-muallimeen eller al-muallimoon (.) who are the teachers who are called
         "al". There are

6   الأساتذة كتير لكن أي أساتذة؟ ليندا، آنا. طلاب ،بس أيا طلاب ؟
         several teachers (.) but which are the teachers. Linda (.) me (1) students (.) but
         which students.

7   مجموعة ٥٥، أنتم ، الطلاب. أقول معلمون بدون التعريف و التحديد.
         <u>you</u> (.) students in group 55 (.5) I say teachers when there isn't a clear definition or
         limit on

8   أيضا هي حالة جمع(كثير) لكن عندما نقول المعلمون... أي معلمون،
         them (.) this is plural (.5) but when we say 'the teachers' then it's in the definite
         form (1) this

9   إيضا ينطبق الكلام عندما نقول الطلاب. طلاب أيضا جمع ولكن أيا
         is also the case when we say 'the students' (.5) 'the students' is also plural (.) but
         which

10   طلاب أنتم أنتم على وجه الخصوص التحديد، الطلاب.
         students. When it's specified and limited (.) then it's 'the students'

11   ärare många (.5) men v<u>i</u>lka (.) Linda (.)   Tina (1) elever (.5)   men v<u>i</u>lka elever (.)
         the teachers many but which ones Linda   Tina   students   but which students,

12   grupp 55 <u>ni</u> (.5) elever<u>na</u>
         group 55 you   the students

13 S2: nu förstår
         now understand

Dovetailing into the teacher's focus on *plurality* (Lines 1 and 3), this MLA's instructional strategy is to contextualize the grammar in the students' personal experience. After pinpointing the focal end syllable of the definite plural form (Line 4), the MLA illuminates both the notion of plurality and the specific, delimited, meaning of the definite form by relating them to the particular teachers and set of students who were present on the outing. With each of her parallel examples in her Arabic explantation, she asks a leading question (Lines 5 and 6) and then breaks down the target structure to the plural component (Lines 5 and 6) before she contextualizes the combined definite and plural components in the specific details of the students' outing experience (Lines 6 and 7). Finally, she provides follow-up metalinguistic clarification (Lines 7, 8, 9 and 10). The final instruction in Swedish – succinct and straightforward – follows the Arabic closely without the metalinguistic explanation (Lines 11 and 12).

This MLA's strategy of contextualizing the language meaningfully is realized partly by reconfiguring a number of contextual resources that she makes communicatively relevant *in situ*. For example, the teacher's co-text (Lines 1 and 3) is not only extended but recycled as an integral part of the MLA's explanation. She invokes the specifically relevant detail from the outing as a contextual resource for generating understanding. Her strategy is also accomplished by an alternation of linguistic resources. The MLA draws from her entire linguistic repertoire. Arabic is sandwiched between two slices of Swedish. This language practice allows the MLA to manage an instructor transition and subsequently language alternation. By initially continuing in Swedish where the teacher broke off (Line 4), the MLA aligns her turn with the teacher's talk so that the instruction passes smoothly from one practitioner to another. Once this transition is secured, the MLA can alternate within her turn to a different language variety without abrasion (Line 5). The sequence suggests that her use of Arabic may well be prompted by the demands of explaining complex grammar in a language the students do not yet know well. Use of Arabic allows the MLA greater expressive capacity and specificity in her explanation. Linguistic items such as *definition*, *the definite form*, *specified* and *limited* in Arabic enable her to make the Swedish label 'bestämd form' (Line 4) more intelligible to the students. Her final move to Swedish signals the end of her explanatory turn and creates linguistic compatibility for passing back instructional responsibility to the teacher. In effect, these instructions are delivered twice and illustrate an instructor's translanguaging practice. In instructional partnership with the teacher, the MLA extends the former's pedagogical range so that students can grasp the meaning of this grammatical form (Line 13).

Thresholding student performance

Since learner agency and effort in producing new language is crucial for grasping how it works in practice and mastering it, the question as to what kinds of opportunity MLAs create for student independent communicative performance in Swedish is critical. In the data, supplying metalinguistic knowledge about the target language and coordinating student orientation to tasks in language they can easily grasp are common forms of launching language use in Swedish. The following extract is taken from interaction in the Arabic language group with a focus on the Swedish negation form and illustrates personally attuned *thresholding* moves geared to accompanying the student to the point at which she can do the language unaccompanied.

Extract 11.7 Thresholding through attuned feedback

1	L:	Ok? Vi testar och pratar i gruppen
		Ok? Let's try and talk in your groups
2	A:	يدكم تحكو هلا عن الجو. شو هلا الجو انو مثلا شو شايفين هلا
		Now we're going to talk about the weather. What's the weather like now? For example, what does it look like now?
3	S1:	هلا هوا هوا
		It's windy now. It's windy
4	A:	أي اعطيني صفه عن الطقس هلا و صفه مو عنو هلا
		Yes, give me a description of the weather now and a description of what it isn't now.
5	S1:	Det är blåser idag
		It (is) winds today
6	A:	°Det blåser°=
		It is windy
7	T:	=Blå:ser=
		Windy
8	S1:	=idag
		today
9	A:	و عطيني شي مو صاير برا شو الطقس هلا
		And give me something that isn't happening outside now. What's the weather like now?
10	S2:	Det är inte bra
		It isn't good
11	T:	Inte bra ((Laughter))
		Not good
12	S1:	DET REGNAR INTE. Det regnar inte
		It isn't raining. It isn't raining
13	T:	aah.
14	S3:	Det kommer regna
		It's going to rain
15	L:	Ja snart
		Yes, soon.
16	S1:	Det snöar inte. DET SNÖAR inte.
		It isn't snowing. It isn't snowing

In this sequence, the MLA unpacks the teacher's instruction (Line 1) progressively in a series of questions and requests (Lines 2, 4 and 9) that elicit a number of student responses (Lines 3, 5, 10, 12, 14 and 16). The student utterances, the first in Arabic (Line 3) and the others in Swedish, demonstrate a lively engagement with the task. By coordinating student comprehension of what the task involves step by step, the MLA creates successive thresholds for students to exercise agency and produce their own meaningful weather descriptions in Swedish.

Moreover, the MLA's feedback treatment of the students' weather reports is an integral part of her *thresholding* work. In Line 4, the MLA affirms S1's answer in Arabic (Line 3) with a 'yes' but her following request for a description of the current weather conditions when S1 has just given her one indicates that she expects a description in Swedish. In line with this meaning, S1 takes the initiative to render her Arabic answer in

Swedish (Line 5). S1 is an elderly student who has been struggling with the target form and who has been treated gently and respectfully by the MLA during group work. This student's report (Line 5) is coherent with the weather conditions (it is windy outside) but irregular in form. In reply, the MLA recasts the ungrammatical part of her utterance quietly in the background (Line 6). This response demonstrates a respectful distance and is followed and confirmed by the teacher (Line 7) who has joined the group. While this feedback does not create opportunity to self-correct, its restricted treatment allows S1 to pin 'today' onto the end of her corrected clause and reclaim her contribution (Line 8). In her next utterance (Line 9), the MLA moves on to request a description of what is not currently happening weather-wise and, in so doing, affirms S1's repaired performance as valid. In other words, by turning the attention of the group onto the second step of the task, this MLA confirms S1's contribution as an acceptable completion of the first task step. This MLA's affirmative and personally sensitive accompaniment pays dividends in terms of thresholding this student's task performance. In Lines 12 and 16, S1 pitches in uninhibitedly with competent descriptions in Swedish of the current outside weather.

Extract 11.7 indicates that the MLA's feedback strategies are sensitive to the student's personal characteristics and socioemotional conditions. S1 in Extract 11.7, an elderly student who has exhibited considerable difficulty grasping the language structure and timidity in front of the other students during group work, is accompanied gently and courteously. In the data, this kind of thresholding constrasts with MLA treatment of confident, talkative younger students who are challenged head-on by brisk accompaniment and direct questioning techniques. Both approaches and the spectrum of strategies in between them lead different students to thresholds of uptake and independent language performance in Swedish. This study aligns with literature on multilingual practitioners that profile the important role they play in supporting learners socially and emotionally (Baker, 2014; Dávila & Bunar, 2020; Rosén, 2018). MLAs recent personal experience of coping as a newcomer to Sweden and learning the language sensitize them uniquely to appreciate the emotional upheaval and sociocultural vulnerability of their students and to prioritize imparting security and hope as a bottom line for learning.

Discussion

As *intermediaries* that 'go-between' teachers and students, MLAs do strategic multilingual, adaptive, inclusive and pedagogical assistance. MLAs adapt and modify teacher approach and performance to make classroom instruction comprehensible for SFI students (Extract 11.1). While this adaptive work addresses criticism that SFI teaching is not sufficiently adapted to individual student proficiency levels and needs (School

Inspectorate, 2018), it raises the question of what this work may deny students. In effect, MLAs routinely do what second language learners become skilled at doing to secure comprehension in interaction with speakers of the target language that simultaneously promotes acquisition (Long, 1983, 1996). Negotiating meaning *for* students (rather than *with* them) and serving them with modified, *comprehensible*, interaction may enact a multilingual pedagogy that fails to empower adult learners as autonomous and successful learners.

As intermediaries, MLAs include students on the periphery of classroom activity by, for example, activating students' prior knowledge related to a theme (Extract 11.5), linking them into ongoing instruction (Extract 11.4) and accompanying students to thresholds of personal engagement (Extracts 11.7). One critical inclusion issue is that there are some students in the class whose language backgrounds are not covered by MLA language competence and as a result may feel marginalized by MLA-mediated classroom support. MLA use of Swedish goes far in bridging this gap but may not go far enough to prevent feelings of unfair treatment and exclusion.

In extending the teachers' pedagogic range, the MLAs do frontline instructional work (Extracts 11.6 and 11.7). However, as with SGMT tutors, there are no formal qualifications required to work as an MLA except command of the language assistance needs to be provided through. Consequently, there is the risk that students may suffer from incongruous approaches and divergent instructional shifts. This pedagogic vulnerability beams up the importance of pre-lesson supervision to equip MLAs for the demands their pedagogic tasks make on their capacities to support students' own learning processes in concert with teachers (see Avery, 2017; Rosén, 2018). All these critical issues imply what the notion of support signifies. *Educational assistance* is not to do learning work for learners. It is the art of including learners in the pedagogic process of engaging their abilities to meet feasible challenges so that they can reap the learning that their own exertions generate.

The image of *intermediary* has also served to identify missing moves in MLA-mediated classroom communication. It has led to the finding that while instructional flow from teacher to students via MLAs is strong, reciprocal communication from students to teachers via MLAs is not regular practice and in need of development if the two-way communicative potential of intermediary work is to be realized. Loss of student voices point to the critical importance of developing strategies for making student contributions accessible to all participants in whole-class interaction and for informing teachers about group work progress in order to enhance relevance and progression in instructional activity. Data point to instructional, organizational and linguistic reasons for this predominantly teacher-to-student communicative current in MLA-mediated classroom instruction. First, without knowing *when* and, crucially, *why* to inform teachers about student meanings and understanding in Swedish, it is unlikely that MLAs will see this task as relevant to their role. Second, the organization of the classroom must position MLAs in readiness to relay student responses rapidly to make teacher uptake possible. Third, with linguistic vulnerability in focus, data underline the importance of pre-equipping MLAs with the language they might need to report in Swedish what students have said in another language but also to the effectiveness of interaction between teacher and MLAs for cooperatively constructing the report *in situ* (Extract 11.5).

How do MLAs deploy their language resources to realize their assistance? MLA assistance is accomplished in and through the alternation of more than one language with an expedient distribution of tasks. Student home languages are chosen to illuminate instructional activity (Extract 11.1, 11.4 and 11.6), to licence student voice and exploration (Extract 11.5), to raise metalinguistic knowledge (Extract 11.6) and to maneuver students into positions where they can do things in Swedish successfully (Extract 11.7). Swedish is used to make teacher talk immediately accessible in whole-class interaction where use of a home language would not reach *all* students in the classroom (Extracts 11.2 and 11.3), to report student contributions to teachers (Extract 11.5), to facilitate teacher-assistant language transitions (Extract 11.6) and to provide feedback on student Swedish performance (Extract 11.7). These extracts show that to achieve student engagement with ongoing teaching and group work, MLA language choice is regulated by both the demands of the pedagogic activity as well as by an orientation to the personal dispositions and affective conditions of the student participants. Thus, using students' home languages is seen to be advantageous for meeting educational goals when it enables students to engage with instructional input and pushes them to produce the target language communicatively. At the same time, MLAs teach us that with the complexity of local interactional arenas configured by pedagogic purpose and a host of learner variables, not least individual characteristics, cultural values and self-confidence, language use and alternation must always be a *local situated decision*.

This pattern of language deployment concords with the four defining purposes of a translanguaging pedagogy outlined by García *et al.* (2017). Extracts presented in this study illustrate that MLA multilingual moves support student engagement with target linguistic practices and create communicative space for students to express their ways of knowing on their own experiential and socioemotional terms. From this perspective, MLAs' assistance is realized in currents of coherent translanguaging supporting student sense-making in the classroom. Moreover, the translanguaging *corriente* (García *et al.*, 2017) signifies that MLA multilingual moves emanate from the teachers' *stance* on the benefits of mother tongue support for their students (see Turnbull & Dailey-O'Cain, 2009). MLA multilingal moves spring from teacher willingness to *design* instruction that entrusts the MLAs with teaching responsibility and to make peda-gogical space for the MLA's autonomous *shifts* of language deployment in the classroom.

With regard to the effects of MLA assistance, Extracts 11.1, 11.2, 11.3, 11.4 and 11.6 unpack some ways that MLA *explanatory* moves create conditions for student understanding and participation in classroom ped-agogic processes. In rationalizing the employment of MLAs, the teachers have stressed learner understanding as a necessary precondition for lan-guage learning and treated understanding in this SFI setting largely because of the MLAs' ability to clarify and make teachers' instruction accessible to students. Bakhtin (1981: 282) challenges the monologic notion of cognition preceding communication by insisting that '[u]nder-standing comes to fruition only in the response'. This stance is underlined in SLA scholarship, highlighting that when learners *language*, strive to make the language work for them communicatively, they come to know significantly more about how to express meaning through language than they are likely to gain by receiving explanation about it (Swain, 2000; Swain & Deters, 2007). With the task of making full use of the students' home languages in this L2 learning setting, MLA mediation raises the question of how much opportunity the learners receive to experience the kind of breakthroughs in understanding that occur when they can explore the potential of new language for communication. The main responsibil-ity for maintaining a balance between understanding *for* language use and understanding *through* language use in MLA-mediated learning environ-ments lies with teachers. Far from making MLAs redundant (see SNAE, 2019), verbal production activities in the target language, such as those illustrated by Extract 11.7, are seen to be effectively realized by the MLAs' ability to encourage students to reach thresholds of autonomous language performance and transformative learning experience.

Note

(1) Key to transcript symbols
   T = Teacher
   A = (ML)Assistant
   S1/2 = Student1/2
   Style Normal: Swedish and Arabic
   Style *Italics*: *Somali*
   (1.5) Silence in tenths of a second
   ((Laughter)) Non-verbal activity
   [Overlapping talk
   <u>word</u> Stress
   = Speakers follow each other without break
   >word< Rapid talk
   <word> slow talk
   wor:d Stretching of the vowel
   °word° quiet talk
   WORD Loud talk

References

Abdulla, A. (2017) Readiness or resistance? Newly arrived adult migrants' experiences, meaning making, and learning in Sweden. Doctoral thesis. University of Linköping.

Avery, H. (2017) At the bridging point: Tutoring newly arrived students in Sweden. *International Journal of Inclusive Education* 21 (4), 404–415.

Baker, C. (2011) *Foundations of Bilingual Education and Bilingualism* (5th edn). Bristol: Multilingual Matters.

Baker, S.B. (2014) The role of the bilingual teaching assistant: Alternative visions for bilingual support in the primary years. *International Journal of Bilingual Education and Bilingualism* 17 (3), 255–271.

Bakhtin, M.M. (1981) *The Dialogic Imagination*. Austin, TX: University of Texas Press.

Bailey, K. (2001) Action research, teacher research, and classroom research in language teaching. In M. Celce-Murcia (ed.) *Teaching English as a Second or Foreign Language* (3rd edn) (pp. 489–498). Singapore: Heinle & Heinle.

Beiser, M. and Hou, F. (2001) Language acquisition, unemployment and depressive disorder among Southeast Asian refugees: A 10–year study. *Social Sciences & Medicine* (53) 1321–1334.

Bourne, J. (2001) Doing what comes naturally: How the discourses and routines of teachers' practice constrain opportunities for bilingual support in UK primary schools. *Language and Education* 15 (4), 250–68.

Cable, C. (2004) 'I'm going to bring my sense of identity to this': The role and contribution of bilingual teaching assistants. *Westminster Studies in Education* 27 (2), 207–222.

Cummins, J. (1996/2001) *Negotiating Identities: Education for Empowerment in a Diverse Society*. Los Angeles: California Association for Bilingual Education.

Cummins, J. (2018) Urban multilingualism and educational achievement: Identifying and implementing evidence-based strategies for school improvement. In I.P. Van Avermaet, S. Slembrouck, K. Van Gorp, S. Sierens and K. Maryns (eds) *The Multilingual Edge of Education* (pp. 67–90). London: Palgrave Macmillan.

Dávila, L.T. (2018) The pivotal and peripheral roles of bilingual classroom assitants at a Swedish elementary school. *International Journal of Bilingual Education and Bilingualism* 21 (8), 956–967.

Dávila, L.T. and Bunar, N. (2020) Translanguaging through an advocacy lens: The roles of multilingual classroom assistants in Sweden. *European Journal of Applied Linguistics* 8 (1), 107–126.

Flyman Mattsson, A. (2018) Andraspråket i utveckling [Second language in development]. In T. Otterup and G. Kästen-Ebeling (eds) *En god fortsättning: Nyanländas fortsatta väg i skola och samhälle* [A Good Continuation: Newcomers' Continued Paths in School and Society] (pp. 141–161). Lund: Studentlitteratur.

García, O. (2009) *Bilingual Education in the 21st Century: A Global Perspective*. Malden, MA: Wiley-Blackwell.

García, O. (2017) Problematizing linguistic integration of migrants: The role of translanguaging and language teachers. In J.-C. Beacco, H.-J. Krumm, D. Little and P. Thalgott (eds) *The Linguistic Integration of Adult Migrants*. Council of Europe. Berlin: de Gruyter.

García, O., Ibarra Johnson, S. and Seltzer, K. (2017) *The Translanguaging Classroom: Leveraging Student Bilingualism for Learning*. Philadelphia: Caslon.

Hjerm, M., Lindgren, S. and Nilsson, M. (2014) *Introduktion till samhällsvetenskaplig analys* [Introduction to Social Scientific Analysis]. Malmö: Gleerups.

Hyltenstam, K. and Milani, T. (2012) Flerspråkighetens sociopolitiska och sociokulturella ramar [The sociopolitical and sociocultural frames of multilingualism]. In K. Hyltenstam, M. Axelsson and I. Lindberg (eds) *Flerspråkighet: En forskningsöversikt* [Multilingualism: A Research Rurvey] (pp. 17–152). Vetenskapsrådets rapportserie 5. Stockholm: The Swedish Research Council.

Kenner, C., Gregory, E., Ruby, M. and Al Azami, S. (2008) Bilingual learning for second and third generation Bengali children. *Language, Culture and Curriculum* 21 (2), 120–137.

Li Wei (2018) Translanguaging as a practical theory of language. *Applied Linguistics* 39 (1), 9–30.

Lindberg, I. (2008) *Andraspråksresan* [The Second Language Journey]. Tredje upplagan. Stockholm: Folkuniversitet.

Lindberg, I. and Sandwall, K. (2012) Samhälls- och undervisningsperspektiv på svenska som andraspråk för vuxna invandrare [A societal and teaching perspective on Swedish as a second language för adult immigrants]. In K. Hyltenstam, M. Axelsson and I. Lindberg (eds) *Flerspråkighet: En forskningsöversikt* [Multilingualism: A Research Survey] (pp. 17–152). Vetenskapsrådets rapportserie 5. Stockholm: The Swedish Research Council.

Littlewood, W. and Yu, B. (2011) First language and target language in the foreign language classroom. *Language Teacher* 44 (1), 64–77.

Long, M. (1983) Native speaker/non-native speaker conversation and the negotiation of comprehensible input. *Applied Linguistics* 4 (2), 126–41.

Long, M. (1996) The role of the linguistic environment in second language acquisition. In W. Ritchie and T. Bhatia (eds) *Handbook of Second Language Acquisition* (pp. 413–68). New York: Academic Press.

Macaro, E., Nakatani, Y., Hayashi, Y. and Khabbazbashi, N. (2014) Exploring the value of bilingual language assistants with Japanese English as a foreign language learners. *The Language Learning Journal* 42 (1), 41–54.

Martin-Jones, M. and Saxena, M. (1996) Turn-taking, power asymmetries, and the positioning of bilingual participants in classroom discourse. *Linguistics and Education* 8 (1), 105–123.

Martin-Jones, M. and Saxena, M. (2003) Bilingual resources and 'funds of knowledge' for teaching and learning in multi-ethnic classrooms in Britain. *International Journal of Bilingual Education and Bilingualism* 6 (3–4), 267–282.

Nilsson, J. and Bunar, N. (2016) Educational responses to newly arrived students in Sweden: Understanding the structure and influence of post-migration ecology. *Scandinavian Journal of Educational Research* 60 (4), 399–416.

Official Inquiry (2019:18) *För flerspråkighet, kunskapsutveckling och inkludering [Into Multilingualism, Knowledge Development and Inclusion]*. Stockholm: Utbildningsdepartementet.

Official Inquiry (2019) *På väg: Mot stärkt kvalitet och likvärdighet inom Komvux för elever med svenska som andraspråk* [On the Way: Toward Strengthened Quality and Equivalence in Adult Education for Students of Swedish as a Second Language]. Stockholm: Utbildningsdepartementet.

Patton, M.Q. (2002) *Qualitative Research and Evaluation Methods* (3rd edn). Thousand Oaks: Sage Publications.

Reath Warren, A. (2016) Multilingual study guidance in the Swedish compulsory school and the development of multilingual literacies. *Nordand* 11 (2), 115–142.

Rosén, J. (2017) Spaces for translanguaging in Swedish education policy. In B. Paulsrud, J. Rosén, B. Straszer and Å. Wedin (eds) *New Perspectives on Translanguaging and Education* (pp. 38–55). Bristol: Multilingual Matters.

Rosén, J. (2018) Bro eller krycka? Studiehandledning som pedagogisk praktik i svensk grundskola [Bridge or crutch? Study guidance in the mother tongue as pedagogical practice in the Swedish compulsory school]. In T. Otterup and G. Kästen-Ebeling (eds) *En god fortsättning: Nyanländas fortsatta väg i skola och samhälle* [A Good Continuation: Newcomers' Continued Paths in School and Society] (pp. 181–198). Lund: Studentlitteratur.

School Inspectorate (2018) *Undervisning i svenska för invandrare* [Teaching in Swedish för Immigrants]. Stockholm: Skolinspektionen.

St John, O. (2018) Between question and answer: Mother tongue tutoring and translanguaging as dialogic action. *Translation and Translanguaging in Multilingual Contexts* 4 (3), 334–360.

St John, O. and Liubinienė, V. (2021) 'This is not my world'. Essential support strategies for newly arrived adult immigrants learning Swedish. *Sustainable Multilingualism*

Straszer, B., Rosén, J. and Wedin, Å. (2019) Studiehandledning på modersmål [Study guidance in the mother tongue]. *Educare – Vetenskapliga Skrifter* (3), 49–61. https://doi.org/10.24834/educare.2019.3.4

Swain, M. (2000) The output hypothesis and beyond: Mediating acquisition through collaborative dialogue. In J.P. Lantolf (ed.) *Sociocultural Theory and Second Language Learning* (pp. 97–114). Oxford: Oxford University Press.

Swain, M. and Deters, P. (2007) 'New' mainstream SLA theory: Expanded and enriched. *The Modern Language Journal* 91, Focus Issue.

Swain, M., Lapkin, S., Knouzi, I., Suzuki, W. and Brooks, L. (2009) Languaging: University students learn the grammatical concept of voice in French. *The Modern Language Journal* 93 (1), 5–29.

Swedish Education Act (2010:800) Stockholm: Utbildningsdepartementet.

SNAE (Swedish National Agency for Education) (2018) *Municipal Adult Education in Swedish for Immigrants: Curriculum and Commentary*. Stockholm: Skolverket.

SNAE (Swedish National Agency for Education) (2019) *Studiehandledning på modersmålet: Att stödja kunskapsutvecklingen hos flerspråkiga elever* [Study Guidance in the Mother Tongue: Supporting Knowledge Development with Multilingual Pupils]. Stockholm: Skolverket.

Turnbull, M. and Dailey-O'Cain, J. (2009) *First Language Use in Second and Foreign Language Learning*. Bristol: Multilingual Matters.

12 Multilingualism in Language Education: Examining the Outcomes in the Context of Finland

Anne Pitkänen-Huhta

Introduction

It is now widely acknowledged that multilingualism in individuals and in societies is the norm rather than the exception. As the Douglas Fir Group (2016: 19) notes, 'multilingualism is as old as humanity, but multilingualism has been catapulted to a new world order in the 21st century'. Multilingualism is thus the state of affairs now, be it age-old or a new phenomenon. Multilingual language use has been studied widely and extensively from various perspectives, and it has also received considerable attention in educational contexts (see, e.g. Blackledge & Creese, 2010; Cenoz & Gorter, 2011; Kramsch, 2009; Li Wei, 2011; May, 2014). When examining multilingualism in education, especially in the European context, we often focus on describing and analysing it as 'change', but we tend to neglect the consequences of multilingualism. What is also notable in the discussion on multilingualism in education is the here-and-now focus on issues. We tend to overlook the historical perspective on multilingualism (May, 2014) and the many consequences or outcomes of multilingualism already having taken place in the educational systems. To fully understand the current situation and to avoid any unwanted consequences of multilingualism for education, such as restricting the use of home languages at school, we need to analyse more systematically the consequences that we have already seen.

When considering the outcome of multilingualism, we first need to understand what we mean by *multilingualism*. As Cenoz (2013) points out, there are numerous ways of characterising and defining multilingualism. Multilingualism can be seen as a societal phenomenon (more than one language used in a certain context), as an individual practice (an individual using different languages) or as an ability (a person's knowledge of different languages). The Council of Europe makes a conceptual distinction between societal and individual multilingualism, calling the latter *plurilingualism* (The Council of Europe, 2007). What is important to note, however, is that any characterisation is also context-dependent and different aspects of multilingualism get more or less weight in defining what multilingualism means in a certain – broader or narrower – context. Recent discussions in the European context concerning 'growing multilingualism' have mostly focused on 'new multilingualism', i.e. the new languages brought in by migration, which has overwhelmingly been forced but also voluntary, often work-based. What has been ignored in this discussion is 'old multilingualism', i.e. the historical perspective and the fact that most societies have various kinds of layers of multilingualism, which have developed over decades and centuries and may thus be difficult to identify as multilingualism.

In recent years, multilingual language use by individuals is often discussed in the conceptual framework of *translanguaging*. The concept of translanguaging is closely related to other concepts that have attempted to describe multilingual language use. These include *metrolingualism* (Otsuji & Pennycook, 2009), *polylingual languaging* (Jørgensen, 2008) and *translingual practice* (Canagarajah, 2013). Translanguaging has been used to describe language practices that step away from the frames of named languages, often connected to nation states, instead adhering to dynamic use of all multimodal and multilingual resources (e.g. Canagarajah, 2011; Cenoz & Gorter, 2019; Creese & Blackledge, 2010; García, 2009, 2019; Li Wei, 2017). In addition to its denotation as a complex theoretical construct (see Cummins, this volume), translanguaging also has more practical denotions that can be identified in the literature. First, it has been used to describe the ways multilingual individuals use different languages or, rather, different linguistic resources. Canagarajah (2011: 401), for example, has defined translanguaging as 'the ability of multilingual speakers to shuttle between languages, treating the diverse languages that form their repertoire as an integrated system'. Li Wei (2017) has further characterised translanguaging practices by adding two concepts of translanguaging namely *Translanguaging Space* and *Translanguaging Instinct*. Both of these relate to how multilinguals use language. He defines the former as a space 'where language users break down the ideologically laden dichotomies between the macro and the micro, the societal and the individual, and the social and the psychological through interaction' (Li Wei, 2017: 15) and the latter as an instinct, which 'drives humans to go beyond narrowly defined linguistic cues and transcend culturally defined language boundaries to achieve effective communication' (Li Wei, 2017: 16–17).

Second, the concept has been used to characterise or to promote certain kinds of pedagogical practices on the basis of how multilingual learners use language (Hornberger & Link, 2012; Paulsrud *et al.*, 2017).

The origin of pedagogical translanguaging lies in bilingual minority contexts, especially the context of Wales, where the concept of translanguaging actually originates (see, e.g. García & Otheguy, 2019). The aim of pedagogical translanguaging has been to offer bilingual learners a space to perform their bilingualism – to be bilingual – in the classroom (García & Otheguy, 2019). Pedagogical translanguaging goes beyond language to issues of power, experience and identity as Li Wei proposes:

> By deliberately breaking the artificial and ideological divides between indigenous versus immigrant, majority versus minority, and target versus mother tongue languages, translanguaging empowers both the learner and the teacher, transforms the power relations, and focuses the process of teaching and learning on making meaning, enhancing experience, and developing identity. (Li Wei, 2017: 7)

For the purposes of this chapter, I follow Hornberger and Link's (2012: 242) definition of translanguaging as 'not only as a language practice of multilinguals, but as a pedagogical strategy to foster language and literacy development'.

In this chapter, I examine the outcome of multilingualism for language education in the specific context of the nation state Finland and if and how the outcomes at different levels are related to pedagogical translanguaging. As pointed out above, multilingualism is a context-bound phenomenon, and it is therefore justified to examine a specific context in detail. A thick description of a particular case reveals dynamics and tendencies, which are potentially applicable in other contexts (e.g. Duff, 2008). In this discussion paper, the outcomes of multilingualism are approached through the examination of different layers of organising language education, and the discussion is divided accordingly into three sections. These are (1) educational policies, (2) policy implementation and (3) the classroom. The first two sections represent the macro-levels of education and the third section represents the micro-level of education. The first two are related to policies, with the first focusing on how policies outline multilingualism (and translanguaging) and second on how this is potentially realised in implementing the policies. The discussion in each section draws on empirical evidence from different sources. In the first section, the data source is the National Core Curriculum for Basic Education (NCC, 2014); the second section draws on statistics concerning the development of language choices at school (Education Statistics Finland) and in the third section, the empirical evidence comes from teacher interviews (Pitkänen-Huhta & Mäntylä, 2020).

Types of Multilingualism in Finland – Past and Present

Before discussing in detail the consequence of multilingualism to language education in Finland, it is necessary to provide an overview of the linguistic landscape of Finland. According to the census in 2018, Finland has 5.5 million inhabitants (Statistics Finland). At the societal level, Finland is officially a bilingual country with Finnish (majority) and Swedish (minority) as the national languages. In addition, the linguistic and cultural rights of Sámi, Roma and Sign language users are guaranteed in the constitution. When looking at the use of individual languages, the census of 2018 (Statistics Finland) shows that 87.6% of the population comprise of Finnish speakers (compared to 92.4% in the year 2000), 5.2% are Swedish speakers (5.6% in the year 2000) and 7.1% speak other languages (1.9% in the year 2000). The largest groups of other languages are Russian (79,225 speakers), Estonian (49,691), Arabic (29,462), Somali (20,944), English (20,793), Kurdish (14,054), Farsi (13,017) and Chinese (12,407). Even though the statistics are rather modest compared to many other European countries, the change in percentages has been quite considerable in the past 20 years. It has to be noted also that in the census in Finland, it is not possible to mark two languages as one's first languages, i.e. bi- or multilingualism does not show in the census, as people need to identify one language as the first language.

When examining multilingualism in the Finnish context, I make a distinction between *old* and *new* multilingualism. The old multilingualism comprises, first, the official Finnish-Swedish bilingualism at the societal level and second, the official status of some 'old' minorities (the Sámi, Roma and Sign language). Old multilingualism – even if not often recognised as such – also includes foreign language (FL) education, which can also be considered elite multilingualism (May, 2019; Ortega, 2019). New multilingualism points to the fairly recent phenomenon of multilingualism brought about by increasing mobility and (mostly forced) migration (May, 2019; Ortega, 2019), which has brought a wealth of 'new' languages into Finnish society.

As Finland officially has two national languages, Finnish and Swedish, schooling is also organised in those languages. The relationship between these two languages dates long back in history to the Middle Ages, when Swedish was used (along with Middle Low German and Latin) for official purposes and Finnish was mainly a domestic everyday language (Salo, 2012). The majority–minority constellation has led to parallel educational systems, where the language of schooling is either Finnish or Swedish, but no bilingual schools are in operation (except for a few schools, which are physically in the same building but students follow different curricula and teaching is organised separately). It has to be noted that in the Helsinki area (the capital), there are also a few schools where the language of instruction is English, French or Russian, for example, even though these languages have no official status in Finland.

Old multilingualism can also refer to minorities that have inhabited Finland for centuries. These include the Sámi ethnic minority and the three Sámi languages spoken in the north of Finland. Since 1992, the Sámi languages have had an official status in the Sámiland in Finnish Lapland. There is Sámi-medium teaching, i.e. instruction in Sámi, only in the Sámi native region, but Sámi language teaching can be offered also outside the Sámi native region in the same way as any other language subject is offered. It is also possible to take the Sámi languages examination in the National Matriculation Examination after upper secondary school.

Another part of old multilingualism is the often overlooked and ignored FL education. Initially, after gaining independence in 1917, ancient or modern languages were only taught in secondary levels of education. First indications of teaching FLs in primary schools can be seen in the form of recommendations in the 1950s and 1960s (Takala & Havola, 1983). With the introduction of the comprehensive school, FLs become a compulsory part of curricula. These were European languages such as German, English, French and Russian. In the 1960s, English gradually overtook German in popularity in secondary education (Leppänen et al., 2011). Still today, the focus in Finnish FL education is strongly on some European languages, but the whole area of FL education is currently shadowed by growing worry about diminishing language repertoires, which I will return to below.

By multilingualism today, we often refer to what I call in this chapter 'new multilingualism'. By this I mean the new repertoires of languages brought about by new migration, be it forced or voluntary. In terms of language education, for newcomers, preparatory education is typically organised in the first year of their arrival at school, and second language teaching is organised either in Finnish or Swedish, depending on the area. Municipalities also organise teaching in the newcomers' first languages (mother tongue teaching). At the moment, such teaching is organised in approximately 50 languages. The metropolitan area around Helsinki has the largest number of different first languages: In some schools, as much as 80% of students have a first language other than Finnish or Swedish. There is, however, great variation in how and in how many languages mother tongue teaching is organised. In 2015, approximately 50% of pupils entitled to first language teaching took part in it (Laakso, 2017).

Old and new multilingualism have led to different ways of acknowledging the languages in the organisation of language education. First of all, official bilingualism in society has led to a dual educational system with the two languages kept separate (Paulsrud et al., 2020). Moreover, both the majority (Finnish speakers) and the minority (Swedish speakers) have to learn the other language as a compulsory school language, Swedish for Finnish speakers starting in Grade 6 (before 2016 Grade 7) and Finnish for Swedish speakers typically in Grade 1. It has been recognised that there are problems with this system as well and – to put it crudely – the attained skills have not been very good and motivation has mostly been poor, especially for Finnish speakers learning Swedish (e.g. Salo, 2012). Partly to remedy the situation (partly for other language policy reasons), various immersion programmes (esp. Swedish) have been set in the coastal areas in particular (Björklund *et al.*, 2014).

Second, the old minority language and cultural groups in Finland, including Sámi languages, Roma and the Sign languages, have guaranteed rights by law. In the past, these linguistic minorities suffered serious oppression (e.g. Ahonen, 2007; Keskitalo *et al.*, 2014; Lindstedt *et al.*, 2009; Pietikäinen, 2012), but these days more value is placed on preserving minority cultures, and the Sámi especially have carried out successful language revitalisation programmes in Sámiland (e.g. Äärelä-Vihriälä, 2017; Olthuis, 2003). Language is increasingly seen as an identity issue, and measures have been taken to ensure rights through legislation. But as with any minority group, the situation is still far from ideal and lack of resources, e.g. finding qualified teachers of the Roma language, hinders development.

Third, traditional FL education has also kept all the languages separate in schools. FL education still largely focuses on a limited selection of languages, with some of the European languages being privileged. This can be characterised as elite multilingualism, which can be described as language learning whereby 'people learn new languages by choice, without any material or symbolic threat to their home languages – and often aided by ample support and in the midst of great praise' (Ortega, 2019: 27). English is usually one party in elite multilingualism (Kramsch, 2014; May, 2019), and as most attention is paid to English, this has led to various kinds of English-medium programmes (large-scale bilingual or language-enriched education) in recent decades.

Finally, the new minorities in Finland have considerably enriched the linguistic landscape of schools (e.g. Lehtonen, 2016). The outcome of this new multilingualism largely remains to be seen. So far, the focus in language education has been on second language learning and to an extent on first language (mother tongue) learning. Similar to the old minorities, issues of identity, cultural awareness and belonging have been prominent in policies (see below), but there is still very little evidence of making use of the new languages in the overall planning and management of language education.

Figure 12.1 summarises the outcome of these four different categories of multilingualism in educational structures in Finland.

Outcome of Multilingualism in Organising and Implementing Language Education

In this section, I examine more closely how old and new multilingualism have led to different kinds of outcomes in organising language education (summarised in Figure 12.1 above), with different kinds of societal regulations and investments in educational policies and implementation of policies. I discuss first how multilingualism (and translanguaging) is visible in

Type of multilingualism		Organisation
'Old' Finnish–Swedish bilingualism	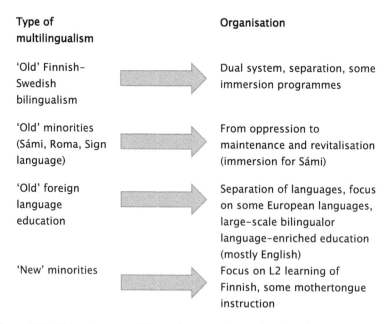	Dual system, separation, some immersion programmes
'Old' minorities (Sámi, Roma, Sign language)		From oppression to maintenance and revitalisation (immersion for Sámi)
'Old' foreign language education		Separation of languages, focus on some European languages, large-scale bilingualor language–enriched education (mostly English)
'New' minorities		Focus on L2 learning of Finnish, some mothertongue instruction

Figure 12.1 Old and new multilingualism as outcomes in education

national language policies, especially in the National Core Curriculum. Second, I focus on how multilingualism appears in the implementation of national policies by using FL education as an example. These two can be seen as the macro-levels of organising language education. Finally, I discuss some micro-level outcomes of multilingualism as seen by FL teachers.

Multilingualism in national education policies

In the Finnish educational system, the core principles and aims of education are outlined in Core Curricula (for pre-primary, basic education and secondary education), which are the responsibility of the National Agency for Education. In addition to the national curriculum, individual schools need to have their own curricula, which are more precise in terms of practical organisation of education. The discussion in this section draws on the National Core Curriculum for Basic Education (NCC, 2014), which was recently renewed and has been effective since 2016. For the purposes of this chapter, the curriculum document was examined through the lens of language education, i.e. sections with guidelines concerning language subjects, language groups or other language-related issues were taken under scrutiny in terms of multilingualism and translanguaging.

The curriculum first outlines some general issues related to basic education such as the mission, goal, operating culture, support, student welfare, the general principles of assessment and the status of minority languages and the different forms of bilingual education. Second, there is a description of all the subjects for Grades 1–2, for Grades 3–6 and for Grades 7–9. One of the principles that guides the development of school culture is cultural diversity and language awareness. Thus, multilingualism is at least implicitly present throughout the curriculum. There is a strong emphasis on language awareness in all language subjects, including first, second and FL subjects (see also Paulsrud *et al.*, 2020). Multiliteracy is mentioned also in relation to other subjects, such as religion, music and visual arts. Literacy is mentioned as health literacy in health education or as environmental literacy in geography.

Cutting across all subjects in basic education are the transversal competences, which are first described generally and then specified for each of the three groups of grade levels. There are altogether seven transversal competences, with slightly differing emphasis in different subjects. These are *Thinking and learning to learn, Cultural competence, interaction and self-expression, Taking care of oneself and managaging daily life, Multiliteracy, ICT competence, Working life competence and entrepreneurship* and *Participation, involvement and building a sustainable future.* What is of significance in terms of multilingualism are especially two of these: *Cultural competence, interaction and self-expression* and *Multiliteracy.* Overall, there is thus an emphasis on language, culture and (multi)literacy in the core curriculum.

The curriculum also includes the special section *Special questions of language and culture*, where overall aims and principles of multilingualism and the specific features of different language groups are taken up. The curriculum states explicitly that each pupil's cultural background and language repertoires are taken into account and the pupil's identity development is supported. The specific objective of education is stated as follows:

> The objective is to guide the pupils to appreciate different languages and cultures and to promote bilingualism and plurilingualism, thus reinforcing the pupils' linguistic awareness and metalinguistic skills. *School work may include multilingual teaching situations where the teachers and pupils use all the languages they know.* (NCC, 2014: 153, italics added)

Even though the Basic Education Act states that the language of instruction is either Finnish or Swedish, the curriculum gives room for instruction to be given in other languages as well. Thus, the principles of translanguaging are given space in the curriculum, although the concept itself does not appear in the document. The official minority languages (Sámi, Roma and Sign language) are mentioned specifically, and it is further stated that instruction may be given in another language as well, 'provided that this does not risk the achievement of the objectives set in the core curriculum' (NCC: 155). Thus, there is room for bilingual education, but the practical decisions are left to municipalities and individual schools.

The core curriculum also focuses on specific language groups and stipulates the principles concerning the instruction of these groups. The language groups gaining specific attention are the Sámi and Sámi language speakers, the Roma, Sign language users and other plurilingual (the term used in the curriculum) pupils. For the Sámi speakers, the objective is formulated as 'supporting the pupils in growing into their language, culture and community and giving them an opportunity to embrace the Sámi cultural heritage' and 'to improve the pupils' capabilities for acting in a Sámi language environment, to learn the Sámi language and to study in Sámi' (NCC, 2014: 155). The description of the organisation of instruction in the Sámi homeland is clearly more detailed than for the other two minority groups. For the Roma, the objective is slightly different from the Sámi, emphasising culture and identity rather than language competence: 'a particular objective is supporting the pupils in developing their identity and awareness of their history and culture [...] promotes the preservation of the Roma language and Roma cultural heritage in cooperation with the homes' (NCC: 156). It is further specifically mentioned that an effort is made to organise teaching in the Roma language, but the reality is that it is very difficult to find competent teachers and only a small minority of Roma pupils receive any instruction in Roma. For the Sign language users, the formulation of the objectives is again slightly different from the two other minority groups, with the assumption that Sign language is already used by these pupils: 'a particular objective is strengthening the pupils' identity as sign language users and their awareness of their own culture and the sign language community [....] makes use of the sign language community and media' (NCC, 2014: 157). For both the Roma and Sign language users, there is an emphasis on relying on the home or the community. There is thus an implicit assumption that the schools may not able to provide instruction to all.

The group of the other plurilingual pupils, who could be considered to be the group of newcomers, differs again from the minority language groups discussed above. The following quote states the objectives:

> Plurilingual pupils are encouraged to use the languages they know in a versatile manner in the lessons of various subjects and other school activities. The learning and use of their mother tongue thus support the assimilation of the content in various subjects, and the pupils also learn to communicate about the contents of school subjects in their mother tongue. Under the Constitution of Finland, each person living in Finland has the right to maintain and develop their own language and culture. An effort is made to offer the pupils instruction of their mother tongue. (NCC, 2014: 159)

In the case of 'other plurilingual pupils', similarly to Sign language users, there is an assumption that the pupils are able to use several languages and they are encouraged to use their resources, i.e. the idea of translanguaging is present but as to how this happens in practice appears to be the responsibility of the pupil and the local practitioners. Similarly to other minorities, the constitutional right to maintain and develop one's own language and culture is highlighted. And again, an attempt is made to provide instruction in everyone's mother tongue, but there is no strict requirement.

A great deal of the responsibility of practical organisation of instruction for specific language groups is left to the local level, as the following shows:

> When formulating the curriculum, local special questions related to languages and cultures should be taken into account and decisions should be made on how the instruction is to be organised. The curriculum should be prepared in cooperation with the pupils, the guardians and the relevant linguistic and cultural communities. (NCC, 2014: 161)

This is understandable, of course, but at the same time, it gives ground to treat pupils differently depending on the resources and willingness of the municipality and school to invest in newcomers' language teaching and to promoting pedagogical translanguaging.

Multilingualism in the implementation of national policies (FLs as an example)

In this section, I move on to discuss the implementation of national policies with FLs as an example. The discussion draws both on the overall organisation of languages in the curriculum as well as statistics concerning language choices (Education Statistics Finland). As could be seen on the basis of the discussion above, many ideas from recent research on multilingualism, including translanguaging, have filtered into key documents guiding educational planning and implementation. Unfortunately, the reality rarely matches the ideals of the policy documents, or rather, policies are in the making in actual implementation practices (Saarinen *et al.*, 2019). A case in point is the organisation of and current changes in FL education in Finland.

Currently, until the beginning of 2020, the languages (foreign and second) in basic education have been divided into compulsory and optional languages (see Table 12.1 below). Since the 1970s, the first FL has started in Grade 3 (i.e. at the age of 9). Starting a FL is compulsory, but students can choose the language among the ones offered. In practice, however, it is most often English, as most municipalities do not offer other languages at this stage. Only the major cities have a wider selection of languages (typically European languages) on offer. There has been a gradual change to this 'compulsory-in-practice' nature of English as the first FL since 1990s, but there are no official guidelines. It has also been possible to offer FLs earlier (Grades 1 and 2) and some municipalities – often again the

Table 12.1 Basic education – languages in the curriculum for Finnish speakers (modified from Nikula *et al.*, 2010)

Year	Grades 1–6 of basic education						Grades 7–9 of basic education			General upper secondary school	
	1	2	3	4	5	6	7	8	9		
LG1 Compulsory	x*	x	x	x	x	x	x	x	x	x	typically English
LG2 optional			(x)	x	x	x	x	x	x	(x)	
LG3 compulsory						x	x	x	x	x	for most Swedish
LG4 optional							(x)	x	x	(x)	
LG5 optional										(x)	

*From 2020 onwards, LG1 starts in Grade 1, earlier in Grade 3

major cities – have made use of the option. In 2020, there is a change in effect to this situation, which will be discussed below. In the lower grades of basic education, it is possible to choose another optional FL in Grades 4 or 5 (depending on local policies). In Grade 6, all Finnish speakers start compulsory Swedish. Swedish speakers start compulsory Finnish earlier, typically already in Grade 1. Newcomers may choose Finnish or Swedish, depending on the area (Finnish- or Swedish-speaking), and in practice, newcomers are often exempted from this second language. It is possible to choose two more FLs, one in Grade 8 and one more in the general upper secondary school. The typical choice of optional languages is German, French, Russian or Spanish.

Even though the possibilities for studying languages in basic education seem broad on paper, in practice the majority of graduates after upper secondary school have studied only English and Swedish (which is compulsory). Due to many changes, which are not all directly related to languages (e.g. division of subjects in the Matriculation Examination), students choose fewer and fewer languages in their programme, and this has led to concern about diminishing language repertoires at the national level. English has kept its position as the most popular choice as the first FL with a constant share of ca. 90%. Figure 12.2 shows that the choice for the other (European) languages has been marginal with percentages ranging from 0.3% to 1.3%.

Figure 12.3 below shows the choices of the second (optional) language. Especially German as a choice has dropped quite dramatically.

The concern about diminishing language repertoires led to a national report by the Ministry of Education on the state of language education in the country (Multilingualism as a Strength, 2017). It gave several recommendations to solve the problem of diminishing language repertoires, but all of them have to pass governmental processes. One of the recommendations was to push the onset of the first FL to the first school year. This recommendation has now passed in the government and as of the beginning of 2020, all first graders start their first FL. Some municipalities have

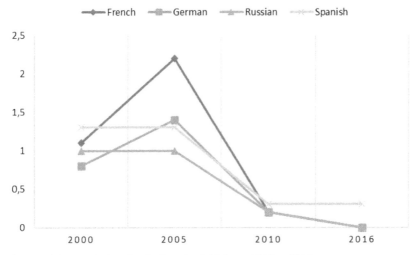

Figure 12.2 LG1 choices (excluding English) from 2000 to 2016

opted to start the first FL at the start of the school year in the autumn of 2019, and others start the language in January 2020, half way through the first school year. One of the aims of the change – along with goals of reaching better learning outcomes with an early start – was to ensure equal access to language learning, as there has been inequality in terms of socioeconomic and geographical factors, i.e. some municipalities or some schools within the municipalities have offered languages earlier than Grade 3 and these have mostly been in the major cities and in affluent areas. Another aim was to make families choose a language other than English as the first FL. English would then start in Grades 3 or 4. As we

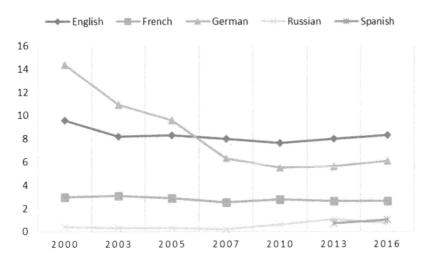

Figure 12.3 LG2 choices from 2000 to 2016

now have this new situation at hand, it is not possible to give facts about the choices, but there are already some indications. In one midsized city, four languages (English, German, French and Spanish) were offered for families to choose in the spring before the start of the first school year in autumn 2019. The minimum size for any language group to start was set at 12 students. The result was that only groups of English were formed. Only a fraction of families would have opted for languages other than English.

To sum up the above discussion, it can be stated that multilingualism may appear in policy documents, but the implementation does not always follow the ideals. The aims of broadening the linguistic repertoires in Finland focus mostly on the European languages traditionally taught in schools and could thus be called elite multilingualism. What can also be seen is that measures are needed to maintain or develop multilingualism through FL education, as voluntariness may easily lead to diminishing repertoires. Moreover, there is very little evidence that the rich multilingual repertoires of the plurilingual pupils (as described in the National Core Curriculum), i.e. new multilingualism, would be visible in organising education. Their presence in classroom practices will be discussed in the next section.

Micro-level outcome of multilingualism: Multilingualism as a problem in the classroom

The discussion in the previous two sections has shown that the outcomes of multilingualism take different forms at different levels of the educational system. While policy documents might adhere to the most recent understandings of language use, language learning and language practices, the implementation does not automatically follow the policies, as there are numerous practical issues – also those not related to languages – that influence implementation. There is, however, one more level that needs attention, namely the level of practitioners, who live with the consequences of multilingualism and the related policies in their day-to-day professional practices. Therefore, the focus gears next towards language teachers, with FL teachers as an example, and how they deal with new multilingualism in their classrooms.

The discussion in this section draws on interview data with seven teachers of English as a FL (EFL) at different levels of basic education.[1] The focus of the interviews was on how teachers acknowledge and support multilingual learners with migrant backgrounds in their EFL classrooms. The data were analysed using qualitative content analysis (e.g. Krippendorff, 2004; for a full analysis of data, see Pitkänen-Huhta & Mäntylä, 2020). All names appearing in text are pseudonyms, and written consent to use the anonymised data for research purposes was received from each participant. For the purposes of this chapter, the data were re-analysed specifically in terms of how multilingualism and translanguaging in the classroom were taken into consideration by the teachers.

The most prominent way of constructing multilingualism was that of *a problem*. This became evident through the various challenges related to multilingualism that the teachers brought up. The teachers had not really consciously considered multilingual learners in their EFL classrooms, but they seemed to tackle problems, if any arose. Seeing multilingualism as an asset which would positively influence classroom practices was not evident in the interviews. In the following quote, Paula (teacher of English and Russian) describes the situation in one of her classes:

> niinku mäkin opetan sitä yläkoulun ryhmää niin mä opetan heille englantia, ja tota se on aika hauskaa ja mielenkiintosta ja tosi vaikeeta siis se opettaminen mun mielestä, kun mä tässä kerrankin katoin että mitä siellä ryhmässä oli sillon paikalla, niin siellä seitsemän opiskelijaa jotka kaikki tuli eri maasta ja kaikilla oli eri äidinkieli ja siis se englannin taitotaso myös aivan eri, ett jotkut puhuu niinku hirveen sujuvaa englantia ainaki suullisesti, kirjotustaito saatto olla vähän heikompi ja eräs just oli oppinu kirjottamaan siis yhtään millään kielellä ja englantia puhu jonkun verran suullisesti mutta ei pystyny mitään kirjottaa tai siis pysty kopioimaan

> *So I teach that upper secondary group, so I teach them English, and well it's quite fun and interesting and really difficult, the teaching I mean, in my opinion, 'cos the other day I checked who were present in the group then, so there were seven pupils who all came from different countries and all had different first languages and well, the level of skills of English were also all different, some use English very fluently, at least orally, writing skills could be a little weaker, and one had just learnt to write, so in any language, and spoke some English, but could not of course write anything, or could copy only.*

This teacher looked at multilingualism strictly from the point of view of English, the target of learning in this class. She mentions the several first languages but focuses merely on English language skills. From that perspective, the constellation of varying proficiency levels was indeed challenging, and the challenges were very often the focus in teacher accounts. This comes up also in the next quote, by the same teacher but now referring to the experiences of a colleague:

> hän on kanssa sano että ihan järkyttävää että taas tuli kolme uutta ja nyt pitäis taas alottaa niitä viikonpäiviä ja numeroita ja värejä ja ja ne muut osaa jo että miten hän nyt niinku sen järjestää että, mut samahan se on siellä valmistavan luokan opettajallakin, kokoajan sinne niiku tupsahtaa porukkaa ja kokoajan pitää eriyttää niinku ihan älyttömästi

> *She [a colleague] also said that it was really shocking that once again there were three new ones and now we should start with the days of the week and numbers and colours, and and the others know them already,*

*so that how could she like organise it, but it's the same with the teacher
of the preparatory class all the time, there's constantly new people
coming in and you have to differentiate all the time like crazy.*

The teacher feels that it is challenging for the teacher to be able to cater
for all levels of proficiency and differentiate her teaching according to
individual pupils' needs. When focusing on the challenges, the issue of
ignoring multilingualism also came up. In the following extract, Lisa
(teacher of English and Swedish in a Finnish-speaking primary school)
ponders whether she should be aware of her pupils' background, thus raising the issue of acknowledging multilingualism or not:

en oo ihan- en oo, en oo siitä varma enkä koe että mun tarvii sitä sen
enempää tietääkään, mut ett ne pärjää sillä suomella niin ett ei meil oo
mitään ongelmaa, että joskus niinku kiva kuulla jos joku sanoo- no yks
romania kakskielinen sano että tää on sama ku englannissa tää sana ja se
on kauheen kiva että ne tuo sillai ite sen esille, mutta mä en haluu sil-
lälailla nostaa ketään että mä nään ihonväristä että toi on erilainen

*I'm not quite- I'm not, I'm not sure and I don't feel that I have to know
any more about that [students' background] but that they cope in Finnish
and then we don't have any problem and that it's sometimes nice to hear
if someone says- well there's one Romanian bilingual child who said that
this word is the same as in English and it's very nice that they bring it up
themselves but I don't want to single out anyone that way so that I would
see from the colour of the skin that this person is different.*

This teacher is unsure whether she even has to know anything about the
pupils' linguistic background, unless there is a problem, i.e. the pupil has
problems with the Finnish language. The teacher further indicates that
she allows natural translanguaging in the class, if the pupils themselves
initiate it. Otherwise, she does not wish to single anyone out on the basis
of different skin colour, for example.

As the previous example showed, translanguging comes up in teachers' talk, too. In the above example, the teacher seems to allow translanguaging in her classroom but does not actively encourage it. In fact, many
practices we might now call (pedagogical) translanguaging, i.e. moving
across languages, have always been present in FL classrooms. These
include translations and comparisons between languages. Typically, these
practices have taken place between the target language and the language
shared with all learners or another language that the pupils are also studying. The textbooks have typically not encouraged comparisons between
any other languages the pupils might know. There has thus been an
assumption that the learner group is linguistically homogeneous. The
sometimes overwhelming number of different first languages in the FL
classrooms today (as became evident in one of the interview quotes above)
may pose problems for teachers in terms of promoting translanguaging

practices. Consider the following quote by Sirpa, a teacher of English in basic education (secondary level):

> esimerkiks just tän virolaisen oppilaan kanssa oli ehkä helpompi tehä sitä vertailua vielä koska oli samantyyliset kielet, mutta sitten taas se on hirveen hankala ett sit näillä muilla on ollu semmoset äidinkielet mistä niinku mulla ei olis pienentäkää hajua, niin sit taas mä en niinku pysty tavallaan sitä kautta auttamaan, että kyllähän sen voi- voin koittaa että mieti että miten sä omassa kielessä mut enhän mä pysty sanoon siihen yhtään mitään ku en mä ymmärrä sitä kieltä että onks se sitten loppuvi- imeks se sama

> *For example, with this Estonian pupil, it was maybe a little easier to compare because the languages are similar, but then again it's extremely difficult with the others who have such mother tongues that I don't have the faintest idea of, so then I cannot in a way help them at all, one could of course – I can of course say that think how it is in your own language but then I cannot say anything about it because I don't understand that language, whether it is the same in the end.*

This teacher does not have anything against the pupils comparing English to their own first languages but what worries her is that she does not know these languages and thereby she feels she cannot help the pupil through translanguaging. There is thus the underlying assumption that the teacher is the only source and support of learning for the pupil. Problems of translanguaging in FL education have been noted more generally as well. Ortega (2019: 32) points out that 'language educators working in FL contexts are generally averse to translanguaging because their main concern has always been with maximising use of the target language during instruction'. The teachers may thus feel that they are not fulfilling their task as teachers of the target language, as was the case in the quote above.

In the classroom, the outcome of multilingualism is naturally context-bound and situated. The above examples from interviews with EFL teachers indicate that new multilingualism is often seen as a problem, or it is consciously tackled only if problems arise. There appear to be mixed feelings as to what can and should be done. Natural translanguaging is allowed, but the multilingualism of learners is not systematically made use of, for the benefit of all learners. Thus, it appears that the ideals of policy documents have not been realised in classroom practices. But this aspect calls for more in-depth research in the classrooms.

Conclusion

The aim of this chapter was to discuss the outcome of multilingualism for language education in the context of Finland and to whether the outcomes are related to translanguaging by examining different layers of organising language education. These were (1) educational policies, (2) policy implementation and (3) the classroom. The discussion drew on empirical evidence from policy documents, statistics and teacher interviews. As pointed out in the introduction, multilingualism is a context-bound phenomenon, and to understand the dynamics of the influences it has on language education, we need detailed examination of specific contexts. Through understanding the outcome of multilingualism – also from a historical perspective – of a specific context reveals tendencies which are helpful in making policy decisions concerning organisation and implementation of language education in other contexts. The discussion showed that there are apparent gaps in the continuum from research to policymakers and to practitioners. The conceptual developments in research filter into educational policy documents guiding educational practices, but whether these materialise in implementation is not always self-evident, and how they become realised at the microlevel in classrooms, is not very well known, as so much responsibility is left at the local level (see also Paulsrud *et al.*, 2020). What also became evident is that when taking a long-term, holistic perspective on how multilingualism is reflected in organising education, there is a great deal of variation, and it seems that different areas of language education (e.g. bilingual education, FL education, minority groups) are in their own silos, which has led to very different kinds of outcomes. In the Finnish context, even the forms of old multilingualism are dealt with differently: There are different degrees of regulation concerning official Finnish–Swedish bilingualism, old minorities and FL education. Then again, issues related to the new minorities are handled through curriculum endorsement, and the main responsibility is at the local level and with the practitioners.

I argue, on the basis of the discussion in this chapter, that in addition to the foci on translanguaging as a practice of individual language users and as an educational practice in classrooms, we need a more holistic approach – a *Translanguaging Mindset* – at all levels of language education to create a smooth continuum from top-level policies to implementation and to classroom practices and vice versa. Pedagogical translanguaging is an excellent tool for catering for all learners, irrespective of their linguistic background (Cenoz, 2017), but if micro-level practices are not supported by macro-level organisation, it is difficult to create collaboration and dialogue between researchers, policymakers and practitioners.

Note

(1) The data were collected in 2013 by the author and Dr Katja Mäntylä.

References

Ahonen, O. (2007) Viittomakielisten äidinkielen opetuksen vaiheita ja nykypäivää [Historical and current issues in the mother tongue teaching of sign language users]. Unpublished MA thesis. University of Jyväskylä.

Björklund, S., Mård-Miettinen, K. and Savijärvi, M. (2014) Swedish immersion in the early years in Finland. *International Journal of Bilingual Education and Bilingualism* 17 (2), 197–214.

Blackledge, A. and Creese, A. (2010) *Multilingualism: A Critical Perspective*. London: Continuum.

Canagarajah, S. (2011) Codemeshing in academic writing: Identifying teachable strategies of translanguaging. *The Modern Language Journal* 95, 401–417.

Canagarajah, S. (2013) *Translingual Practice: Global Englishes and Cosmopolitan Relations*. Abingdon: Routledge.

Cenoz, J. (2013) The influence of bilingualism on third language acquisition: Focus on multilingualism. *Language Teaching* 46 (1), 71–86.

Cenoz, J. (2017) Translanguaging in school contexts: International perspectives. *Journal of Language, Identity & Education* 16 (4), 193–198.

Cenoz, J. and Gorter, D. (2011) A holistic approach to multilingual education: Introduction. *The Modern Language Journal* 95 (3), 339–343.

Cenoz, J. and Gorter, D. (2019) Multilingualism, translanguaging, and minority languages in SLA. *The Modern Language Journal* 103 (Supplement 2019), 130–135.

Creese, A. and Blackledge, A. (2010) Translanguaging in the bilingual classroom: A pedagogy for learning and teaching? *The Modern Language Journal* 94 (1), 103–115.

Council of Europe (2007) From linguistic diversity to plurilingual education: Guide for the development of language education policies in Europe. https://rm.coe.int/16802fc1c4 (accessed April 2020).

The Douglas Fir Group (2016) A Transdisciplinary framework for SLA in a multilingual world. *The Modern Language Journal* 100 (Supplement 2016) 19–47.

Duff, P. (2008) *Case Study Research in Applied Linguistics*. New York: Routledge.

Education Statistics Finland. See https://vipunen.fi/en-gb/basic/Pages/Kieli--ja-muut-ainevalinnat.aspx (accessed January 2020).

García, O. (2009) *Bilingual Education in the 21st Century: A Global Perspective*. Oxford: Wiley-Blackwell.

García, O. (2019) Translanguaging: A coda to the code? *Classroom Discourse* 10 (3–4), 369–373.

García, O. and Otheguy, R. (2019) Plurilingualism and translanguaging: commonalities and divergences. *International Journal of Bilingual Education and Bilingualism* 23 (1), 17–35.

Hornberger, N. and Link, H. (2012) Translanguaging in today's classrooms: A biliteracy lens. *Theory Into Practice* 51 (4), 239–247.

Jørgensen, J.N. (2008) Polylingual languaging around and among children and adolescents. *International Journal of Multilingualism* 5 (3), 161–176.

Keskitalo, P., Lehtola, V.-P. and Paksuniemi. M. (eds) (2014) *Saamelaisten kansanopetuksen ja koulunkäynnin historia Suomessa* [The History of Teaching and Schooling of the Sámi in Finland]. Turku: Siirtolaisinstituutti. http://www.migrationinstitute.fi/files/pdf/A50.pdf (accessed April 2020).

Kramsch, C. (2009) *The Multilingual Subject. What Foreign Language Learners Say about Their Experience and Why It Matters*. Oxford: Oxford University Press.

Kramsch, C. (2014) Teaching foreign languages in an era of globalization: Introduction. *The Modern Language Journal* 98 (1), 296–311.

Krippendorff, K. (2004) *Content Analysis: An Introduction to Its Methodology* (2nd edn) Thousand Oaks, CA: Sage.

Laakso, H. (2017) Vieraskieliset perusopetuksessa (Foreign language speakers in basic education). In M. Portin (ed.) *Vieraskieliset perusopetuksessa ja toisen asteen koulutuksessa 2010-luvulla* [Foreign Language Speakers in Basic and Secondary Education in 2020s] (pp. 27–36). Helsinki: Opetushallitus [National Agency for Education].

Lehtonen, H. (2016) What's up Helsinki? Linguistic diversity among suburban adolescents. In R. Toivanen and J. Saarikivi (eds) *Linguistic Genocide or Superdiversity? New and Old Language Diversities* (pp. 65–90). Bristol: Multilingual Matters.

Leppänen, S., Pitkänen-Huhta, A., Nikula, T., Kytölä, S., Törmäkangas, T., Nissinen, K., Kääntä, L., Räisänen, T., Laitinen, M., Pahta, P., Koskela, H., Lähdesmäki, S. and Jousmäki, H. (2011*) National Survey on the English Language in Finland: Uses, Meanings and Attitudes*. Studies in Variation, Contacts and Change in English, vol 5. Helsinki: Research Unit for Variation, Contacts and Change in English.

Li Wei (2011) Multilinguality, multimodality, and multicompetence: Code- and modeswitching by minority ethnic children in complementary schools. *The Modern Language Journal* 95 (3), 370–384.

Li Wei (2017) Translanguaging as a practical theory of language. *Applied Linguistics* 39 (1), 9–30.

Lindstedt, J., Hedman, H., Huttu, H., Lindgren, A., Lindgren, M., Vuolasranta, M., Åkerlund, T., Granqvist, K. and Hänninen. A. (2009) *Romanikielen Kielipoliittinen Ohjelma* [Language Policy Programme for the Roma Language]. Helsinki: Kotimaisten kielten tutkimuskeskus. http://scripta.kotus.fi/www/verkkojulkaisut/julk10/romanikielen_kielipoliittinen_ohjelma.pdf (accessed April 2020).

May, S. (ed.) (2014) *The Multilingual Turn. Implications for SLA, TESOL and Bilingual Education*. New York: Routledge.

May, S. (2019) Negotiating the multilingual turn in SLA. *The Modern Language Journal* 103 (Supplement 2019), 122–129.

Multilingualism as a Strength (2017) https://minedu.fi/documents/1410845/5875747/Multilingualism_tiivistelm%C3%A4.pdf/be86bffa-d55f-4935-bff4-2fd150c82067/Multilingualism_tiivistelm%C3%A4.pdf (accessed January 2020)

NCC (National Core Curriculum for Basic Education) (2014) Finnish National Board of Education.

Nikula, T., Pöyhönen, S., Huhta, A. and Hildén, R. (2010) When MT + 2 is not enough: Tensions within foreign language education in Finland. *Sociolinguistica* 24 (1), 25–42.

Olthuis, M.-L. (2003) Uhanalaisen kielen elvytys: esimerkkinä inarinsaame [Revitalizing endangered languages: Inari Sámi as an example]. *Virittäjä* 107 (4), 568–579. https://journal.fi/virittaja/article/view/40298 (accessed April 2020).

Ortega, L. (2019) SLA and the study of equitable multilingualism. *The Modern Language Journal* 103 (Supplement 2019), 23–38.

Otsuji, E. and Pennycook, A. (2009) Metrolingualism: Fixity, fluidity and language in flux. *International Journal of Multilingualism* 7, 240–254.

Paulsrud, B., Rosén, J., Straszer, B. and Wedin, Å. (eds) (2017) *New Perspectives on Translanguaging and Education*. Bristol: Multilingual Matters.

Paulsrud, B., Zilliacus, H. and Ekberg, L. (2020) Spaces for multilingual education: Language orientations in the national curricula of Sweden and Finland. *International Multilingual Research Journal* 14 (4), 304–318. DOI: 10.1080/19313152.2020.1714158

Pietikäinen, S. (2012) Kieli-ideologiat arjessa. Neksusanalyysi monikielisen inarinsaamenpuhujan kielielämäkerrasta [Language ideologies in the everyday. A nexus analysis of the language history of a multilingual Inari Sámi speaker]. *Virittäjä* 116 (3), 410–440.

Pitkänen-Huhta, A. and Mäntylä, K. (2020) Teachers' negotiating multilingualism in the EFL classroom. *European Journal of Applied Linguistics*. Published online. DOI: https://doi.org/10.1515/eujal-2018-0020

Saarinen, T., Nuolijärvi, P., Pöyhönen, S. and Kangasvieri, T. (eds) (2019) *Kieli, Koulutus, Politiikka. Monipaikkaisia Käytänteitä ja Tulkintaa* [Language, Education, Policy. Multisited Practices and Interpretations]. Tampere: Vastapaino.

Salo, O.-P. (2012) Finland's official bilingualism – a bed of roses or of procrusters? In J. Blommaert, S. Leppänen, P. Pahta and T. Räisänen (eds) *Dangerous Multilingualism. Northern Perspectives on Order, Purity and Normality.* Houndmills, Basingstoke: Palgrave MacMillan.

Skinnari, K and Nikula, T. (2017) Teachers' perceptions on the changing role of language in the curriculum. *European Journal of Applied Linguistics* 5 (2), 223–244.

Statistics Finland https://www.tilastokeskus.fi/tup/suoluk/suoluk_vaesto_en.html (accessed November 2019)

Takala, S. and Havola, L. (1983) *English in the Sociolinguistic Context of Finland.* Bulletin 240. Jyväskylä: University of Jyväskylä, Institute for Educational Research.

Äärelä-Vihriälä, R. (2017) Kielipesissä elvytetään uhanalaista saamen kieltä [Revitalizing the endangered Sámi language in language nests]. *Kieli, Koulutus ja Yhteiskunta*, 14.9.2017 (Syyskuu). http://www.kieliverkosto.fi/article/kielipesissa-elvytetaan-uhanalaista-saamen-kielta/ (accessed April 2020).

Afterword

Is translanguaging a broadening of (socio)linguistic perspective, a new ontology of communication or a component of a scholarly rebranding campaign (e.g. Grin, 2018; MacSwan, 2017; Otheguy *et al.*, 2015; Pavlenko, 2018)? It is an exciting time in applied/educational linguistics for vigorous theoretical and intellectual conversations about the nature of human language(e)ing. While the conceptual underpinnings are important, what the pre-service teachers with whom I have worked in both Sweden and the United States are hungry for is what translanguaging offers for their practice.

These future teachers recognize the linguistic diversity among the student populations they will teach and the concomitant need for a pedagogy that fosters equity and justice and fights against linguicism. As an educational linguist and a teacher educator, I want to help them develop approaches for such a pedagogy through my courses. Many teacher candidates discover translanguaging on their own, before ever being exposed to it in course texts, through discussions in their local communities of educators or in professional publications they read online. They come to class excited and intrigued by the term as well as by the prospect of finding ways to bring the fullness of their students' repertoires into the classroom.

Translanguaging has been powerful in capturing the imagination of today's (future) teachers to think beyond monoglossic paradigms much like previous work on code-switching and plurilingualism in the classroom did for earlier generations of teachers and teacher educators internationally (e.g. Goodman & Tastanbek, 2020; Lau & Van Viegen, 2020; Lin, 2013; Martin-Jones, 1995; Pinho & Andrade, 2009; Vallejo & Dooly, 2020). In this way, at least, it is evident that translanguaging continues a long legacy of multilingual education by drawing teachers' attention to students as active multilingual agents whose linguistic resources are sociopolitically situated. As Li Wei (2018) explains,

> Translanguaging was never intended to replace code-switching or any other term, although it challenges the code view of language. It does not deny the existence of named languages, but stresses that languages are historically, politically, and ideologically defined entities. It defines the multilingual as someone who is aware of the existence of the political

entities of named languages and has an ability to make use of the structural features of some of them that they have acquired. (Li Wei, 2018: 27)

As Cummins (this volume) notes, 'the recent theoretical focus on translanguaging, together with earlier multilingual instructional initiatives, has resulted in a significant increase in educators' (p. 14) interest in exploring ways in which minoritized students' home languages can be incorporated productively into instruction.' The translanguaging conference that has emerged in Sweden is a prime example. Each of the three iterations thus far has brought together researchers and educators in conversation about research-based practice for pedagogical translanguaging. This synergy is prominently reflected in the themes of each conference: 'Practices, Skills, and Pedagogy' (Dalarna University in 2015; see Paulsrud *et al.*, 2017), 'Researchers and Practitioners in Dialogue' (Örebro University in 2017; see Adinolfi *et al.*, 2018) and, most recently, 'Translanguaging in the Individual, at School and in Society' (Linnæus University in 2019) from which the present volume stems. The hunger for such research-practice discussions is further reflected in the attendance of teachers and researchers from Sweden as well as scholars from throughout the world, which has continued to grow with each successive event. Indeed, the fourth event, scheduled again for Dalarna University in 2021, will be known as the International Conference on Translanguaging.

It is, perhaps, fitting that a regular translanguaging conference is gaining footing in the Nordic context whose countries are often mischaracterized internationally as stereotypically monolingual and monocultural while being far from either. With the (post)colonial history of Sweden and Finland, diverse regional and minority languages, migrant languages, regional and dialectal variation and inter-Nordic communication across Danish, Norwegian and Swedish, it is a region long touched by the many guises of bilingualism, multilingualism, code-switching and translanguaging (e.g. Börestam Uhlmann, 1996; Boyd & Huss, 2001; Hult, 2004, 2010, 2017; Hult & Pietikäinen, 2014; Modiano, 2003; Palviainen, 2012; Quist & Svendsen, 2010; Røyneland, 2020; Thingnes, 2020). At the same time, it is also a region that continues to be challenged by issues of racism, classism and ethnocentrism that intersect with language and education (e.g. Boyd, 2003; Clark, 2013; Hällgren, 2005; Hübinette & Räterlinck, 2014; Hübinette & Tigervall, 2009; Pred, 2000; Tholin, 2014) and thus very much in need of the kind of socially responsive pedagogy represented by pedagogical translanguaging.

The strength of the present collection, for Swedish and international readers and for teachers and teacher educators alike, is in providing research-based documentation of socially situated pedagogical translanguaging in practice across a wide range of instructional contexts. In addition to contributions that address theoretical foundations (Cummins) and processes of school-based research on a meta-level (Källkvist &

Juvonen; Sundqvist *et al.*), chapters span the full range of primary and middle grades (Carbonara & Scibetta; Pitkänen-Huhta; Svensson), upper secondary schools (Reath Warren; Wedin; Sierk) and adult education (Rosén & Lundgren; St John) as well as a spectrum of foci from mainstream and content area classrooms to second language and mother tongue instruction. In all, the volume offers a robust smörgåsbord to satisfy a hearty appetite for practical insight into what pedagogical translanguaging can be.

Francis M. Hult
Baltimore, Maryland, USA
7 October 2020

References

Adinolfi, L., Link, H. and St John, O. (eds) (2018) Translanguaging: Researchers and practitioners in dialogue [Special Issue]. *Translation and Translanguaging in Multilingual Contexts* 4 (3), 331–421.

Anderson, J. (2011) Reshaping pedagogies for a plurilingual agenda. *Language Learning Journal* 39 (2), 135–147.

Boyd, S. (2003) Foreign-born teachers in the multilingual classroom in Sweden: The role of attitudes to foreign accent. *International Journal of Bilingual Education and Bilingualism* 6 (3 & 4), 283–295.

Boyd, S. and Huss, L. (eds) (2001) *Managing Multilingualism in a European Nation-state: Challenges for Sweden.* Clevedon: Multilingual Matters.

Börestam Uhlmann, U. (1996) Språkligt detektivarbete: om problemkällor i interskandinavisk kommunikation. *Språk och stil* 6, 51–62.

Clark, G. (2013) *What is the True Rate of Social Mobility in Sweden? A Surname Analysis, 1700–2012.* Retrieved from http://faculty.econ.ucdavis.edu/faculty/gclark/The%20Son%20Also%20Rises/Sweden%202014.pdf

Dávila, L.T. and Bunar, N. (2020) Translanguaging through an advocacy lens: The roles of multilingual classroom assistants in Sweden. *European Journal of Applied Linguistics* 8 (1), 107–126.

Goodman, B. and Tastanbek, S. (2020) Making the shift from a codeswitching to a translanguaging lens in English language teacher education. *TESOL Quarterly.* https://doi.org/10.1002/tesq.571

Grin, F. (2018) On some fashionable terms in multilingualism research: Critical assessment and implications for language policy. In P.A. Kraus and F. Grin (eds) *The Politics of Multilingualism: Europeanisation, Globalization and Linguistic Governance* (pp. 247–273). Amsterdam: John Benjamins Publishing Company.

Hällgren, C. (2005) 'Working harder to be the same': Everyday racism among young men and women in Sweden. *Race Ethnicity and Education* 8 (3), 319–342.

Hübinette, T. and Räterlinck, L.E.H. (2014) Race performativity and melancholic whiteness in contemporary Sweden. *Social Identities* 20 (6), 501–514.

Hübinette, T. and Tigervall, C. (2009) To be non-white in a colour-blind society: Conversations with adoptees and adoptive parents in Sweden on everyday racism. *Journal of Intercultural Studies* 30 (4), 335–353.

Hult, F.M. (2004) Planning for multilingualism and minority language rights in Sweden. *Language Policy* 3 (2), 181–201.

Hult, F.M. (2010) Swedish Television as a mechanism for language planning and policy. *Language Problems and Language Planning* 34 (2), 158–181.

Hult, F.M. (2017) More than a lingua franca: Functions of English in a globalised educational language policy. *Language, Culture and Curriculum* 30 (3), 265–282.

Hult, F.M. and Pietikäinen, S. (2014) Shaping discourses of multilingualism through a language ideological debate: The case of Swedish in Finland. *Journal of Language and Politics* 13, 1–20.

Lau, S.M.C. and Van Viegen, S. (eds) (2020) *Plurilingual Pedagogies: Critical and Creative Endeavors for Equitable Language in Education*. Cham, Switzerland: Springer.

Li Wei (2018) Translanguaging as a practical theory of language. *Applied Linguistics* 39 (1), 9–30.

Lin, A. (2013) Classroom code-switching: Three decades of research. *Applied Linguistics Review* 4 (1), 195–218.

MacSwan, J. (2017) A multilingual perspective on translanguaging. *American Educational Research Journal* 54 (1), 167–201.

Martin-Jones, M. (1995) Code-switching in the classroom: Two decades of research. In L. Milroy and P. Muysken (eds) *One Speaker, Two Languages, Cross-disciplinary Perspectives on Code-switching* (pp. 90–111). New York: Cambridge University Press.

Modiano, M. (2003) Euro-English: A Swedish perspective. *English Today* 19 (2), 35–41.

Norman, K. (2018) *Sweden's Dark Soul: The Unravelling of a Utopia*. London: C. Hurst and Co.

Otheguy, R., García, O. and Reid, W. (2015) Clarifying translanguaging and deconstructing named languages: A perspective from linguistics. *Applied Linguistics Review* 6 (3), 281–307.

Palviainen, Å. (2012) Lärande som diskursnexus: Finska studenters uppfattningar om skoltid, fritid och universitetsstudier som lärokontexter för svenska. *Nordisk tidskrift for andrespråksforskning* 1, 7–36.

Paulsrud, B., Rosén, J. Straszer, B. and Wedin, Å. (eds) (2017) *New Perspectives on Translanguaging and Education*. Bristol: Multilingual Matters.

Pavlenko, A. (2018) Superdiversity and why it isn't: Reflections on terminological innovation and academic branding. In B. Schmenk, S. Breidbach and L. Küster (eds) *Sloganization in Language Education Discourse: Conceptual Thinking in the Age of Academic Marketization* (pp. 142–168). Bristol: Multilingual Matters.

Pinho, A.S. and Andrade, A.I. (2009) Plurilingual awareness and intercomprehension in the professional knowledge and identity development of language student teachers. *International Journal of Multilingualism* 6 (3), 313–329.

Pred, A. (2000) *Even in Sweden: Racisms, Racialized Spaces, and the Popular Geographical Imagination*. Berkeley, CA: University of California Press.

Quist, P. and Svendsen, B.A. (eds) (2010) *Multilingual Urban Scandinavia: New Linguistic Practices*. Bristol: Multilingual Matters.

Røyneland, U. (2020) Regional varieties in Norway revisited. In M. Cerruti and S. Tsiplakou (eds) *Intermediate Language Varieties: Koinai and Regional Standards in Europe* (pp. 31–54). Philadelphia, PA: John Benjamins.

Thingnes, J.S. (2020) Making linguistic choices at a Sámi university: Negotiating visions and demands. *Current Issues in Language Planning* 21 (2), 153–174.

Tholin, J. (2014) 'Swedishness' as a norm for learners of English in Swedish schools: A study of national and local objectives and criteria in compulsory schools. *Scandinavian Journal of Educational Research* 58 (3), 253–268.

Vallejo, C. and Dooly, M. (eds) (2020) Plurilingualism and translanguaging: Emergent approaches and shared concerns [Special Issue]. *International Journal of Bilingual Education and Bilingualism* 23 (1), 1–112.

Subject Index

Milton Keynes UK
Ingram Content Group UK Ltd.
UKHW022033070923
428247UK00005B/363